China Against the Tides

China Against the Tides

Restructuring through Revolution, Radicalism and Reform

2nd Edition

Marc Blecher

continuum
LONDON • NEW YORK

Continuum
The Tower Building, 11 York Road, London SE1 7NX
15 East 26th Street, New York, NY 10010

British Library Cataloguing-in-Publication Data
A catalogue record for this book is available from the British Library.

ISBN: 0–8264–6422-X (hardback) 08264–6421–1 (paperback)

Typeset by RefineCatch Ltd, Bungay, Suffolk
Printed and bound in Great Britain by The Bath Press, Bath

For Sharon, Joel, Jacob and Ian
Scholars,
artists,
citizens,
companions
and swimmers against the tides.

This second edition is dedicated to Tang Tsou
Scholar extraordinaire
Sage teacher
Proud citizen of China and the USA
Adroit, serene navigator of rip tides.

Contents

List of Figures

List of Tables

Preface to the First Edition

Work on this book began with the intention of modestly revising and updating *China: Politics, Economics and Society: Iconoclasm and Innovation in a Revolutionary Socialist Country* (London: Pinter, 1986). Like China, it ended in a rather different and unexpected place. I failed to anticipate the depth of the changes that had occurred in the course of a decade in China. In retrospect, I did not take seriously enough my own arguments in the earlier book about China's extraordinary propensity to change course in startling ways. I also did not realize just how much my thinking would have to change to cope with these developments.

Chapters 1 and 2 draw most heavily on *China: Politics, Economics and Society*; the rest are new. Like its predecessor, though, *China Against the Tides* is intended to offer an interpretive survey of China's revolution, its sustained experiment with radical state socialism and its efforts at equally radical structural reform. The approach remains interdisciplinary, weaving together history, politics, society, economics and culture. Though written for readers with no particular background in Chinese affairs, it does not try to be merely introductory. Rather, it offers arguments and analyses informed by social science theory and by a comparative perspective. It strives both to inform and to challenge.

Acknowledgements for the First Edition

What soon grows old? Gratitude.
                          – Aristotle

In the individualistic, alienated world that we have created, it is easy to forget that all we are and do are products of the efforts of an incalculable number of people both historically and at present. This book, surveying my thinking about China over almost thirty years, has been shaped by all the scholars who have taught me so much, from my first undergraduate course to their latest articles and letters.

Tang Tsou, my teacher at the University of Chicago, contributed more than I know. Over and over, I have encountered the same feeling of astonished disconcertment whenever I have picked up his scholarly writings, or my scribblings from his lectures, and discovered that what I had come to think of proudly as my own interesting, novel ideas originated instead with him. His achievement as a mentor is all the greater because he so assiduously eschewed turning his students into disciples, insisting instead that we have the latitude to pursue our own interests and visions – which is one reason why it is so hard to fathom how profoundly he contributed to how and what we think. John Wilson Lewis first excited me about China, and about the power of social science for illuminating it, during my undergraduate days at Cornell. In graduate school at Chicago I was also fortunate to have the opportunity to learn so much from Jeremy Azrael, Leonard Binder, Philip Kuhn, William Parish, Kenneth Prewitt, Lloyd Rudolph, Suzanne Rudolph and Philippe Schmitter.

Over the years I have been privileged to have a core of brilliant, sympathetic colleagues with whom to share and develop ideas. My collaborations on books with Vivienne Shue and Gordon White were scintillating experiences. My professional and personal lives have been immeasurably enriched by Phyllis Andors, Steve Andors, Bob Benewick, Randy Coleman, Cui Zhiyuan, Chris Howell, Ron Kahn, Ira Katznelson, David Kelley, Dan Kelliher, David Laitin, Hong Yung Lee, Li Lianjiang, David Love, Mitch Meisner, Michelle Mood, Kevin O'Brien, Suzanne Pepper, Mark Selden, Steve Volk, Wang Shaoguang, Lynn White III, Harlan Wilson, Scott Wilson, Brantly Womack, Christine Wong, Yue Ming and David Zweig.

I also have a scholarly debt to my students at Oberlin College and the University of Chicago. The high level of intellectuality that they brought into my classrooms and office provided the crucible in which many of the ideas in this book were catalysed and then refined. They have made a teacher's work rewarding and thrilling. Their constant search for complex, committed understanding has informed the approach taken in this book, and also helped inspire much of its substance. It is my deepest hope that *China Against the Tides*, drawn so much from them, will help sustain and develop such inquiry among their successors.

Turning the work and study of so many years into this volume also required some specific help. Frances Pinter, Iain Stevenson and Nicola Viinikka provided the considerable encouragement I needed in order to be persuaded to take the project on. So did Phil Shively's timely and gratifying invitation to contribute to his project on

Comparative Governance. Petra Recter and Fiona McKenzie oversaw the editorial work with aplomb and professionalism. Reid Wood once again offered invaluable technical help with great generosity and characteristic good cheer. Turning from essence to existence, from consciousness to the material base, Oberlin College and the National Endowment for the Humanities (Fellowship #FB-32277–95) provided the time for contemplation, research and writing. No thanks to the Republicans in the US Congress for shamelessly and needlessly gutting the NEH, making it so much more difficult for scholars in the future to have the opportunity to develop and share their reflections on a world ever more badly in need of reasoned analysis.

China Against the Tides is dedicated to my family. If ultimately I could keep my head above water, it was only with their nurture, their cheerful willingness to put up with the demands on my time, energy and spirit, and the inspiration and stimulation provided by their own scholarly achievements.

Oberlin, Ohio
9 May 1996

Preface and Acknowledgements for the Second Edition

Six years after the completion of the first edition of this book, China continues to swim against the tides. In 1996, a spasm of rapid growth and relative openness was fuelling intense optimism in the country and among foreign observers. With the economy bursting at the seams, and proposals for further economic and even political reform finding relatively receptive ears at the very highest levels of the leadership, could a democratic transition be far off? Was it not bound to be the product of an ever more pluralistic, educated, well-informed, self-employed, resourceful and independent-minded citizenry? Would the People's Republic of China go the way of the USSR and so many other state socialist countries: to the dustbin of history, replaced by something more familiar and welcome to the Western-dominated post-Cold War world? Or would it embark on the pathway of gradual democratization that had swept over Taiwan, South Korea and much of Latin America in the 1990s?

The first edition of *China Against the Tides* ended on a far more cautious note, wondering whether China could not swim against this optimistic tide of both modernizing forces and opinion about them. A plausible and even somewhat probable outcome seemed to be that the country would 'muddle through'. 'Market Stalinism' could prove more resilient than its wishful opponents, both in China and abroad, would hope.

China has indeed muddled through the last six years. It continues to grow, and at a more moderate and sustainable pace than its breathless, overheated pace of the mid-1990s. Foreign capital pours in unabated. The country survived the 1997 Asian financial crisis far better than most of its neighbours. It has matured in its relations with foreign countries, joining the WTO and demonstrating its capacity to patch up its differences with an initially hostile Republican government in the USA. The country has stabilized: business practices have normalized somewhat, and daily life is perhaps a bit more predictable. Yet a host of problems – inequality, corruption, unemployment, environmental crisis – have continued unabated or even grown more serious. Protest is on the rise. Politics remains repressive.

All this is not an argument that further stasis is on the cards. It is a caution. China is a great historical civilization and, after more than a century of profound crisis and collapse, it has become a great and increasingly self-confident economic and political power on the world scene. It marches to a drummer that, while surely not immune to the forces around it, is very much its own. It is most assuredly not 'inscrutable' – it can be understood by outside observers. They must, however, equip themselves with both a deep working knowledge of the country's past, a willingness to try to grasp reality the way people in China grasp it, and the theoretical and analytical tools of modern social science. Only such an approach has a chance to explain China's penchant for confounding so many expectations over the past 150 years – a penchant that is likely to continue.

I dedicate this second edition lovingly and reverently to the late Professor Tang Tsou, who taught me this and so much more. Born and raised in a deeply cultured and sophisticated family in China, and educated in the best schools there, he developed and always maintained as profound a grasp of the country as anyone could. Taking his graduate training at the University of Chicago, where he went on to teach for decades, he possessed an equally deep appreciation for, and ever expanding command of, social science. He was always telling us graduate students to read the latest book on political participation in the USA, or on rational choice theory, and then showing us what it could explain about China even while warning us that it needed considerable, creative adaptation to make any sense in a Chinese context. In addition to everything else he imparted to me, in the last year of his life, while he was pitting his irrepressible intellect and drive against ever failing health, he read chapters of the first edition of *Tides* with his characteristic intensity and attention to detail. I remember hours upon hours of conversation about what needed to be changed and strengthened, peppered of course with the usual reading list of works without which I could not understand the problems at hand. Improvements that readers may find in this edition owe much to his intellect and labours.

I also wish to thank colleagues and students who have read and considered the first edition, from whose questions, comments and criticisms I have learned so much. Their interest allowed me to think that the book might be worth a second edition. So too did Professor Hua Qingzhao, Chun Byong-gon and Jung Hwan-woo, who helped develop the Chinese and Korean editions. Indispensable to this bandwagon as well were Continuum Publishers, and my editors Alexandra Webster and Caroline Wintersgill. Professor Robert Benewick has been a very special help through thick and thin. I have borrowed time from a research grant from the American Philosophical Society to prepare this revision, and I thank colleagues and staff there for both their generosity and flexibility. Erika Cline provided cheerful, yeo-woman research assistance. As always, my wife Sharon and my sons Ian, Jacob and Joel – each of them now accomplished scholars and published writers – have provided sustenance as inspirations and as exemplars, which every writer and scholar must have, of what it truly means to be human in an ever more inhuman world.

Guide to Romanization and Pronunciation

This book adopts the official and now widely used Pinyin system of romanization. The only exceptions are some names of famous people and places, such as Sun Yatsen and Hong Kong, which are commonly used to render their Cantonese names into English phonetically. (In romanized Mandarin, they would be Sun Zhongshan and Xianggang respectively.)

Pinyin romanization is not strictly phonetic in English. The following may aid in efforts at correct pronunciation:

Pinyin	Phonetic English
x	sy
z	dz
zh	j
c	ts
ong	ung
ian	ien
ui	way
i	ee (after most initials)
	r (after ch, r, sh, zh)
	deep '-uh' or no sound after c, s, z

Introduction

For millennia, China's politics, economics and society were the most enduring in the world. Yet, repeatedly in the nineteenth and twentieth centuries, China has, to use a phrase favoured by Mao Zedong, moved against the tides (*fan chao liu*) of its own great history and of wider international forces. Sometimes it even challenged the waves of revolution that it had itself set in counter-motion to previous currents. China has probably undergone more thoroughgoing, iconoclastic and innovative change than any other country. Its state went from an imperial monarchy to a short-lived republic, then to weak and decentralized proto-Fascist authoritarianism, then to revolutionary state socialism and finally to structural reform.[1] Its economy underwent repeated, spasmodic shifts from unparalleled crisis to very rapid growth and modernization of both agriculture and industry. Its society and culture were sundered by imperialism and profound class struggle, and were subject to the contortions of war and modernization, including explosive urbanization, population movement, technological change and transformation of values, first in a collectivist, socialist direction, then in an individualistic one more associated with capitalism. How can these changes be comprehended? Why and how did they happen? What has been their effect on China, the world's most populous country? And what is their significance for political, economic and social change in the rest of the world?

Focusing on China's resistance to the tidal forces acting on it, on its tendency to break with its own history and with existing models, often in surprising and innovative ways, is not obvious or uncontroversial. It challenges the argument that Chinese state socialism has essentially been just the most recent incarnation of the country's age-old tradition of highly centralized and absolutist state power. By this account, first Mao Zedong and then Deng Xiaoping are the latest embodiments of Chinese emperors, and the vast party and government organizations are the heirs to the centralized imperial bureaucracy that supported and enforced monarchical power for millennia. *China Against the Tides* will argue, by contrast, that despite some surface continuities in, for example, the cultural norms that appear to infuse political life or the leaders' personal demeanour, as a state the People's Republic of China – in both its Maoist and Dengist variants – represents a sharp departure from the past in its objectives, organizational forms, political reach and effects in transforming society, economy and culture.

Moreover, our emphasis on China's resistance to the dominant tides of history challenges the view that Chinese state socialism is at bottom an adaptation of the model marked out first by the Soviet Union. For decades, comparative communist studies took the view that there was a single model of totalitarian rule by a centralized state, led by a Communist Party, that had complete control of the economy and society. The Cold War encouraged such a theory, going so far as to give credence to the idea of an internationally organized communist movement of monolithic states, even though serious differences and conflicts among them became apparent by the mid-1950s. In fact, China's was one of the most unusual of the world's many state socialisms. Unlike the Soviet Union and Eastern Europe, Chinese state socialism emphasized the peasantry and rural development, rural industrialization and, until the end of the Maoist period (1949–78), local and international economic self-reliance. Politically, though like them it possessed a powerful state led by a mighty Communist Party, its politics also evinced strongly participatory and anti-bureaucratic features. While the Soviet Union and the Eastern European state socialist systems sought politically quiescent populations, stable administration and ironclad control of political life,[2] the leadership associated with Mao Zedong believed in 'uninterrupted revolution' directed even against its own state. It encouraged popular participation in campaigns to topple class enemies, criticize 'rightists', build and operate communes, wipe out schistosomiasis and study political philosophy, among many others. The Cultural Revolution of the late 1960s, a mass movement encouraged by the Maoist leadership to attack bureaucratism and élitism among state officials, went so far as to topple many leading Communist Party and government leaders, including President Liu Shaoqi and Party General Secretary Deng Xiaoping. So many Chinese people came forward with so much relish to attack the state – and each other – that ultimately Mao himself had difficulty bringing the Cultural Revolution to a halt.[3] If the politically quiescent state socialism of the USSR and Eastern Europe was an icon that Soviet leaders and, indeed, the West, too, expected other countries under Communist rule to follow, China chose instead to smash it.

Soon, though, China would move decisively against the tide of radicalism that it itself had caused to rise. If China's was among the most iconoclastic and innovative state socialisms through the 1970s, it would also engage in the most profound structural reform in the 1980s and 1990s. While a few Eastern European state socialist systems, most notably Hungary, developed serious economic reform blueprints and began to implement them, on the whole their vision and action pales by comparison with China's profound effort starting in 1978.[4] This is one reason the Chinese Communist Party and its state outlasted those of the Soviet Union and Eastern Europe.

We have already begun to see, then, that Chinese state socialism has also undergone far greater gyrations and reversals than any other. The very nature of socialism was debated and struggled over more seriously and passionately than anywhere else. Political conflict among élites was fairly standard fare in state socialist countries, as it is among capitalist ones. But in China these disagreements led to deeply contradictory approaches to economic development, social policy and political life. The highly participatory land reform of the late 1940s and early 1950s was followed in 1953–57 by the First Five Year Plan which, modelled on that of the Soviet Union, emphasized bureaucratic authority and draconian workplace management. Disillusionment by many leaders with this approach led to the Great Leap Forward of 1958–61, which aspired to bring about true Communism, including an end to inequality, bureaucracy and the division of labour. The disasters of the Leap brought about from 1962–65 a return to central planning in the cities and, in many places, decollectivization of farming. But no sooner had life begun to settle down again when the Cultural Revolution broke out. Though the most extreme mass movements were over by 1968, its radicalism dominated politics until Mao's death in 1976. After a hesitant interregnum, thoroughgoing structural reform began in 1978. But that too has been characterized by cycles of stop-go economic policies and shifting winds of dilatory political reform and tough crackdown.

There is yet another important way to look at China's repeated tendency to swim against shifting tides other than in the contexts of its history and of state socialism. For it is also a late industrializing, economically developing country. Like many countries in Africa, Asia and Latin America, China has faced problems of deep poverty and a late start on economic modernization. Yet China's approach to development differed from most other places in the Third World. Since 1949, the Chinese state shared with many other countries a forceful commitment to economic development. But, unlike many of them, during the Maoist period it married to this goal both a profound commitment to economic equality and balance, and also the capacity of a very powerful state to mobilize vast social and economic resources in pursuit of development. As a result, China enjoys a well-deserved reputation for some stunning developmental successes, including among the very highest life expectancy and literacy rates in the Third World.[5] In the Maoist period, China achieved a level of economic equality unprecedented among countries of substantial size and low level of economic development. In the Dengist period (beginning 1978), China achieved astonishing rates of economic growth that have rivalled and even exceeded those of the capitalist success stories such as Taiwan and South Korea.

Thus, somewhat surprisingly, we have already introduced capitalism as a fourth optic (besides China's own history, state socialism and the late developing countries). Since 1978, China has been busy adding elements of capitalism to its economy, and eyeing enviously the achievements of its capitalist neighbours in Japan, South Korea, Taiwan and Singapore. Most production and commerce is now conducted through markets. Entrepreneurs have been encouraged to open private businesses. Managers of government enterprises have been given significant autonomy in making economic decisions and controlling resources. Unlike in the Maoist past, when enterprises were judged by their ability to meet production quotas, profitability has now become the key indicator of performance. Unprofitable firms are being restructured or even closed down, and millions of workers are unemployed, with many more facing that grim prospect.

Yet, Western observers and ideological pundits may have jumped a little too quickly to the ideologically self-satisfying view that China has been swept up in the worldwide tide of capitalism. Much productive capital is still in the hands of central and local governments. Some markets and prices remain under state regulation. In the cities, millions upon millions of Chinese still work in government enterprises. While in the countryside farmers have become far more independent in their day-to-day economic activities, central and local governments still have decisive power over their access to land, decisions about the crops they plant on it, the prices they pay for inputs and receive for outputs and many other facets of life.

3

Is China following the new icon of the capitalist success stories of Japan, Taiwan, South Korea and Singapore? It is more like their mirror image. Where those countries added significant elements of state planning and regulation to an essentially capitalist economy, China is groping for a new hybrid by grafting markets and limited spheres of private ownership and initiative onto state socialism. It continues to resist the tide of unbridled capitalism.

As we strive to understand the distinctiveness of contemporary China in terms of its own history, of state socialism, of Third World development and of capitalism, we will draw on the methodological and epistemological perspectives both of Sinology – which views China as a world unto itself and strives to understand it in its own terms – and also of social science – which views countries in a comparative context. On the one hand, we will endeavour to comprehend how Chinese people experience and interpret their world. We will try to put ourselves in the position of China's leaders and people, to grasp, insofar as it is possible, the motivations, hopes, fears, obstacles, opportunities and sense of history that they had in mind as they acted in a particular situation. After all, their sensibilities are an important contributor to the events we wish to understand. Moreover, striving to put ourselves in the place of others can help us overcome the biases and blinders imposed by our standpoint as outsiders. Doing so may also help us to find a rationality in what might otherwise appear bizarre or exotic, even if that rationality is very different from our own or at times can be judged to be downright irrational. We will be much the wiser if we can, for example, understand the Great Leap Forward or the Cultural Revolution as the result of the actions of serious, rational leaders and people seeking their goals in a specific situation, rather than as a product of collective dementia. Finally, seeking the participants' perspective may help us avoid analytical blunders or blind alleys that can result from imposing our own values, often unknowingly, on another country where they do not fit. In the heat of the 1989 protests, most media pundits and even many China specialists predicted the imminent collapse of the Chinese state and the triumph of democracy. This mistaken analysis was, to a significant degree, the product of vision blurred by observers' own Western political values and hopes.[6]

There is also much to gain from maintaining the objective perspective of comparativists. Concepts and theories drawn from the study of other situations can often help reveal what those embroiled in a situation cannot see. Comparison allows the world to surprise us, alerting us to the importance of phenomena that might not otherwise appear significant. For example, a Chinese worker may regard it as perfectly ordinary, natural and fair that incentive bonuses are distributed equally to everyone in the plant; but, to an American social scientist (not to mention an American manager or worker!), this would be a very strange phenomenon that would have huge implications for shaping and explaining day-to-day life and authority relations in the plant. It would also be one piece in analysing the anaemic economic performance of Chinese industry. Moreover, theoretically informed social science comparisons can help explain the reasons for these phenomena. To return to an example deployed above, while the perspective of participants in the

Cultural Revolution helps us get beyond its deranged appearance, to grasp the dynamics of the Cultural Revolution we will also refer in Chapters 2 and 5 to dispassionate statistical analysis of social science data on the factors shaping participants' political behaviour. People who thought that as individuals they were acting for ideological or personalistic reasons turn out also to have been acting in ways that correlate strongly with their class background and levels of education (Blecher and White, 1979). The task of unearthing such underlying dynamics comes more naturally to a social scientist with no particular stake in the situation than to a person caught up in the events.

Thus, *China Against the Tides* will seek to combine both the internal perspectives of the actors themselves with the external standpoint of the social scientist. Each approach helps compensate for the shortcomings of the other. The Sinological perspective helps us arrive at a suitably textured and accurate understanding of Chinese realities. It also helps ensure that our social science concepts and theories are appropriate and unbiased ones. And the social science perspective helps us transcend the narrowness and self-referentiality (of Chinese or of foreign specialists who identify with them) that comes from an approach that treats China as unique in and of itself. China is, of course, unique; but so are all countries. But, like other countries, its distinctiveness can best be grasped by observing it from outside as well as from within.

Chapter 1 examines the Chinese revolution, seeking to explain it in the context of the specific social formation within which it appeared. It asks why an urban-based bourgeois revolution grounded in a rising capitalism failed to materialize, and why a revolution with a rural base and a broadly popular participatory politics – both significant departures from earlier world revolutions – could succeed. It also suggests some of the theoretical and practical implications of these specific qualities of China's revolution. Chapter 2 traces the history of China's socialist transition and development during what is called its Maoist period, from 1949 to 1978.[7] Chapter 3 continues the story for what is called the Dengist period, from 1978 to at least the time of this writing in late 2002.[8] These chapters attempt to find the rational bases for the many apparently strange twists and turns in policy and politics. They also try to ferret out the underlying continuities that reach across the ostensible ruptures between and even within the Maoist and Dengist periods. In doing so, the analysis tends to emphasize the material forces at work in the society and economy that shaped and were expressed in political and ideological terms. Chapter 4 covers the institutions of the Chinese state, including most prominently the Chinese Communist Party and government administration. Chapter 5 focuses on society, sketching some of the major cleavages, most prominently class, gender and urban vs. rural areas. Chapter 6 covers political economy, comparing the Maoist and Dengist periods. The discussion of politics within the state, and between it and society, comes next, in Chapter 7, on the view that politics in a state socialist country like China are fundamentally bounded by the institutions in which they take place, while also being shaped by conflicts in society and over issues of political economy. Finally, Chapter 8 looks at the major crises facing China and the country's prospects for dealing with them.

CHAPTER 1

Imperial Legacy, Capitalist Failure and Socialist Triumph

Let us begin with a puzzle. Why did Chinese history fail to develop a successful capitalism, which has provided other countries with the conditions for the development of representative politics led by rising middle classes?[1] There are good reasons to have expected China to be among the first capitalist countries in the world. Historically, it had a highly developed structure of markets that systematically connected the humblest hamlet to the greatest cities. During the Song dynasty a millennium ago, Chinese merchants established regular international trade routes as far as Africa. Culturally, China has long traditions and extensive experience in business entrepreneurship. Other parts of East Asia – such as Hong Kong, Japan, Singapore, South Korea and Taiwan, that historically shared many of China's social, economic, political and cultural forms – have produced some of the most vibrant capitalisms in the world.

Why did China produce instead one of the world's most massive and far-reaching socialist revolutions, and why did this revolution have a rural base and a more popular character than many others? This too is paradoxical. Marx, of course, predicted that socialist revolutions would be the product of the crisis of developed capitalism, which China has never experienced. He also projected that the industrial working class would provide the social base of the revolution when it did break out. Moreover, China's long history of imperial authoritarianism and bureaucratic centralization hardly presaged the participatory politics, orientation to local conditions and anti-bureaucratism that were distinctive features of the Communist-led revolutionary movement. And, more generally, China's profoundly conservative and durable traditional state seems an unlikely breeding ground for a revolution more radical than even the French and Russian.

This chapter explores these paradoxes. Ultimately it also addresses three analytical problems about Chinese state socialism. First, how can the triumph of state socialism in China, with its specific characteristics, be explained? Second, how did China's history affect its state socialism once it did triumph? And third, what does the Chinese case tell us about the preconditions and bases for socialist revolution and transformation more generally?

IMPERIAL CHINA AND ITS FAILURE

The Chinese imperial state, which had been in existence for two thousand years, collapsed in 1911.[2] It failed to provide the basis for China to make a smooth transition to a new state. It would take nearly four decades for China to re-establish political unity and coherent governance, and that would only come under as unlikely a successor as the Chinese Communist Party (CCP). Why did China's imperial state, which had succeeded better than any system in world history in establishing continuous rule for nearly two millennia, and which had presided over the development of the most advanced economy and culture on the planet for much of that time, finally collapse in the late nineteenth and early twentieth centuries? Why did it not prepare the ground better for its succession?

The structure of the gentry-dominated social formation

The answer to these questions has much to do with the interrelated structures of state and class in imperial times. The term 'ruling class' has probably never been more applicable than in the case of traditional China. The intelligentsia, members of the state bureaucracy and landowners formed a close-knit social class known as the gentry, which exercised robust hegemony over all the important levers of economic, political and social power.

Landlords of course owned large amounts of land, which they rented to peasant tenants, but in whose cultivation they played no significant part. The size of their holdings was subject to wide regional variation, rendering general statistics somewhat artificial. Still, the fact that, in the land reform of the late 1940s and early 1950s, 44 per cent of China's arable land was redistributed may give a rough idea of the order of magnitude (Bo, 1952: 151–2, cited in Lippit, 1974: 3). By the second and third decades of this century, around one-third of China's peasant households were tenants, and around 85 per cent of the land they rented was owned by landlords. The rest was rented from what the Communists would later call 'rich peasants' – farmers who owned more land than they could cultivate. and who therefore rented some out – and from less well-off peasants who could not work their own land, such as elderly widows or the infirm. Like so much else in China, regional variation was tremendous: tenancy rates ranged from a low of around 10 per cent of households in Shandong and Hebei Provinces to around half in Sichuan and Guangdong (Esherick, 1981: 395). Landlords also controlled rural credit; it was to them that peasants turned for loans, often in the form of rent deferrals with usurious interest, when times were bad, or even near the end of many routine growing seasons when food stocks were low and market prices for grain high. Many peasants who could not repay lost their land this way, since they had to put it up as collateral. Finally, the landlords were in command of grass-roots politics. Because the state was not formally organized below the county (*xian*) level, it depended on landlords to discharge the tasks of village government, such as tax collection and maintenance of order. This they did through control of lineage and 'civic' organizations and local militias. And, of course, when they carried out governmental service such as tax collection on behalf of the state, they made sure to retain a share for themselves by charging the peasants considerably more than was actually owed.

Landlords, however, also needed support from the state. The implicit threat of its coercive power helped underpin the exploitative tenancy system, and imperial armies were used to put down peasant revolts throughout Chinese history. Land-lords also depended on the state to construct and maintain the large water-control systems on which the cultivation that gave their land value depended. They needed political influence so they would not become vulnerable to economic squeeze and harassment by state officials. Perhaps most important, state power was, even more than land, a major source of wealth. Official salaries – between 33 and 180 taels annually for various civil service ranks in the late nineteenth century – were a mere pittance compared to the income from expense accounts, perquisites of office and open corruption, which brought in 30,000 to 180,000 taels annually. (By contrast, the average peasant earned in the neighbourhood of ten taels a year.) The average state official earned far more than the average landlord, then; and in aggregate terms, the gentry class derived around half of its income from governmental ser-vices and the like, but only around one-third from rent (Chang, 1962: 36, 40, 329).

In order to assure themselves some influence with the state and to partake of the riches that could be garnered there, landlords often sought to have a member of their family join the state bureaucracy. Office holders were recruited through the examination system, in which candidates were tested on their mastery of the Con-fucian classics. This is where the intelligentsia entered the picture. Landlords needed them to train sons, nephews or sometimes even adoptees for the rigours of the examinations. The scholars in turn either needed the landlords to employ them, or were themselves landowners or retired state officials. Preparing a boy for the examinations required wealth, to pay the scholar-tutor and to forego the income that the candidate could otherwise produce during years of training. Thus the children of ordinary peasants, even relatively well-off ones, were effectively barred from entering the state bureaucracy (unless they were co-opted by a wealthy land-lord who would sponsor their education, in return, of course, for expected loyalty and service in the future).

Once a real or adopted child of a landlord managed to pass the examination and enter the state bureaucracy, his links with the landlord class were only strength-ened.[3] He usually used his high income to purchase land or enlarge existing hold-ings. Although the state, to increase its control, forbade its officials to hold posts in their home areas, landlords could call on them to intervene informally with the magistrate in their home area on behalf of their relatives. And, as noted above, state officials needed the cooperation of landowners in the areas where they did serve to carry out the functions of local government at the grass roots.

Thus the landlords, state officials and scholars were bound together in a complex web of mutually reinforcing roles and self-interest. They controlled land, wealth and political power, and officially defined knowledge. They also maintained their position in the social hierarchy through the reproduction of Confucian culture,[4] through kinship organizations (which bound peasants of the same lineage to them, in a subordinate position, of course) and by manipulation of myriad local cultural symbols. The gentry's domination over the peasantry was nearly total.[5]

They also managed to keep the merchant class small and weak by restricting and pre-empting its development, devaluing it in social and cultural terms and co-opting it into the structure of gentry power. The state claimed for itself exclusive monopolies over the highly profitable salt *gabelle* and foreign commerce. It also imposed all manner of taxes and levies on trade. Confucian morality ranked commercial and manufacturing pursuits even lower than cultivation of land. The nexus of gentry power was so prepossessing that businessmen who could afford to do so often bought land themselves and tried to join the economically more idle gentry. This is one important element in China's historic failure to develop a bourgeoisie, as an initially much more economically and commercially backward Europe did.

Another factor in the historic weakness of the Chinese bourgeoisie is the nature of the state and its relationship to urban space. In Europe, feudal states were weak, having dispersed land and much political power to a warrior nobility. In the interstices of the royal domains, there developed towns and townspeople (the literal meaning of the word *bourgeoisie*) who undertook trade and manufacture in places beyond the reach of the monarch or the local nobility on their estates. Thus, there was physical and political space for autonomous bourgeois development within European feudalism. In China, by contrast, the central state occupied the towns, establishing local government offices and keeping a watchful eye on the rise of alternative sources of economic or political power among town dwellers.

Another element in the country's failure to develop capitalism has to do with the puzzle of Chinese technology. Historically, Chinese science and technology were extremely advanced. By the fourteenth century at the very latest, and probably many centuries earlier, China possessed all the knowledge and technique needed to invent modern industry. It also had a vast range and quantity of the necessary natural resources. Why then did it not do so? The answer lies in the country's political, social and economic structures. On the side of the supply of technology, the best young minds in China were generally channelled not into science, but into the study of Confucian classics in order to pass the bureaucratic entrance examinations. The Confucian world-view's emphasis on the virtues flowing from the natural order of the world also tended to discourage scientific or technological efforts to reshape nature. On the demand side, there was only a limited market for new inventions and technology, since the gentry were uninterested, the merchants more involved in trade than manufacture and the peasants generally too poor.

In conclusion, the society that the gentry ruled had reached the highest levels of economic, political, scientific and cultural development on the planet for many centuries after the collapse of the Roman Empire. This contributed to its astonishing longevity. Yet for all its sophistication and power, which were still intact as late as the middle of the nineteenth century, imperial China was unable on its own to make the economic and political breakthroughs that were achieved in Europe in the last few centuries. Nonetheless, it probably could have survived a good deal longer but for the rise of new challenges from abroad. Yet the very same forces that prevented China from making a breakthrough to economic, social and political modernization also made it impossible to survive the challenge posed by Europe and Japan which started in the middle of the nineteenth century.

The failure and collapse of the gentry-dominated social formation

The Qing dynasty had begun to run into difficulties by the latter half of the eighteenth century, due to rising population pressure, devolution of financial and political power away from the central government toward the regionally and locally based gentry, and peasant-based rebellions. Though these problems seem to have been of the sort that could threaten a dynasty, from the perspective of millennia of Chinese history there appears nothing so new in them as to threaten the very structure of the social and political formation itself. Yet a fresh ingredient was soon to make itself felt: China's first defeat by the West in the Opium War of 1839–42.

The Achilles' heel that imperialism found in China was not so much economic or social as political. While scholars of imperialism in other parts of the world – especially Africa and Latin America – have often tended to emphasize economic exploitation and social dislocation, in China the major damage done by imperialism was to the state. To be sure, foreigners made large fortunes in China. They also caused tremendous social damage by, for example, introducing opium on a wide scale (despite strenuous efforts by the Chinese state to resist it). The Chinese economy, however, was so vast and so deeply entrenched historically that imperialism was not sufficient to undermine, much less reorganize, it. Economic imperialism was restricted mainly to trade at first. Foreign firms did not begin to build factories in China on a significant scale until after the Sino-Japanese War, by which time the Chinese state was already in severe decline. International trade did not drastically transform the structure of the Chinese economy, the way, for example, that British imperialism did in India by destroying important rural sidelines such as spinning. Sidelines were a very important part of the rural economy in China too, and in some localities they were wiped out by foreign competition. More generally, though, by the 1930s, the volume of imported goods (other than textiles) that could compete with rural handicrafts was less than 5 per cent of the volume of handicraft production (Perkins, 1975: 121, cited in Lippit, 1978: 279).

The major impact of imperialism on China was to weaken it politically, by creating challenges that heightened its internal political and social contradictions, forcing attempts at change that made those contradictions manifest. Specifically, imperialism posed for the Chinese state the problem of political and economic reform, a project on which it and its gentry supporters would prove decidedly ambivalent. It also created new social forces – such as a nascent bourgeoisie – and mobilized others – such as provincially and locally based gentry and rebellious peasant-based mass movements – that gradually undermined the state.

The first concerted response to the West – specifically to the British victory in the Opium War – was the 'self-strengthening' movement of the 1860s. The two-decade delay is indicative of China's difficulty in responding to imperialism. The movement was centred on the construction of a domestic armaments industry by the state. Yet this resulted only in increased dependence on foreign armament manufacturers for advice and equipment, and in debt to the West for loans to finance the project. Moreover, the rise of a Chinese military industry did not spur wider industrialization that could have provided resources to pay off the debt later.

The loss of the Sino-Japanese war of 1894–95 revealed China's weakness in a particularly humiliating way. In 1898, a movement to modernize education and government administration was later dubbed the 'Hundred Days' because it was nipped in the bud by the arrest of its leaders by the Empress Dowager Cixi, who was supported by conservative-minded gentry and officials. By 1901, though, reformers had the upper hand again. The state undertook a major effort at conservative modernization, heavily influenced by the Japanese model, to make over China's governmental, military, educational and financial systems. It was supported by some gentry (including the Empress Dowager, who by 1905 had had a change of heart) and a small but growing Chinese bourgeoisie that was linked closely to the state and encouraged in its development by imperialism.

In Western Europe, the bourgeoisie and the state had provided the historical impetus for economic modernization.[6] We have seen how the nexus of gentry–state power made it difficult for China to undertake state-sponsored modernization. Yet China was not the first country with a strong conservative coalition between landed élites and the Crown. England and France also had such alliances at early moments in their pathways to modernity. In both countries, however, bourgeois forces paved the way for the development of modern industrial economies. In China, they proved too weak to overcome even the declining imperial state and its gentry base.

To be sure, a Chinese bourgeoisie did begin to develop in the second half of the nineteenth century. Its early leaders were men who had managed some of the first state-sponsored industries.[7] They struck out on their own, but also maintained their ties with the state, creating a close connection that would continue until the founding of the People's Republic in 1949.[8] The developing bourgeoisie also recruited Chinese merchants, bankers, manufacturers and compradors who had served as intermediaries with foreign business. Interestingly, many gentry – particularly those who lived in the environs of the coastal *entrepôts* – joined, contributing capital and sometimes even becoming entrepreneurs themselves. The Chinese bourgeoisie both collaborated with its foreign counterpart – a common phenomenon in late developing Third World countries subject to economic imperialism – but also gave foreign business interests very stiff competition. In 1933, Chinese-owned factories outnumbered foreign-owned ones by a factor of ten, employed nearly three-quarters of the industrial working class, and produced two-thirds of China's industrial output (Lippit, 1978: 264).

Yet this bourgeoisie was unable to exert the political hegemony needed to take a leading role in modernizing the Chinese economy and state. It was too little, too local, too late and too landed. First, in the vastness of predominantly rural China the bourgeoisie was too small to be able to generate the financial resources that were needed to transform the Chinese economy. A strong, centralized state – along the lines of Bismarckian Germany or even Napoleonic and post-Napoleonic France – was therefore required.[9] In China, however, the power of the regionally and locally rooted gentry to block the formation of such a state or state policies proved too formidable for modernizing political élites and the small Chinese bourgeoisie to overcome.

Second, building on China's long tradition of guild organization, the bourgeoisie was organized locally, in financial, kinship and home-place networks around individual cities. Rivalries between localities, based in nativism, linguistic and cultural differences and economic competition, helped prevent the bourgeoisie from forming a significant national political leadership or organizational presence (such as a political party of its own). Thus, even during the heyday of the Republic of China, the Chinese bourgeoisie was at least as much a subject and even victim of the militarist state's power as it was a force that could influence the state (Coble, 1980).

Third, by the time of China's political crisis and industrial take-off, imperialism had already entrenched itself in the country's economy and polity. This posed some fundamental difficulties for the Chinese bourgeoisie. Foreign powers occupied many key coastal cities, which their capitalists used as bases to occupy the commanding heights and most profitable sectors of the economy, such as finance, mining and shipping. Through those activities, as well as the control over collection of customs duties that they had won in various unequal treaties, foreigners appropriated a great deal of China's wealth. Some of this would otherwise have been available to finance China's development. In addition, the distinctive pattern of imperialism in China – under which several foreign countries established geographic spheres of influence – only further fragmented the country.

Finally, the Chinese bourgeoisie never fully separated itself from the gentry-ruled state or from the land. Indeed, its development was based heavily on both of these. If some of its capital came from land rent, some of its profits also returned to the land, as businessmen bought or enlarged estates as a hedge against the political and economic uncertainties of the day, and in accordance with Confucian values emphasizing the virtues emanating from land. Moreover, since some of the leading merchants had close ties to the imperial state – or to families with such ties – as a whole, the bourgeoisie was unable to mount a unified opposition to the state. To be sure, some bourgeois Chinese did, but many did not, continuing to ally themselves with the imperial state by buying offices, for example. For all these reasons, the Chinese bourgeoisie did not fully separate itself from, and therefore could not break through, the conservative nexus of gentry–state power. Thus, a major pathway toward China's economic modernization remained blocked.

What, however, about popular movements and their capacity to bring down the state, thereby removing a major obstacle to modernization? There was certainly no shortage of uprisings in the nineteenth century. Peasant rebellions accompanied the rise of the Taiping 'Heavenly Kingdom', a counter-state that actually ruled vast parts of central China (and even received foreign envoys) in the 1850s and 1860s. Around the same time, the Nian Rebellion, which took its name from the secret society that provided its leadership and organizational core, gained wide popularity for its Robin Hood-style appropriations and redistributions of government and landlord property. Ethnic minorities such as the Hui (Moslems) and the Miao also participated in rebellions, as did followers of various other secret societies. From 1898 to 1900, in the wake of the imperialist expansion that followed the loss of the Sino-Japanese War, the 'Boxer Rebellion' – a popular movement that was made up largely of peasants – gained control of major parts of Hebei Province, besieged

Beijing with the connivance of foreign powers and killed numerous foreign missionaries and businesspeople. Ultimately, a joint expedition of the armies of the foreign powers was organized to put down the Boxers. They went on to massacre thousands of Chinese and to demand from the imperial government the payment of a massive indemnity of 450 million taels. This burden, which came on top of the 250 million paid to Japan after the Sino-Japanese War, further weakened the already shaky imperial finances.

During the latter half of the nineteenth century, then, popular movements based on the active participation of tens of millions of peasants posed a serious threat to the empire. In the end, though, their lack of coordination, their mutual disagreements and inconsistencies and their inability to challenge the basic structure of gentry power within the villages prevented them from overthrowing the empire. None of the rebellions involved systematic attacks on the structure of gentry power. Ideologically, they were oriented to millenarian or quasi-religious, syncretic themes, not to class conflict. Politically, local élites were often the leaders of the rebel forces, recruiting peasants into rebel armies on the basis of lineage or secret society organizations that they dominated. When the imperial forces – often with the help of the foreign powers' troops – were able to defeat the rebel armies, local gentry easily restored the pre-existing relations of class domination that, as we have seen, provided the bedrock of the state. Still, the series of mass uprisings seriously weakened the Chinese state by draining it of resources needed to quell the rebellions, by making manifest its inability to command broad support and by providing opportunities for imperialism to strengthen its position in China.

THE FAILURE OF THE CHINESE REPUBLIC

The 1911 Revolution marked the end of the Qing Dynasty and, more significantly, also the end of all imperial dynasties in China. It was less a coordinated movement to create a new government or society than a snowballing series of regional revolts. It began with a mutiny of troops of the anti-Manchu Hubei New Army in Wuchang (now part of metropolitan Wuhan) on 10 October, a date now considered to mark the beginning of the post-imperial era. By November, uprisings led by several different groups had occurred in eleven provinces from Yunnan in the south to Shandong in the north. Meetings in December among leaders of the various uprisings ended in disagreement on a nominee for president of a new republic. Finally, Sun Yatsen, who in the interim had returned from a trip to Europe and the USA, was chosen, and inaugurated as China's first President on 1 January 1912.

From the point of view of class relations, three points are significant about this juncture of Chinese history. First, because the gentry's power was doubly rooted in the centralized bureaucratic imperial state above and the localities below, many of its constituent elements – particularly the local landowners and the provincial leaderships they supported – could survive the collapse of the state, at least for a time. Indeed, sections of the gentry could prosper in the short run from the dissolution of the imperial state, as they were then relieved of state exactions, regulation and harassment. That is part of the reason they helped bring it down. The active role of the gentry in the 1911 Revolution lent a conservative character to any régime that would replace the Qing.

Second, the bourgeoisie could only join the gentry in bringing down the Qing; they could not do the job themselves or provide the main leadership. Their presence in the revolutionary coalition was enough to make it impossible to re-establish an imperial government (though an abortive attempt was made by Yuan Shikai). Yet their economic and political power was not strong enough to establish a bourgeois state in its place. From 1911 to 1949, the accommodation of a dying conservative landed élite and a sickly bourgeois infant – foetus would be a better metaphor, since it had not separated itself clearly from its gentry parentage – produced a sustained and contradictory political crisis. This crisis had two tendencies: near anarchy, warlordism and a political vacuum on the one hand, and fascistic authoritarianism and militarism on the other.

Third, the lower classes were not really represented in or by the leadership or political programme of the 1911 Revolution. Their support was mobilized around anti-Manchu and anti-foreign slogans by the gentry and bourgeois élites who led the revolt. Workers and peasants, however, were not part of that leadership, and their interests were not seriously addressed in the revolutionary programme. The 1911 Revolution, then, could bring down the empire, but it could do little to address China's deepest and widest base of discontent.

For more than a decade after 1911, no stable or legitimate national government could be formed. Beijing was the site of endless political intrigue, coups and counter-coups. In effect, there was anarchy at the national level in China by the late teens and into the twenties. The closest thing to coherent governance was exercised by warlords over their regional satrapies. Of course, the weakness of the political centre only perpetuated China's problems both at home and abroad. Unrest continued to simmer and then began to boil over. When word reached China that the Allied Powers meeting at Versailles had given Germany's special rights in its Shandong sphere of influence to Japan instead of returning them to China, an historic demonstration took place in Beijing on 4 May 1919. The movement that took its name from this date swept rapidly and spontaneously over China, involving general strikes and demands for political reform, intellectual and cultural renewal and progressive social change. Hundreds of political societies were formed, including a group of thirteen radicals who gathered in Shanghai on 1 July 1921 to form the Chinese Communist Party.

In this climate of nationalist and reformist fervour, the Guomindang (Nationalist Party), under the leadership of Sun Yatsen, emerged as a leading force. Based in Canton initially under the protection of a sympathetic warlord, Chen Qiongming, Sun began to build a 'national' government and an army that would unify China under it. To achieve this he forged an alliance with the CCP and received assistance from the Soviet Union. At this time the Guomindang-led coalition comprised a very broad range of political forces, including conservative, locally based but nationalistic warlords and gentry, liberal-minded elements of the bourgeoisie, radical political activists, intellectuals, peasants and workers.

Of course, so profoundly contradictory a coalition could not last long. Sun died before the military unification campaign could get under way, and the politically conservative and militarily minded Jiang Jieshi emerged at the top of the leadership scuffle that followed. The 'Northern Expedition', a military campaign for political unification, began in 1926. Along the way, the left and right in the Guomindang split, and in April 1927 Jiang moved to eradicate the left in the 'White Terror', a bloody purge that left thousands of radical workers and liberal and radical intellectuals and political leaders dead. The Guomindang was now in the hands of its conservative wing of military and political leaders, warlords and their various landlord and bourgeois supporters. It proclaimed the formation of the Republic of China on 18 April, with its capital in Nanjing.

It was a weak, hollow institution. In order to 'rule', it had to ally itself with various warlords in the provinces, delegating considerable autonomy to them. More a loose confederation of regional satrapies than a national government that could command legitimacy and authority from its citizens and political leaders, it was unable to carry out even the most basic functions of government. Five military offensives were required against the main Communist base area in Jiangxi Province, and even the last was successful only in driving out, but not destroying, the CCP. The Guomindang also proved incapable of defending the country against invasion and occupation by Japan. During the war, it exercised no significant control over the countryside; indeed, it could not even collect taxes there, leaving that prerogative to its warlord allies. Plagued with administrative and political problems, the government and military became increasingly corrupt, inept and reactionary. The Guomindang presided over one of the worst hyperinflations in history, a product of its inability to raise the funds it needed to finance its military efforts and simultaneously to line the pockets of so many of its functionaries. A political rhetoric and form of popular organization with a strong resemblance to Fascism developed. For example, the Guomindang undertook mass campaigns – against spitting, for example – to promote discipline and cleanliness among its citizens. It organized gangs of 'Blue Shirts' to keep opposition in line.[10] It temporized in defending the country against Japan; while its armies did tie down the bulk of Japanese forces, they could never have driven them back home without the military exertions of the Communists and, in the Pacific military theatre, the United States. Following the defeat of Japan, the Guomindang military waged an unsuccessful civil war against the Communists, which it promptly lost by 1949, far sooner than either side had expected. Its leadership managed to escape to the island province of Taiwan, where, under American protection, it was able to consolidate what to this day it still formally claims to be China's only legitimate national government.

This debacle was the natural product of the class basis of the Guomindang government – in particular, its attempt to rule with the support of the landlords in the countryside and the bourgeoisie in the cities and, therefore, without the support of the peasants and workers. The landlord class, of course, wanted to maintain the rural status quo in class relations and its political autonomy from the central government. It was indifferent to any plans for national economic reform that might threaten its dominant economic position by, for example, taxing away part of the surplus it appropriated from the peasants, or building industries that might entice them to leave the land.

The bourgeoisie had a more complex and contradictory set of interests. Objectively, it needed a strong national government to help economic modernization. This meant, at minimum, national unification and peace (to stabilize markets, currency and transportation), and authoritative government (to assure labour discipline, guarantee contracts and defend against imperialism). It could also have gained from positive state activity to foster economic growth, such as building or financing needed transportation and energy infrastructure, developing technology and promoting the creation, stabilization and rationalization of markets. Yet such a programme would require putting vast financial resources under central administration. Because of landlords' hostility to modernization and their desire for localized autonomy from the Guomindang government, these resources could not be raised from the countryside. Therefore they could only be supplied by the cities, which meant putting pressure on the working class but also on the bourgeoisie. This the Guomindang did, though not to promote development but rather to finance its military and to enrich itself. In the process, it alienated many members of the bourgeoisie, and drove quite a few out of business. Thus, the Guomindang faced a double contradiction in its relations with its own class constituency: it was hamstrung by the opposing interests of the bourgeoisie and the landlords, a dilemma that in turn only exacerbated its conflicts with each of them.

In this situation, its authoritarian and militarist character can be explained in class terms. Historical situations in which a bourgeoisie and conservative landed class must find political accommodation have routinely produced strongly authoritarian governments, for example in Franco's Spain, Salazar's Portugal, Fascist Italy and Nazi Germany.[11] The Guomindang had few resources at its disposal besides military and coercive force. Perhaps if it had been able to mount a more effective army capable of subduing the warlords and the Communists, and of keeping the Japanese at bay, it could have then settled down to preside over a conservative programme of economic modernization that would also have accommodated the landlords. Yet the multiple crises facing the Guomindang – warlordism, landlord opposition to strong central government, an ambivalent bourgeoisie, rising peasant and worker discontent, civil war, Japanese invasion and a very weak economy – posed insuperable obstacles to the construction of a strong, effective military.

THE RISE AND TRIUMPH OF THE COMMUNIST-LED REVOLUTION

The analytical problem of the Guomindang state is thrown into relief by comparison with the Communist-led movement, which faced many of the same difficulties (such as civil war, Japanese depredations and economic crisis). Armed with better leadership, more appropriate military strategy and, perhaps most important, a class basis more suited to the goal of building a strong state that could begin to tackle China's many-faceted crisis, the Communist Party succeeded where the Guomindang failed. In some ways its success was also a product of Guomindang failure, as the Communists took advantage of Guomindang blunders.

The Chinese Communist Party, founded in 1921, began its quest for revolution mainly among China's proletariat. This was the terrain prescribed by Marx's own work, and its revolutionary potential had been stunningly confirmed by the Bolshevik Revolution in Russia just a few years before. Because of a combination of its own newness, the formidability of the fluid and confusing political situation in China at the time and advice from the Soviet Union, the Party entered into a 'united front' with the Guomindang, which in the early 1920s had not yet made its rightward turn and was the leading revolutionary force in the country. This obviated the need for the CCP to expend its energies on forming its own military organization. Instead, many of its members joined the Guomindang army, often as political commissars. The alliance also allowed the CCP to concentrate its early efforts on organizing unions and strikes.

The united front strategy was sensible for the new party so long as the Guomindang leadership remained pluralistic and reliable, and Soviet aid helped guarantee the CCP's safety. Yet it left the Party defenceless against the 'White Terror', when Jiang tried to crush the Communists while Stalin, valuing his alliance with the would-be Chinese government more than his commitment to proletarian internationalism, opportunistically looked the other way. The CCP learned a lesson that decisively influenced its future: that it needed its own armed forces.[12] Some CCP activists, including a young organizer named Mao Zedong, also learned from the April events the impossibility of making a proletarian-based revolution in the conditions prevailing in China at the time. Yet it took the Party Central Committee as a whole quite a while to reach this conclusion. In fact, the Party continued to lead urban uprisings through the rest of 1927. The reasons were several: the continuing importance of Marxist and Leninist theories; a still extant organizational base in other Chinese cities; the hope that the non-Communist left of the Guomindang might yet triumph over the Jiang Jieshi-led right; and a steady stream of advice from Moscow not to abandon the cities or the Guomindang (that continued even as the Communists were being slaughtered there by the GMD). Thus the centre of gravity of the decimated CCP did not shift away from the cities until 1931, when the Central Committee moved its headquarters out of hiding in Shanghai and into the Jiangxi countryside. Orthodoxies die hard, sometimes harder than the people who hold to them.

The CCP in the countryside: 1927–34

Mao Zedong and a few like-minded comrades were able to liberate themselves from the failed orthodoxy sooner than others. Though not the first Chinese Communist to promote a rural strategy – Peng Pai had been organizing peasant unions in eastern Guangdong since 1925 – Mao had urged the Party to pay attention to the peasants by March 1926, sharpening his position with the publication of a report on his rural investigation in Hunan in March 1927 (Mao, 1967, 1: 13–59). Thus the Party put him in charge of the Autumn Harvest Uprising there in the autumn of that year. When the revolt was crushed by the Guomindang, Mao and his small armed band retreated to the remote mountainous region of Jinggangshan, on the Hunan–Jiangxi border. He was joined there soon after by Zhu De and his armies, also on the run after defeats by the Guomindang.

In their early months in Jinggangshan, Mao and Zhu sought their first base of support in alliances with local outlaws, bandit gangs and secret societies. Initially these alliances had as much or more to do with the need to survive in a hostile area than with revolutionary strategy. Nevertheless, three points are significant about this decision for understanding the Communist Party as it would operate under Mao's leadership in later years. First, it demonstrated a supreme pragmatism which Mao would often emphasize in word and deed,[13] a trait that coexisted uneasily throughout his entire life with his propensity for radicalism. Second, the decision to ally with bandits shows Mao's flexibility on questions of the class basis of the revolution. Already by this time Mao had evinced this flexibility (or heterodoxy, depending on one's perspective) when he had called the Party's attention to the peasantry. Now he was allying with the rural counterpart of the lumpenproletariat.[14] Later, Mao would seek the support of middle and rich peasants and even patriotic landlords.

Third, Mao's alliance with the Jinggangshan bandits reveals a basic difficulty posed by the agrarian structure of Chinese society for rural revolution in China. The Chinese peasantry was at once under the organizational and political control of the local landlords, and lacking in bonds of solidarity with each other. Kinship ties (made concrete in formal clan associations in the villages), clientelism and tenants' need to cultivate the favour of their landowners to ensure that they would have land to rent all bound peasants to landowners in a pattern of authority that was reinforced and legitimated or at least justified by Confucian morality. These vertical ties across class lines, combined with the relative openness of the Chinese village in a rural structure in which the multi-village marketing area was the basic unit of commercial and social life, also served to weaken the solidarity of the peasants of a given village (Moore, 1966: 201–27; Skocpol, 1979: 147–54). In short, Chinese agrarian structure posed serious obstacles to any Communist efforts to organize peasants in their villages. The Party would eventually solve this problem, but only with patient, arduous, persistent effort and much experience. In the interim, Mao and Zhu could find their early allies only among marginal groups like bandits, who lived outside that landlord-dominated agrarian structure.

Gradually, the Communist movement in Jinggangshan began to broaden its support, as it was joined by Communist cadres who had survived Guomindang attacks in 1927, and as it recruited miners, railwaymen, peasants and soldiers from other Northern Expeditionary armies.[15] It adopted a very radical policy under which all land was to be confiscated and redistributed. This frightened off many rich and middle peasants, who were the mainstays of production in this very poor area. Mao favoured a more moderate policy under which only landlords would have land expropriated, while farmers with surplus land would be permitted to sell it (rather than have it expropriated).[16] Implementation of the radical land policy went slowly, and was not completed before the Jinggangshan base had to be abandoned in early 1929 under the pressure of a Guomindang blockade that helped create serious food shortages. The Jinggangshan Communists moved eastwards to a new base area straddling the border between Jiangxi and Fujian Provinces, establishing their headquarters at Ruijin.

In the meantime, the Party centre held firm to its proletarian strategy for the Chinese Revolution. At the Sixth Party Congress – held in Moscow (for reasons of security but also politics) concurrent with the Sixth Congress of the Moscow-dominated Communist International (Comintern) – the CCP stated that the working class was the most revolutionary force in China, and that the rural-based guerrilla armies were to help nurture a national revolutionary army that could attack and hold China's cities. The Party continued clandestine organizing in urban areas, particularly Shanghai, trying (with little success) to rebuild 'red' unions (to counter the Guomindang-run 'yellow' ones). A wave of strikes after 1928, which accelerated after 1930, did help underpin the case of those Communists arguing for proletarian revolution; but, in fact, most of these strikes were spontaneous affairs and had a predominantly economic rather than political character. The Party planned a military offensive by its rural-based armies on the cities of Changsha, Wuhan and Nanchang in 1930. Yet when the first attack, at Changsha, was routed, Mao and Zhu refused to carry out the assault on Nanchang with which they had been charged. In the wake of this defeat, and under continuing pressure from the Guomindang police in Shanghai, the Central Committee of the Party finally also moved its headquarters to Ruijin in 1931.

The Jiangxi Soviet undertook a series of agrarian reforms that was variable but on the whole quite radical. The 1930 policy, set by Mao and his comrades, was less extreme than that of the Jinggangshan years. All land was to be confiscated from the landlords and rich peasants. However, rich peasants, their dependants and even some landlords were allotted shares of redistributed land equal to those received by the 'masses'. This principle of protecting the interests of rich peasants in order to help ensure their continuing contribution to production would be upheld by Mao for most of the remaining years until the Party's 1949 victory. At this time, though, it was controversial within the CCP. These policies were reversed by the 1931 land law, drafted by a group of Moscow-trained CCP leaders known as the '28 Bolshe-viks', who were influenced by Stalin's stringent anti-kulak policy.[17] The law provided for the redistribution of only the poorest land to the rich peasants, and none at all to landlords, who were also subject to being drafted for forced labour.

The radicalism of agrarian policy in the Jiangxi Soviet was coupled with difficul-ties in implementation. Instructions were sent down from higher to lower-level organs, with little room for those below to convey information and views back upward. Sometimes this resulted in problems in carrying out the movement, includ-ing excessive and unrestrained mass radicalism. A major problem was the definition of exploiters. Generally, it was straightforward enough to classify landlords (those who owned land but did not work it), rich peasants (those who owned more land than they worked, renting out the rest) and poor peasants (those who had to rent land in order to survive). Matters became more complex, however, when it came to deciding who would be classified as middle peasants, a category defined as those who worked all their land, neither renting any in nor out. The matter was important, for middle peasants were not to have any property confiscated in the land reform. At the village meetings held to determine the classifications, poor peasants often wanted to classify middle peasants as rich peasants, so that their property would become available for redistribution. This damaged the productive energy and capacity of a large segment of China's most productive farmers, in turn undercutting production and, therefore, dealing a blow to the revolutionary movement. Moreover, some landlords and rich peasants were killed, which often frightened off wavering supporters. Then there were other mistakes which resulted from too little popular participation rather than excessively radical popular impulses. For example, the size of landlord and rich peasant holdings was sometimes assessed simply by asking the rich to testify about themselves and their neighbours. This resulted, of course, in understatements of their holdings, in turn reducing the amount of property that could be redistributed to the poor. In the Jiangxi Soviet period, then, the CCP first began to recognize the complexity and difficulty of mixing leadership and popular participation in order to carry out agrarian reform effectively. It was a problem with which the Party would continue to struggle for many years, and the experience garnered in Jiangxi would prove invaluable in refining and defining its distinctive style of mass work during the Yan'an period.

From the Jiangxi Soviet to the Long March

The CCP also faced growing pressure from the Guomindang throughout the Jiangxi years. In late 1930, Jiang Jieshi launched a military 'extermination' campaign. This and three more, each successively more massive and sophisticated, were repelled by the Communists. Finally, a fifth campaign launched in late 1933 managed to blockade the Jiangxi base, choking it economically and militarily.

The radical approach to the rich peasants had undercut the economic base of the region's economy by attacking its most productive class. It has been argued, especially in light of the subsequent Yan'an period's greater moderation and success, that a less radical or more effectively implemented policy would have helped attract more mass support in dealing with the blockade. The causality, however, could also run in the opposite direction. One lesson the CCP would learn from its failure in Jiangxi is that the peasantry would participate much more willingly in an agrarian reform if the military security of the area could be assured, so that the peasants would not have to worry about retribution by a returning pro-landlord government. This was, in fact, the actual meaning of Mao's widely misinterpreted statement that 'political power grows out of the barrel of a gun'. The relationship between success in garnering support for agrarian reform and for armed defence was reciprocal.

In any event, the Guomindang succeeded in driving the CCP out of its Jiangxi-Fujian base area, though it failed in its goal of 'exterminating' the Communists. It came close to realizing this grisly objective during the next two years, when the CCP undertook its famous 'Long March'. To say that the Party and its armed forces were decimated would understate the damage. Of the 100,000 or so who left the Jiangxi base, only 8,000 arrived in Shaanxi Province in late 1935. It was something of a miracle that the Communist movement survived at all. Even today, the Long March, filled with so much heroism and sacrifice, is revered in Chinese historical consciousness. There is something extraordinary about those who survived it, and it stands as symbol of the indefatigability of the Chinese Revolution.[18]

More concretely, the Long March proved to be a double climacteric for the Party. First, it represented the end of the conventional military strategy of positional warfare that had been used in the defence against the fifth Guomindang extermination campaign, and against which Mao and others had been arguing for several years. Mobile guerrilla tactics were adopted and perfected in the many battles against the pursuing Guomindang armies that punctuated the Long March. Second, the '28 Bolsheviks', who had led the Jiangxi Soviet and were now blamed for its military mistakes as well as its errors in agrarian policy, were replaced by a new leadership group headed by Mao. He retained the top Party post until his death 41 years later.

The Yan'an period

The Second United Front

In the wake of the Long March, the focus and direction of the Chinese Revolution underwent two major shifts. The first was the formation, amazingly enough, of a united front with the Guomindang against Japan. In 1931, Japan had invaded Manchuria, occupied it with no resistance from the Guomindang or its warlord allies and established a puppet government. On the first day of 1933, Japanese forces moved into the North China Plain, occupying large parts of present-day Hebei and Inner Mongolia. A rising tide of anti-Japanese protests and sentiment in 1935 and 1936 produced widespread demands for cooperation among Chinese of all political persuasions to resist and expel the Japanese.

The CCP had issued such a call in 1935. In December 1936, Jiang Jieshi was placed under house arrest by General Zhang Xueliang, the Manchurian warlord whose warlord father had been assassinated by Japanese officers, and who wanted to forge a stronger national anti-Japanese united front. In a brilliant display of statecraft and political acumen, the CCP persuaded Zhang to release Jiang, the Party's old arch-enemy who had betrayed it in the bloodbath of the 'White Terror' a decade before and who again had nearly 'exterminated' it just two years earlier before and during the Long March. With this spectacular demonstration of the CCP's commitment to the anti-Japanese struggle, and with popular patriotism at fever pitch, Jiang Jieshi was hard put not to sign a second united front pact with his arch-nemesis, the 'Communist bandits'. An agreement was signed in July 1937, one day after the new Japanese invasion. The CCP armies were to be left intact, and incorporated formally into the troops of the Nationalist government. In other words, the Guomindang and Communist armies were no longer to fight each other, and were to cooperate in fighting the Japanese.

The Yan'an way

The second major shift of the Yan'an period was the development of a new class constituency, agrarian policy, political institutions and leader–mass relationship that came to be known as the 'Yan'an way', after the rural Shaanxi town at which the CCP established its headquarters.

Class policy

The Party now came to see its class policy in the Jiangxi Soviet as excessively radical, having failed to promote the broad popular support and level of economic production needed to sustain the revolutionary base. Moreover, such a policy was no longer consistent with the CCP's shift toward the anti-Japanese struggle, for which it had called upon all patriotic groups in Chinese society – including even the Guomindang – to unify with it. Now CCP policy called for the support not only of the poor and middle peasantry and the working class, but also of rich peasants, the petit bourgeoisie, intellectuals, national capitalists and even a newly created class category called 'enlightened landlords', i.e., those who would not collaborate with the Japanese occupation forces or their puppet governments.[19] Of course there were not many members of the national bourgeoisie who actually participated in the CCP movement, since its base areas were primarily rural. Likewise, few landlords fitted the 'enlightened' category; most allied themselves with or at least complied with the Japanese or pro-Japanese political forces. The CCP did elicit support, however, from many non-Communist intellectuals, who left their homes in the major coastal cities that had come under Japanese occupation and headed for Yan'an because they felt that the Party was the leading patriotic force in the country.

Agrarian policy

The changes in class policy and constituency required concomitant changes in agrarian policy. No longer was the hard line taken in Jiangxi against rich peasants and landlords appropriate. Private property – a principle dear to the petit and national bourgeoisies, many liberal intellectuals and even (and, perhaps most important to the rural revolution) middle peasants – was now to be scrupulously respected. Thus, summary expropriations and redistributions of land and property were replaced by campaigns for rent reduction and usury control. Landlords were to be subject to taxation, sometimes heavy or retroactive, but they kept their land. Rich creditors of poor peasants were often penalized by repayment moratoria, but the debts were not cancelled.

Political organization and leader–mass relations: the mass line

The greatest innovations and most decisive break with past practice came in the area of political organization and leader–mass relations. The 'mass line' developed in Yan'an was a radically new approach that involved closer and more democratic relations between revolutionary leaders and institutions on the one hand and the people on the other. This effort would become a lasting feature of Chinese politics in the Maoist period, and one that distinguished it sharply from state socialist politics in the Soviet Union and Eastern Europe. It became influential in Third World socialist countries such as Mozambique, South Yemen and Vietnam.

The most concise statement of the mass line was made by Mao in 1943:

> Communists must . . . combine the leadership with the masses . . . all correct leader-ship is necessarily 'from the masses, to the masses'. This means: take the ideas of the masses (scattered and unsystematic ideas) and concentrate them (through study turn them into concentrated and systematic ideas), then go to the masses and propagate and explain these ideas until the masses embrace them as their own.
>
> (Mao, 1967, 3: 117–19)

In Yan'an the mass line took several concrete forms. First, government administration was streamlined and decentralized. The Chinese Communist Party was heir both to millennia of imperial centralized bureaucracy and the newer Leninist (and, more particularly, Stalinist) form of democratic centralism that was generally far more centralist than democratic (see Chapter 4). From its inception, it had by and large organized itself and its movement along lines of vertical political organization and power. Lower-level units were primarily, if not exclusively, responsible to higher-level ones. Democratic centralism focused the attention of local officials on carrying out instructions they received from above, often with little regard for the policies' suitability to local conditions or their palatability and popularity with the people. In the language of policy studies, this had resulted in difficulties in receiving timely 'feedback' on 'performance'. In terms of politics, it had hampered popular expression and influence. Now county and grass-roots-level leaders were given expanded latitude and coordinative power in carrying out higher-level instructions in accordance with local needs, conditions and opinions. In a famous essay entitled *Oppose Book Worship*, Mao urged them to start thinking for themselves (Mao, 1966). Elsewhere he wrote:

> [T]he person with overall responsibility in the locality must take into account the history and circumstances of the struggle there . . . ; he should not act upon each instruction as it comes down from the higher organization without any planning of his own . . . [I]t is hoped that comrades will themselves do some hard thinking and give full play to their own creativeness.
>
> (Mao, 1967, 3: 121–2)[20]

Higher-level organs were reduced in size and complexity, and told to limit their instructions to their subordinates.

> Nor should a higher organization simultaneously assign many tasks to a lower organ-ization without indicating their relative importance and urgency or without specifying which is central, for that will lead to confusion in the steps taken by the lower organizations.
>
> (Mao, 1967, 3: 121)

Party officials were, in another phrase Mao used to title an essay, to stop writing 'eight-legged essays' (a strict template used in Confucian commentary writing) and instead make shorter, more direct reports to reduce red tape (Mao, 1967, 3: 53–68). The combination of streamlined centralized leadership and local discretion and coordination known as 'dual rule', first implemented in Yan'an, would return to China in 1958 during the Great Leap Forward. It has produced its own characteristic political tensions (see Chapter 4). Yet dual rule also mitigated against some of the worst problems of one-sided authoritarianism and bureaucratism that were the bane of state socialism in the Soviet Union and Eastern Europe.

A second form of the mass line was the campaign to send cadres 'to the villages' (xia xiang). Many of the middle and higher-level officials whose positions were abolished in the administrative simplification, along with many of the intellectuals who had flocked to Yan'an, were assigned to posts at the grass roots. They were to help strengthen local governments and the political capacities of peasants and indigenous local leaders. To ensure that these cadres would not simply take over local affairs (which could have the opposite effect intended by the decentralization), and because of Mao's professed belief that leaders could lead best when the existential distance between them and the masses was reduced, these cadres were expected to participate regularly in production alongside the peasants, live in similar circumstances with them and in general share their experiences. The cadres were supposed to learn directly from the peasants about rural life in order to be able to lead them more effectively in carrying out the Party's policies of rent reduction and usury control, building up local governments and the peasants' political abilities to participate in politics (e.g., through literacy campaigns, newspaper reading groups, and political discussions) and resisting and driving back the Japanese.

Third was the effort to enhance the democratic and representative character of local governments by separating them from the Party and by ensuring significant representation of non-Party people in them. Secret ballot elections were held regularly at village, township, county and regional levels, with universal suffrage for all men and women over eighteen years of age. The only restriction was the 'three thirds' principle, according to which one-third of offices was to be filled by CCP members, one-third by non-CCP leftists and one-third by progressive-minded people who were not required to be particularly leftist in their political orientation. Even Guomindang members, members of the bourgeoisie and landlords were eligible for the latter category. In the Yan'an base, only a quarter of those elected in 1941 to representative positions at all levels were CCP members. Of course, the CCP did have greater representation in the higher levels of government: 57 per cent of the members of the regional congress (covering the entire Yan'an base) were Communists. Yet compared with the previous governmental monopoly held by the Party, and in the light of the decentralization of much power downward to lower levels where CCP members occupied proportionally fewer posts, the Yan'an electoral system was significant in promoting democracy and in reflecting and reinforcing the new breadth of the political base in the liberated zone.

Fourth, the forms of popular political expression and the range of issues on which such expression could take place were also broadened. Village mutual aid teams and nascent urban co-operatives were run on a participatory basis. In Yan'an, the 'wall poster' (bi bao), on which citizens could write their views on any subject and post them up in a public place for all to see, first came into serious use. Known after 1957 as the 'big-character poster' (*dazibao*), this form of citizen expression, distinctive to Chinese socialism, would go on to become extremely important in the Cultural Revolution decades later (see Chapter 2).

Fifth, in a continuation of practices developed during the Jiangxi Soviet, the armed forces were to play an important role in civilian affairs, in a way that subordinated them to civil authority. They were mobilized into production drives, and continued to abide by the 'three rules for attention' and 'eight points of discipline', according to which, for example, soldiers were to take nothing from the people ('not even a needle and thread'), return all borrowed items, speak courteously, pay fair prices for all purchases and not take liberties with women.

The mass line placed tremendous demands on cadres, which they could not always fulfil. Reared in the authoritarianism of traditional Chinese political culture, brought to political maturity in a Leninist-style Communist Party and thrust into the exigencies and unfamiliar circumstances of rural life and revolution, it was easy for them to act in ways inconsistent with the goals of the mass line. 'Deviations' occurred, including: 'commandism' (seeking compliance by issuing orders rather than by the use of persuasion, which could easily occur in the heat of battle or other emergency situations); 'tailism', its opposite (following the immediate wishes of the masses without engaging people in analysis of their views); 'subjectivism' (making decisions or formulating opinions without full investigation or consultation); 'élitism' (acting as if one were superior to others); 'bureaucratism' (carrying out orders and sticking to cumbersome official procedures); and 'localism', its opposite (acting in disregard of central directives and the wider political situation).

To deal with these problems and help cadres perfect their mass-line leadership styles, the CCP launched a 'rectification' (*zhengfeng*) movement in 1942. The orientation was to be constructive – Mao used the metaphor of curing the sick – rather than punitive. As such, it was not a purge – the emphasis was not on show trials and summary expulsions. At the centre of the rectification was 'criticism and self-criticism', in which all cadres – not just pre-selected targets – were to analyse their own actions, receive public criticism from other members of the work unit and then make a public self-criticism before the unit. In this process, then, the standards of mass-line leadership were specified by cadres' own colleagues in a group process. Criteria were developed successively by dealing with each person's specific case, and then applied through public deliberation and evaluation. This was direct mass democracy in action, though always in the context of guidelines from the Party centre – in particular, from Mao himself. The result of the rectification was the reinforcement, not diminution, of most cadres' attachment to the Party and the revolution. The rectification movement also helped improve cadres' leadership skills. It elevated Mao himself as a model leader in a way that had not been done before. Finally, it firmly established the principle of criticism and self-criticism, which was to become a hallmark of CCP politics that, like so many other innovations of the Yan'an years, would distinguish Chinese state socialism from its counterparts in the Soviet Union and Eastern Europe.

Military struggle in the Anti-Japanese War

The CCP's popularity during the Yan'an period stemmed in part from its innovative and flexible strategies on class relations, agrarian policy, political organization and leader–mass relations. Its stature was also enhanced by the leading role it took in the Anti-Japanese War. The Guomindang's contribution to the resistance was passive and defensive by comparison. It used the 1937 united front agreement with the CCP more to strengthen its position vis-à-vis the Communists than to join with them to fight the Japanese. For example, Jiang Jieshi assigned his best armies to blockade the Yan'an base. Guomindang forces often avoided engaging the Japanese, preferring massive retreats (justified by the slogan 'trading land for time') that left much of China under Japanese control by 1941. The Guomindang capital had to be moved far inland to Chongqing, in Sichuan Province. While this way of (not) waging the war involved good measures of cowardice and cunning betrayal (by saving energy to fight the CCP, while allowing it to bear the brunt of the Anti-Japanese War), objectively speaking it had a material basis too. The Guomindang armies were corrupt and incompetent, and their command and coordination structures unworkable. Many of the rank-and-file soldiers were impressed into service by force, and treated horribly – fed and housed minimally, and put on lengthy forced marches during which many died before the enemy was ever engaged. Thus, morale and commitment were low, to say the least. The officers were generally no better than the soldiers. Many sold arms to the Communists to line their own pockets. Generals were known to lose battles on purpose so as to make a financial (as well as human) killing by driving down the value of government bonds they had sold short on the Shanghai exchange. They also inflated figures on the number of troops under their command so they could enrich themselves with larger budgetary allotments from the Chinese government and its foreign allies, especially the USA. The need to rely on alliances with semi-autonomous warlords made unified command and military coordination difficult. It became self-evident to most Chinese that the Guomindang could not and would not prosecute the Anti-Japanese War effectively.

By contrast, the CCP armies concentrated their military energies on fighting the Japanese in their own way. They used the mobile guerrilla tactics they had developed during the Long March to wage coordinated campaigns (such as the famous Hundred Regiments Offensive of 1941), while also engaging in sustained harassment behind Japanese lines. Though the CCP could not really damage the powerful Japanese war machine until Japan had been weakened by a declining position in the Pacific War, Communist efforts did help keep Japanese armies at bay in many base areas. More important than their military effect was their political one: they established the Communists as the leading anti-Japanese force in China.

Nationalism and revolution

Analysts of the communist movement disagree about the reasons for its rapid growth in power and popularity from 1937 to 1945. Some have argued that the Communists owe their popularity to their nationalism, not to their programmes of agrarian and political change – in other words, that patriotism, not revolution, was their main source of popular appeal (Johnson, 1962). This argument is founded on the premise that a clear distinction can be drawn between the national and revolutionary struggles. It cannot. The Japanese invasion exacerbated aspects of the class struggle, and in turn the class struggle against landlords was also a patriotic struggle against collaborators. Many landlords collaborated with the Japanese and thus became associated with their hideous depredations against civilian populations (such as the scorched earth policies of 'kill, burn and destroy everything'). The CCP-led production drives and the political reforms were the major source of relief from the Japanese blockades of the base areas. The effectiveness of the CCP's guerrilla struggles against Japanese forces was based on its revolutionary mass-line policies. In short, the class and national struggles were so tightly intertwined as to render untenable the argument that patriotism but not revolution was the basis of the CCP's appeal and success.

Civil war and the triumph of the CCP: 1945-49

At the end of the Second World War, the CCP had a large reservoir of popular sympathy, but it still controlled only its inland base areas, many of which were poor to begin with and had become more completely immiserated during the war. With the help of an American airlift, the Guomindang regained control of China's industrial and financial centres, as well as its richest farmlands, in the coastal areas and in the north-east. It also enjoyed much other support from the United States, the most economically powerful country in the world after the war. Looking at this strategic balance, the CCP did not anticipate a revolutionary victory just yet. It hoped, rather, for the formation of a coalition government with the Guomindang, to give it breathing space to marshal its forces. In the USA, many officials were growing aware of the structural weaknesses and practical incapabilities of the Guomindang; and the growing US–Soviet rivalry fuelled concerns about Soviet aspirations in the Far East. So the USA too sought to forge a CCP–Guomindang coalition. Yet Jiang Jieshi, as always ideologically fanatical and inflexible in his anti-Communism, and confident of his ability to command American support even if he resisted a coalition, was intransigent.

In 1946–47, his armies undertook a major offensive against the Communists, driving them out of many of their wartime bases, including Yan'an. This was not, however, a devastating defeat for the CCP. Yan'an, a remote rural area, was important only symbolically, and the Guomindang advances were partly the result of the CCP's now perfected strategy of shunning positional battle and the fixed defence of territory in favour of mobile warfare. The CCP took up a new base in the far more prosperous Shanxi Province, from which it launched a counter-offensive that by late 1947 had enabled it to control most of Shanxi, Hebei and Shandong Provinces. Shijiazhuang, a strategic railway junction and capital of Hebei Province, became the first major city taken by the CCP.

Meanwhile, the Guomindang's domestic base began to crumble rapidly. Unable to finance its military exertions, its corruption and its normal governmental operations with an irregular, inefficient, leaky revenue system, it resorted to print-ing worthless currency. Prices rose to more than six thousand times the 1937 level. Workers joined shopkeepers in staging riots and strikes in Shanghai in protest against the rising cost of food and declining standard of living. Peasant unrest grew even in areas under Guomindang control. Jiang responded with a wave of repres-sion that shocked and alienated even many anti-Communists. Key liberal leaders, including Song Qingling, Sun Yatsen's widow, began to withdraw their political support.

In the expanding Communist base areas, the class struggle heated up. Late 1945 saw a renewal of the rent and interest reduction campaigns. 'Anti-traitor' move-ments attacked landlords who had collaborated with the Japanese, confiscating and redistributing their property and cancelling debts owed to them. This was the first land reform since Jiangxi. In the older liberated areas under secure CCP military control, land reform was gradually extended, based on popular mobilizations using the mass-line methods developed in the Yan'an period. Showing its characteristic flexibility on class relations, however, the CCP adopted a much more moderate line in the newly liberated zones, which were more urbanized than the older base areas. It sought the support of the middle classes, capitalizing on their disillusionment with the Guomindang. By late 1948, the CCP succeeded in signing an agreement with centrist anti-Guomindang political parties to establish a national Political Consultative Conference. On the military front, it began to occupy major industrial centres in Manchuria. Through 1949, the Communist armies gained control of all the major urban centres in east and north China. With the tide turning, many Guomindang generals switched allegiance to the CCP. Those remaining loyal to Jiang Jieshi followed him to Taiwan, where they remained, laying a *de jure* claim, that continues to the present, to be the government of all of China. Formally China would remain in a state of civil war between rival governments. But, in reality, the CCP victory was complete. On 1 October 1949, Mao Zedong stood on the rostrum of the symbolically crucial Gate of Heavenly Peace (*Tiananmen*) in Beijing and proclaimed the foundation of the People's Republic of China.

CONCLUSION

The questions posed at the outset of this chapter can now be addressed. First, why did the Chinese empire collapse, after enduring for two millennia and achieving the highest levels of political, cultural and economic development in the world for most of that time? Second, why did it collapse the way it did: in utter political and economic crisis in which no government capable of ruling the country in a unified way could coalesce for nearly forty years, during which time the country was wracked by civil war, foreign conquest and revolution? Third, why did capitalism not take hold as a robust mode of production on which a politically viable state could be founded? Fourth, why did the Chinese Communist Party succeed, where the landlord class and the bourgeoisie had failed, in creating a new state with political coherence and power? Fifth, why did the revolution led by the CCP find its base in the countryside rather than the cities, and its form in a movement that mixed popular and participatory elements with Leninist-style leadership? Sixth, what implications does this long and complex legacy have for Chinese socialism under the CCP? And, finally, what implications does it have for our theoretical understanding of the preconditions for socialist revolution?

The collapse of gentry society

Explanation of the first problem – the fall of the gentry-dominated social formation after millennia of dominance – revolves around the structure of gentry hegemony in imperial China and its transformation under new conditions in the nineteenth and twentieth centuries. The gentry's command of economic, social, political and cultural levers of power was so strong and complete that it could rule China for two thousand years. It effectively undercut the development of any social, economic and political forces that rivalled its power. In particular, through a combination of pre-emption, co-optation and economic regulation, the gentry was able to prevent the rise of an independent bourgeoisie from among China's mercantile strata.

In the nineteenth century, the European powers posed a threat to China's sovereignty and territorial integrity that could only be fended off by industrialization. Yet under gentry hegemony, China was incapable of a timely economic transformation. The country could not industrialize sufficiently before the state had been undermined and the economy opened to imperialism. Industrialization has everywhere required a strong bourgeoisie and/or leadership from a modernizing state. Gentry hegemony had prevented China from generating a bourgeoisie. It also prevented the state from taking the lead in fostering industrial modernization, in several ways. The gentry used its political leverage to block reform. It clung to and continued to reproduce an anti-modern Confucianism. Structurally, its local bases of political power were a powerful obstacle to the political and financial centralization that state-sponsored industrialization would require. In short, the robust hegemonic power of the gentry was also at the root of its inability to respond to the new challenges of industrialization of the nineteenth and twentieth centuries. This incapacity led to its demise.

We can now turn to our second problem: why did the gentry-dominated social formation fall the way it did? Specifically, why was no smooth transition to a next stage possible? Why, instead, did China become a political centrifuge, breaking up into rival satrapies for almost four decades? Again, explanation begins with the structure of gentry domination. In China's vastness and variegation, the gentry had ruled by developing locally and centrally based levers of power: controlling land and other economic resources, social organization, culture and politics in the villages, and controlling the state above them. When, for reasons we have discussed above, the centre fell, the gentry, maintaining their levers of local control, did not have to fall with it. The support among many gentry for the 1911 Revolution indicates that they sensed this clearly. Thus, the gentry-dominated social formation could collapse slowly, one layer at a time: first the state, and then the rural mode of production, class structure and ideology. This helps explain the protracted nature of the Chinese Revolution. It also explains the centrifugal character of its collapse: when the gentry's central base of political power evaporated, but landlordism did not, the only place from which it could continue to exercise power was its local and regional bases.

Finally, the survival of the rural élite into the post-imperial period also contributed to the political and social tendentiousness and persistent conservatism of the transition. After 1911, the political field contained organizations not only of the bourgeoisie, working class and peasantry, but also of the gentry. Their presence only complicated and exacerbated what would even without them have been an explosive struggle, in at least three ways. First, unrestrained by the moderating influence of the imperial state, and in the context of the need to build and defend local satraps against each other as well as would-be state builders at the centre, the landlords stepped up their exploitation of the peasantry, whose capacity to endure it was reduced by the depredations of civil and Anti-Japanese War. So the survival of the gentry as landlords only sharpened the objective bases of rural class struggle.

Second, the landlords' continued presence after 1911 weakened and conservatized the bourgeoisie and exacerbated its political crisis. We have seen how they blocked construction of a modern and modernizing state by the bourgeoisie or on their behalf. This political failure only deepened the transitional crisis by undercutting the development of China's industry. It also reproduced the centrifugal nature of the polity in two respects: weakening the bourgeoisie so much that it could not form a coherent national base of power; and tying them to land and therefore reinforcing their localism. Third, the survival of the landlords forced the Guomindang to balance them against the bourgeoisie. This combination, in China as elsewhere, was the social basis of fascistic authoritarianism.

The failure of capitalism

In discussing the structural factors that caused China to fracture after the fall of the empire, we have already touched upon the third question: why did capitalism fail in China? The Chinese bourgeoisie faced formidable structural obstacles to constructing a robust capitalism. First, its development had been hampered by millennia-old gentry hegemony. Second, the bourgeoisie maintained close ties to the landed élite: it received investment from them, and in turn purchased land and imperial office. When the gentry began to collapse in the late nineteenth century, the bourgeoisie had great difficulty erecting the minimal political preconditions for a functioning, integrated capitalism, such as national government to provide unified currency, legal guarantees for contracts and civil peace. The presence in China of a more industrially advanced West only made prospects for a bourgeoisie-led capitalism dimmer, in two ways: by providing stiff competition, and by further weakening and even dismembering China. These same factors, combined with the continued political power of a largely conservative and anti-modern landed élite, and the incapacitation of the Chinese state due to Western and Japanese imperialism, domestic uprisings, civil and international war and the political centrifuge of warlordism, also undercut the alternative possibility of a state-sponsored capitalism in China.

The nature and success of the Chinese Revolution under the CCP

The fourth question concerns the reasons why the CCP could succeed where the Guomindang had failed in establishing and consolidating state power. This is all the more puzzling since many of the structural conditions within which the CCP had to work were notably unfavourable to its revolutionary project – which is one reason why the Party and the revolutionary movement it led came close to destruction not once but twice from 1927 to 1936. The working class, though capable on occasion of considerable radicalism, was small in the national scheme of things. The peasantry was enmeshed in landlord-dominated vertical structures – such as tenancy relationships, kinship associations, patron–client networks and secret societies – that made it very difficult for it to attain class consciousness or organizational unity (Skocpol, 1979: 148–50). Peasant support did not drop into the lap of the CCP like a ripe fruit. Quite the contrary, it had to be worked for very hard against considerable odds. It took quite some time and many mistakes before the 'mass line' as a way of attracting and mobilizing peasant support could be made effective in eliciting the active popular following that was required for successful revolution in China. Yet, in the end, the substantive reforms, which produced genuine material gains for the majority of rural people in the wartime bases, and the mass-line process that went along with them, proved popular with a broad range of classes and groups. That support in turn provided an important bedrock of support for the CCP through 1949 and beyond.

There were also some structural features of transitional China that were conducive to its revolutionary aspirations. First, the peasantry was increasingly exploited after 1911. Structurally, this exploitation was occasioned by the fall of the Chinese imperial state, which had restrained the landlords somewhat. Its absence opened up a competitive politics that fuelled landlord avarice. Second, worsening rural oppression took place within an essentially unchanged agrarian structure. Unlike England, for example, where the eviction of peasants from the land and the commercialization of agriculture took place as peasants were being thrust into new lives in the industrializing cities, in China the peasants remained together on the land, in a pre-commercialized, pre-modernized agriculture, to suffer under the landlords. Peasants are likely to be more radical when their pre-existing way of living and making a living is preserved but strained to the breaking point than when that way of life is uprooted (Moore, 1966: Ch. 9).

Third, there was a structural weakness at the bottom of the landlord–peasant relationship that made China more prone than many other agrarian societies to peasant rebellions. While Chinese peasants were, certainly, under the pervasive dominance of the landlords, such power was more broad than deep. The landlords did not take part in or make a meaningful contribution to agriculture or peasants' livelihoods. When push came to shove, the Chinese peasants did not need their landlords. Thus, they were structurally predisposed to rebellion when things got bad enough, as they did in the first half of this century (Moore, 1966: 201–27). Of course, it is a long way from rebellion to revolution, but peasant rebelliousness could provide a starting point for revolution (Thaxton, 1983). Fourth, the disintegration of the Chinese polity in these years was a great boon to the CCP, affording it the opportunity to establish base areas in remote regions in which it could test out its policies and nurture its resources. It is no accident that these base areas were often founded in border regions, so that the mobile political and armed forces of the CCP could more easily elude provincial leaderships who lacked coordination by central state authorities.

Fifth, the protractedness of the post-imperial transition, which we have traced to its structural contradictions, gave the CCP badly needed time to overcome some of the structural obstacles it faced, to learn from its mistakes and to develop experience in government administration and political organization and mobilization.

The CCP victory was also aided by the failures of the Guomindang. It profited from the influx of a large number of patriotic but previously non-Communist intellectuals and students who became disillusioned with the Guomindang's failure to defend China against Japan, its gross corruption and its inability to lead China forward toward modern economic and social development. The CCP took cunning advantage of the military blunders and inappropriate strategies of the Guomindang armies. It turned the misery caused by the economic policies (and non-policies) of the Guomindang, such as the hyperinflation and utter lack of developmental action, against not only the government but also against the landlords associated with it.

When all the favourable and unfavourable structural factors are totted up, though, it still remained for a skilful and committed leadership blessed with some fortuitous historical conjunctures to overcome the obstacles and take advantage of the opportunities with which the Chinese social formation presented the Communist Party. Without the Japanese invasion, Jiang Jieshi might well have been able to concentrate his military resources on the Communists and reach his most treasured goal of 'exterminating' them; after all, he nearly did it even with the Japanese on the scene. The Japanese invasion also provided the impetus for the major shifts in CCP class and agrarian policies and political methods that proved successful where previous ones had failed. This brings us to the political brilliance of Mao Zedong and his like-minded comrades in formulating those innovative policies and leadership methods, and the extraordinary commitment of thousands of CCP cadres in carrying them out under the most difficult circumstances. The Chinese Revolution was a triumph of historical and class forces, but it was also a triumph of human will against such forces.

The fifth question, concerning the rural base and popular participatory character of the CCP movement, has already been mentioned. Neither of these features of the Party's revolutionary strategy came easily to it. Indeed, it took years of failure with an urban and more strictly Leninist approach before the CCP officially found its own road. One could argue that the rural and popular character of the revolution was structurally determined: the working class was too small and weak to be the main base of the revolution, the urban-based Guomindang was bound to betray it and the peasantry could only be won over with something like the mass line.[21] Yet there is something a bit too deterministic about this. The Chinese working class might have been able to grow into a more formidable revolutionary force if it had not encountered an enemy ruthless and shrewd enough (at least in the short run) to destroy its radicalism early. And there was nothing that compelled the Guomindang to act as it did toward the urban left, which was actively supporting the Guomindang's Northern Expedition at the time. The April 1927 'White Terror' against the Communists and coup against the Guomindang left was very much the work of Jiang Jieshi, and it did not have the support of many liberal-minded Guomindang leaders of the day. So one could argue that it was as much Jiang Jieshi and his right-wing allies in the Guomindang as it was the inexorable forces of history that undercut the CCP's proletarian base and drove it – very hesitantly and reluctantly at first – into the arms of the peasantry.

It is also circular and functionalist to argue that the mass line was formulated and implemented successfully because it was the only way the rural revolution could be consummated.[22] After all, the revolution need not have succeeded. Or it could have attracted much less active support than it did and still have won by default. The failures of the Jinggangshan and Jiangxi days were eventualities of this sort. One can conclude from those failures and from the successes of Yan'an that rural revolution required strong popular participation to succeed fully. Yet it took creative leadership and committed supporters to make this discovery in the crucible of China's revolutionary praxis. Mao and his comrades were not mere products of history; they also made that history.

History, revolution and socialism

How did China's past affect the way the CCP made the future? This is our sixth question: what implications did China's complex history have for the distinctive brand of socialism we will be studying in succeeding chapters?

First, China's vastness and variegation, which have expressed themselves in different ways throughout China's history – such as the reliance on locally based élites in imperial days, and the centrifugal forces of the transitional period – have also been manifest in its revolution and, as we shall see, in the structure of its socialist political economy. A Communist Party operating in nearly twenty base areas spread over all of China could not have sustained the highly centralized structure of command and discipline associated with Leninism. That the CCP and its revolution were so dispersed was a function of the difficulty that weak and hostile political forces had reintegrating the vast Chinese polity. The relatively decentralized nature of the CCP, at least in revolutionary days, is, therefore, partly attributable to China's size and differentiation. In addition, the structure and character of local politics in China since 1949, in which grass-roots organs, their officials and even ordinary people have definite degrees of political manoeuvrability, and in which local cadres with political bases in their constituencies below and the state above have been important in mediating between state and society (see Chapter 7), resonates to the political structure of imperial days. China's size and complexity have set real limits to totalitarian state domination of society.

Second, the populism and voluntarism of China's revolutionary past shaped the Maoist approach to socialism and development. The mass line forged in Yan'an days would find expression in the political campaigns, periodic Party rectifications and egalitarian approach to leader–mass relations that are, as we shall see, hallmarks of Chinese socialism. The miracle of the Party's survival after April 1927, the unstinting exertions of the Jinggangshan, Jiangxi and Yan'an periods, the heroism of the Long March and the surprising triumph of the poorly equipped and ragtag Communist forces against the US-backed Guomindang all lent to Chinese socialism a potent voluntarism – a belief that nearly anything was possible with enough hard work and commitment. This found expression in Mao's very popular (or at least highly popularized) essay on 'The Foolish Old Man Who Moved the Mountain', in which he drew an analogy between the CCP and a fabled man who single-handedly tried to move Mounts Taihang and Wangwu because they were obstructing his doorway (and who, for his efforts, was given God's help in clearing them away):

> We must persevere and work unceasingly, and we, too, will touch God's heart. Our God is none other than the masses of the Chinese people. If they stand up and work together with us, why can't these two mountains [imperialism and feudalism] be cleared away?

> (Mao, 1967, 3: 322)

This faith in the power of the organized and committed people would inform many of the key developments of Chinese socialism, such as the Great Leap Forward and the Cultural Revolution.

Yet juxtaposed with this popular impulse was a third, contrary inheritance: the élitist character of traditional political culture and the absence during the transition of the development of any serious liberal impulse. To its credit, the CCP did develop its own form of mass-line politics, but it was devoid of any concept of individual rights, and it remained enmeshed in the élitism and authoritarianism that were characteristic, albeit in very different ways, of both imperial and Leninist politics. As a result, the mass line could not grow into a democratic politics that could protect citizen rights while also forging and articulating class interests. Moreover, mass-line politics have repeatedly encountered resistance from more bureaucratic and authoritarian political styles and practices, as we shall see. Even Mao could take the most extreme positions in favour of mass democracy – announcing during the Cultural Revolution that 'rebellion is justified' – but, soon after, call in the army to quell the fighting. At the symbolic level, too, the persona of Mao Zedong as a man respected like an emperor but revered for his faith in and commitment to populism and egalitarianism manifests this contradiction in Chinese socialism. Even in death this remains so. Mao's tomb, built in the centre of Tiananmen Square, which is the centre of Beijing (and which in turn is the centre of China, which is the centre of the universe in Chinese cosmology), is no less prepossessing than that built by any emperor. Yet there is a great difference: where the ordinary citizen was forbidden to cast eyes upon the emperor, now the depressing sight of Mao's cadaver is on display for one and all to see. The popular democratic and authoritarian elements of Chinese politics would form one of its central contradictions.

A fourth historical legacy affecting Chinese socialism is the question of nationalism. China's history provides it with among the greatest, and certainly the oldest, national heritage in the world. Yet its nationhood was threatened by the failure of timely industrialization. Neither capitalism nor socialism could take hold in China unless they could re-establish and defend China's national sovereignty. That required building up the country's industry. This imperative has posed deep structural problems for Chinese socialism, which has also been committed to raising living standards and to serving the interests of the peasantry that comprises the vast majority of the Chinese people and was the primary basis of the revolution. As we shall see, industrialization under state socialism created a vast bureaucracy that stood in sharp contradistinction to Maoist populist impulses. The contradiction between these two forms of politics shaped the most extraordinary, and in many ways the defining, moments of the Maoist period – the Great Leap Forward and the Cultural Revolution. Moreover, the irreconcilability of this tension helped incline China away from both bureaucratic state socialism and popular participation in the Dengist period.

A fifth and related problem inherited from the past is the failure of agricultural commercialization. Agrarian society underwent little structural change until the land reform. The revolution liberated from landlord domination a country of peasants still living in their traditional villages, with strong ties to land, village and kin. This liberation affected the way in which rural development and change could proceed. With the brief (and disastrous) exception of the Great Leap Forward, the Party chose to develop the countryside basically within the old social structure. As we shall see in Chapter 2, peasants were not uprooted from their homes, collectives were formed along boundaries conforming to pre-existing residential contours and the traditional family was preserved and put at the service of collective production, to name just a few instances. In other words, there was something distinctly traditional about China's rural transformation. For a time the Dengist leadership argued that the preservation of this agrarian structure set real limits to its efforts to modernize China. For example, it has sometimes been difficult to replace old village leaders, whose power was based on political loyalty, kinship or patron–client networks, or just effective social skills, with technocratically capable ones. In other cases it proved difficult to get some rural producers to give up the peasant mentality of economic self-provision and fully join the wider commodity economy as modern farmers. Yet even the reforms that were intended to commercialize Chinese agriculture fully based themselves upon the household, the most basic unit of China's traditional agrarian structure.

Implications for theory of revolution

China's was the first socialist revolution to draw its social base from the countryside, refuting the orthodox Marxist emphasis on the revolutionary primacy of the proletariat. The condescension with which Marx and many Marxists regarded the peasantry, and the view that it is basically reactionary, have had to be completely rethought. That these statements seem commonplace today testifies partly to the power that the Chinese Revolution had in inspiring rural-based socialist revolutions in other countries.

The Chinese Revolution has much to teach us about the role of peasants in revolution. First, and contrary to the view that China's was a 'peasant revolution', the Chinese Revolution is yet another case of the inability of the peasantry to make revolution on its own. Chinese history is full of peasant rebellions, but the attempt to make a revolution – a 'basic transformation of a society's state and class structures'[23] – requires a leadership with an analysis of the past, a vision of the future and a political strategy and organization to lead society from the former to the latter. The Chinese case puts particular emphasis on the importance of creative, insightful and committed leadership, which could forge a revolutionary base even in an agrarian social structure that was decidedly lacking in the peasant solidarity and autonomy conducive to revolution.

Yet in China even a peasantry inclined toward or capable of revolution, and a revolutionary leadership, was not enough. The CCP's success was in part a product of the multifaceted Guomindang failure. The CCP did not bring the Guomindang down alone. In that feat it received much help from Japan and from the Guomindang itself. With better leadership and without the Japanese invasion, it is conceivable, even though structurally unlikely, that the Guomindang could have stabilized its rule and co-opted or 'exterminated' the CCP. Skocpol's argument that successful revolutions depend very heavily on a profound state crisis is apposite in the Chinese case (Skocpol, 1979).

The Chinese Revolution also indicates how important it is for rural revolutionaries to establish their own armed forces and to use them to establish secure base areas within which popular support can be built, experience gained and revolutionary resources nurtured. This lesson may seem self-evident today, in the light of China's own history and that of almost every other successful revolution (and many unsuccessful ones too) of the twentieth century. Yet before the CCP learned it, it nearly paid for its ignorance with its life – as the vast majority of its members and so many sympathizers and activists did.[24]

The Chinese Revolution also suggests the importance of a flexible and modulated policy on class relations and struggle. The CCP's radical attacks on landlords and rich peasants in Jinggangshan and Jiangxi did not advance the revolution, and may even have set it back. Its Yan'an policy of broad class coalition – 'uniting the many to oppose the few' – proved much more salutary. The land reform, which attacked the landlord class and finally wiped this last remaining stratum of the gentry off the stage of history, came only at the very end of the revolution.

This suggests a larger methodological point: the need for care in thinking about the importance of class struggle in the grand dialectics of revolutionary theory, in actual revolutionary praxis and in social science analysis of revolutions. Clearly, the CCP, inspired by Marxist theory, gave class struggle pride of place in conceiving its revolutionary strategy. At the level of social science, too, our class-structured analysis of the fall of gentry hegemony and the failure of the bourgeoisie suggests the importance of class relations and struggle at the foundation of the Chinese revolutionary dynamic. Yet in our analysis of the actual course of the CCP-led movement, class struggle took a seat alongside the quality of leadership and historical contingency in explaining revolutionary success. The Chinese Revolution demonstrates that there need be no contradiction between class conflict and class compromise – and, more positively, that tactical class compromise can often be the most effective way of leading and prosecuting a strategy of class struggle.

CHAPTER 2

The Triumph and Crises of Maoist Socialism, 1949–78

1949–52: RECOVERY AND CONSOLIDATION

The founding of the People's Republic of China on 1 October 1949 occasioned euphoria among the leaders and participants in the revolution, and elicited a good deal of optimism among workers, peasants and even many patriotic people in the middle and upper classes. Yet these feelings went hand in hand with difficult problems facing the country and its new leaders, and with rapidly shifting currents within which those problems would have to be confronted. The civil war was still raging. Land reform was incomplete in many places, and had not even begun in others. The CCP had little experience in urban administration and leadership, and none in national government, while its relations with the working class were weak. The economy was in disastrous shape after almost forty years of revolutionary and civil war and a century of imperialism and declining political capacity. Unemployment, inflation and back-breaking poverty demanded urgent solutions. Deeper structural problems of underinvestment, shortage of skilled personnel and multiple economic imbalances would also have to be tackled. Society, too, was in deep crisis. Disease, prostitution, drug addiction, illiteracy, corruption and gangsterism were epidemic, and social services were non-existent or in utter disarray. To compound the difficulties, China would soon find itself embroiled in the Korean War, which brought it face to face with the military might of the USA, and which prolonged the civil war by strengthening the USA's resolve to defend and support the Guomindang and its efforts to retake the mainland from its Taiwan redoubt.

The proportions and nature of the crisis are similar in some ways to that facing the Bolsheviks after November 1917, when they too faced economic and social breakdown, and ongoing civil and foreign war. The CCP, however, responded quite differently. Where the Bolsheviks initiated 'war Communism' – a period of radical transformation, including rapid, sweeping nationalizations, tight central control of the economy and summary and sometimes forced appropriation of food from the peasantry – the CCP moved much more cautiously and moderately. It continued its practice of forging broad class coalitions and limiting class struggle. Nationalization was carried out selectively, and centralization of levers of economic power proceeded gradually. Just as the Chinese Revolution had proceeded very differently from the Russian, so now in power Chinese state socialism took its first steps on what would continue to prove to be a very different trajectory of development.

Rural transformation: the land reform

The Chinese land reform is perhaps the most sweeping and successful rural transformation in history. In one stroke it relieved exploitative tenancy and provided poor peasants with land, completed the four-decade-long collapse of the Chinese gentry and galvanized a new kind of mass-based politics and government at the grass roots. Moreover, the Chinese land reform did so without precipitating a production crisis, always a grave danger in land reform. On the contrary, it actually helped promote the recovery of the rural economy. Finally, land reform managed to avoid a bloodbath. Though violence was done to many landlords, the vast majority remained physically unhurt, and survived into the state socialist period as owners of small plots that they had to learn to work like the peasant cultivators they had exploited for millennia.

All this was accomplished in the face of serious obstacles. One was structural. As we have seen in Chapter 1, the Chinese peasantry was historically bound up in a web of vertical relationships and institutions dominated by landowners, including kinship associations, patron–client ties, religious institutions and secret societies. This undercut the potential for peasant solidarity against landlords, and gave the landlords considerable leverage with which to oppose the land reform.

In this situation, matters would have been much easier if the landlord class had simply evaporated, as it largely did in Korea when the Japanese, who owned much of the land, withdrew after their defeat in the Second World War. Yet China was not blessed with such a conjuncture. The Chinese landlords were, by and large, still on the scene, and they used all the levers of political and social power at their disposal to undermine the land reform. They were expert at bribing and blackmailing Communist cadres. For just one doubly oppressive example, some commanded their wives and daughters to seduce local activists, after which the landlord exposed them, undermining their credibility as allies of the poor. The landowners also attempted to enforce tenancy relations through co-optation, promising favourable treatment to peasants who would oppose the land reform, persuade others to do so and continue to pay rent secretly. They attempted to conceal their holdings by burying gold and transferring formal land titles to poor relatives or 'non-profit' institutions such as religious or kinship organizations. They threatened physical violence against land reform cadres and their peasant supporters, and hired thugs to make good this intimidation. Perhaps their most potent threat was the possibility of a return to power by the Guomindang, which was by no means an impossibility. Many peasants, beaten down by centuries of oppression, felt weak and feared they might again become dependent on landlords to rent them land or loan them money; their fear of a 'change of sky' dampened their willingness to join in attacks on their exploiters. Dialectically, this fear presented the CCP land reform leadership with an opposite problem as well: once they had persuaded peasants to join in the land reform, often the peasants were inclined to commit deadly violence against their landlords, to prevent future revenge.

To ascertain the full extent of landlord holdings, build solidarity among the structurally fragmented peasantry and overcome the peasants' difficulties in coming forward to attack the landlords, the CCP relied on the mass-line methods developed in Yan'an. In the archetypical pattern, land reform cadres would begin by locating potential activists – people with strong anti-landlord feelings, the capacity and inclination to articulate them and the social skills and stature needed to persuade others to join them. Confidential conversations with such people were used to build networks of support and eventually to prepare the ground for a village-wide meeting. Here peasants were encouraged to join a revolutionary bandwagon, by confronting their landlords directly and publicly, exposing their holdings and measuring and denouncing their exploitation and other depredations. Through this direct confrontation, peasants would break through their awe and fear of the landlord, striking a decisive blow against the political, social and cultural aspects of landlord hegemony. This was genuine empowerment, both for individual peasants and simultaneously for the peasantry as a class. Then the landlord's property would be seized and, through another series of mass meetings and deliberations, redistributed.

Of course, land reform almost never went this smoothly in practice; archetypical was not typical. Mistakes and setbacks were frequent. Mass meetings were sometimes called prematurely, and their failure to evince serious attacks on landlords set events back to square one or even short of it. Landlords, too, could play the game, and sometimes mobilized their supporters to defend them or to attack the activists. Then there were excesses: peasants often wanted to attack rich peasants and even middle peasants too, to enlarge the stock of property to be redistributed. A particularly difficult moment was the division of the 'fruits' of the struggle. Bitter disputes ensued over thorny issues. Should activists receive more or better property as a reward or just desert for having led the way in the movement? What about cadres who appropriated more or better property for themselves or their friends or kin? What was to be done if there was not enough confiscated property to provide for the needs of all the poor, a situation that was quite common, especially in north China where tenancy was much lower than in the south? What about special individual cases, such as poor widows who had no choice but to rent out their land because they could not work it themselves? How was a middle peasant, who was not entitled to receive any redistribution, to be distinguished from a poor peasant, who was? And how was the Party to exert leadership and provide guidance in dealing with these matters without dampening the popular initiative and power that was required to make the land reform successful in the first place?

To minimize and deal effectively with these problems, the land reform required a complex mix of Party leadership and popular participation. Cadres armed with the latest Party instructions and clarifications had to make peasants aware of the problems and persuade them to abide by the Party's policies. Yet they also had to listen carefully to peasants' opinions and complaints, and to report them to their superiors. At other times they had to subject themselves to criticism from the peasants for mistakes they had made. Sometimes parts of the land reform process had to be repeated to resolve errors made in the first go-round.[1]

In the end, the Chinese land reform was a stunning success, partly despite these difficulties and partly because of them. First, the structure of land ownership became far more equal (though, by design, it drew up far short of complete egalitarianism, a point to which we shall soon return). Landlords, who comprised 2.6 per cent of households, saw their land holdings drop from 28.7 per cent to 2.1 per cent of China's crop land. The holdings of poor peasants and landless labourers, who comprised 57.1 per cent of the households, doubled from 23.5 per cent of cultivated land to 46.8 per cent. Tools and livestock were also redistributed.

Second, the rural economy made a rapid recovery during the land reform. In general, land reforms pose a great danger to production, as peasants and landowners unsure of their future holdings disinvest in the land, fail to maintain it or actually refuse to put it under crops. They may also destroy productive resources like seed or livestock, and drain down reserves of food, preferring to eat them rather than see them expropriated. Yet the Chinese land reform did not precipitate an economic crisis. On the contrary, it provided the conditions for rapid recovery. Grain production grew from 113 million tons in 1949 to 164 million in 1952 (which exceeded the previous all-time record), cotton production tripled and fish production nearly quadrupled, to mention just a few important indicators. Gross value of agricultural output increased nearly 50 per cent. Such a record would be impressive at any time, but it is especially remarkable in the context of a massive land reform.

Of course, the increase was in part a result of what from a purely economic point of view was the depressed level of production in 1949 due to decades of war and political dislocation. With the advent of peace and political stability for the first time in decades, the economy could easily rebound, as existing but unused or underutilized capacity was brought into play and as farmers could concentrate on farming rather than fighting. Yet other factors specific to the land reform were at work as well in fostering the rapid recovery. The CCP's efforts to reassure the peasantry, and its insistence on protecting the holdings of the most productive strata of rich and middle peasants, were of great help. The speed and timing of the land reform were also important. To help maximize peasant participation and minimize crop damage, the winter slack season was often used to carry it out. Once prepared, the movement in a particular village was put on a fast track, to minimize the time that property owners would have to destroy or sell off their assets and to prepare their defences. Finally, the land reform liberated the productive energies of the peasantry and the investment resources at their disposal. In 1933, one of the last years for which comprehensive and reliable statistics exist, the Chinese rural economy was producing a surplus of more than 25 per cent of national income (Riskin, 1975). Much of this had gone to subsidize the extravagant consumption of China's gentry. Now this surplus accrued to the peasantry, who could and did use it to invest in expanded reproduction of the agrarian economy.

Third, the landlord class was destroyed, but most individual landlords were not. What does this mean? Classes, though made up of individuals, are much more than the sum of their parts. They are structures of power. If a ruling class loses its power, it may be dead as a class even though the individuals who comprise it live on. In the land reform, the landlord class[2] lost its power. This was accomplished not merely by expropriating the landlords' property, though certainly that was an important element. In Chapter 1 we saw that the landlords' power was multifaceted. Aside from resting on land, it also involved their political control of the peasantry through vertical institutions (such as kinship associations) and through the complex of Confucian values, local customs and traditional ways of acting and thinking that comprised a culture of gentry hegemony and peasant subordination. These levers of power operated, then, not just in economic relations, but also in political and social relations and in consciousness. So that is where the CCP attacked them, through the mass-line process of having peasants confront their landlords personally and publicly. Marx's third thesis on Feuerbach contains a relevant insight: 'The coincidence of the changing of circumstances and of human activity can be conceived and rationally understood only as *revolutionizing practice*' (Marx, 1959: 243; emphasis in original). Here Marx is noting that revolutionary action can, dialectically, change the world ('circumstances') and also the people who are changing it. In other words, revolution revolutionizes the revolutionaries – it is a verb as well as a noun. The land reform not only changed the 'circumstances' of land tenure, but also involved 'human action' that changed the way the tenants thought about their landlords and themselves. In doing so, land reform struck at an important, if non-material, underpinning of landlord hegemony. With the land reform, the last remnants of the gentry class – whose fall after millennia of domination had begun with the collapse of the imperial state four decades earlier – finally had their remaining sources of political, social and cultural as well as economic power cut out from under them. The class power of the tenacious old ruling class was at last extinguished.

The death of the landlord class also involved the death of many, though not most, individual landlords. There is a grisly, polemical debate, based on very poor and highly politicized data, about precisely how many landlords died in the land reform. Somewhere in the range of half a million to a million landlord deaths is about the best one can conclude from it. Evaluation of these awful numbers involves thorny moral questions. Should one take into account the fact that many of the landlords who were killed were themselves guilty of serious crimes, or that the tenancy system they supported was responsible for the deaths of untold numbers of peasants through physical exhaustion and deprivation? Then there is the issue of who is responsible for violence against landlords. Certainly, during radical periods before 1949, CCP policy did produce peasant violence against landlords even though it often explicitly discouraged it. In September 1947, for example, what the Party deemed an excessively slow pace of land reform was blamed on landlord and rich peasant infiltration of the Party, and the masses were mobilized to criticize and reverse this. The change resulted in physical attacks against landlords. In January 1948, Mao himself wrote:

> [W]e must insist on killing less and must strictly forbid indiscriminate killing. To advocate more and indiscriminate killing is entirely wrong; this would only cause our Party to forfeit sympathy, become alienated from the masses and fall into isolation. Trial and sentence by the people's courts . . . must be carried out in earnest.
>
> (Mao, 1967, 4: 185–6; translation slightly altered to improve accuracy and readability)

In fact, landlords were specifically to be allowed to retain small plots of land sufficient to sustain themselves and their families. Mao argued that they could be used 'as a labour force for the country', while the Party could also 'save and remould them'. Perhaps he also had in mind their function as a living symbol of the reversal of the old exploitative class structure. In any event, Mao concluded: 'Our task is to abolish the feudal system, to wipe out the landlords *as a class, not as individuals*' (Mao, 1969, 4: 186; emphasis added).

The fourth result of the land reform was the development of new political leadership and institutions at the grass roots. Activists and local cadres were recruited to carry out the movement. These new local leaders as well as older ones were put through some of the most difficult tests of their leadership skills and their commitment. The experience they gained would prove invaluable in later years. Many of China's corps of grass-roots cadres who would preside over local affairs during the succeeding decades of collectivization and rural transformation got their start in the land reform.

In addition to these peasant leaders, the land reform also gave many urban activists their first exposure to conditions in the countryside. To help guide the movement and correct its 'deviations', the Party organized 'work teams' composed of urbanites, some of whom were Party and government officials, but many of whom were simply young people from the newly liberated cities who had little or no prior involvement with the Party or the revolution but were sympathetic to them. The work teams were given brief training and then dispatched to the countryside for several months or more to help the peasants carry out the land reform. Service on the work teams proved to be a real eye-opener for many urban Chinese, who had spent little time in the rural areas before, and who had no appreciation of the gravity of conditions and the nature of peasant culture. It was the first step in the Maoist attempt to bridge the gap between rural and urban life and consciousness, an effort that would prove to be one of the boldest and most distinctive themes of Chinese state socialism.

The land reform also helped develop and invigorate local political institutions. Peasant associations in villages came to life. The village-wide meeting, a strange new phenomenon in the fragmented and landlord-dominated society of Chinese villages, became a central forum of political action during the land reform, and continued as such for the next three decades. Above the grass-roots level, township (*xiang*) and especially county (*xian*) Party and government institutions, charged with overseeing the land reform, acquired a political weight, coordinative capacity and network of linkages with grass-roots political leaders and institutions that they have retained up to the present day.

A fifth result of the land reform was its legacy of class relations and inequality. Though it struck a great blow toward greater equality by expropriating and redistributing most landlord property, land reform stopped well short of full equalization. This was no accident or policy failure. The Party had rejected radical egalitarianism since its setbacks in Jinggangshan and Jiangxi. In fact, the ability of the Party to resist poor peasants' pressure for a more radical distribution of property was a major policy success. The land reform specifically protected rich peasants. The 1950 Agrarian Reform Law targeted landlords, and stipulated that:

> Land owned by rich peasants and cultivated by them or by hired labor, and their other properties, shall not be infringed upon. Small portions of land rented out by rich peasants shall also be retained by them.
>
> (H. Hinton, 1980, 1: 63)

Only if they were renting out more land than they were working could the rich peasants be subject to expropriation, and even then only the rented portion was to be touched. The property of middle peasants (including 'well-to-do middle peasants') was fully protected. No industrial or commercial property was to be expropriated, even if it was owned by landlords.

As a result, post-land reform society contained certain class (not to mention spatial) inequalities carried over from the past. Rich peasants, who comprised 3.6 per cent of rural households, still held 6.4 per cent of crop land (down from 17.7 per cent before the land reform). The 35.8 per cent of households classified as middle peasants ended up with 44.8 per cent of land, while poor peasants and landless labourers – 57.1 per cent of households – had 46.8 per cent. These aggregate figures do not reflect a rather more inegalitarian situation in many villages – especially in north China – that had relatively fewer landlord holdings and more rich peasant ones. There and elsewhere many poor peasants were left with minuscule plots, some even too small to provide subsistence. They would soon be forced to rent additional land. This set up a new dynamic of exploitation that provided the basis for future political conflicts. Dialectically, those conflicts in turn spurred the Party's decision to promote mutual aid and collectivization, the next stages of socialist transformation.

Transition in the cities: social reform, nationalization, and political consolidation

Compared with the epoch-making changes in rural class relations, the early changes in the cities were much less striking than those in the countryside. The sheer magnitude of crisis in the urban centres, the Party's inexperience and lack of strong political and social bases there, the drain on its energies caused by the land reform and the Korean War and its general propensity to move gradually at this time all contributed to the CCP's decision to adopt a cautious approach to urban class conflict. Thus the Party characterized the political nature of the period as 'new democracy' based on a coalition of the national and petit bourgeoisies as well as the peasantry and the proletariat. Still, the quality of urban life and government was vastly improved by the CCP's skill in constructing and consolidating new political institutions, and by its radical – in the strict sense of root-seeking (rather than extreme or leftist) – approach to social problems.

Prostitution, gambling and opium addiction had reached epidemic proportions in many of China's large cities by 1949. The new government used combinations of carrot and stick, and of popular mobilization and state power, to strike swiftly and deeply at these problems. Regarding prostitutes and drug addicts as victims of the social crisis engendered by colonialism and Guomindang reaction and incapacity, it sought not to punish but to help them through rehabilitation programmes. Petty pimps and drug dealers were let off with a stern warning and organized criticism by their neighbours. Serious offenders, though, were subjected to public trials and severe punishment. Meanwhile, campaigns were organized to educate the public about the evils of prostitution, gambling and drugs, while the major centres of such activities in the urban neighbourhoods were raided and closed down. Within two years, these major social problems were basically eradicated. In doing so, the new government also eliminated an important node of political opposition. The Guomindang had cooperated with organized criminals who ran these operations, using them for political intelligence, repression and corruption. Thus the socialist state's attacks on this rot were important not just socially but also politically: they struck at a core of residual Guomindang support and sabotage, while also helping the CCP prove its effectiveness and benevolence to the urban population at large.

The new state also moved vigorously to reform family relations and strike a blow against the oppression of women in both the cities and the countryside. Under the new Marriage Law, women were given the right to own property, hold employment and divorce husbands who had maltreated or abandoned them. Concubinage and forced marriage were made illegal. The law was also designed to protect children. Infanticide and the sale and betrothal of children, which had victimized girls and poor families, were forbidden. Children born out of wedlock were given equal legal protection. Mass campaigns to promote the new family relations and criticize abusive husbands and fathers were organized.

Economic nationalization proceeded much more slowly. After the defeat of Japan, which had occupied China's industrial heartlands, control of heavy industry and mining had been consolidated under an amalgam of state control and private profit for Guomindang élites. The CCP referred to this sector as 'bureaucratic capitalism'. When most of its leaders fled to Taiwan, leaving their productive assets behind, it was natural and easy to nationalize this sector. Indeed, there was little else that could be done with it. Foreign-run firms were also nationalized, though through a process of negotiation and compensation that kept the factories running, provided training for Chinese technicians, managers and workers to run them and even protected future business relations with the foreign firms. Thus, in short order the new government found itself in control of the industrial core of the economy, which accounted for about one-third of industrial output value, more than three-quarters of fixed capital and about 700,000 employees.

Still, Chinese heavy industry was poorly developed, and the lighter sectors bulked much larger in the urban economy. (Outside of Manchuria, consumer goods production made up more than 90 per cent of industrial output.) These were under the control of the national capitalists (also translated as 'national bourgeoisie'), who were not closely tied to the Guomindang. They were designated as part of the CCP's class coalition during the period of 'new democracy', so their interests were scrupulously protected. The CCP leadership realized that it needed their technical, managerial, commercial and entrepreneurial expertise to effect the economic recovery that was a central goal of the period. Moreover, with the sharp constriction in China's access to world markets during the Korean War, it became particularly important for the CCP to seek economic allies wherever it could. Thus, the national bourgeoisie's assets were not subject to nationalization, and they could continue to make and appropriate profits. As early as 1947, the Party had actually criticized nationalizations undertaken by newly victorious cadres, armies and workers. Leaders and workers were told to get down to work in the name of national economic recovery. In return, they would be rewarded in other ways, as the national capitalists now came under new forms of regulation concerning wages, working conditions and even pricing and marketing practices, over which control was also exercised through gradual nationalization of wholesale – but not retail – trade.

Despite their reduced autonomy, the number of private industrial firms increased sixfold to 150,000 between from 1949 to 1953, by which time they employed over two million workers – three times the number employed in the state sector. This was in addition to the plethora of petit bourgeois enterprises, such as self-employed artisans and service providers, who continued to operate and proliferate unencumbered. It is clear, and more purposeful than ironic, that the CCP was successful in promoting business and political confidence among the bourgeoisie and petit bourgeoisie. Thus, by 1952 China's urban economy was a mixture of state and private ownership. The state sector accounted for 56 per cent of gross industrial output value, 27 per cent was produced in what was called the 'state capitalist' sector (comprising some joint state–private firms but mainly private firms operating under state contracts and instructions) and 17 per cent in purely private capitalist firms.

The urban-based industrial and commercial economy performed very well in the recovery years of 1949–52. The hyperinflation that resulted from the Guomindang government's inability to finance itself was quickly brought under control. The state budget was balanced as taxes were simplified and revenues raised from industrial profits of the state sector. Gross value of industrial output increased two and a half times, with heavy industry outpacing light. Retail sales volume doubled. Even world trade volume increased 50 per cent, despite the US-led Western embargo. Perhaps most significant for the future, investment in capital construction increased almost fourfold, to 20 per cent of net domestic expenditure by 1953.

The CCP leadership also moved vigorously to establish and consolidate its political control in the cities. Since during the revolution it had not been able to establish its own organs of government and administration in the cities, it was forced to utilize many of those it inherited from the Guomindang state. Most lower-level officials had stayed on after 1949. The new government placed these institutions and bureaucrats under its political control, subordinating them to new government ministries and assigning Party members to supervise them. For example, the police were now placed under the authority of the Ministry of Public Security, and Party cadres were assigned to key command posts. At the same time, the CCP leadership moved to create new grass-roots organizations. In the neighbourhoods, urban residents committees were made responsible for public information and propaganda work, dispensation of municipal services, local dispute arbitration and judicature and gathering intelligence and information for the state. They were valuable in the campaigns against prostitution, drug addiction and organized crime. Women's and students' federations and trade unions were also formed. The women's federation was particularly important in promulgating and enforcing the new policies on gender and family relations.

Of course, the CCP had acquired its own special appreciation of the political truisms that institutions are no better than the people in them, and that institutions can reshape those people in undesirable directions. In fact, Mao and his followers would prove downright suspicious of bureaucracy itself as a breeding ground of ideological, social and economic stagnation and even counter-revolution. The early 1950s saw the use of political campaigns to galvanize the personnel of the new state and purge from them certain tendencies deemed unhealthy by the Party leadership. A 'three-anti' (*san fan*) campaign was launched to fight corruption, waste and élitism among officials held over from the Guomindang state, new Party recruits and even old Party cadres. A 'five-anti' (*wu fan*) campaign against bribery, tax evasion, fraud and theft of government property and economic secrets was directed at members of the national bourgeoisie who were not complying with the plans the state had for them. In both campaigns the familiar mass-line methods of persuasion and discreet solicitation of information along with public mass criticism were employed. These were not purges in the Stalinist sense. They were not used by top élites to eliminate political rivals. Less than one cadre in twenty was formally censured in the *san fan*, and most of these were simply demoted or dismissed rather than imprisoned. In a similar vein, penalties under the *wu fan* – meted out to three-quarters of the businesses in the major cities – were mainly financial. Though broad in scope, this was not a frontal attack on the national bourgeoisie in the way the land reform attacked the landowners. Yet it did put China's capitalists on notice that their position in socialist China was becoming more tenuous.

SOCIALIST TRANSITION, 1953–57

With the recovery complete, the consolidation of the new state well in hand and the end of the Korean War, the conditions for the next stage of China's state socialist development were in place. Industrial and agricultural output were back to the all-time highs of the 1930s (levels that were still quite low in absolute terms). The rapid rates of growth of the first three years of the People's Republic were, in part, statistical artefacts of the very depressed baseline of 1949. They also resulted from the mobilization of existing but underutilized resources. To be sure, the CCP's policies in 1949–52 had been sensitive and skilful in fostering the conditions under which those resources could most effectively be brought into play. Yet economic growth via resuscitation could only occur once. Now new ways would have to be found to propel the Chinese economy forward on a sustained basis. Like the revolution and the earliest years of CCP governance, this stage would be characterized by rather different approaches in the countryside and the cities. It also involved some new departures from the political directions that the leadership had steered to bring China to this point. Specifically, the next five years saw the creation of Soviet-style bureaucratic central planning and management in industry and commerce, and very rapid collectivization in agriculture. Moreover, for the first time in Chinese history, agriculture began to be used systematically as a source of capital to finance industry.

Industrial centralization: the First Five Year Plan, 1953–57

The First Five Year Plan involved several elements that departed from previous Chinese practice. First, planning was to be highly centralized, in contrast to the local and regional self-reliance that had grown out of revolutionary wartime conditions. The economy was to be administered by vertically organized government ministries, with almost no role for horizontal coordination by local or regional political authorities. In other words, 'dual rule', the combined vertical and horizontal organizational gridwork of Yan'an days (see Chapter 1), now gave way to a more singularly vertical pattern of authority.

Second, investment priority was given to heavy industry, while agriculture was left to fend for itself. The huge amount of investment capital required for industry was to come in small measure from the Soviet Union, but primarily from the Chinese countryside. The USSR provided credit and technical assistance for 156 major projects, in what was perhaps the largest transfer of technology ever carried out by any country. Yet this was just a drop in the vast bucket of China's plans for high-speed industrialization, amounting to only about 3 per cent of total state investment. Moreover, most of this came as loans (with short-term repayment periods), not grants. So the major part of the cost of industrial investment during the First Five Year Plan was to be paid by the Chinese people. And most of them were peasants.

This does not mean, however, that the livelihoods of China's farmers were sacrificed to pay for industrialization. Total tax collections from the countryside declined from 17 per cent of output in 1949 to 13.2 per cent in 1952; thereafter, the agricultural tax was fixed in absolute terms at the 1952 level for each household, so that with increased production the proportion paid as tax declined (Shue, 1980: 122, 136). Of course, states have many other ways to extract resources from the countryside besides taxes. One that has been used in many countries is to require farmers to sell crops to the state at artificially low prices. Starting in 1953, with the policy of unified grain purchase, the Chinese state set quotas for each locality to sell grain to the state. Prices were set at the prevailing market level, however, and the price ratio between agriculture and industry moved in favour of the farmers through 1955 (Shue, 1980: 222). Moreover, the state did not take advantage of unified purchase to raise the level of extraction from the countryside: total grain marketings as a percentage of total output remained fairly steady through 1958 (Lardy, 1983: 34). Overall, living standards and rural reinvestment rose significantly during the First Five Year Plan (Lardy, 1983: 144; Shue, 1980: 212n). So while the First Five Year Plan did transfer considerable resources out of the countryside to finance industry, and disadvantaged the rural sector compared with what would have occurred under different investment priorities, the burden borne by the rural sector was moderate enough to permit growth of rural accumulation and income too, as we shall see. Moreover, when the total extracted from the countryside to fund industrial investment was spread over the vastness of rural China, it did not cause significant pain to China's farmers.

In a third departure from the revolutionary past, the new heavy industry was to take the form of enormous complexes concentrated in a few large cities. For example, the steel centre at Anshan attracted almost one-third of the Soviet-aided projects, and 35,000 new workers; by 1957 it would produce two-thirds of China's steel. Such massive concentration of production reinforced the state's capacities for central planning and control of the economy. This pattern also tended to pre-empt industrial development in medium-sized cities. Finally, the size of these enterprises was unsuited to participatory management.

Fourth, in contrast to the incremental approach of 1949–52, the pace of socialist transformation was accelerated. By June 1952, Mao had already concluded that the national bourgeoisie ought no longer be included in the class coalition of the socialist state. In 1953, the state began to convert many private firms to joint state–private ownership. It subjected them to the same state planning and management as the state-sector plants; the only significant difference was that in the joint state–private plants the former owners were often retained as managers and were paid dividends out of part of the firms' profits. By 1956, the private sector in industry, including both large factories and small handicraft workshops, had been eliminated. Two-thirds of gross industrial output value was now produced in state-run plants, and one-third in joint state–private firms. Commerce and services had also been socialized. Large retail and wholesale operations had come under state ownership, and small private shops engaged in retail trade and services (such as barbers and tailors) had been converted into co-operatives.

Fifth, in contrast to the decentralized and participatory approach to leadership of revolutionary days, factory management was consolidated in the hands of managers who were given tremendous authority. A more participatory form of industrial management known as the Shanghai or East China system, which had been employed selectively and experimentally since 1947, gave way to 'one-man management' along Soviet lines.[3] This was a natural result of the fact that the industrial nationalizations were carried out by administrative fiat rather than through a popular movement (as in the land reform). One-man management was based upon strict hierarchical, bureaucratic command in industrial administration and management. Factory directors took orders from their superiors in the ministries, and exercised tight control over the workers in their factories. They frequently employed piece-rate and quota systems to control and motivate the labour force, which atomized and depoliticized workers both by pitting them against each other while simultaneously intensifying work.[4] During the first two years of the plan, Chinese economists boasted of a 42 per cent rise in labour productivity as against a 7 per cent rise in workers' real incomes. (Incidentally, these figures show that the burden of financing industrialization was borne not only by farmers but also by workers.)

It is surprising that China's leadership embarked on a programme of industrial development that so explicitly aped the Soviet model. From 1927 onwards, relations between the CCP and the Soviet Union had been stormy. Stalin and the advisers he sent to China had persistent doubts about the agrarian base of the revolution. Within the CCP there were many bitter struggles between Soviet advisers and party leaders affiliated with them on the one hand, and other party leaders, many affiliated with Mao, on the other. After the defeat of Japan, the USSR raced the CCP and the Guomindang to receive Japanese surrenders. Soviet troops even went so far as to loot industrial enterprises under Japanese control, packing up as much equipment as possible and shipping it back to the USSR. This infuriated Chinese on both sides of the civil war. On Mao's first visit to the USSR in 1950, he was humiliated by being forced to cool his heels for days at a time to get in to see Stalin. The Soviet Union manoeuvred China into the position of doing most of the fighting in the Korean War. In his own leadership of the Chinese Revolution, Mao had already shown his doubts about the bureaucratism, centralization and élitism that characterized the USSR under Stalin, though he would not openly critique the Soviet system for such ills until the late 1950s.

Chinese leaders adopted this Soviet-inspired and in many ways uncharacteristic plan for several reasons. They utterly lacked experience in industrial development; and, given China's isolation in the world, the only available source of advice was the USSR. In fact the Soviet Union was a rather attractive model because of its impressive performance in a context originally quite similar to China's. In the 1920s, the USSR had embarked on industrialization in a large, poor and war-torn country that had a very late start compared with the West and had relatively little infrastructure with which to work. Like China, the USSR was severely threatened by the West – both countries had found themselves under attack from Western capitalist countries soon after socialist governments had been established – and thus faced the task of industrializing while isolated from Western sources of capital, markets and technology. Yet the USSR had achieved dazzling results in rapid industrialization. Within the short span of a quarter of a century, it had built a modern industrial economy powerful enough to enable the country to drive back Germany and emerge from the Second World War as a superpower that could contend with the USA. The prospect of equally rapid growth of its industry and defence capability had strong appeal to the nationalist as well as to the socialist proclivities of China's leaders. They began to talk brashly of overtaking Great Britain economically. Finally, the prospect of Soviet aid, at a time when China was strapped for resources and when no other sources of credit or grants were available, was not to be taken lightly. Of course, however, Soviet aid came only with Soviet-style industrial planning and organization.

The First Five Year Plan produced results that were impressive enough to sustain the Chinese leaders' dreams. Industrial output grew 15.5 per cent per year, faster even than their audacious target of 14.7 per cent. Heavy industrial output nearly tripled, while light industry grew 70 per cent. Railway freight volume more than doubled. Of course, agriculture could not grow at anything like this pace. Its gross output value grew only at an average of 2.1 per cent per year, a sharp decline from the heady rate of 14.1 per cent during the recovery years of 1949–52. Output of key crops grew very slowly in 1953 and 1954, and erratically thereafter (see Table 2.1).

Though agricultural production and rural economic conditions were not in deep crisis, this level of performance was a thin reed upon which to rest grandiose plans for rapid industrialization. It would be difficult to sustain the high rate of accumulation demanded by the Soviet-style strategy – already about a quarter of output (see Figure 6.3) – if agriculture were stagnant or growing only marginally. Markets for industrial output would also pose a problem. China's urban population and labour force had grown around 50 per cent from 1952 to 1957, putting great stress on food supplies. In purely economic terms, the imbalance between agriculture and industry could threaten the success of an industrialization strategy that gave primary emphasis to industry.

Economics aside, Soviet-style industrialization also posed deep political problems. The Soviet Union had paid a very high price for its industrial achievements: the devastation of its peasantry (including seven to ten million deaths), which was looted for investment capital, contributing to the long-term stagnation of its agriculture. It was politically possible for Stalin to pay this price because the Russian peasantry was not the leading component of the revolutionary coalition that brought the Bolsheviks to power and sustained them. The Bolsheviks had little feeling for, understanding of or organizational base in the peasantry. It was much more difficult for the leaders of China's rural-based revolution to exploit the peasants. The experience of the revolution and the mass line also made it difficult for many Chinese leaders – particularly those in agreement with Mao – to accept the bureaucratization, hierarchy, inegalitarianism and concentration of authority that accompanied the Soviet model. Meanwhile, the decline of dual rule at the expense of vertical, technocratic authority reduced the role of the Party vis-à-vis more apolitical government institutions and bureaucratic officials, some of whom were trained and had risen to their posts under the Guomindang.

Finally, the First Five Year Plan's dependence on the Soviet Union grated on the nationalist sensibilities of the Chinese leadership and people, while difficulties in

Table 2.1 Annual Growth Rates of Grain and Cotton Output, 1953–57

Year	Growth of foodgrain output over previous year (percentage)	Growth of cotton output over previous year (percentage)
1953	1.6	−9.9
1954	1.3	−10.1
1955	8.9	42.5
1956	0.3	−5.7
1957	4.9	13.5

Source: Computed from Eckstein, 1980: 63.

day-to-day social relations between Russian and Chinese officials and experts caused irritation. The deep concern about Soviet influence in China was expressed perhaps most pointedly in the first purge of a top Party leader since the establishment of the People's Republic. In late 1953, the Party Politburo expelled Gao Gang, the head of the Party and government in Manchuria. The charge was that he established an 'independent kingdom' there. (Manchuria has a long border with the USSR, and had recently been under Japanese rule for over a decade.) Gao was particularly close to the Soviet leadership, having visited the USSR several times. He had gone further than any other Chinese leader in implementing Soviet-style industrialization. So the anti-Soviet overtones of his purge were clear.

The Chinese leadership undertook the Soviet-style strategy of rapid industrialization with some ambivalence. It was indirectly yet clearly criticized by Mao in a major 1956 speech entitled 'On the Ten Major Relationships', where he evinced concern about imbalances between, among others, inland and coast, centre and locality, and, most prominently, industry and agriculture (Mao, 1977: 284–307).[5] This last cleavage was causing serious controversy among planners and politicians, and was at the root of the unexpected decision to promote rural co-operativization.

The socialist transformation of agriculture, 1953–57: mutual aid teams, grain and credit market control and co-operativization

The land reform destroyed the landlord class, but, as we saw above, left in place a definite class structure, in which poor peasants had less land and capital than middle and rich peasants. These inequalities soon began to provide the basis for new kinds of class exploitation in many places. Poor peasants whose holdings were too small to get by were forced to borrow money or rent land from rich peasants, sell their labour to them and in some cases – for example, when loans could not be repaid – even lose their land to them. The state viewed these developments with alarm, and took several innovative steps to stop them.

First, it began in the early 1950s to promote the development of mutual aid teams (MATs). Voluntary associations of five to ten or so households, they exchanged labour and resources with each other on a temporary, seasonal or year-round basis. The MATs had several benefits. They helped raise production through shared knowledge and rationalized use of resources. For example, households with more land than they could farm efficiently could combine with those with too much labour, to the advantage of both. MATs gave peasants in economic straits a way to resolve their problems without having to turn to rich peasants for 'help'. They were also a first step towards the collective forms of organization that the Party had vaguely in mind for the future. The formation of MATs was promoted in several ways: through mass-line methods of persuasion, mobilization and emulation; by designing them in conformity with the traditional contours of society, i.e., along kinship or neighbourhood lines; and by offering material benefits such as preferential marketing opportunities and credit to MATs and their members. Rich peasants and landlords were excluded, to help ensure that they would not exploit their poor neighbours through the MATs. In fact, to the extent that the MATs denied rich peasants opportunities for exploitation by providing the poor with other ways to solve their problems, they constituted the first step in the gradual, state-led attack on the rich peasants as a class, which was the next phase of the Party's leadership of China's class struggle.

A second step in this attack was the institution of unified grain purchase and supply in late 1953, under which the state made itself the sole buyer and seller of grain. A primary motivation for this policy was the stabilization of grain prices. Peasants were now required to sell specified quotas of grain to the state. Surpluses could be saved, sold to the state at premium prices, sold to local supply and marketing co-operatives, sold in government-regulated markets or exchanged in limited quantities with neighbours. To encourage production, prices were set in accordance with local market conditions, and quotas were set at levels well within the productive capacities of each household. Private grain merchants were closed down. All sales of grain to cities were now handled by government agencies. Unified grain purchase and supply had a double effect on class relations in the countryside. First, it gave poor peasants a place to turn when they were short of grain, so they did not fall into the clutches of rich peasants or merchants. Second, unified grain purchase made it difficult for traders and rich peasants to profit by taking advantage of the seasonal ebb and flow of grain prices.

A third measure the state took against the rich was the establishment of rural credit co-operatives. Like unified grain purchase and supply, the state was trying to end the private credit market. By providing an alternative source of finance to farmers, credit co-ops undercut one more in a shrinking repertoire of mechanisms by which the rural rich exploited the poor. By 1954, mutual aid, unified purchase and supply and credit co-operatives had put in place formidable obstacles to exploitation through rent, speculation and moneylending. Within the parameters set by the unequal ownership of land, it was increasingly difficult to get rich or stay rich except by working the land.

The stage was now set for co-operativization, which began in a gradual way. In 1954, the year in which the transformation began in earnest, just one in nine rural households became co-op members. These early co-ops averaged around 30 households. Yet their size was set flexibly so that, in the interests of providing a workable social base, the composition of the co-ops would fit the traditional contours of society. For example, a co-op would normally be formed around a small hamlet or a neighbourhood of a larger village. Where lineage rivalry could interfere with the smooth operation of the co-op, membership might be organized so as to separate clans. Toward this same end of maximizing social support, the co-ops were organized through a participatory and voluntary process. The Party generally used its time-honoured mass-line methods of persuasion and mobilization. There is no evidence that coercion or administrative fiat were employed to any serious degree.

Moreover, the early co-ops were a transitional institution between private and collective forms. Known as lower-stage agricultural producers' co-operatives (LAPCs), they were 'semi-socialist' in ownership and method of distributing income. At village meetings not unlike those used in the land reform to divide up property, co-op members tendered each other shares in the co-op according to the value of property they had contributed. The co-op's net income (after taxes and expenses) was distributed partly according to shares owned, and partly according to work done. Thus, the socialist principle of 'pay according to work' coexisted with the capitalist principle of 'pay according to ownership'. On average, one-quarter of the co-ops' income was distributed according to share ownership. To minimize the effect – to prevent the co-ops from being used for what in strictly Marxist terms would be economic exploitation of those with fewer shares by those with more – rich peasants were to be excluded from membership, and prosperous and propertied middle peasants were to be drawn into the co-ops only gradually.[6]

Reminiscent of the extremism of some of the land reforms, though, in many villages poor peasants and cadres sought to drive middle and rich peasants into the co-ops while undervaluing their property. This resulted in the destruction of property, especially livestock that middle peasants slaughtered before it was expropriated. The tendency to undervalue middle and rich peasants' property also undercut their willingness to deploy their productive energies and talents, which damaged production. To make matters worse, the weather was unusually inclement in 1954.

Thus, in early 1955 the Party slowed the pace of co-operativization. A small number of the most troubled co-ops were even disbanded. The problems of the transition to co-operative farming were discussed openly in the press, and the leadership urged flexibility and local initiative in balancing the interests of richer and poorer villagers. Progress continued, albeit more slowly than in 1954; by the middle of 1955, 15 per cent of peasant households were in co-ops, up from 4 per cent at the end of 1954.

This measured approach to co-operativization was also motivated by the concern of the apparently dominant group in the leadership with the wider economy, especially the issue of industrialization. For them, a primary purpose of co-operativization was to ensure grain supplies to the state in order to feed workers and finance industrialization. These leaders advocated a gradual pace of co-operativization so as not to damage production or induce any peasants – especially middle and rich peasants and traders – to consume or conceal the surpluses that the country needed. In line with their overriding concern for production, the advocates of this position also argued that it made little sense to form co-ops until they could be equipped with modern inputs from industry (such as tractors, cement and chemical fertilizer), so their larger scale could be best put at the service of increased production. President Liu Shaoqi was the most prominent person associated with this view; he criticized the 'premature' establishment of co-ops and ordered the disbandment of the weakest ones. In mid-1955, Vice-Premier Li Fuchun's report to the Second Session of the First National People's Congress summed up what appeared to be the leadership's consensus:

> Only when agriculture . . . turn[s] *gradually* from individual to collective management, and on this basis equip[s itself] . . . with modern technique, can the productive forces of agriculture be greatly developed, its capacity for reproduction increased and output raised *to meet the demands of the nation's industrialisation.*
>
> (Li, 1955: 47 emphasis added)

Yet this view was soon challenged. Where Liu and those agreeing with him could be seen as focusing on co-ops mainly in order to collect from the peasants, more radical leaders like Mao were more interested in collectivizing them to advance revolutionary progress. For them, the major purpose of co-ops was not so much to serve industrialization as to combat rural class inequality and stratification (mainly by eliminating the rich peasant class, to which notion we shall return), and to transform private ownership and management to co-operative forms. To head off snowballing class restratification, no time could be lost in forming co-ops, Mao and like-minded leaders argued. Moreover, they felt that co-ops did not need to await the availability of modern inputs. Like MATs, the co-ops could register increases in production by rationalizing the use of existing resources, and especially by tapping the people's presumed enthusiasm for socialism.

Within weeks of Li's speech stressing moderation, Mao countered with his own. In place of the original goal of increasing the number of co-ops from 650,000 in mid-1955 to 1,000,000 by the end of 1957, he now pressed for 1,300,000 by the autumn of 1956. Mao took direct issue with his opposition:

> An upsurge in the new, socialist mass movement is imminent throughout the country-side. But some of our comrades, tottering along like a woman with bound feet, are complaining all the time, 'You're going too fast, much too fast.' Too much carping, unwarranted complaints, boundless anxiety and countless taboos – all this they take as the right policy to guide the socialist mass movement in the rural areas. No, this is not the right policy, it is the wrong one.
>
> (Mao, 1977: 184)

To be sure, Mao spoke of the productive benefits that would accrue from co-operativization, and that in turn would aid industrialization (Mao, 1977: 197). Yet he also emphasized:

> As is clear to everyone, the spontaneous forces of capitalism have been steadily grow-ing in recent years, with new rich peasants springing up everywhere and many well-to-do middle peasants striving to become rich peasants. On the other hand, many poor peasants are still living in poverty for shortage of the means of production, with some getting into debt and others selling or renting out their land. If this tendency goes unchecked, it is inevitable that polarization in the countryside will get worse day by day. Those peasants who lose their land and those who remain in poverty will com-plain that we are doing nothing to save them from ruin or help them out of their difficulties.
>
> (Mao, 1977: 202)

Mao was able to triumph partly because of his political skill and prestige among the leadership, and partly because of the energies that rapid co-operativization ignited at the grass roots and the middle levels of the state. Local leaders were eager to move ahead for several reasons. Many shared the ideo-logical commitment to socialism that had propelled them through the victorious revolution. Some wanted to demonstrate their loyalty to the Chairman, or at least took their cues from him. The establishment of co-ops also created new institu-tions in which local leaders could exert political power. For poor villagers, the co-ops would provide a hope of security in bad years. Cooperation was also a way to gain some access to the property of their wealthier neighbours. Finally, many simply responded to the enthusiasm of their neighbours. In this light, the puzzle of why peasants would be willing to part with the land they had only just won in such a long, hard struggle turns out not to be so puzzling after all. Co-operativization now accelerated rapidly. Within six months, 1,900,000 LAPCs had been organized, half again as many as Mao had called for even in his upwardly revised target.

The LAPCs constituted an attack on the rich peasant class even though rich peasants were precluded from membership. With poor peasants busy tending co-op fields, the supply of people for rich peasants to hire or to rent land to began to dry up. In this way the rich peasants' property, the last remaining source of their wealth (after unified purchase and credit co-ops had deprived them of other exploitative opportunities), was also made less of an advantage. Co-ops sometimes dramatized this point by mobilizing their members to help rich peasants work the land they were unable to work themselves. Not only did this increase production, but by not accepting any payment for this work, the co-op members also humiliated the rich peasants, and provided a living lesson to both themselves and the rich peasants about the superiority of co-operative farming. While the co-ops were attacking rich peasants from below, the state attacked from above through increasingly onerous taxes on private farmers. Caught in a pincer movement, many rich peasants began to feel ready to throw in the towel and join co-ops.

The momentum of the co-op movement, the high spirits of the poor peasants and local leaders and the increasing isolation of the rich helped set the stage for the next phase, known as the 'high tide' of co-operativization. Many poor peasants were growing unhappy with the semi-socialist character of the LAPCs. Why, they wondered, should their wealthier neighbours receive more income merely because they had come out of the land reform with more property to contribute to the co-op? These feelings and questions in the villages, and the growing confidence of the radical leadership in the centres of state power, propelled China toward the nationwide movement to form higher-stage agricultural producers' co-operatives (HAPCs). They were much larger than the LAPCs, averaging 160 households. They were also fully socialist in character: shares were abolished, and distribution was solely according to work. By mid-1956, eighteen months sooner than the target date the Party had set that January (and that was itself advanced from earlier targets by one to two years), 90 per cent of the peasantry had joined almost half a million HAPCs.

This moment is seen by many people in China and the West as a turning point in the history of Chinese state socialism. They argue that the gradualism, flexibility, voluntarism and common sense that generally infused the politics of Yan'an days and the early years of the People's Republic now gave way to ideologically driven radicalism that was cut off from reality. This shift is seen as presaging the Great Leap Forward and the Cultural Revolution, both of which are understood, with some justification, as human and political catastrophes. In this interpretation, the rapidity of the movement, which violated the step-by-step approach of the past, could not have occurred without state coercion, threats or administrative fiat (Selden, 1982).

While there is no doubt that co-operativization underwent a radical acceleration in 1955 and 1956, questions still arise about how much the high tide was a break with the Party's past. The tendency to 'strike while the iron is hot', returning later to 'rectify' mistakes and 'deviations', was, after all, deeply rooted in Maoist political practice (Shue, 1980: 323 and *passim*). It is also not clear how much the high tide of co-operativization was accomplished by pressure from above. It did not involve the use or even threat of military force, physical violence or mass deportations, as were employed in the Soviet collectivization. Nor did Chinese peasants respond with the widespread sabotage or passive resistance that their Russian colleagues did. As a result, the Chinese rural economy was not thrown into anything like the economic crisis that occurred in the USSR. Though growth in grain production in 1956 was slow (partly because it was so high in the previous year), it was very good in 1957 (Table 2.1). Moreover, the argument that use of coercion, threats or administrative fiat must have been used assumes that farmers were unwilling to join the co-ops. No doubt some peasants felt this way: many (though, we have seen, not all) rich and middle peasants stood to lose out, and no doubt some poor peasants had their doubts about the wisdom and workability of the large new co-operatives. There is no question but that forcible means were sometimes used to get such people into co-ops. The Party regularly and vociferously criticized such tactics, branding them as 'commandist' and therefore inconsistent with the mass line. Moreover, the Party's policy (enunciated often by Mao) had always been that each new stage could only be taken if the likely result would be increased income for 90 per cent or more of those involved. The logic of co-operativization was, then, predicated on economic self-interest and its consonance with co-operative economic organization. If farmers had to be pushed into co-ops, then more work needed to be done to persuade them of the economic benefits that they were sure to receive.

The Party's confidence that farmers would support co-operatives was based only partly on its general conviction that socialism was economically superior to capitalism. It also took concrete steps to make the co-ops economically attractive, by offering credit, tax and marketing advantages to them. In some cases, for example, rich peasants actually raised their incomes by joining the HAPCs, because the heavy taxes they had been forced to pay as individual farmers exceeded their incomes from property ownership. And while available data are incomplete, it is very likely that the poor peasant majority saw its income rise with each new socialist advance. It is not at all clear that rapid higher-stage co-operativization was broadly unpopular. On the contrary, it probably advanced the economic interests of most peasants, including even some rich peasants, at least in the short run.

At the same time, the higher-stage co-operativization dealt yet another blow to the rich peasant class by undermining the last major element in the structure of private ownership and enterprise on which its economic power was based. Rich peasants were now to be taken into the co-operatives, but they had to leave behind their ability to earn income through land ownership. By 1956, then, the goal of complete equality of ownership of productive resources within villages, which during the land reform just a few years earlier had been cherished by many of the poor but resisted by the Party, was realized.

It is frequently argued that, in general, economic equality and growth are incompatible. Yet the Chinese co-operativization advanced both. It did not harm agricultural production in the short run (Table 2.1), as such radical transformations of property relations can often do. It also laid the foundation for further development of agriculture in the future. By enlarging the fields, it facilitated mechanization. The larger scale of organization made it possible to rationalize resource utilization. The capacity of the co-ops to coordinate large amounts of labour and resources also enabled them to undertake infrastructure projects (such as farmland reclamation and water conservancy) that were beyond the scope of individual households or smaller collectives but that were necessary for further agricultural development. The elimination of payments to property (i.e., rent and interest), which even under the LAPCs had amounted to nearly one-quarter of output, freed up resources to help finance such development projects. The co-ops provided an institutional context for developing and promulgating new agricultural techniques and information. There is also another dimension to technological development: while most individual households would not be willing to take the risks involved in trying a new technique, the co-ops could do so by allocating a small amount of resources to experimentation, reducing the risks involved by spreading them over a large number of households.

Overall, then, the socialist transformation of agriculture can be counted among the successes of Chinese state socialism. That evaluation is strengthened by the fact that even the Dengist leadership, which criticized so much of Maoist development, and which oversaw the dismantlement of China's rural collective economy, has not broadly criticized it. Nonetheless, these achievements were made in a way that began to open serious divisions within the Chinese leadership. These rifts would become cataclysmic during the Cultural Revolution, only a decade hence.

Political conflict, 1956–57

As the Second Five Year Plan for 1958–62 began to be considered, leaders on both sides of the debate about the first plan began to focus on intellectuals to advance their positions. Yet of course they did so in very different ways. Leaders who wanted the second plan to follow the basic contours of the first emphasized the need for the scientific and technical intelligentsia to contribute their talents and skills to make it work effectively. Inventions, better techniques and more scientific management would all contribute to the industrialization effort. The Party would have to adopt policies to encourage these intellectuals, by allowing them latitude to select and pursue their work and by encouraging scientific exploration and debate. Other leaders who were concerned with the political implications of the first plan – such as bureaucracy, élitism and authoritarianism – saw intellectuals as a potent source of criticism of these tendencies. In this context, a movement to encourage more intellectual autonomy and freedom of expression – in Mao's now classic turn of phrase, to 'Let a hundred flowers bloom, a hundred schools of thought contend' – was launched in 1956. Naturally, the direction and scope of the movement were hotly contested. China's intellectuals were caught and eventually wounded in the crossfire.

Many top Party leaders, and most middle-level Party and government officials, sought to restrict the Hundred Flowers movement. At best it threatened their growing political prerogatives, subjecting their authority in ministries and factories to scientific scrutiny. Bureaucrats and political leaders alike would now have to justify their actions to economists, factory managers to engineers, editors to writers and so forth. At worst, the movement opened the prospect of a broad-gauged political critique of the way power was organized and wielded in an increasingly bureaucratic China. Socialism itself could come under attack. The leadership was haunted by the spectre of Hungary, where critical intellectuals had been at the heart of an uprising that was only put down with (Heaven forbid, the more patriotic among them must have thought!) the 'help' of the Soviet Union. So they had little interest in hearing from scientists and technical specialists, much less from more socially and politically minded critics. The Hundred Flowers movement was given formal approval at the CCP's Eighth Congress, but then put on the back burner. It was actually suppressed in early 1957.

Mao was concerned with precisely this sort of bureaucratic defensiveness. In February, he went on the attack. In an important speech he warned of the rise of 'contradictions' between the Party leadership and the people, and began to speak of class struggle under socialism.[7] In Marxist discourse the concept of class struggle carries a specific dialectical grandeur, connoting nothing less than revolution. Mao was, therefore, opening a Pandora's box whose contents were new and, to the leadership, most dangerous: the prospect of revolution in a socialist state pitting the masses against their leaders. For now, Mao felt that the main battleground of such conflict was ideological, so he stopped short of trying to mobilize mass uprisings (a stage to which he would elevate the struggle within a decade, during the Cultural Revolution). He contented himself with trying to draw out the ideological issues and cleavages by inviting comments and criticisms from the intellectuals.

The speech was not published immediately, and in the next few months the Party bureaucracy tried to downplay it, while Mao pressed the point. Once again Mao prevailed. A Party rectification campaign was launched, and intellectuals – who at first had held back, fearing the consequences and remembering that the Hundred Flowers movement had been put on hold – finally came forward with a torrent of criticism. Ad hoc organizations of students, writers and liberal political figures sprang up, public forums were held and 'big-character posters' (see Chapter 1) and underground newspapers appeared, often carrying scathing attacks. The Hundred Flowers movement was revived and accelerated.

The content of many of the criticisms shocked and worried even Mao. Of course, intellectuals levelled the attacks on bureaucracy, élitism and authoritarianism that he had sought. Yet many critics went further, attacking the CCP and its government for failing to live up to socialist ideals in general or, even more serious, critiquing socialism itself. By June, the Party, with Mao's support, launched an 'anti-rightist' campaign. Mao's February speech was published at last, but in a revised version that now contained criteria by which to identify impermissible criticisms. Specifically, they were to help promote 'socialist transformation', 'people's democratic dictatorship', 'democratic centralism' and the Party, among others.

The anti-rightist campaign came down most heavily on outspoken writers who had demanded that literature and art conform to actual rather than socialist realism, i.e., that it reflect actual, not ideal, conditions. Ding Ling, the brilliant leftist writer who had been an important Party leader in cultural affairs, was expelled from the Party, banished to labour reform and had her works taken out of circulation. Others, including liberal politicians and ideologists who had joined the government and been bold enough to use the opportunity to voice deep criticisms against state socialism or the Party's socialist character, were 'sent down' (*xia fang*) to the countryside for 're-education', or subjected to popular criticism (in some cases by their own children) and self-criticism. Most resumed their work within a few years. Yet the effect of the anti-rightist campaign on the intellectuals and on the possibility of legitimate dissent in socialist China was chilling.

This series of events points up just how difficult it was for Chinese state socialism to subject itself or be subjected to sympathetic critique – i.e., criticism that proceeded from a commitment to core socialist values. Partly the problem was a lack of consensus within the Party on what those values were or ought to be. Partly it stemmed from the inability of the Party leadership to accept and tolerate criticism that pushed up against or beyond the indistinct boundaries of socialist commitment, and to recognize that others may have drawn the boundaries differently.

At its core, then, Chinese politics began now to display a fundamental contradiction. On the one hand, the state had a penchant, promoted by no less powerful a figure than Chairman Mao Zedong, for raising publicly the most fundamental questions about socialism, and for maintaining values of popular participation and anti-élitism not only in theory but also in practice. Yet, on the other, it was unable to find ways to tolerate serious criticism from society or debate among the leadership. Neither Mao and his supporters, nor his opponents and theirs, nor the leaders and functionaries at the middle and lower levels of the state, showed any willingness to do so. And no political institutions were ever built to create an environment hospitable to such discussion. This conundrum would continue to plague Chinese politics. It would also give Chinese politics its distinctive character among state socialist countries: its repeated tendencies toward broadly participatory, radical movements that raise the most fundamental issues and press outward the limits of socialism, that produce feisty, unruly politics full of unanticipated cross-currents, and that therefore have eventuated more than once in a coercive crackdown.

THE GREAT LEAP FORWARD

By 1957, the basic transformations in China's class structure and institutions of political economy were complete. The gentry, rich peasantry and various bourgeois strata had been dispatched, industry and commerce nationalized or co-operativized and agriculture co-operativized. This had all been accomplished without economic crisis, and the security of the socialist state had been preserved against active foreign threats. The early phases of socialist transition and consolidation could be said to be complete.

Now attention had to be turned to deeper structural questions. In agriculture, there were the long-standing problems of underemployment and low labour productivity. They were partly a product of China's enormous population and its limited space – even today China must support over 20 per cent of the world's population on less than 10 per cent of the world's arable land. Throughout the 1950s, no efforts were made in China to restrict population growth; in fact, the warnings of some demographers were drowned out by Maoist paeans to the virtues of a large population, and by obstreperous, dogmatic denunciations of Malthusian theory as bourgeois ideology. Underemployment and low labour productivity also had to do with the fact that Chinese agriculture still had to make a breakthrough to modern technology. China's traditional agriculture was, certainly, one of the most advanced in the pre-modern world, having achieved very high land yields through the accumulation of centuries of experience and the very intensive application of labour to land. Much Chinese farming could more aptly be called gardening. For this reason, the country's agriculture was butting up against the limits of its traditional technological base, a phenomenon known as a 'high-level equilibrium trap' (Elvin, 1973: 298–316). Without introducing modern technological inputs, Chinese agriculture could produce no more than around 185 million metric tons of grain, a level it had reached by the mid-1950s. The reorganization effected by co-operativization had rationalized the use of existing resources, enabling more to be squeezed from them than ever before; but it had not itself introduced the new ones that were needed. In 1957, China was not yet able to begin a breakthrough to modern agriculture. Much Western agricultural technology – which was oriented to the more extensive, less labour intensive agrarian systems of the USA and Western Europe – was inapplicable to Chinese conditions. The 'green revolution' technology of advanced seed strains and associated inputs was just beginning to be developed. Chinese industry was not oriented to production of modern agricultural inputs, so a simple shift in sectoral priorities toward agriculture would not have helped agriculture very much.

Industry had problems of its own, too. The capital-intensive strategy of heavy industrialization – which was to be continued in the Second Five Year Plan – would require huge investments. Yet with agricultural growth levelling off after the post-war recovery, it was increasingly difficult to rely on extraction of a surplus from the countryside to finance further expansion of the industrial base. Meanwhile, urban unemployment was rising, partly as a result of the migration of peasants to cities.

Yet industry's capital-intensity would also not create employment as quickly as a more labour-intensive approach.

The existence of these structural problems in the economy was accompanied by a conjunctural predicament in politics. Relations with the Soviet Union were deteriorating after 1956, as the Chinese leadership began to distrust Khrushchev, whom they regarded as unpredictable and unreliable (because of his surprise denunciation of Stalin) and potentially dangerous (because of his invasion of Hungary). Moreover, China had actually begun to register negative balances in its economic relations with the USSR after 1956, as it repaid earlier loans. So at best the USSR could not be counted upon to assist China in solving its economic problems, and at worst the Soviet Union was beginning to pose an ominous new threat.

These structural economic issues and the growing concern about the Soviet Union set the stage for a complex political debate that, surprisingly, led to something of a broad compromise on what would become the Great Leap Forward. In response to the First Five Year Plan's bureaucratic centralization and foreign dependence, some leaders responsible for finance and commerce proposed reforms that would allow a greater, though still only supplementary, role for the market. Mao supported them, because of his hostility to bureaucracy, his suspicion of the Soviet Union and his economic populism and flexibility. Ultimately, this approach faltered, largely because in the face of the anti-rightist campaign it became difficult to advocate marketization and a reduced role for the state in the economy. Yet if the reformers failed to solve the problems, they did succeed in posing them. Leaders responsible for economic planning and heavy industry – the main proponents and beneficiaries of the First Five Year Plan – could no longer carry on as before. To defend their bailiwicks, they proposed economic decentralization of planning to lower levels (primarily, provinces), higher priority for small and medium-sized firms, more emphasis on industry serving agriculture and reduced dependence on the Soviet Union. Mao and other top leaders went along with what would soon become the core priorities of the Great Leap Forward. They did so partly because they lacked an alternative at this point. More positively, though, through this approach they could realize some of their goals, such as opposition to overly centralized planning, desire for greater national self-reliance and concern for agriculture and light industry. Thus, although the Great Leap Forward would ultimately come to represent an effort to make an unrealistically radical vault to true communism, it was not originally conceived as such by Mao or other leaders. Instead, it developed out of much more normal processes in which leaders sought to develop measured, realistic reform policies, and then engaged in political jockeying and, ultimately, compromise around them. In other words, in important respects the Leap would turn out to be a bizarre and disastrous unintended consequence of some reasonable and even potentially beneficial policy proposals (Bachman, 1991).

As these principles were put into practice in a complex process involving middle and local-level leaders and ordinary farmers and workers, the logic of the Leap came to involve five basic elements. First, the priority on heavy industry was to be replaced with a simultaneous emphasis on heavy industry, light industry and agriculture. Second, though, this was not just a matter of sectoral priority in a macroeconomic plan. For the very distinction between industry and agriculture, and between city and countryside, was to be overcome not only in the economy but also in social life and consciousness. Farms were to have industries, and peasants were to work in them; urban factory workers were to raise food, and to help peasants harvest crops in the busy seasons. Third, the emphasis on capital intensity, which was proving difficult to sustain financially while also failing to address China's employment problem, was now to be reversed. Economic growth was to be fuelled by mobilizing labour, the resource with which China was most well endowed. Fourth, central planning, which took the entire economy as its focus, and which sought to maximize efficiency and comparative advantage nationally, was to give way to a more decentralized pattern with local and regional horizons of calculation and self-reliance. And fifth, Chinese economic planners and administrators, engineers and technicians, managers of factories and farms, and workers and peasants were to eschew help from the Soviet Union, relying instead on their own initiative, ideas and sheer hard work.

In the countryside, the Great Leap involved the creation of large units known as people's communes. They were the product of spontaneous popular creativity as well as radical leadership. Farmers and local cadres at the grass roots had begun experimenting with amalgamations of HAPCs in early 1958, and in the context of an excellent summer harvest the movement acquired a momentum of its own over the summer. It caught the attention of Mao and his associates, who dubbed these new units 'people's communes' and put their imprimatur on them. The pace of events caught the more circumspect of China's leaders off guard, and by August an enlarged session of the Party Politburo had no choice but to trumpet its approval.

The communes departed from the co-ops in several important respects. First, they were combined units of political, social and economic organization. They incorporated township governments and local units of Party organization, which had remained distinct from the co-ops. Second, they provided an expanded array of social services and functions, such as childcare, health services, education, food and, in places, even housing. Third, they combined agriculture and industry. They had their own factories and workshops, and integrated them with farming not only in management and finance but also planning, turning out industrial inputs for agriculture and industrial products using agricultural outputs. Fourth, the communes were much larger than co-ops. When first formed in 1958 they averaged around 5,000 households. After being reduced to a more manageable size in 1959, they still averaged 1,600 households, ten times the HAPC average of 160.

Nevertheless, in its August document the Party specified important continuities with the co-ops. Communes were owned collectively (by their members), not by the 'whole people' (i.e., the state). Organization and management of day-to-day work were to take place at the level of the 'production brigade' – roughly equivalent to the HAPC – that in turn was broken down into 'groups' (*zu*) roughly the size of an LAPC.[8] The principle of distribution was to be socialist (according to work), not communist (according to need). Though small plots of privately retained land were to be gradually eliminated, private ownership of other small but important productive resources (such as pigs, chickens and fruit trees around houses) and personal effects was preserved.

In addition, the Party repeatedly urged prudence, caution and flexibility in the pace of the transition to and the institutional form of the new communes. Yet these admonitions were not to be heard. The last half of 1958 was one of the most radical periods in Chinese state socialism. By its end almost every Chinese peasant was a commune member. Vestiges of private ownership of productive resources and even many consumer goods were eliminated. Communist principles of distribution came into use in many places, with allocation according to need (e.g., the 'free supply' of grain in communal dining halls) or to strict egalitarianism. Rural industries sprouted up everywhere, and in some very unlikely lines of production (including the infamous 'backyard steel furnaces'). Huge contingents of workers, including a massive mobilization of female labour, were set to work on infrastructure projects both during the farming months but especially in the slack winter season. By 1959, women were accounting for 40–45 per cent of the labour days outside the home, and 70 per cent of China's children were cared for in nurseries. Popular educational efforts, including part-time and evening schools, short courses and work-study programmes, were established to diffuse industrial skills among the peasantry. Campaigns were carried out emphasizing the basic equality of peasants on the one hand and cadres and intellectuals on the other. These movements actually went beyond the level of propaganda to attempts to prove the point in practice. For example, peasants were encouraged to write, paint and even read and discuss philosophy. Militia work was integrated with production and education. It was a time of genuine enthusiasm and very high hopes. New horizons were opened up on all fronts, as many peasants gained their first experience outside farming or the narrow confines of the village of their birth. As one peasant recalled: 'Those were great days! Great days! ... Every time I recall those days I am filled with happiness' (W. Hinton, 1984: 217–18).

In the cities, too, there was an attempt to construct people's communes – integrated units of agriculture and industry, and of political, economic and social organization. Yet they proved unfeasible. Workers simply could not find land, time or energy to grow crops. This abortive movement aside, though, urban industry underwent its own momentous changes. First, following the original reform plans discussed above, there was a major decentralization of state planning and administration. Provincial and local authorities were now permitted to retain up to 20 per cent of certain taxes and of the profits of state industries. They were also given greater latitude in spending these funds. This amounted to a shift away from the one-sided policy of vertical rule under the First Five Year Plan back toward dual rule, with horizontally organized authorities at the provincial and local levels gaining some financial resources and administrative power. Second, a similar change took place at the factory level. The heavily vertical one-man management in the factories, which had already come under attack from workers in 1956 and 1957, was replaced by a more dualistic one known as 'responsibility of the factory manager under the administration of the Party committee'. This also enhanced Party authority vis-à-vis that of the bureaucracy and technocracy. Third was a set of factory management reforms known as 'two participations, one reform and triple combination': i.e., participation by managers in manual labour and by workers in management, reform of the complex factory rules established in the previous years and the formation of teams comprised of workers, technicians and political cadres at various levels of organization and spheres of work. Fourth, more collectivist forms of distribution and material incentive were implemented (such as providing services or increased income to an entire workshop that had increased production), and were supplemented by non-material incentives (such as awards and public recognition). Fifth, popular education, propaganda and cultural campaigns like those undertaken in the countryside were carried out, emphasizing the equality of workers and cadres and the evils of social differentiation.

1958 set a new record for grain production, which may in the end have been unfortunate since it masked some of the deep problems with the communes that would soon make themselves apparent. Yet there were also more purposive forces that concealed the difficulties. In the flush of enthusiasm backed up by intense political pressure, a wave of overreporting of production results by local cadres broke out. Outlandish claims were made, such as reports of grain production reaching 270 tons per hectare (compared with an average of 1.6 in 1957). They prevented the leadership from learning in a timely way that the situation was actually growing worse. In 1959, total grain production was back to the level of 1953, 1960 was the worst year since 1950 and the 1958 level would not be surpassed until 1966. Per capita figures were even more disastrous. The Chinese population suffered a net loss of 20 to 25 million people in 1960 and 1961, including both deaths as well as expected births that did not occur due to deferral of pregnancy, conception failures and miscarriages. The Great Leap resulted in human suffering on a gargantuan scale.

The causes of the collapse were many and varied. It proved difficult for the relatively inexperienced and untrained rural cadres to administer finances and manage production in a unit as large as the commune. The communes' scale also undercut the peasants' ability to monitor each other's work, as had been possible in the face-to-face scale of social organization of the co-ops. Incentives suffered in other ways. With much income being distributed collectively (e.g., in the form of free food in dining halls) and equally (e.g., in the form of free services), the link between work and reward was broken or at least weakened severely. The combination of formerly richer and poorer co-ops and villages into one unit acted as a disincentive for both: many people from poor villages felt less need to work while they enjoyed a windfall from being thrown together with the rich, while people from richer villages were demoralized from being dragged down by the poor.

Incentives were, however, far from the whole problem. For the Great Leap Forward was also a time of intensification and mobilization of labour on an unprecedented scale. In haste and in ignorance of the requirements of construction, much of this labour was squandered. Many of the huge industrial and infrastructure projects were poorly planned. Agriculture was often left to women, who worked hard but were so inexperienced in farming (due to years of oppression that kept them at home) that their labours did not come to much. Nature did not help: 1959 through 1961 saw some of the worst weather of the century in China, with 60 per cent of cultivated land suffering drought or flood. Even in the absence of the Great Leap these would have been years of human disaster on a massive scale.

Industry, too, suffered, though somewhat differently and with much less human cost. Industrial output value rose rapidly through 1960, but then went into free fall (Figure 6.4). Yet output figures do not tell the full story. Even the early gains were achieved at tremendous cost and at the expense of output quality. The most infamous instance was the 'backyard steel furnaces', in which peasants produced three million of the national total of eleven million tons of steel in 1958. The steel was so poor in quality that it often proved utterly useless. As some farmers complained, it could not even be made back into the cooking pots that had been melted down to make the steel in the first place. Fuel and ore were used wastefully or were gathered in ways that had deleterious effects on the environment and resource reserves: forests were stripped for wood, and coal and iron were mined without regard to future access. Financial costs were very high, but this was not apparent at the time since so many of them – e.g., the value of locally gathered fuel and ore – went unaccounted. Under Chinese state socialist organization, they were 'free' to the commune, which could obtain them simply by mobilizing its own labour to work on its own mines and forests. In hundreds of other, smaller ways, efficiency, cost economy and quality were sacrificed on the almighty altar of gross output. These problems were exacerbated by the sudden pull-out in 1960 of all assistance from the USSR, whose leaders and technicians were baffled by industrial policies they could only regard as foolhardy, and exasperated by the lack of cooperation and anti-Sovietism they sometimes received from their hosts.

Though the overall balance sheet is certainly negative, the Great Leap Forward did have a few positive results. Valuable infrastructure, including many railway lines and water conservancy projects, was built, and much of it is still in use today. Peasants received their initial experience with industry, taking the first steps toward what would become China's unique and hugely successful rural industrialization. The Great Leap also began to modulate the hegemony of the Soviet-style heavy industrialization strategy that had been tried in China during the First Five Year Plan. Agriculture and light industry would subsequently get a slightly higher priority, and attempts would be made to integrate them into a more balanced approach to economic development.[9] Finally, the Great Leap Forward created the integrated unit of political, economic and social organization known as the people's commune. After some organizational readjustment, it would prove to be one of the most successful institutions of collective agriculture in the history of state socialism.

RECOVERY, READJUSTMENT AND POLITICAL CONFLICT

By early 1959, there was a growing consensus in the top leadership that the commune movement had developed serious excesses, but also disagreement about their seriousness and nature. At a Party meeting in March, Mao himself criticized the appearance of a 'Communist wind', which was manifest in 'levelling poor and rich, . . . excessive accumulation and labour responsibilities, and . . . "making public" all sorts of "property"'. (This last phrase was a play on the word 'communism', which in Chinese comprises the characters for 'public' and 'property'.) He called for distinctions between proper and improper public ownership, and stressed that any private property taken over by the communes must be paid for, since it had belonged to peasants, not exploiters. He condemned ownership and management at the level of the large commune, stressing instead the need for gradual development based on the smaller brigades and teams (Mao, 1969: 279–88). Others in the Party – most prominently Peng Dehuai, the Chief of Staff of the People's Liberation Army – thought Mao's criticisms of the Great Leap did not go far enough. Peng condemned the commune movement outright as 'petit bourgeois fanaticism', arguing that it had alienated the Party from the people and destroyed central control of the economy.

Mao and Peng confronted each other in July and August 1959 at a Party conference in Lushan, where both suffered political setbacks. Mao assumed the blame for many of the problems of the Great Leap, including the 'backyard steel furnaces', which he called a 'great catastrophe'. 'The chaos caused was on a grand scale and I take responsibility.' He admitted that, 'I am a complete outsider when it comes to economic construction, and I understand nothing about industrial planning'. He invited criticism ('If you don't agree with me then argue back') though probably without much sincerity, as we shall soon see. Yet he also sought, with some justification, to spread responsibility for the Leap's errors among other leaders at the centre and localities. As we have seen, the Great Leap Forward was a product of compromise among various leaders and groups in the top leadership. After returning to power many years later, Deng Xiaoping would admit that he too had supported it at the time. Thus, while Mao acknowledged that 'the one with the most responsibility is me', he also blamed others in the top leadership as well as radical cadres in the communes and counties, 'who extorted things from production brigades and teams. This is bad. The masses disliked it . . . Comrades, you must all analyse your own responsibility. If you have to shit, shit! If you have to fart, fart! You will feel much better for it.' He even held out for a more balanced view of the Great Leap: 'It is not a complete failure. Is it mainly a failure? No, it's only a partial failure.' He credited the Party with having stemmed much of the 'Communist wind' (i.e., the excessively rapid transition beyond socialism to Communism) since earlier in the year, when he had criticized it (Schram, 1974: 131–46).

In perhaps the most stunning remark of this remarkable speech, Mao struck back at Peng Dehuai, and in the same breath threatened the Party with nothing less than civil war if it challenged him.

> If we do ten things and nine are bad, and they are all published in the press, then we will certainly perish, and will deserve to perish. In that case, I will go to the countryside to lead the peasants to overthrow the government. If those of you in the Liberation Army won't follow me, then I will go and find a Red Army. But I think the Liberation Army would follow me.
>
> (Schram, 1974: 139)

By invoking his own popular base, disarming his critics through self-criticism, reminding the rest of the Party leadership of its own involvement in the Leap and, implicitly, the erosion of its own political base, and playing upon its desire for political stability and fear of civil strife, Mao was able to ride out the political storm. Peng Dehuai and his followers were removed from office and publicly vilified for organizing an 'anti-Party clique'. Yet Mao too took a fall. Liu Shaoqi was appointed Chairman of the People's Republic, a position held by Mao until just a few months before. For the next several years, Mao had to be satisfied with the role of *éminence grise*. From behind the scenes he participated in shaping the general direction of policy and ideology, while leaving administration of the affairs of Party and government to others, supreme among them Liu. He would later complain that during these years he was rarely consulted, and in general was 'treated as a dead ancestor' (Schram, 1974: 266–7).

In the context of the sharp criticisms of the Great Leap that had emerged at the Party centre in 1959, and of the deepening economic crisis of 1959 and 1960, systematic retrenchments took place on all fronts. The fleeting experiments with urban people's communes were abolished. Under a major financial retrenchment, thousands of construction projects were cancelled, many in midstream. In factories, worker participation in management gave way to greater authority for managers, and draconian individual material incentives were revived. Central planning was restored, as 'trusts' – in effect, vertically integrated state monopolies – were established and held to stricter financial accountability. Urban employment was cut back by evicting the approximately twenty million peasants who had taken up jobs and residence in the cities. They were now expected to return to their villages and get to work producing badly needed crops.

In the countryside, the communes were reduced in size by one-third through 1959 and 1960. A 1962 organizational scheme and set of regulations known as the Sixty Articles codified many changes that had already taken place (Selden, 1979: 521–6). The 'basic accounting unit' – the level of collective organization at which actual production was managed, accounts kept and income shared – was lowered from the large commune to the brigade (by then reduced to a size roughly equivalent to the former HAPC) and then to the team (roughly the size of the former LAPC). 'Private plots' were restored,[10] and strict limits were set on the collectives' accumulation and welfare funds. In important respects, then, ownership, management and distribution reverted to forms similar to those of the HAPCs, but on a scale more like the LAPCs.

Yet there were important differences too. The production teams were now part of a three-tiered commune structure with significant political, economic and social roles. Politically, they incorporated local Party leadership (over key aspects of production, political campaigns and political study and propaganda, for example) and government administration and finance (e.g., taxation, population and residence control and public security). In the economy, the brigades and communes were involved in state planning, regulation of various kinds and projects beyond the scope of the team (such as water conservancy, agricultural experimentation and rural industry). In social life, they organized health care, cultural and recreational services, education and youth and women's work. Much more than in the co-op period, under the commune China's villages were bound up closely with the state and made responsible for a comprehensive and integrated set of leadership and administrative responsibilities.

There was, however, also a countervailing trend. With the devolution of responsibility and authority to the teams, and an increase in their number (from 198,000 in late 1960 to 440,000 a year later), it became difficult for the Party to monitor grassroots affairs. Some teams adopted strict piece-rates and other pay schemes designed to maximize incentives, at the expense of egalitarian considerations. Many teams divided up their land, contracting it to individual households in return for a share of the output the team needed to meet its tax and compulsory grain sales quotas. As the collectives lost control over production and distribution, and in the face of deep economic crisis, they atrophied in other ways too. Work on infrastructure projects was drastically reduced, collective industries, workshops, schools, clinics and nurseries were closed or cut back, and economic guarantees and support for the poor were curtailed or eliminated. In the face of the crisis, many peasants turned back to traditional practices such as witchcraft, superstition and ancestor worship. Gains obtained by women through collective organization and work in the early Great Leap were lost. Black markets, speculation and hoarding also resumed. Many peasants fled the countryside to find work in the burgeoning urban informal sector.

These phenomena exacerbated class inequality in the countryside. Many former rich and middle peasants helped fuel the retrenchment, arguing – no doubt persuasively – that collective agriculture had proved a failure. Many poorer peasants turned back to their formerly wealthier neighbours as natural leaders of the village, now that the leadership associated with the revolution and collectivization was discredited (Thurston, 1977). All this, coupled with the Party's new stress on raising production, elevated the political prestige of the former middle and rich peasants at the grass roots. They were sometimes able to use their rising stature to gain control of the allocation of property contracts, obtaining for themselves the most or best land. In other cases, a disproportionate share of productive resources was allocated to them because they had more labourers in their families (since the wealthier peasants could afford more children, or had been able to afford to have their children sooner after the land reform). Some teams, out of desperation, exhausted resignation or desire to avoid controversy, decided to allocate productive resources to those who had owned them before the co-ops had been formed. To the extent that former middle and rich peasants still possessed a disproportionate share of agricultural acumen, commercial contacts and labour power, they could also benefit the most from the expansion of private plots and household contracting.[11]

Class cleavage did not simply run along the lines of 'former' rich and middle vs. poor peasants, though. During the co-operative period new divisions had emerged too, as some former poor peasants – including many rural cadres – prospered more than others. Many of these people were well positioned to take advantage of the retrenchment. Grass-roots cadres sometimes arranged favourable contracts for themselves. 'New middle' and 'new rich' peasants who were not cadres were able to benefit from the retreat from collectivism in the same ways that 'former' rich and middle peasants did. Meanwhile, many poorer peasants had little but the collective sector to rely on in the face of the economic crisis. Yet the recovery of the rural areas was taking place precisely at the expense of the collectives.

A consensus soon started to develop in the Party leadership that the 'spontaneous capitalist tendencies' in the countryside were dangerous and had to be stopped. Yet a split developed over their significance and the attendant solutions. Where Liu Shaoqi and Deng Xiaoping saw a problem of local leadership, Mao saw a class struggle. Liu and Deng perceived 'deviations' by cadres taking advantage of a specific crisis situation by lining their own pockets, ignoring their public duties or wavering in their commitment to socialism. Mao too saw all this, but he offered a more radical analysis that traced the roots of these phenomena to incipient capitalism. Specifically, he began to develop more fully the theory he had advanced in his criticisms of the First Five Year Plan in 1956, that despite the triumph of the CCP and the establishment of the People's Republic, China was still in a period of struggles between classes and, therefore, between socialism and capitalism. Now he pushed the analysis further than before. In the past, Mao had felt that the forces of capitalism operated primarily in the form of unreconstructed consciousness among certain strata (including many in the Party and government leadership). He now began to develop a theory of its material basis. This he located not in property relations, as a strict Marxist analysis of capitalism would, but in political relations between leaders and masses. This did not mean that he was of one mind with Liu and Deng, who also emphasized the political in their concern with local leadership. Mao endowed his concept of the political conflict with all the grandeur of class struggle and, eventually, revolution, while Liu and Deng saw little more than a need for some cadre rectification.

This theoretical debate was played out in the Socialist Education Movement of 1962–65. It got off to a slow start, partly because of the relatively low priority that Liu and Deng, at the helm of day-to-day Party and government activities, assigned to it in the face of continuing economic difficulties. Moreover, the state machinery was understandably reluctant to take up a campaign that could damage many of its officials. As in the past, it was Mao who galvanized the campaign. In May 1963 he issued a major document called the 'First Ten Points'. It began with a critique of recent Party policy on rural problems, which, he argued, failed to take account of 'other problems that have yet to be solved' and 'were not presented in a clear-cut or systematic way'. It reminded readers that Mao had argued in 1962 that 'in this stage [of history] there still exist class, class contradiction and class struggle; and that also existent is the struggle between socialism and capitalism and the danger of a comeback of capitalism.' The document went on to stress that victory in this struggle would depend, like earlier phases of the Chinese Revolution, on 'the poor peasants and the lower-middle peasants' (H. Hinton, 1980, 2: 952–60).[12] Thus, poor and lower-middle peasant associations should be organized at the grass roots, and these should undertake investigations of local affairs and uncover cadre abuses, which were in turn to be dealt with through popular criticism and cadre self-criticism. Mao was calling again for mass mobilization.

Deng Xiaoping countered a few months later with his own document, which took issue with Mao even in its title. The 'Later Ten Points' gave the highest priority to the 'organization and training of work teams'. Cadre meetings were mentioned next, while mass mobilization was fifth on Deng's list, and mass organization eighth. In general, the stress was on Party leadership to identify and replace corrupt, lackadaisical and incompetent local cadres (H. Hinton, 1980, 2: 961–74). Liu followed a year later with his own 'Revised Later Ten Points', that urged more concerted action in the face of sluggish results of the movement; but the form of action was similar to that advocated by Deng a year earlier (H. Hinton, 1980, 2: 974–88).

In early 1965, Mao countered in a document known as the 'Twenty-three Articles', that upped the ante not just numerically but also politically and theoretically. It returned to the theme of struggle between classes and modes of production, this time identifying the class enemy as:

> people in positions of authority in the Party who take the capitalist road . . . There are some people in the communes, districts, *hsien* [counties], special districts, and even in the work of the provincial and Central Committee departments, who oppose socialism.

Mao had already decided by this time that Liu Shaoqi would have to be removed from office, though the document made no mention of this. Yet Mao was not one for simple Stalinistic purges that only removed a rival from the élite. So now, as before, class struggle was to be undertaken, in which 'capitalist roaders' would be attacked in a broad mass movement. Whereas earlier the movement had concentrated on 'four clean-ups' – of corruption and incompetence in work points, local accounts, distribution of supplies and warehouses in the teams – now the four areas were redefined much more broadly as 'clean politics, clean economics, clean organization and clean ideology'. 'We must boldly unleash the masses', Mao urged. The work teams were not to run the movement themselves, but, in classic mass-line fashion, were called on to 'arouse the poor and lower-middle peasants, organize class ranks, discover activist elements and train them to form a leadership nucleus, and work together with them'. Mao went so far as to speak of forcible, even armed, political struggle.

> [W]here leadership authority has been taken over by alien class elements or by degenerate elements who have shed their skin and changed their [class] nature, authority must be seized, first by struggle and then by removing these elements from their positions . . . [T]hese elements can be fired from their posts on the spot, their Party membership cards taken away, and they may even, if need be, be forcibly detained . . . In places where authority must be seized, or under conditions where the people's militia organisation is critically impure, we should adopt the method of turning over the weapons and ammunition of the people's militia to reliable elements among the poor and lower-middle peasants.
>
> (H. Hinton, 1980, 2: 989–92)

So radical a mass movement did not yet break out, which only heightened Mao's resolve to break through the barriers erected by those leaders whom he felt must be restraining it. He was feeling more angry, desperate and, at least as far as the state leadership was concerned, helpless. Yet Mao was not given to despondency and inaction. On the contrary, he was an activist and an optimist. He would not wait long to make one more stunning attempt to lead history forward. The analysis of class struggle under socialism that had informed the Twenty-three Articles, and its call for radical methods of mass mobilization and even uprising, set the stage for the Great Proletarian Cultural Revolution. Launched the following year, it was to rock China to its core, and provide the most remarkable and thoroughgoing effort at radical change yet to occur in any state socialist country.

THE GREAT PROLETARIAN CULTURAL REVOLUTION

Historically unprecedented events often reveal much about history. Such was the case with the Cultural Revolution. It was played out with many of the elements of politics that had appeared since 1949: a radical supreme leader attempting to draw strength from an inchoate constituency of 'the masses'; political and bureaucratic élites advocating a more organizationally routinized and stable politics, using their control of state apparatuses to block or blunt radical thrusts; citizens being drawn headlong into popular movements with little leadership, preparation or organization, and adding their own genuine spontaneity and energy, all of which resulted in extremism and chaos; and the inability of the polity to produce serious debate in which opposing views are aired fully and calmly, while the political rights of advocates on all sides are protected. The Cultural Revolution also gave political expression to a complex of social, economic and political cleavages that had been incubated in Chinese socialism since 1949, including those between rich and poor, former exploiters and exploited, new élites and ordinary citizens, intellectuals and politicians and those of more and less radical ideological persuasions, to name just a few. None of these cleavages was clear-cut in practice. They were more like continua along which many people found themselves in various middling positions. Moreover, they cut across each other in myriad ways. Thus, we must resist simple or simplistic analyses of the Cultural Revolution as a 'two-line struggle', a conflict of 'radicals' vs. 'moderates' or 'pragmatists', a problem of charismatic vs. rationalizing authority or a mere power struggle among élites – interpretations that have been propagated in the West and China alike.

There is still much to learn about the Cultural Revolution, and it will require a greater fullness of time for research and reflection before it can be learned. The complexity and persistent uncertainty surrounding the movement were crystallized in a memorable conversation I had with a Chinese friend in 1979. Born a peasant, he was admitted to one of China's foremost universities during the Cultural Revolution, when emphasis was laid on recruiting students from peasant and worker backgrounds. He proved to be adept at languages, and was now a rising star in the Foreign Ministry. When he began to criticize the Cultural Revolution, using the standard arguments then being advanced in official media, I replied that, were it not for the Cultural Revolution, he would not be where he was and indeed would probably be working in a rice paddy. He paused, flustered and deeply disturbed, and was unable to reply for quite some time. Finally, with a sad and serious voice, and without a hint of evasiveness, he said, 'Yes, it will take us Chinese a very long time to fathom the Cultural Revolution.'

The Cultural Revolution can be periodized two ways, both of which are valid. It often refers to the three years from 1965 to 1968, during which intense conflict at the very highest levels of the state expanded into widespread conflicts among ordinary Chinese, tearing apart the country's political and social fabric and disrupting the economy. It is also dated through to 1976, to include the years of ongoing political wrangling among leadership groups whose conflicts in the early, hot years remained unresolved until Mao's death finally created the opportunity for a denouement.

Popular mobilization, participation and struggle, 1965–68

At the January 1965 Politburo meeting at which he had presented the radical Twenty-three Articles, Mao had begun to speak in vague terms of the need for a 'cultural revolution'. A 'Cultural Revolution Small Group', a task force of five top leaders, was formed, with Beijing Mayor Peng Zhen – who would soon become a victim of the movement – in the chair. At this point the Party confined the movement mainly to cultural affairs, so it did not attract broad concern. Matters heated up considerably in November, with the publication of a critical review of Wu Han's 1961 play _Hai Rui Dismissed from Office_. The script had obliquely (and, according to come scholars, unintentionally) criticized Mao by portraying the unjustified purge of an upright official (in the modern analogy, representing Peng Dehuai) for supporting poor peasants (hurt by the Great Leap Forward) against corrupt and high-handed officials. The author of the critical review of the play was Yao Wen-yuan, a relatively unknown left-wing literary critic who would later become a major protagonist in the Cultural Revolution (and one of the 'Gang of Four' radical leaders subsequently vilified for their role in the movement). Yao's article was reprinted in all the major newspapers, causing a political storm that culminated with Wu's public self-criticism only a month later. Peng Zhen, speaking for the Party leadership, retorted in February with a report that obliquely criticized Yao: 'We must not behave like scholar-tyrants who are always acting arbitrarily and trying to overwhelm people with their power.' Henceforth the Cultural Revolution was to be carried out 'under leadership, seriously, positively and prudently'. Fusillades were to be fired with restraint: 'Public mention in the press of names for major criticism must be made with care, and in the case of some people the approval of the leading bodies must first be secured.' The scholarly principle of 'seeking truth from facts' was emphasized alongside that of class struggle (H. Hinton, 1980, 3: 1380–1).

The left responded publicly on 16 May 1966, with a document that revoked the February outline report, vilified Peng Zhen and has come to mark the official start of the Cultural Revolution. It broadened the scope of the movement, locating cultural affairs squarely within a framework of political and class struggle.

> [Peng's] purpose is to channel the political struggle in the cultural sphere into so-called pure academic discussion, as frequently advocated by the bourgeoisie. Clearly, this . . . opposes giving prominence to proletarian politics.

It targeted 'representatives of the bourgeoisie who have sneaked into the Communist Party', including 'a number . . . in the Central Committee and in the Party, government and other departments at the central . . . level', branding them as 'counter-revolutionary revisionists'. Responding to the February criticism of 'scholar-tyrants', it argued: '[I]f the proletarian academic work overwhelms and eradicates bourgeois academic work, can this be regarded as an act of "scholar-tyrants"?' (H. Hinton, 1980, 3: 1508–11).

In the next few months, the struggle in the top leadership sharpened, the Maoist position became increasingly radical and, perhaps most significantly, groups of ordinary citizens ('the masses') began to participate in Cultural Revolution politics. On 25 May, a radical Beijing University philosophy instructor named Nie Yuanzi put up a big-character poster denouncing University President Lu Ping for the suppression of criticism of Wu Han, and calling upon students and intellectuals to join the battle. Mao, in a classic example of one approach to the mass-line principle of 'from the masses, to the masses', seized upon Nie's words as pointing in precisely the direction he advocated, and had the poster republished and broadcast nationwide on 1 June. As a result, students all over China formed themselves into groups that came to be known as 'Red Guard' organizations. Educational administrators everywhere came under direct criticism from students and the radical faculty. The dismissal of Peng Zhen and his associates was announced. On 18 June, college entrance examinations were postponed for six months, in order to allow the student movement to blossom untrammelled.

On 1 and 2 August 1966, the Party Central Committee approved a 'Sixteen-Point Decision' that laid down the guidelines for the Cultural Revolution. It repeated earlier themes about the target being counter-revolutionaries and bourgeoisie in the Party. It also stressed that they were to be rooted out not, as in the past, by work teams or by Party rectification, but rather by self-organized, aroused organizations of Red Guards and new Cultural Revolution groups that were to become permanent organs of popular political power. Moreover, they were to be formed not only on campuses, but in production and administrative units of all kinds. Big-character posters were to be used to register popular criticism publicly. In fact, on 5 August Mao put up his own poster on the door of the Central Committee meeting hall, in which he issued what would become his (in)famous call to 'bombard the headquarters'. On 18 August, hundreds of thousands of Red Guards from all over China – many of whom had reached Beijing by commandeering trains and trucks – rallied in Tiananmen Square at the centre of the capital. Mao, donning a Red Guard armband, received them personally. The two-pronged attack on the state leadership – from Mao above and the radical mass groups below – continued unabated in the closing months of 1966, as President Liu Shaoqi and Party General Secretary Deng Xiaoping came under direct personal attack as the 'leading' and 'second leading person[s] in authority taking the capitalist road'. Liu was never again seen in public after November.

Party and government officials, sensing the need to adopt new tactics to defend themselves against the Red Guards, organized their own Red Guard groups comprising supporters, and used them to attempt to divert criticism from themselves and onto former landlords and capitalists. This was a shrewd move. Quite a few of the most radical Red Guards were young people with 'bad' class backgrounds who had suffered all manner of discrimination since 1949. They were seizing upon Mao's call for rebellion to get back at the officials who had been making their lives so difficult. Thus, the more radical Red Guard groups focused their attacks on Party and government officials for their alleged corruption, authoritarianism, élitism and bureaucratism, and generally for forming a new 'bourgeoisie' under socialism. For some of the radicals, this was genuinely felt ideological and political criticism; for others, it was a conclusion they drew on the basis of years of personal mistreatment; for still others, it was mere rhetoric used to legitimate a desire for revenge. By contrast, what came to be known as the 'conservative' Red Guard groups focused instead on the more familiar concept of historical class backgrounds. They sought to expose the fact that some of the radicals came from capitalist, landlord and rich peasant backgrounds, and that those radicals with worker and poor peasant backgrounds were nonetheless tainted as the allies of the former class enemies. The conservatives also led the infamous attacks on the 'four olds' (old ideas, culture, customs and habits) that led to the destruction of temples, shrines and historical artefacts. (This aspect of the Cultural Revolution was later condemned, hypocritically but no less vociferously, by the Dengist leadership, even though many of their supporters actually fuelled it at the time.) Such moves diverted attention away from the actual class structure that had been developing under state socialism itself, which was the radicals' focal point and the established leadership's great fear. In colleges, universities, offices and factories all over China, the mass movement factionalized, with some Red Guard groups supporting local, regional and national Party and government officials, and others attacking them. The situation became very confused: children of former class enemies were among the 'radicals', while children of workers, poor peasants and loyal Communists filled the 'conservatives'; moreover, groups on both sides claimed loyalty to Mao and competed in producing and iterating ever more extreme positions.

Until the end of 1966, the initiative rested – albeit decreasingly – with the leaders on both sides, who were able to define the issues and provide guidance to the various Red Guard groups. Yet in early 1967 the mass movement acquired momentum of its own, and was no longer subject to leadership direction. Even Mao lost control of the radicals, and he would soon criticize them for having gone too far. In January, radical Red Guard groups stormed the leading offices in schools, colleges, factories, farms and offices. In these 'power seizures', authorities were dismissed and often incarcerated by radicals who set themselves up in their place. Official files were opened to scrutiny, which only produced more evidence to substantiate the radicals' criticisms against the former leaders. The Shanghai government was reorganized on the model of the Paris Commune. In most of China, the Party and government organizations simply stopped functioning. This was nothing less than a political revolution in the most literal sense. The major difference from the standard model of a revolution is that this one was being encouraged by the supreme leader of the state that was being attacked.

Mao and other radical leaders, not to mention less radical Maoists such as the broadly popular Premier Zhou Enlai, began at this point to have doubts about the mass movement. In mid-February, just days after the proclamation of the Shanghai Commune, Mao summoned its leftist leaders Zhang Chunqiao and Yao Wenyuan to Beijing, where he told them that 'the slogan of "Doubt everything and overthrow everything" is reactionary'. 'Doing away with all heads [i.e., leaders]', as demanded by the radicals and incorporated in the idea of a Shanghai commune, was 'extreme anarchism'. Mao argued that communes ought not be established beyond Shanghai, and that even Shanghai ought to 'transform itself into a revolutionary committee' (Schram, 1974: 277–9).

The revolutionary committee was to be a new kind of institution based upon a 'triple alliance' of Red Guard groups, revolutionary cadres and the army. In proposing it, Mao was saying four important things, some consistent with his previous statements and long-standing views, and some not. First, he was reaffirming the importance of political leadership alongside mass participation. Second, Mao was stressing that not all Party leaders were 'capitalist roaders'. He had been saying from the beginning that they constituted a minority, a position he had reiterated as recently as August. Third, he wanted an end to Red Guard factionalism. A broad, unified mass movement ought to be able to ascertain who the 'capitalist roaders' were, though he never specified how (since the masses were to 'educate themselves' in the course of the movement). It ought then to unite with the remaining majority of upright leaders to deal with them. The fractures in the mass movement had in fact made it impossible for the masses to 'educate themselves' or to identify the true 'capitalist roaders'. On the contrary, they had resulted in a chaotic situation in which nearly everyone became suspect. Now Mao wanted the mass movement to act in a more unified way. Fourth, and most novel, he was giving the army the key role in forging the new coalition among factionalized masses and revolutionary cadres. This was a major retreat from his position of just a few months before, when, in the August 'Sixteen Points', he had stated that 'it is the masses who must liberate themselves. We cannot do the things for them which they should do themselves' (H. Hinton, 1980, 3: 1566).

Mao called on the army for several reasons. First, it was the only state organ left capable of acting in a decisive way. It had not experienced the same sort of attacks from below that the Party and government had. Second, since in many places armed struggles had broken out among rival Red Guard groups, the job of restoring political authority required coercive muscle. Third, the armed forces were firmly under Mao's political control. After the Lushan Plenum during the Great Leap Forward, at which Mao purged Chief of Staff Peng Dehuai, the armed forces had come under the command of Lin Biao, one of Mao's closest political allies.[13]

The army faced a formidable, and in some ways impossible, set of tasks: to reconcile Red Guard groups that had often become the bitterest enemies between whom violent armed combat had all too often broken out. In this hostile context the army was asked to make political judgements about which leaders and mass organizations were truly revolutionary and which were not. Middle and lower-level commanders could not be blamed for confusion about what a truly Maoist position was at this point. Since Mao had now begun to emphasize the restoration of order, many commanders sided with more conservative factions and leaders in the grassroots units they were sent to supervise. Others attempted to strike compromises between conservatives and radicals. In either event, the army was greeted with hostility and opprobrium by the radicals, who had had the initiative in January, just a month earlier. At minimum, the army's presence gave the conservatives breathing room. In other cases, it enabled them to score victories that would have been impossible without the army on the scene. This period was later dubbed by the radicals as the 'February adverse current'.

Tensions heightened through the spring of 1967, a period of contradictory tendencies during which neither side could gain a decisive advantage. On the one hand, Mao continued to urge 'power seizures' against capitalist roaders, while on the other he urged stabilization under the revolutionary committees. Attempts were made to resuscitate the paralysed state apparatus at the centre, but centrifugal forces prevailed in the provinces, only four of which (aside from Beijing and Shanghai) could establish revolutionary committees at the level of the provincial government by the end of April. Even the popular Premier Zhou Enlai came under attack. Central government offices, including the Foreign Ministry, were raided and had their files opened by Red Guards. Demands for a national commune continued to be heard.

In July, hostilities reached a terrifying climax. General Chen Zaidao, the regional army commander in the industrial metropolis of Wuhan, had helped the more conservative mass organization there lay siege to its radical rivals. Two top Beijing leaders, carrying orders signed by Zhou (who by this time was firmly allied with Mao), instructed Chen to lift the siege. He refused, and arrested both of Zhou's emissaries, one of whom was severely beaten. Zhou himself tried to intervene, but his aeroplane was not permitted to land in Wuhan. Ultimately, superior infantry, airborne and naval units were ordered to converge on Wuhan. Chen capitulated before they were to attack. In the succeeding weeks, the Foreign Ministry was seized by rebels, who appointed their own Foreign Minister. The British Chancery in Beijing was burned to the ground. The People's Republic of China could no longer conduct its foreign relations. Already in the throes of revolution, the country was on the brink of civil war and political anarchy.

Mao now moved decisively to restore order. On 5 September, a joint order of the top Party, government and army leaderships, signed by Mao personally, ordered all mass groups to turn in their weapons to the army, and to obey military authority in carrying out its paramount task of restoring order. On 1 October, the eighteenth anniversary of the founding of the People's Republic, Mao greeted crowds in Tiananmen Square alongside many top military commanders who had been denounced by radical Red Guards in the previous months. Days later, schools and universities were ordered to reopen, and students were told that it was time to get back to their studies.

Throughout 1968 the mass movement sputtered and the leadership moved to consolidate the situation. Factional fighting continued, reaching severe proportions in places. Mao summoned Red Guard leaders to Beijing in July and told them that they had disappointed him and the peasants, workers and soldiers of China. 'Mao Zedong Thought Propaganda Teams', staffed by workers and led by the army, were sent to quell campus disputes. In an attempt to narrow and then draw to a close the mass criticisms of top leaders, the arrests of major officials, including Liu Shaoqi, were belatedly announced at last. A programme for sending urban youth and guilty cadres to the countryside was announced. An official cult of Mao, reaching new heights of deification, was propagated as a way of mollifying radical popular sentiment. By April 1969, the Party was able to hold its first national congress since 1958. The army took a plurality in the new central committee. To help stabilize the political situation and pre-empt a succession struggle, the new constitution designated Lin Biao as heir to Mao's leadership.

Ongoing political conflict, 1969–76

Yet political stability was not to be so easily found, and Lin's succession was to prove ephemeral. As Mao moved to rebuild the Party by bringing back into the fold many of those criticized in the Cultural Revolution, as Zhou Enlai worked in parallel to restore the government apparatus and as a new initiative in foreign policy was forged that involved, of all things, overtures to the USA, Lin Biao and other leftist leaders became alarmed. The dispute is shrouded in mystery. It appears that at a Party plenum at Lushan in August 1970, Lin attacked Zhou Enlai's foreign and domestic policies in a speech that he failed to clear with Mao in advance. Lin apparently tried to divide Mao and Zhou, and also to undercut the institutions of Party and government, by asking the Party formally to deify Mao as a 'genius'. He also allegedly asked to be appointed state chairperson, a post that Liu Shaoqi had held and that Mao wanted to abolish. Lin lost badly at Lushan. He and Chen Boda, who had been a major left ideologist, chairperson of the Cultural Revolution Small Group and Mao's personal secretary, were criticized. Chen was soon to be vilified as an 'ultra-leftist'. No appointment of a state chairperson was made. In foreign policy, the principle of 'peaceful coexistence' was enshrined alongside opposition to the USA and the USSR.

During the months after the Lushan plenum, great progress was made in re-establishing Party committees in the provinces and in thawing Sino-US relations, both of which must have appalled Lin. In September 1971, he dropped out of sight. Only the following July would the electrifying story be revealed: Lin Biao had plotted a *coup d'état*, attempted to assassinate Mao and, when the plot went awry, fled by jet to the USSR, only to have his plane crash in Mongolia.

Lin's disgraceful fall posed complex problems for the leadership, provoking equally complex political manoeuvring. His disloyalty tarnished the Cultural Revolution left, even as his disappearance created opportunities for other leftist leaders. With the left on the defensive in the months immediately following Lin's demise, Premier Zhou Enlai seized the moment to urge economic stabilization. Factory managers, for example, had become unwilling or unable to enforce discipline on the shopfloor because of workers' attacks during the Cultural Revolution. Zhou tried to encourage managers to get the workers back to work regularly. He also attempted to call into question radical advances in the countryside, such as collectivization of private plots and efforts to raise the level of collectivism from the production team to the larger brigade. Zhou also worked to restore educational and scientific standards. At every turn he met opposition from the left, who were still backed by Mao. Fearing that the tide was in danger of shifting too much against the left after a year of challenges led by Zhou, Mao now made some extraordinary moves. To help invigorate the left leadership, in the autumn of 1972 he promoted a handsome, energetic, radical young factory official named Wang Hongwen, who had already risen to de facto leadership over Shanghai, to a position of prominence in Beijing.[14] (Because of his meteoric rise, Wang came to be known by the nickname 'helicopter'.) Moreover, where Lin Biao's 'ultra-leftism' had been a weapon used by the right to attack Cultural Revolution radicalism, Mao declared in December that Lin had been an 'ultra-leftist' only in form, but in essence was an 'ultra-rightist'. Nonetheless, ever something of a political balancer, at the same time Mao approved the rehabilitation of Deng Xiaoping, the leading survivor of the leadership that had come under the attacks of the Cultural Revolution radicals.[15] Many of the Party and government officials who had fallen from power in the Cultural Revolution were also returning to their posts. The cult of Mao's personality was criticized, apparently with Mao's own approval. At the Tenth Party Congress in August 1973, a collective leadership, including elements of the Cultural Revolution left as well as veteran Party and government officials, was confirmed, replacing the unitary figure of an appointed successor like Lin.

Party congresses had often served to draw a line under previous periods of conflict, and to consolidate the position of the leadership and its policies for the proximate future. Yet the turmoil opened up by the Cultural Revolution could not be so easily put to rest. The left asserted itself through a public campaign to 'criticize Lin Biao and Confucius'. In an oblique expression of its opposition to the return of the pre-Cultural Revolution leaders, it attacked Confucius' call to 'revive states that have been extinguished'. Mired in confusing cross-currents and played out in the popular press in academic debates about ancient Chinese history that must have seemed arcane to most readers, the campaign never attracted a mass following. The only popular chord it struck was among advocates of women's rights, who used the opportunity to level criticisms against the continuing sexism of Chinese society rooted in Confucian ideology. Yet as an attempt by the left to formulate a political analysis and ideological critique on which to base a new mass movement, the campaign to criticize Lin Biao and Confucius fizzled. The left was on the defensive in élite politics too. In July 1974, Mao denounced his wife Jiang Qing and three other top left leaders – Wang Hongwen, Yao Wenyuan and Zhang Chunqiao – as a 'Gang of Four', a term implying the cardinal sin of factionalism among the political élite. She soon moved out of his quarters. In January 1975, Deng Xiaoping, with Mao's support, was elevated to the Politburo Standing Committee as Party Vice-Chair, a position that put him in day-to-day control of the Party and government.

Yet Deng's strength remained uncertain and the overall situation unsettled, especially in view of the advancing cancer of Zhou Enlai.

The left made several efforts to assert itself in 1975. It encouraged labour protests in several major cities. Jiang Qing convened a national conference calling for radical advances in agriculture, including class struggle and economic and political egalitarianism. In March and April 1975, Yao Wenyuan and Zhang Chunqiao published major articles in *Red Flag*, the Party's theoretical journal (Yao, 1975; and Zhang, 1975). They struggled to formulate an argument about the material and historical-dialectical basis of bourgeois recidivism and capitalist restoration under socialism. Zhang hearkened back to Marx's concept of the persistence of 'bourgeois right' – for example, private ownership of consumer goods, circulation of money and commodity production – in only partially transcended form during the post-revolutionary transition. Showing some moderation and political maturity, he argued that bourgeois right was bound to be a part of Chinese socialism, and that the best that could be done was its gradual restriction. His short article contained the kernel of a sophisticated idea that required much more development and critical debate, not to mention testing in the crucible of political practice.

Unfortunately, the opportunity for such contemplation and discussion never materialized. China's highly polemical ideological climate – created by radicals like Zhang himself – was inhospitable to the intellectual complexity and reasoned disagreement that can lead to a theoretical breakthrough of the sort that may have been immanent in Zhang's argument. Political tension and uncertainty too continued to rise, as a series of deaths of major Party figures soon brought the Chinese polity to a crossroads at which it would have to confront and resolve the disagreements that had simmered for so long. Dong Biwu, the last surviving founder of the Chinese Communist Party, and Kang Sheng, a long-standing close associate of Mao, died in 1975. Zhou Enlai, the irrepressible and adroit administrator and diplomat, and one of the few top leaders who occupied something of a middle ground on the political spectrum and could therefore help forge compromises, finally succumbed to his cancer in early 1976. Zhu De, the Red Army leader and another widely venerated figure, died a few months later.

The pent-up pressure came to a head on 5 April 1976, when a ceremony was held to lay wreaths in Tiananmen Square at the centre of Beijing in honour of Zhou Enlai. This was no doubt an affair planned and supported by more centrist leaders and their mass supporters. A crowd of those with more leftist sympathies moved in to try to remove the wreaths, and a riot broke out. It was quelled by the army and militia, and the left agitators were duly condemned. Hua Guofeng – a political beneficiary of the Cultural Revolution but himself not a prominent leftist, who had been elevated by Mao to the position of Acting Premier – attempted to strike a middle ground by having Deng Xiaoping dismissed from all his posts two days later. In August, the left sought to capitalize on Deng's second fall with a press campaign against rehabilitated cadres.

In this context of renewed conflict between the left and its more centrist opponents, Mao's death on 8 September 1976 provoked a furious struggle. The manoeuvring in the succeeding weeks was intense. On 6 October, Hua had the

Gang of Four arrested on a charge of trying to foment civil war by allegedly arming the Shanghai militia and planning an attack on the organs of state. In a sad but laughable example of the crudeness of China's propaganda apparatus, the radicals' images were now airbrushed out of photographs of Mao's funeral, even though earlier versions of the photos with the four in plain view had just been published a few weeks earlier. The next day Hua was confirmed as Party Chairman. He soon formally drew the curtain on the Cultural Revolution, which he declared – with a good deal of truth – had lasted more than a decade.

THE HUA GUOFENG INTERREGNUM: FAILED COMPROMISE, 1976–78

For the next two years, Hua Guofeng attempted to stake out a middle ground between the rival policy positions and their respective leaders and supporters. He presided over a campaign to criticize the Gang of Four and their leftist supporters, but at the same time continued to pass favourable judgements on the Cultural Revolution. He associated himself squarely with Maoist models of agricultural and industrial organization. In 1978, he put forward a new ten-year plan emphasizing a relative balance of industry and agriculture, and high targets to be achieved mainly by dint of great sacrifice and effort. Yet Hua tempered all this by setting it in the context of economic modernization – actually, not one but 'four modernizations' (of agriculture, industry, science and technology and the military), a slogan associated with Zhou Enlai that was now being adopted by the re-emerging Dengist leadership. Deng Xiaoping made his second political comeback in mid-1977, when, at the Third Plenum of the Tenth Party Central Committee, he was restored to all the posts he had held until the previous April.

A middle path was not to be forged, however. The animosities that rent China's leadership during the Cultural Revolution proved, understandably, too difficult to overcome. In addition, many political leaders, together with the trained professionals who advised them, felt that China's economy needed radical surgery and deep restructuring, not mere readjustment – an issue to which we shall return in Chapter 3. Thus, they sought a decisive political victory rather than a mere compromise with Maoist politics, policies and institutions. (In this sense, the word 'reform', which has come to denote the subsequent changes, is inadequate in capturing the depth of the coming transformation.) Finally, there is politics. Hua Guofeng simply lacked the political support, acumen, experience and sheer, sometimes ruthless, determination that Deng Xiaoping had developed over his very long career in the revolution and the Maoist years. All Hua had was the imprimatur bestowed on him by an ailing Mao: 'With you in charge, I'm at ease.' Yet from his display case in the grand mausoleum built for him in the centre of Tiananmen Square, even a man as formidable and tenacious in life as Mao Zedong could not in death exert his will over a country that was beginning to question the ways in which Maoist politics had shaken China to its very core. Deng understood Hua's political weakness. He sensed the political opportunity to undertake the thoroughgoing change that he believed, correctly, would be welcomed by so many Chinese leaders and ordinary people. Throughout 1978, Deng and his supporters took full advantage of their vast political networks and experience to manoeuvre themselves into position. At the Third Plenum of the Eleventh Party Central Committee in December 1978, they scored their victory. They returned to key positions of leadership in the Politburo and its Standing Committee. Class struggle was replaced by modernization as the main ideological principle guiding politics and policy. Radical advances in rural collectivization were rejected, and the importance of private plots and markets was reaffirmed. Hua's grandiose plans for rapid development of heavy industry were scrapped in favour of a more balanced and measured approach. In short, the way was now cleared for China's programme of 'reform' – in truth, a rip tide of profound restructuring – in pursuit of socialist modernization.

CHAPTER 3

The Triumph and Crises of Structural Reform, 1979 to the Present

The commonplace term for the vast changes that have taken place in China since 1978 is 'reform'. It is appropriate insofar as it refers to aspects of the process by which these transformations have occurred. Change has been pursued gradually and without large-scale violence. 'Reform', however, can hardly capture the depth and breadth of the substance of the changes. Since 1978, China has not merely been tinkering with, perfecting or toning down Maoist state socialism. Something far more thoroughgoing has taken place. The country has excised, root and branch, many of the basic elements of its Maoist polity, economy, society and political culture. It has questioned almost everything that went before. Its leaders and people have sought to create new forms of political authority, economic activity, social organization and cultural expression that have no precedent in China or indeed the world. If revolution is defined as a 'basic transformation of a society's state and class structures' (Skocpol, 1979: 4), then what China has been undergoing is no mere 'reform', but rather something that would more aptly be called a peaceful revolution. Another, perhaps less oxymoronic, term to capture China's gradual and peaceful process toward 'basic transformation of the state and class structures' is 'structural reform'.

DISMANTLEMENT OF MAOIST LEADERSHIP AND IDEOLOGY

Even with their stunning successes at the Third Plenum, the Dengists still had their work cut out for them. They had acceded to leading political positions, but now it remained for them to use their power. First, they still had to root out Maoist ideology, politics, policies and institutions, which appeared to be no mean feat. Maoist ideology was, after all, the set of principles and values on which the Chinese Revolution had ultimately been fought, and which had guided Chinese state socialism for three decades. Indeed, ideological factors probably played a greater role in driving socialism in China than they did in most other countries, with the possible exception of Cuba.[1] Politically, many leaders whose careers had developed in the Maoist period, and who linked themselves with Maoist ideology and policies, were still in place – from Hua Guofeng and many others at the very pinnacle of the state to officials at the middle and grass-roots levels of the vast Party and government apparatuses. Most difficult of all, Maoist policies and institutions were deeply entrenched in all aspects of political, social, economic and cultural life. Finally, if the task of clearing away the Maoist system were not formidable enough, the new leadership also faced the much more challenging task of replacing it with something new.

Since political change was a precondition of change in ideology, policy and institutions, and also the arena the Dengists knew best, they began there. Mere days after the Third Plenum wound up, Wang Dongxing, Mao's personal secretary and a leading protagonist in the political intrigues of the Cultural Revolution, was removed from his key position as head of the Party Central Committee General Office. At the Fourth Plenum, in September 1979, many prominent leaders associated with Mao were demoted. Dengist replacements – Zhao Ziyang and Hu Yaobang, who would soon accede to the top government and Party posts respectively – were promoted. Particularly symbolic was the return to the Politburo of former Beijing Mayor Peng Zhen, one of the earliest and highest officials to fall in the Cultural Revolution. One bad plenum for the Maoists led to another: at the Fifth, in February 1980, Wang Dongxing and three other key Maoists – known as the 'Little Gang of Four' – lost all their Party and government positions. Chen Yonggui, the peasant who rose from being a village leader in Maoist-period rural model Dazhai in the 1960s to a Vice-Premiership, dropped out of sight. In April, two more Maoist Vice-Premiers were removed. Now isolated at the top, Hua Guofeng was replaced in August 1980 as Premier by Zhao Ziyang. At the Sixth Plenum, Hua lost his remaining positions as Chair of the Party and the Military Affairs Commission (MAC). Hu Yaobang took over the leading Party position. Deng, preferring to lead from a position less vulnerable than the very top, and hoping to encourage his older colleagues to relinquish their power, shrewdly contented himself with the MAC Chair and a Vice-Premiership. He was now clearly the key figure in Chinese politics, however, and remained so for the better part of the next two decades.

The leadership changes at the Third through to the Sixth Plenums were accomplished not only with surprising swiftness and decisiveness, but also in a new way. In the years both before and after 1949, losers in leadership shake-ups found themselves stripped of all their posts, and were often made the objects of public campaigns of vilification for their alleged ideological or personal offences. Yet the rising Dengist leadership, themselves having been victimized *in extremis*, now sought not revenge but rather a novel approach that would spare both themselves and their enemies any repeat of their previous agonies, and that would also help normalize and stabilize Chinese politics. Thus, though Hua Guofeng was subjected to serious criticism within the Party, no large-scale campaign was launched against him or most other surviving Maoists. Hua's move was presented as a resignation, after which he remained a Vice-Chair of the Party Central Committee as well as a member of the powerful Politburo Standing Committee. Yet this new approach to fallen leaders would be pursued inconsistently. In late 1980 and early 1981, the Gang of Four were subjected to a televised show trial and their final public condemnation and humiliation. And in the wake of the 1986 and 1989 nationwide demonstrations, Hu Yaobang and Zhao Ziyang respectively were publicly criticized, though no mass struggle movement reminiscent of Maoist days was pursued against them (and, indeed, Hu even kept his seat on the Politburo).

As the Maoist leadership was being shunted aside and the Dengists were able to consolidate their positions, they turned their attention next to ideology. A momentous move had already been made at the Third Plenum, when class struggle was displaced in favour of socialist modernization as the guiding principle of Chinese state socialism. In early 1979, Wu Han's play *Hai Rui Dismissed from Office*, the criticism of which had been the opening salvo of the Cultural Revolution, was re-evaluated positively. Toward the end of that year, in a speech approved in advance by the Party at its Fourth Plenum, Vice-Premier Ye Jianying, one of the three most senior leaders of the Party, criticized the Cultural Revolution as having been a calamity. The choice of Ye was significant not only because of his high position; since Ye was one of the few senior leaders who had not come under attack during the Cultural Revolution, the Party was showing the breadth of its negative consensus on the movement.

Thornier by far was the question of Mao. More than even a predominant leader, Mao was a founder of the People's Republic of China, the author of its central body of doctrine and a cult figure. It would not be possible to break with the leadership, policies or institutions of the Maoist period without rethinking Mao's own writing and leadership. Yet doing so had obvious hazards, and was a matter of the greatest sensitivity. In the same speech in which he had announced the Party's negative verdict on the Cultural Revolution, Ye Jianying praised Mao. This put both Ye and the Party, for which he was speaking, in a contradictory position, since everyone knew that without Mao the Cultural Revolution would never have taken place. At the same time, however, Ye did criticize three key incidents in which Mao had been prominent, albeit without naming Mao: extending the 1957 anti-rightist campaign, making rash plans during the Great Leap and strenuously attacking senior officials at Lushan in 1959. Continuing to tread carefully but deliberately, at the Fifth Plenum a few months later, Liu Shaoqi – Mao's arch-enemy in the late Socialist Education Movement and the Cultural Revolution – was posthumously cleared.

It took another year and a half of careful preparation before the new leadership felt it was ready to take the perilous and problematic step of attacking Mao directly. Finally, in June 1981, at the Sixth Plenum of the Eleventh Central Committee, a major document entitled 'On Questions of Party History', that had been drafted and debated in the Party for the previous fifteen months, was issued (*Beijing Review*, 6 July 1981: 10–39). It criticized Mao's political ideas in relation to the Cultural Revolution.

> [T]he history of the 'cultural revolution' has proved that Comrade Mao Zedong's principal theses for initiating this revolution conformed neither to Marxism-Leninism nor to Chinese reality. They represent an entirely erroneous appraisal of the prevailing class relations and political situation in the Party and state.[2]

Mao's actions too were criticized. He was again taken to task by name for his attack on Peng Dehuai at Lushan. He was also berated for becoming 'arrogant' and élitist during the Cultural Revolution, when he 'divorced himself from practice and the masses, acted more and more arbitrarily and subjectively and increasingly put himself above the Central Committee'.

Nevertheless, Mao was still hailed in the document:

> Comrade Mao Zedong was a great Marxist and a great proletarian revolutionary, strategist and theorist . . . [I]f we judge his activities as a whole, his contributions to the Chinese Revolution far outweigh his mistakes. His merits are primary and his errors secondary.

As with its handling of Hua's dismissal, here again the Dengist leadership chose to deal with its political enemies differently than in the Maoist period. Though the balanced assessment was no doubt motivated by a political desire to maintain as broad as possible a base of support during a very risky break from the past, it was nevertheless a refreshing change from the Manichaean, polemically charged approach to problems that had stifled serious debate on key issues of state socialism in China as well as many other socialist countries.

Difficult as these offensives to unseat Maoist leaders and ideology were, they were accomplished with surprising swiftness and smoothness. It is difficult to say how much this is testimony to the bankruptcy of Maoism, how much to the political skill of the Dengists and how much to the tendency of those under attack in Chinese politics not to stand and fight but to draw back, regroup and wait for a propitious moment to reassert themselves. Whatever the case may be, the Dengists' determination and surefootedness in moving swiftly to transform politics and ideology in the first two and a half years after the Third Plenum led to high expectations for their capacity to transform policy and institutions.

THE STRUGGLE FOR STRUCTURAL REFORM

To adopt a phrase from the CCP's own lexicon, 'history proves' that this would be a far thornier task. Some of the policies and institutions that were set in place during the first thirty years of Chinese state socialism, including, most prominently, collective agriculture and the strictures against markets, were transformed rather easily. Others, such as the vast state bureaucracy, state-owned industry and guarantees of a decent livelihood to state officials, functionaries and workers, proved far more resilient. Part of the difficulty would turn out to be structural. Reform in many areas proved exceedingly complex. Sometimes it was downright contradictory, conjuring up some old problems (such as developmental imbalances and inequalities) and some new ones (such as powerful inflationary pressures and rampant corruption). Moreover, it was difficult to discern or arrive at suitable alternatives for many Maoist-period policies and institutions. For example, competitive markets, which were to replace state planning, often did not develop smoothly or naturally. No substitute for state-owned industry appeared readily on the horizon.

No means could easily be found to replace the ways that the state had come to provide housing, education, health care or retirement income.

Reform of Maoist-period policies and institutions also faced serious political obstacles. Many powerful senior leaders had deep reservations about the rise of the market, the social and economic inequalities and the Westernization of Chinese society and culture that the reforms brought in tow. Many ordinary people who were being left behind by the reforms found numerous ways to make their opposition felt. For example, farmers often refused to plant the crops the state demanded, or to sell their produce to the state at the prices being offered. Often they resorted to violent protest, including killing and maiming tax collectors and even staging uprisings. Strikes and slowdowns began to appear in industry. Two serious waves of public protest took place on a national scale, one of which – the 1989 movement – mesmerized the world. The many struggles involved in the reformers' plans to restructure Chinese politics, society, economy and culture will preoccupy us throughout the remainder of this book.

Early initiatives, mixed results: 1979-83

In the glow of the Third Plenum in 1978, 1979 dawned with lively ferment for reform on all fronts. Optimism about reform, both in China and abroad, was fuelled by high hopes and by inexperience with the complexities involved. Chinese society and its political and economic institutions, however, held surprises in store for both supporters and opponents of the Dengist initiatives. The country's initial four years of grappling with structural reform would produce almost unimaginably deep changes in the countryside. It was all the more startling, then, that at the same time changes in politics and the industrial economy – arenas thought to be most directly under central control – would encounter such unanticipated obstacles and equivocal results.

Rural structural reform on the fast track

Perhaps the most remarkable early success of structural reform took place in the countryside. Beginning in early 1978, some farmers and local officials, particularly those in poor places, spontaneously started experimenting with contractual relationships. The farmers, individually or in groups, signed up to do a specified task for their team or brigade in return for a specified payment. Under the most extreme form, individual households contracted for the use of collective property – usually a piece of land, but also possibly a fish pond, orchard, tractor or workshop – in return for a payment to the team in cash or kind. The farmers could keep all the profits, and were responsible for their losses. Thus the new contractual relationship came to be known as a 'responsibility system'.

These developments on the ground took place spontaneously, in advance of any policy initiatives from the state. The leadership was divided over the prospect of converting collective agriculture to a contracting system. After all, collective agriculture had been the key rural institutional creation of the Maoist period. It had many adherents in the Party and government, including most prominently

Vice-Premier Chen Yonggui, who had been a lowly village leader until the 1960s. Collective agriculture also had some substantial economic achievements to its credit. Finally, as we saw in Chapter 2, support for the rural contracting that emerged spontaneously in the wake of the Great Leap Forward had been condemned at the time by both Mao and the more cautious President Liu Shaoqi.

In the villages, too, particularly in places where communes had been relatively successful, collective agriculture had strong supporters. Some came from grass-roots leaders. As self-interested local politicians, they knew that decollectivization would mean loss of their institutional base. And, as people responsible for and deeply interested in local development, many were worried about the effect of dividing up the land. They worried about the inefficiencies that would result from people working individually on strips of land instead of collectively on large fields. They feared what would happen to collective investments in farm machinery and water conservancy infrastructure, or collective services such as schools and clinics. Many farmers also asked themselves these questions, and wondered how they would endure the 'responsibility' for their possible losses on their own.

Thus, Deng Xiaoping – who in 1962 had supported rural contracting with his famous words, 'it doesn't matter if the cat is black or white, so long as it catches mice' – had difficulty moving forward. Even the triumphantly reformist Third Plenum of late 1978 forbade responsibility systems. Meeting almost a year later, the Fourth Plenum went no further than allowing teams to assign tasks to groups of households. However, payment was still to be in work points (i.e., shares of collective income), a far cry from assigning farmers some property to use, charging them for it, giving them a claim on its output and holding them responsible for their losses.

Yet by the late 1970s, household responsibility systems were gaining momentum in many poor areas. A fascinating political dynamic of popular initiative and political influence was now set in motion. It was not quite democratic in the Western sense, and it closely resembled the mass line except that it did not produce the socialist advances that Mao assumed it would. Step by step, villagers and local leaders in various parts of the country moved ahead in developing contracting systems that were more and more comprehensive and individualistic. Each time they were actually crossing the boundaries permitted by state policy at the time. The results they achieved were usually significant increases in production. Party and government leaders sympathetic to radical rural reform would visit or receive favourable reports about these places, and use these villages' experiences as fuel to argue for further reform. After several iterations of this process, in September 1980 the State Agricultural Commission for the first time permitted the use of full contracting to individual households. This only fuelled more debate, from the highest levels of the leadership to the grass roots. The reformers won the day. At the centre, they signalled the importance and decisiveness of their position by issuing, as their very first pronouncement of 1982, Document #1. It pronounced not only that the household responsibility system was permissible, but that it was consistent with socialism. In the villages, the political dynamic now shifted. What had been a spontaneous movement from below toward decollectivization now became a programme actively propagated by the leadership, and in many places even forced on unwilling farmers and recalcitrant leaders, in ways not so dissimilar from those used to promote rapid collectivization in 1956. By mid-1982, almost three-quarters of production teams were engaged in household contracting, and the process was virtually complete by the end of 1983.[3]

Two concomitants to this process also moved relatively quickly. First, as decollectivization proceeded, many restrictions on private commerce were gradually lifted. Markets quickly sprang back to life, and the state pulled back its regulation of them. Where it used to set prices for a wide range of goods, now the state mostly just set maximum prices (with the exception of some key commodities such as grain and cotton). Even the number of goods with state-set maxima declined gradually. Second, the rural economy was depoliticized. As we shall see, class labels such as 'capitalist' and 'rich peasant' were abolished, so that enterprising and prosperous contractors could not be stigmatized. Economic and political administration were separated institutionally. As the responsibility systems proliferated, communes began to lose control to farmers of concrete production issues such as cropping choices and labour allocation. China's fourth constitution, adopted in late 1982, spoke of town and township governments instead of people's communes. As we saw in Chapter 2, the communes were originally established during the Great Leap Forward to help put 'politics in command' of agriculture. In 1958, they had replaced township governments, from which rural co-ops had been relatively autonomous. Now CCP Document #1 of January 1983 spoke anew of such a separation. By the end of 1984, communes were a thing of the past.[4] Yet, as we shall see in Chapter 6, state political control of agriculture and of many aspects of rural life would not disappear quite so easily.

The swift pace of rural institutional reform surprised many people, including, as we have seen, even its supporters in the top levels of leadership. If they concluded from this success that further transformation of China's polity and economy would be a smooth ride, they were in for another surprise. Structural reform of politics and the industrial economy has proved far more difficult, and in some cases intractable. Indeed, efforts in this direction have encountered frequent setbacks, and have provoked crises that have threatened the very existence of the People's Republic. Those processes and dangers are ongoing.

Abortive political reform

Structural reform of Chinese politics began as the Third Plenum had begun with a simple, bold and momentous move: it relegated class struggle to the back burner. Throughout the Maoist period, every Chinese had a formal class label originally fixed in the late 1940s and early 1950s. These labels had been the basis for significant differences in the ways that the state had treated people and distributed scarce resources. For example, capitalists, landlords and rich peasants and their children had been targeted for special abuse during various political campaigns. They were often discriminated against when it came to admission to schools and universities or to allocation of housing. In villages, former landlords were frequently vilified in public as reminders of the bad old days, and were forced, for example, to work in the fields during major holidays when everyone else celebrated. As we have seen, class background was one of the most important issues in the Cultural Revolution (also see White, 1989), and perhaps the single most important factor in accounting for why Red Guards joined the factions that they did (Blecher and White, 1979). As we shall explore more fully in Chapter 7, class had become nothing less than hegemonic in Maoist-period China.

In laying these categories aside, the Dengist leadership was accomplishing several goals related to political and economic restructuring. Most generally, it was distancing itself from the ideology, policies and deepest principles of the Maoist period at perhaps their most pivotal point. The new leadership was also eliminating an issue that had become a large and painful thorn in its own side during the Cultural Revolution. It was trying to reassure all Chinese people, no matter what their class background, that they would no longer suffer ferocious attacks based on their position in a society that had been overturned three decades before. The change would help create the conditions for social and, therefore, political stability by disposing of an issue that had rent China asunder. The leadership also had its eye on the rise of a new class of entrepreneurs who would help develop China's prospective market-based economy. These people, however, would be reluctant to come forward so long as the sword of class struggle was held over their heads. Abandonment of class categories and their political mobilization would also help encourage intellectuals, whom the state would need in its plans for China's technological modernization. The Dengists were shrewd to make this simple but profound move, as it met with instant and very broad, if quiet, approval from a public disillusioned with the crude, perverse form that class struggle took during the Cultural Revolution. Thus, even though class struggle in its more standard form had proved extremely popular during the Chinese Revolution, in late 1978 it died with not even a whimper but rather a sigh of relief.

Neither this stunning move, nor the rapid changes in the central leadership discussed earlier in this chapter, involved structural reform of the political system (such as the introduction of rights, reformulations of the Party system and government organization and transformations in state–society relations such as genuine elections or interest-group organization and politics). Indeed, the changes that eventually took place barely even merit the simpler term 'reform'. There was some minor tinkering with Party organization at the top. The basic ideological and institutional features of the Maoist-period Leninist political system were preserved, however. China would remain a country in which the Communist Party dominated political life, firmly resisting the rise of alternative organizations, citizen political rights and new forms of state–society relations.

At the outset of the Dengist period, such an outcome was not obvious. Even before the landmark Third Plenum, structural political reform actually reached the political agenda with a loud thump. In mid-November 1978, during a central Party work conference that was preparing for the plenum, big-character posters[5] began going up on a Beijing street corner just blocks from Zhongnanhai, the residence of the top Party leadership. While at first they merely expressed support for Deng Xiaoping, within a week they were raising larger issues of democracy and rights.

'Democracy Wall' became a site of lively political debate among Chinese and, even more novel, between Chinese and foreigners. Some Chinese visiting the wall went so far as to ply Western journalists with questions to put to Deng in their upcoming interviews with him. Soon some participants outgrew the format of the big-character poster, and moved on to editing and publishing newsletters and magazines, and even to forming independent political organizations.

Initially, Deng supported the concept of Democracy Wall; after all, many of the writers were directing their critiques against his Maoist opponents. In a sad repetition of the Hundred Flowers, however, Deng and most of his colleagues soon began to worry that much of what was being said, as well as the concept of independent publications and organizations, was out of bounds. By the spring of 1979, Deng emphasized the 'four cardinal principles': the socialist road, the dictatorship of the proletariat, the leadership of the Party and Marxism-Leninism-Mao Zedong Thought. He referred to some of the people engaged in the democratic activities as 'bad elements' – an epithet echoing one of the class-like categories that were then being abolished, thereby hearkening back to Maoist-period political struggles, including the Cultural Revolution. When a Beijing zoo electrician named Wei Jingsheng, who had been participating actively in the Democracy Wall project, criticized Deng's turnabout, he soon found himself sentenced to fifteen years in prison. Freedom of speech and association, a potentially crucial element in structural political reform, and certainly one that could stimulate other changes, was once again off the political agenda.

If the Dengist leadership was not ready for such basic transformations of the political system, even its small steps met with mixed results. In 1982, the Twelfth Party Congress took up two major issues. First was the transfer of top positions from the elderly patriarchs of the Chinese Revolution to the next generation. A new body – the Party Central Advisory Commission – was created to give them an honorific way to relinquish their direct power and serve instead as wise, experienced advisers only. Most, however, were unwilling to go so soon, and so they joined only on the condition that the powers of the new Commission were strengthened. (In the 1989 events, the Commission became a central player in the decision to crack down.) Second, to reduce the power of any one individual at the very top of the Party, a Central Party Secretariat was revitalized to replace the posts of Chair and Vice-Chair of the Central Committee. Its General Secretary was to be constrained by other members of the Secretariat. At the National People's Congress at the end of the year, socialist China's fourth constitution was adopted. It emphasized rationalized institutions and leadership processes that would be regulated by law. The functions of various bodies were spelled out and separated more clearly, and top leadership positions were now given term limits and prohibitions from holding concurrent posts. As would soon become clear, none of this significantly altered the power of China's political élite or the way it conducted its business. As to the question of normalizing the treatment of top leaders who were ousted from their positions, an issue with serious implications for the way that China's leaders conduct themselves while in office, results were also equivocal at best. As we have already seen, Hua Guofeng was eased out and allowed to retain a political role, but the Gang of Four were vilified. Premier Zhao Ziyang, who would lead China with Deng's imprimatur through the 1980s, but who was purged after the 1989 protests, remains under house arrest as of this writing in late 2002, along with his Chief of Staff Bao Tong. Party General Secretary Hu Yaobang, purged after nationwide student protests in 1986, was never heard from again (although students mourning his death in 1989 certainly were).

The conundrums of industrial reform

Like political and rural economic reform, industrial reform was the focus of lively activity at the outset of the Dengist period. There were good reasons to expect swift, deep changes. After all, there was a broad consensus among the top leadership, most experts on the economy and many enterprise managers that China's system of state ownership, planning and management of industry was technically backward, deeply inefficient and unable to meet the developmental and consumption needs of the country (issues discussed in Chapter 6). Moreover, the fact that industry was too tightly under central political control could perhaps be used by the reform-minded leadership to change it. Such expectations, however, would prove naïve. Industrial reform quickly showed itself to be a terrain of protracted conflict among leaders, experts, middle-level officials and workers, a quagmire of rhythmic policy reversals and a roller coaster of economic outcomes. Among other effects, these problems helped to catalyse the 1989 protests that threatened to topple the People's Republic.

Things got off to a rousing start in 1979, when a major conference of experts from various state agencies and think-tanks met, after careful preparation at smaller, regional convocations, in the picturesque and prosperous city of Wuxi to discuss economic reform. They criticized China's economic planning system for being overly centralized, and for not allowing enough space for enterprises to take the initiative. Basing economic planning on political criteria had, the participants argued, often led to the wild pursuit of unrealistic goals, wreaking havoc in the process. Over time it had produced structural irrationalities such as excessive emphasis on heavy industry, or a price system that did not help producers and consumers make rational choices. Instead, planning should be grounded firmly in market-like realities such as actual economic capacities, scarcities and preferences, i.e., in supply and demand. Moreover, markets should not just be simulated by planning; they should actually be allowed to develop to complement this new, more realistic planning process.

The ink was barely dry on this marketizing manifesto when the sparks began to fly. Critics, led by no less prominent a person than Vice-Premier Chen Yun, had a rather different vision, emphasizing 'readjustment' of planning more than development of markets. They worried, presciently, that marketization would cause inflation, since market prices of many commodities, especially essential ones such as foodstuffs, clothing or many basic industrial and agricultural inputs, would surely rise much higher than the low prices set by the state. Critics also feared that the more goods moved outside planned state channels, the more difficult it would be for the state to extract the revenues it needed, which could bring about financial deficits. They mainly wanted to change planning priorities to pay more attention to agriculture and light industry and less to heavy industry. They also wanted to raise standards of living by allocating a greater share of the country's output to consumption and less to investment. This meant scaling back some of the grandiose production plans that Hua Guofeng had put forward. They were open to the possibility that certain peripheral sectors of the economy, such as some retail trade in non-essential goods, could be conducted on markets. That is a very different matter, though, than doing overall planning in a way that simulated markets. Finally, of course, they opposed marketization itself on ideological grounds.

These critics won out for the time being. In the second half of 1980, anxiety about the rise of the Solidarity movement in Poland reinforced the position of those taking a political and ideological hard line. That made it difficult to argue for marketization. At a central Party work conference in late 1980, economic reform was put on hold. In the spring of 1981, experiments with reform of enterprises were halted, and a campaign against 'bourgeois liberalization' linked economics and politics by emphasizing the pernicious political and social effects of markets. This tendency – called, strangely, both 'conservative' and 'leftist' because it sought to conserve key features of the Maoist-period political and economic institutions now that they were shorn of their radical, mobilizational thrust – dominated through to the end of 1982.

If 1979 to 1982 evinced a cycle of reformist advance and then defeat, a similar movement and countermovement took place, this time at a faster rhythm, within the single year of 1983. With several years of political quiescence having passed, and with the surprising successes of rural reform in raising production apparent to one and all, reformers were able to go on the offensive early in the year. Party General Secretary Hu Yaobang understood the important role that intellectuals would have to play in economic reform. After all, many of the supporters of the early, shelved marketizing reform plans had been social scientists. They would need reassurance from the highest levels of the leadership to encourage them to participate actively in the politically contentious process of reform, especially in light of the repressive closure of Democracy Wall. Hu tried to do so by offering his public support for a reformulation of Marxism, put forward by leading intellectuals, that focused on its early, humanistic phase (as opposed to its later, more hard-nosed emphases on class conflict, from which intellectuals had suffered during the Maoist period). In this view, '*Socialist* humanism implies . . . upholding the equality of all before truth and the law, and seeing that the personal freedoms and human dignity of citizens are not infringed upon' (Wang, 1983).

Concurrently, Premier Zhao Ziyang promoted economic reform by arguing, in a major speech at the opening session of the Sixth National People's Congress (in June 1983), that prices, taxes and credit had major roles to play in regulating the economy. To reduce further the political control of enterprises, Zhao also introduced a new system of state revenue collection. Instead of enterprises handing most of their profits over to the ministries that supervised them, they would now pay taxes according to a standardized, predictable scale; after-tax profits would be theirs to keep. This clever stroke was intended to increase the power of enterprises vis-à-vis the planning agencies in a way that allayed the critics' fears that reform would cause state budget deficits. At this same meeting, 'conservative' ideological leaders struck back, launching a campaign against the 'spiritual pollution' produced by market society and Westernization. They continued in this vein through to the end of the year. Then the worm turned once again, as Zhao Ziyang said the campaign was threatening foreign investment, and he went so far as threatening to resign if it were not curtailed.

Thus, five years after the landmark Third Plenum of 1978 announced the dawn of a radically new political direction in China, the country had been through at least two cycles of reformist political and economic offensives, each met by strong counter-offensives from leaders bent on maintaining tighter political control and major elements of economic planning. Moreover, even setting political disagreements aside, some of the complexities and contradictions of reform were coming into focus: e.g., the rise of markets vs. the dangers of inflation and deficit; the state's need for intellectuals to develop and deploy their skills vs. its concern about political liberalization; the widely shared desire to attract foreign capital vs. the concern about the corrosive effects of Western consumer culture. At the end of this period, if no clear resolution was yet found to the controversies and conundrums of reform, at least the battle lines were drawn, the boundaries of permissible disagreement were being set and the structural obstacles were elucidated.

The rhythms of market Stalinism

1984–89

In other words, by early 1984 the outlines of Dengist China's political economy were emerging. Thereafter, China's reform policies would score many achievements, engender many problems and cause some massive crises. As these emerged and came to their political resolutions, often painfully, the political and economic systems' boundaries and the rules of the game crystallized. The process has evinced a two-dimensional rhythm. First, the space for structural economic reform was incrementally widened. With each advance, there would come criticism and a temporary stall, followed by yet another advance. Second, the upbeat/downbeat of economic reform stimulated another rhythm in which demands for deep political change emerged and were met by crackdowns. Dengist China was lurching tortuously toward a new system that can, with both irony and accuracy, be called 'market Stalinism'.[6]

As 1984 dawned economic reformers were back on the offensive. Politically, 'leftism' came under attack in the official press. The Party made efforts to promote a phalanx of younger leaders. A more permissive atmosphere of cultural expression was tolerated, putting before the public precisely the images – such as Western dress and artistic nudes – that the anti-'spiritual pollution' campaign had attacked. By the end of the year, the value of Marxism itself was being openly questioned in no less important a place than the flagship *People's Daily*. In the economic realm, the year began with Deng's highly publicized trip to the special economic zones (SEZs) of south China. Soon after, the 'factory director responsibility system' was highlighted as a way to induce enterprises to follow market logic rather than the political wishes of their Party committees. Enterprises were also given expanded autonomy. In the countryside, land contracts were extended from under five years to fifteen. Then, amid the euphoria of a bumper harvest, the three-decade-old system of quota grain sales was to be replaced by a new system of contracts negotiated freely between farmers and the state. In finance, enterprises were now allowed to keep 70 per cent of their depreciation funds under their own control. The system of paying taxes rather than remitting profits was further rationalized. In production planning, the number of products subject to state control was drastically reduced. Enterprises were permitted to make their own decisions about all above-quota output, and to negotiate prices for disposing of it. Many of these policies were advanced by a group of young economists who, profoundly influenced by their experience with structural reforms in the countryside, emphasized microeconomic factors – price reform, marketization and enterprise reform – as against the primacy the 'conservatives' placed on macroeconomic issues such as planning balances, investment rates, state finance and inflation.

Precisely those issues would now be called to the forefront, not so much by critics of reform as by the economy itself. Starting in late 1984, inflation spiked, alarming leaders and ordinary Chinese who had not experienced it for three decades. Many of them linked rising prices not so much with the abstract issues of structural economic reform as with something more palpable: the increasing number of small private merchants and workshops. This perception imparted a specific, class-based character to the general unhappiness and worry over inflation. Meanwhile, foreign exchange reserves began to run short due to profligate imports of foreign equipment and consumer goods. Much of the problem resulted from rising corruption, as relatives of high officials took advantage of their positions to make fortunes on import deals.

The result was that the reformist upbeat of 1984 moved on to an equivocal but detectable downbeat of reaction and retrenchment. In ideology, the *People's Daily* retracted its critique of Marxism, lamely claiming a misprint. Campaigning against 'bourgeois liberalization' renewed. Economically, the central government undertook concerted efforts to bring investment under control and to reduce inflation and the rate of economic growth. As it became clear that the 1985 harvest would decline from the previous high, wide criticism of the contract grain sales system extended to an unprecedented public disagreement between Deng Xiaoping and 'conservative' leader Chen Yun at a National Party Conference in September. Chen sounded a nationalist theme, denouncing the reform for making China dependent on foreign markets for its food. Politically, an ongoing party rectification drive shifted its focus from rooting out remnants of Maoism to corruption and the lesser sin of officials being overly zealous in their entrepreneurialism at the expense of their political duties.

Yet a political countercurrent was also in evidence. In the summer, Deng Liqun, the leading 'conservative' ideologue who had spearheaded the drives against 'bourgeois liberalization' and 'spiritual pollution', was replaced by Zhu Houze, who, like his patron Hu Yaobang, had defended the intellectuals against such attacks. This initiated a period of cultural and intellectual flowering that would last for over a year. Pushing the political boundaries outward yet further, a series of public outbursts took place starting in the spring. Young urbanites who had been relocated to the countryside during the Cultural Revolution held sit-down protests in Beijing, demanding permission to return home. Consumers publicly voiced gripes about inflation. Students demonstrated on a motley range of issues, including poor food and dormitory conditions, Japanese imperialism, nuclear weapons testing, African students dating Chinese and the continued presence of troops who had moved to campuses in 1967 to quell Cultural Revolution battles. The response from the highest levels of state leadership was not yet to crack down, but instead to continue to pursue moderate forms of political change that directly challenged 'conservative' elders. Several technocratically inclined leaders in their fifties and sixties were promoted to key positions. They were receptive to recommendations from the Chinese Academy of Social Science for civil service reform and further separation of the state from the economy.

As had happened just a year or so earlier, the advancing cadence of reform was again slowed not so much by political criticism as by structural factors such as the economic downturn and the increasingly apparent contradictions inherent in reform. The retrenchment policies of 1985 slowed economic growth rates, which bottomed out in early 1986. Opinion surveys showed significant dissatisfaction with the economic inequalities resulting from reform. When the government promulgated new regulations to eliminate lifetime employment and welfare guarantees for workers in state factories, putting them instead on contracts, a wave of strikes and slowdowns broke out. Economic reform found itself caught in a thicket of debate over its structural complexities. How should ownership and price reform be sequenced? If enterprise reform took place without price reform, enterprises could not really pursue efficiency through marketized operations. If price reform took place first, however, still unreformed, monopolistic enterprises could make windfalls without improving efficiency. Or how fast should growth take place? Too high a rate of growth would cause overheating, i.e., inflation and excessive, often unproductive investment, in turn further driving down consumption levels; too low a rate of growth had recently produced recession and serious employment problems. Or how much attention should go to large state-owned industries? Too much would only further encourage many loss-making firms, requiring continued subsidies; too little would put the employment and living standards of the large core of China's working class at risk. In one concrete example, a Bankruptcy Law, passed in order to create a way for the most problematic state enterprises to be closed down, could not be implemented for lack of an Enterprise Law stipulating the nature of enterprise property, rights and obligations. Several of these issues had significant implications for political reform: for example, ownership and enterprise reform went to the heart of the role of the state in the economy, and resonated to the issue of corruption. At several major convocations in the autumn, no resolution or clear direction emerged.

If this tense stalemate was produced in large measure by structural factors, it was soon exploded by a political intervention from one of China's most prominent and outspoken intellectuals. In late 1986, Fang Lizhi, one of China's leading astrophysicists, went on a speaking tour of several university campuses. He pressed beyond the limits of public political discourse by ridiculing Politburo members by name, denouncing socialism as a failure and calling for 'complete Westernization', including democracy, individual rights and popular sovereignty. Vice-Premier Wan Li was immediately dispatched to Fang's home campus, where he soon found himself on the losing end of an extemporaneous public debate with the popular professor. Within days, student protests involving many thousands broke out across China, lasting a month.

The leadership waited out the protests, once again eschewing a crackdown. Once the demonstrations dissipated in early January 1987, the leadership swung toward a hard line by underscoring in the clearest terms its commitment to tighter political boundaries. No less a figure than Party General Secretary Hu Yaobang was removed from office for having helped create a political atmosphere in which such extraordinary things could be said and done. Significantly, Hu was also criticized for contributing to economic overheating, i.e., excessive rates of growth without concomitant increases in productivity, leading to inflation. A new campaign against 'bourgeois liberalization' – a phrase that links political and social ills with their economic roots – was launched. In a clear indication of continuing lack of consensus in the top leadership, Premier Zhao Ziyang, now appointed General Secretary of the Party as well, announced that the campaign would be conducted only within the Party, and not in society more widely.

Perhaps because the leadership had put the political system back in the deep-freeze (or at least thought it had), it was willing to take its most serious crack yet at the politically dangerous question of structural economic reform. By 1988, Deng Xiaoping decided that the time was ripe for price reform, a move that he admitted publicly was sure to bring serious inflation and popular political opposition in tow. Marketization of all the basic factors of production – labour, capital and land – were also stressed; they too would have their own versions of price reforms: floating wages, interest rates and rent. Structural reforms of ownership and enterprise management, and deflationary policies such as constriction of investment and the money supply, were shelved, even though their advocates included Zhao Ziyang and many other influential leaders and economists. On the political front, there was talk of various reforms to control bureaucracy, to decentralize, and to strengthen the civil service and the role of law. The leadership also spoke of the need for dialogue with the people, who, it was recognized, had increasingly diverse opinions. If all this was intended to allay or pre-empt public concerns, it failed. In the event, none of this talk translated into significant new policies or practices.

As had happened several times before, economic crisis ultimately brought a halt to economic reform, this time specifically to Deng's bold plans to marketize not just commodities but also labour, capital and housing. This time the leadership's internal disagreements, combined with its recognition of the sheer complexity of structural reform, delayed the denouement for many months, during which the country's political and economic troubles only heated up more. Inflation began to climb again in early 1988. Through the first half of the year, factories experiencing difficulties coping with the new environment began laying off workers and defaulting on their debts and tax obligations. Some closed up under the pressure.

It was no surprise that all this resulted in expressions of discontent, but the extent and forms of the outcry began to shock the leadership. Once again, students demonstrated and workers struck. Opinion surveys showed thunderous disapproval for the country's political institutions. Physical attacks on managers and tax collectors rose. Crime was on the rise. Moreover, the spirit of defiance was not restricted to the people. Even delegates to the Seventh National People's Congress in March 1988 showed some independence: more than 10 per cent, an unprecedented number, voted against the Party's leadership's choice for Vice-Premier. In the summer, the national television network aired *River Elegy*, a six-part series that inveighed against China's historical insularity and backwardness while it extolled the West. It elicited strong reactions on all sides, and ultimately the very highest levels of the leadership weighed in against any future broadcasts.

Through all this turmoil, Deng Xiaoping continued to insist that price reform be put through. As prices rose, the Chinese people heeded their economic interests far more than their leaders' appeals, a reaction that should hardly have surprised a leadership that had been exalting the market principle. Depositors drew their money out of the banks en masse – causing a minor financial crisis – and people went on spending sprees in anticipation of rising prices. One old-timer standing in a long line awaiting the opening of a Beijing department store, when asked what he was shopping for, said that he was just going to grab anything he could find, because he was sure he could resell it soon at a handsome profit. The wave of panic buying must be understood not only or even mainly as predatory speculation; people were also striving desperately to protect the value of their meagre savings against an inflation whose dimensions they could not fathom. Everyone remembered that the demise of the Nationalist government on the mainland in 1949 was precipitated by a hyperinflation that killed off the last remnants of public acquiescence.

In this frenzied atmosphere, the top leadership bundled itself off for its annual conclave at the beachfront resort of Beidaihe. Zhao Ziyang asked for the authority to declare martial law,[7] and threatened to resign if it were not granted. Deng began to back away from responsibility for the situation, and encouraged his colleagues to blame Zhao. Li Peng, a 'conservative' – he was the adopted son of Zhou Enlai – who had been elevated to the Premiership just months before, quarrelled with Zhao over the rapid pace of growth. Faced with runs on its banks and shops, deep divisions in the leadership and the prospect of having to call out the army, the leadership got cold feet. The price reforms, which had been heralded so long and so loudly by so powerful and prominent a figure as Deng Xiaoping, were shelved. Zhao Ziyang limped out of the meeting. The country's top leadership was also badly bruised from its internal battles, the public visibility of its disagreements, the failure of its economic policies, the damage those policies had done to the people and to its relationship with them and its humiliating reversal.

Economic policy now returned to familiar 'conservative' themes: price freezes and deflationary monetary policy, slower growth, renewed emphasis on state-owned industry, centralization of economic control and a reduced role for the market in favour of greater state control of the economy. Economic reformers, lacking alternatives, countered by advocating large-scale privatization as a way to undercut the power of the state in the economy. In September 1988, at the Third Plenum of Thirteenth Central Committee, Zhao Ziyang attacked 'bureaucratic racketeering'. In eloquent testimony to the triumph of 'market Stalinism' that had emerged out of all the twists and turns that had occurred by this time, it soon became clear that economic reformers had completely given up on democratic political reform. Their political programme was 'neo-authoritarianism'. In this vision, the political and economic roles of the Chinese state could only be cut down to size by the rise of a powerful leader.[8] Ironically and naïvely, some had Gorbachev in mind. Odder yet, in this same vein many people also began fondly to remember Chairman Mao, whom they associated with a time when China was free of inflation, corruption and crime. Thus, an official ideological campaign of adulation for Mao in late 1988 found significant, if surprising, resonance in society. In fact, Mao became the object of quite a fad, complete with music recordings, statues, publications, pictures, posters and, of course, badges.

The movement of 1989

The new year dawned with a palpable air of crisis. The deflationary, statist economic policies adopted in the wake of the price reform debacle did nothing to alleviate either the structural problems of the economy or its short-term difficulties. Double-digit inflation continued to roar, and people remained fearful of losing their employment and the social guarantees such as housing, medical care and education that went along with it. Ideologically, there was an array of competing visions in the air – backward to Mao, outward to Gorbachev or to the West – none of which was either realistic or thoughtfully developed. Politically, none of these had any resonance to a serious leader, organization or programme. Moreover, the leadership was widely known to be weak and divided. As it turned out, it would require rather little for the situation to explode.

Starting in the final days of 1988, demonstrations and eventually riots erupted on Beijing and Nanjing campuses as thousands of male Chinese students once again attacked African men for dating Chinese women. Coincidentally, leading intellectuals campaigned publicly for the release of China's political prisoners, including Wei Jingsheng, who was Deng Xiaoping's *bête noire*. That they sometimes did so in international forums must have particularly rankled the nationalistic top leadership. In February, Beijing police prevented Fang Lizhi from attending a dinner to which he had been invited by US President Bush. In early March, a demonstration in Lhasa, the Tibetan capital, resulted in the declaration of martial law. Few suspected that it would prove but a trial run for several more such declarations in succeeding months.

The pace quickened in April with the death of Hu Yaobang, who was seen by intellectuals and political reformers as having been their leading supporter in the

Party's top leadership before his 1987 purge. Students mourning his death poured into central Beijing's Tiananmen Square. They quickly went well beyond merely honouring a deceased hero. Within just three days of Hu's death, over 10,000 took the unprecedented step of demanding entry to Zhongnanhai, the residential compound of China's top Communist Party leaders, to discuss an agenda that included re-evaluation of the 1986 protests and Hu's role in them, financial records of top leaders and their children, political freedoms and educational funding. When rebuffed, they actually clashed with the armed military guards at the gate. A few days later, they repeated their call to meet with Premier Li Peng during Hu's funeral, being held in the Great Hall of the People, flanking a Tiananmen Square now filled with tens of thousands of demonstrators. When Li refused, they mockingly crawled on all fours – as had been customary in approaching the emperor – to deliver their petitions. Meanwhile, demonstrations were spreading to many of China's largest cities.

A turning point came on 26 April. The leadership published a major manifesto on the editorial page of the *People's Daily*. Drafted on the basis of a statement by Deng Xiaoping, it took a hard line in denouncing the students as 'hooligans' led by 'evil' people bent on fomenting 'turmoil' (*Renmin ribao* [*People's Daily*], 26 April 1989). The demonstrators were not so easily cowed. On the contrary, on the very same day they formally established the Beijing Students' Autonomous Federation. The next day, their spirit of defiance only strengthened by the leadership's efforts to intimidate them, the number of demonstrators doubled to around 100,000. By early May, the social base of the demonstration broadened to include many office and shop staff, workers and even journalists. There were 150,000 in Tiananmen Square each day.

The leadership now changed tactics. Zhao Ziyang, with Deng's permission, made a conciliatory statement, calling students' demands 'reasonable' and urging a 'democratic and legal' response (*Renmin ribao* [*People's Daily*], 5 May 1989). By helping divide the movement, this approach appeared more deft than the heavy-handed threats of the previous week. (As we shall see, though, splitting the opposition would ultimately prove a disastrous course.) By appearing reasonable, the editorial began to encourage those who were tiring of the daily excitement to return home and await the start of a more orderly process of political change. (Students' final examinations were also coming up.) By changing course, the leadership appeared weak and polarized precisely at a moment when it also seemed to be receptive to popular demands. This only encouraged the more radically inclined protesters, while also attracting new and decidedly adventurous groups to their ranks, including lumpenproletarians like pickpockets, gangsters and out-of-towners who had high energy, more political *naïveté* and fewer local networks to restrain them. Reflecting this growing division, by mid-May the number of protesters began to wane at the same time that the movement became more provocative. Showing their shrewdness in political symbolism and use of mass media, on 13 May, just two days before the planned state visit of Soviet President Gorbachev, the student leadership upped the ante, declaring a hunger strike by 3,000 in Tiananmen Square. The image of noble students starving themselves in supplicant self-sacrifice before an intransigent, unpopular, corrupt government elicited deep sympathy from hundreds of thousands of urbanites of all backgrounds, who now flocked to Tiananmen, reversing the previously declining turnout. The resurgent movement combined with the arrival of Gorbachev put China on the centre stage of international media attention.

On 16 May, Zhao Ziyang sent an emissary to the square to convey a sympathetic understanding of the protests and to promise no reprisals if the protest would end. Most of the participants were willing to declare a victory and make the deal. However, under the students' consensus rules, a small number of the most uncompromising hunger strikers and their supporters obstructed a settlement. The next day, at a Politburo Standing Committee meeting, Zhao Ziyang proposed a further concession – retraction of the hated 26 April editorial – in the hopes that doing so would sway enough protesters to the side of compromise. Deng, inclined in the opposite direction, instead persuaded his colleagues to authorize Premier Li Peng to declare martial law when he thought necessary.

Before resorting to this extreme, though, the leadership tried one more time for a compromise. The following day (18 May), Zhao, Li and other top leaders paid a highly publicized visit to hospitalized hunger strikers to express their sympathy. Li and other leaders also agreed to a live televised meeting with the students' representatives. It did not go well. Though Li Peng had become a personal target of the demonstrations, he began calmly and diplomatically. The students replied by excoriating him and refusing, when he offered, to shake his hand. Wu'er Kaixi, one of the most charismatic and radical leaders, who had come to the meeting replete with his intravenous feeding apparatus, collapsed. The Premier finally lost his composure, and stalked out in a huff. Zhao Ziyang, who had not been present at the televised meeting, went to the square in the small hours of the morning of 19 May, where he confessed his inability to find a compromise and bade farewell to the protesters and to public life. When dawn came, Premier Li announced the imposition of martial law in the capital.

As had happened in response to the 26 April editorial, this hardline offensive again backfired. At the bottom of the Chinese polity, tens of thousands of Beijingers came out to their neighbourhood intersections to block the troops' advance. The confrontations were stunning, for by and large they were sympathetic rather than hostile. The urbanites appealed to the bewildered troops not to act against the noble, precious and emaciated young people in Tiananmen. Meanwhile, at the top, the only surviving People's Liberation Army marshals – Nie Rongzhen and Xu Xiangqian – publicly praised students' patriotism; and seven other senior generals drafted a statement, signed by over a hundred senior officers, maintaining that the army would never fire on the Chinese people. Astonishingly, the military advance stopped.

Deng Xiaoping now took decisive action. Having shrewdly retained the position of chair of the Party Military Affairs Commission, he was able to call an emergency meeting of the regional military commanders in the central city of Wuhan, far from the madding crowd in Beijing. Zhao Ziyang was sacked as Party General Secretary on 24 May. With troops still ringing the city, and the numbers of demonstrators in the square again beginning to decline from their astronomical, unsustainable levels, several top student leaders proposed a way out. The protests would end on 30 May with a huge victory celebration. In what would now prove a fateful, tragic juncture, once again a minority of extremists scuttled the plan, vowing to soldier on into late June, when the National People's Congress was scheduled to meet next door in the Great Hall of the People. In an inspired tactical gambit deploying postmodern iconography and media politics, on 29 May they fortified their own spirits and galvanized world attention by erecting the 'Goddess of Democracy', which combined aspects of the benevolent traditional deity Guanyin with the Statue of Liberty. The same day, the most radical protesters – mainly workers and lumpenproletarians rather than students – began to be taken into custody.

The arrests triggered a new development, noteworthy in its own right and also reflecting a serious shortcoming of the movement that few had noticed before. Only after the arrests of workers' leaders on 29 May did autonomous workers' associations begin to attract significant support. Workers now came forward, with a very different agenda from the students' and other urbanites' demands for democracy. They focused on job security, wages, challenges from burgeoning rural and private enterprises and attacks on their modicum of power on the factory floor. Where intellectuals and other urban middle classes tended to see the solution to corruption and authoritarianism in increased economic and political reform, workers were more inclined to think that excessive reform was threatening the gains they had made under state socialism. Where students erected the 'goddess of democracy', workers marched proudly under portraits of Chairman Mao. Thus the alliance of intellectuals, government and shop staff and other urban dwellers on the one hand with workers on the other – the leadership's worst nightmare[9] – never came off. In the end, this missing link would prove to be one of the protest movement's two Achilles' heels.

The other was, as we have seen, its inability to reach a decision, desired by most of its members and leaders, to declare victory in time to return home safely and begin to plan for the future of their movement. Having allowed an extremist minority to dig in its and everyone else's heels, it was now too late for anything but an unhappy ending. With Zhao out of the way and the infuriated hardline leadership now fully in charge, the military crackdown got under way on the night of 3–4 June. The death toll could never be ascertained, but the best estimates are around a thousand (Munro, 1990). The vast majority were not students but workers and other Beijing residents, who were killed in their encampments at major intersections of the city ringing Tiananmen as they tried to prevent troops from reaching the students in the square. Several dozen people died in the immediate vicinity of the square, and a few actually in it. The casualties in Tiananmen were not higher because most students left by a pre-negotiated exit route. More intangibly but no less significantly, colossal damage was also done to the popular reputation of the state and its leadership.

Though this was surely its climax, the movement of 1989 was not over yet. In another stunning example of how repression only increased the protesters' determination, two days later renewed protests broke out in cities all across China. A dominant image from the earlier Beijing protests was the lone man who stopped the advance of a line of tanks by stepping in front of them. By contrast, in Shanghai, a group of protesters blocking a railway track was run over by a train that would not stop. The train was attacked and burned, killing several more people. In Chengdu, the capital of Sichuan Province, up to 300 people may have been killed in what was probably the most violent confrontation. Many leading intellectuals now fled the country, while Fang Lizhi, the firebrand astrophysicist so fond of inciting his students to anti-government protest, took refuge in the US embassy. During the last two weeks of June, there was more violence, this time perpetrated by the state. Dragnets resulted in thousands of arrests, and around fifty people were summarily executed. Significantly, most were workers and lumpenproletarians. The state took a different approach to disciplining the intelligentsia. A 'most wanted' list of protest leaders, comprising mostly students, was widely distributed. Some were caught and sent to prison, but none was executed. In eloquent testimony to the declining capacity of the state to control the Chinese people, quite a few of the 'most wanted' managed to escape the country, aided by many sympathizers and by gangs of smugglers hired by Hong Kong support groups.

Through the summer, the leadership adopted several attitudes toward its public. It attempted to mollify them by launching a new drive against corruption, including not just words but some concrete action: expulsion of many Party members, fines on several large companies (and closure of one) engaged in questionable business deals and a ban on the business activities of the offspring of high officials. The leadership tried persuasion by a massive propaganda campaign, including a skilfully produced video portraying genuine facts, such as the presence of foreign spies amid the protesters, and violent attacks on troops. Of course, it also resorted to coercion and retribution. The size of the incoming class at Beijing University and other institutions was drastically reduced, and the students were required to fulfil an extended period of special military training before enrolling.

Even in this repressive atmosphere, society and even some officials lobbed attacks back at the state as well. Snipers took occasional potshots at soldiers. Beijing University students protested against the safe target of cuts in the education budget. At one meeting, middle-level government officials hissed a senior military officer who had come to explain the Tiananmen events. These small protests, however surprising and courageous, could not dilute the overwhelming victory of the political hardliners.

During the first decade of the Dengist period, impulses for structural reform of the polity and the economy had proceeded by ebb and flow. The two dimensions of change had often moved in tandem. Yet, as the events of 1989 drew the decade to a close, it became clear that economic change had advanced faster than political change. Put differently, the leadership had proved to have broad consensus on the need to transform the Maoist-period economic system, even as it disagreed on what ought to replace it. By contrast, although the Dengists evinced a broadly shared enthusiasm for abandoning Maoist-period ideology and radicalism, they had also ended up with a commitment to maintain the basic political institutions of the Maoist period: monopolistic rule by the Communist Party and tight restrictions against civil liberties and an autonomous political sphere of civil society. In a nutshell, what emerged from the fits and starts of the 1980s were the clear outlines of market Stalinism. It would only be consolidated even further in the coming years. For, even though the immediate aftermath of the 1989 events was economic retrenchment, before long the market would emerge more triumphant than ever, while, and indeed partly because, political reform would remain in the deep-freeze.

CHINA SINCE TIANANMEN

1989-91: political and economic deep-freeze

Since in broad outline those leaders most hostile to political reform also tended to take a less radical position on economic reform, it is no surprise that their ascendance marked the start of an extended period of economic retrenchment. For two and a half years after the crackdown, economic policy emphasized austerity, slowed growth to tame inflation and circumscription of the market. Industrial investment was curtailed by tightened credit and fiscal policies. Such investment as was to take place focused on state-owned enterprises rather than on the collective or private sectors. In fact, many rural industries were ordered to close or were choked by restrictive credit and tax policies and stiffened regulation. Renewed investment priority was given to agriculture, for several reasons. Agricultural growth had been stagnant in the years following 1984, as we shall see in Chapter 6. This had alarmed 'conservative' leaders, including of course the hardliners, who feared rural discontent and, as we have seen, dependence on foreign markets. Food price subsidies – provided to keep urban prices low (and with them, political discontent) while maintaining higher prices paid to farmers to keep them content as well – were consuming a huge portion of the state budget, contributing to a growing deficit and financial crisis. The situation was so serious that state grain-purchasing agencies lacked funds to pay the farmers; when they resorted to issuing IOUs, they incurred both the farmers' wrath and also the risk that even less human energy and material resources would be put into agriculture. Rural infrastructure such as water conservancy projects were deteriorating, threatening future disasters. Meanwhile, for both producer and consumer goods, price controls were reinstated; to this same deflationary end, the money supply was shrunk. In both the countryside and the cities, propaganda campaigns stressing the need and virtues of plain living were launched.

Throughout this period, politics remained tightly under wraps as well. By the winter and spring of 1990, the leadership extended a few olive branches (twigs, in fact) to society. Martial law was lifted in Beijing and Lhasa, some arrested demonstrators were released and Fang Lizhi was permitted to leave China. No one mistook any of this for a change in the leadership's commitment to strict political control. Laws and regulations restricting demonstrations were promulgated. Ideological campaigns for 'socialist spiritual civilisation' and against 'bourgeois liberalization' were renewed, this time with ominous overtones that the liberalizers might be class enemies. Yet the leadership also understood the need for some internal house cleaning. It emphasized the need to improve its relationship with the masses, to the point of returning to some time-honoured Yan'an and mass-line measures such as periodically sending cadres to the grass roots. Renewed anti-corruption drives and ideological study campaigns were directed toward this same end. Intellectuals were reminded of their responsibility to serve the state.

1992–98: renewed rhythms of market Stalinism

Perhaps the success of these repressive measures in achieving two years of political quiescence persuaded the leadership that it could now risk reopening the economy. Whatever the cause, in early 1992 economic reform picked up renewed momentum. In January, the conservative Premier Li Peng declared that the period of 'improving the economic environment and rectifying the economic order' – i.e., economic austerity – was over (*BBC Daily Report* [1992] FE/1276; quoted in *China Quarterly*, 130: 469). A week later, Deng Xiaoping embarked on another widely publicized tour of southern China, during which the economic dynamism of Guangdong Province – the most marketized in China – was singled out for special endorsement.[10] Once again Deng's trademark ideological pragmatism was on display, as he now trumpeted the view that markets are not to be equated with capitalism, and that 'socialism's real nature is to liberate productive forces' (*BBC Daily Report* [1992] FE/1326; quoted in *China Quarterly*, 130: 456). This time around, though, in order to broaden the base of political support for the new policies, Shanghai was to be included. It would bring in tow the huge and economically dynamic lower Yangzi Delta region. In fact, Deng now admitted that it had been a mistake not to do so earlier, suggesting that disagreement over previous economic liberalizations had had a political dimension. Shanghai's ascendance was no doubt also a result of the rise of many key leaders from the city, including Party General Secretary Jiang Zemin. By the end of the year, the target for economic growth was raised from 6 to 9 per cent.

Price and market reforms were now put into gear. The number of products under state planning was cut back to just 72. State-set prices of basic commodities and utilities were raised; for example, grain prices in state shops rose an average of 50 per cent in most provinces. In the summer of 1992, a pilot plan to free grain markets completely in 400 counties (out of around 2,200) was announced. Crop planning was cut back. In the autumn, the leadership took a big risk by deciding to lift grain price controls in order to stimulate lagging production. Political change was far slower, although in October, at the Fourteenth Party Congress, the Party Central Advisory Commission, a bastion of the conservative elders, was abolished, and a younger, better educated group of officials was promoted.

By 1993, these economic policies had resulted in serious overheating of the economy. Officially, inflation reached 13 per cent. The state's financial crisis continued unabated, and once again local governments often had no alternative to giving farmers IOUs for their crops, despite official condemnation of the practice. The political situation in the countryside now became explosive. For example, in June 1993 spontaneous protests by farmers in Renshou County (Sichuan) against road construction levies led, according to a government report, to 'beating, smashing and looting ... [in which] some people ... stormed the district and township governments and schools, beat up cadres and teachers, smashed public and private property and illegally detained grass-roots cadres and public security personnel' (*BBC Daily Report*, 14 June 1993). When police responded with tear-gas, some were taken hostage by the angry crowd, and police cars were set on fire. A month later, an effort by a county government in Hunan to requisition land along a railway line prompted farmers to seize weapons, including semi-automatic rifles, from the local armoury; several hundred troops and armed police were drawn into a battle in which 35 people were wounded (*BBC Daily Report*, 6 July 1993). Meanwhile, crime was on the rise nationally, and there had been riots in Tibet and Qinghai by disaffected national minorities. Grain prices soared – around 35 per cent in Beijing in just one December week – as farmers and traders worked the market.

With inflation and crime soaring, and significant parts of society literally going ballistic, the leadership became obsessed with the need, in General Secretary Jiang Zemin's words, to 'take forceful measures to maintain social and political stability' (*China News Digest*, 27 December 1993). Thus, as had happened several times before in the 1980s, it was economic crisis as much as political criticism from 'conservatives' that put the brakes on economic reform. In the summer of 1993, banks were ordered to call in loans, interest rates were raised and infrastructure investment budgets were slashed. The financial resources thus shepherded were to be used in part to put cash rather than IOUs behind state grain purchases, amid repeated warnings that farmers were being dangerously overburdened by high input prices, local government levies, corruption and low remuneration for their sales. In the autumn and winter, the vaunted abolition of grain price controls was abandoned.

The retrenchment measures failed to work, an indication that the economy was starting to spin dangerously out of control. In 1993, gross domestic product (GDP) grew 13.5 per cent, almost 50 per cent higher than the targeted figure of 9 per cent. Inflation ran at over 13 per cent by official figures, and probably much higher in actuality. The following year, the economy overheated even further: GDP grew 12.6 per cent, and was severely unbalanced between industry (17.4 per cent) and agriculture (3.5 per cent). Inflation spiked to 22 per cent by official reckoning, more than double the target of 10 per cent. This resulted in even further expressions of discontent in both the countryside and, increasingly, in the cities too. While visiting Mao's birthplace, no less a figure than Jiang Zemin himself was surrounded for nearly an hour by unhappy farmers seeking to give him their petitions. The Ministry of Labour admitted that in 1994:

> the number of large-scale labour-management disputes exceeded 12,000. In some 2,500 cases, workers besieged plants, set fire to facilities, staged strikes, or detained bosses or leaders. Such events directly threatened the personal safety of party leaders in various factories and mines. In the Jixi Mining Bureau, enterprise leaders did not dare go to the pits for fear that they might be attacked by the workers.
>
> (*Dangdai*, 15 May 1994)

Adding to the leadership's anxiety over the uncontrollability of the economy, and the rising discontent it engendered, was the spectre that inchoate social protest was showing signs of becoming organized. Unofficial trade unions were forming and, shrewdly, began to engage in legal activities such as running employment services and petitioning the National People's Congress. Even more ominous, intellectuals began working with these organizations – an alliance that, as the leadership knew, had helped account for the victory of Poland's Solidarity. Dissidents became more openly active on a number of other fronts as well, including education law and anti-corruption work.

In this context, political repression remained in place. Wei Jingsheng, the electrician who had emerged from the 1978 Democracy Wall movement as China's most prominent dissident, and who had been released in 1993 after serving fourteen years of his fifteen-year prison term – he was paroled as part of the state's charm offensive connected with its bid to host the 2000 Olympics – was rearrested in the spring of 1994. His new trial only occurred at the end of 1995, when he was sentenced to another lengthy term. Other dissidents were rounded up as well. To demonstrate its commitment to shutting down any autonomous political organization, in early 1996 all places of worship were required to register with the government; the rationale was that 'some people are trying to take advantage of more freedom in religion with the aim of overthrowing the government and dividing the nation', an extremely serious charge (*China News Digest*, 17 January 1996). In February, rules for police use of firearms were relaxed.

In its efforts to enforce social discipline and political compliance, the leadership did not rely only on naked force. It also tried to appeal to popular sentiments on two large, safe issues. First, its public campaign against official corruption has continued noisily (if largely ineffectively), focusing on some very high-profile cases. Beijing Vice-Mayor Wang Baosen committed suicide in April 1995 on the eve of the publication of charges that he embezzled funds worth a quarter of a billion yuan ($\approx$US\$35,000,000). Soon after, Beijing Mayor and Central Party Politburo member Chen Xitong was removed from office and then arrested on sensational charges of being involved with Wang, embezzling funds worth over a billion yuan, keeping several apartments for his mistress and helping her escape to Hong Kong. Since corruption is so salient an issue for many Chinese, who are victimized by it in myriad, palpable ways, the state probably would regain appreciable support from society by rooting it out to any significant degree. Yet in a society like China's, characterized by serious scarcity and inequality, very rapid growth opportunities, continued close state involvement in the economy, a weak legal system, a crisis of ideology and public values and a state with a declining political capacity, eliminating corruption is a tall order.

Second, the leadership attempted to win public sympathy by taking an increasingly hard line on nationalist issues. It gleefully adopted an uncompromising posture over Hong Kong, going so far as to erect a huge clock in Tiananmen Square to count down the seconds until the very moment of planned reunification. To show its resolve to retain control over Tibet and prevent any autonomous organization there, in late 1995 it reacted forcefully when monks linked to the exiled Dalai Lama chose a new Panchen Lama. The hapless boy whom the clerics had identified disappeared, other monks were brought to Beijing to deliberate over the choice of the successor and the Chinese people were treated to the bizarre sight of its Communist government publicly, and with great fanfare, anointing its own boy as the reincarnation of the Panchen Lama. The leadership also engaged in several rounds of menacing sabre-rattling, replete with war games, in response to elections in Taiwan in late 1995 and early 1996. Yet many Chinese had become more interested in emulating Taiwan's economic success than in overrunning it.

Ultimately, however, the key to maintaining public support, or even just acquiescence for the state, lies where Deng Xiaoping always said it did: in the condition of the economy. Thanks in part to the shrewd macroeconomic policies overseen by Vice-Premier Zhu Rongji, as well as Zhu's political forcefulness in imposing them, in 1995 the economy did achieve a soft landing from its dangerous altitude during the previous two years. GDP, which had grown at an extraordinary average annual rate of 13.4 per cent from 1992–94, slowed to 10.5 per cent. Overall inflation was reported at 14.8 per cent, less than the 15 per cent target and 21.7 per cent level of 1994. Urbanites' cost of living, however, rose 22 per cent (*China Daily*, 27 February 1996). Farmers harvested a record 466 million tons of grain, rebounding from the 445 million of 1994, which actually had declined from the previous record of 456.5 million tons in 1993. The 1995 harvest helped reduce upward pressure on grain prices, which, it will be recalled, had threatened calamity just two years earlier.

In subsequent years, economic policy continued its march toward structural reform. With price reform having been successfully accomplished in the early 1990s, the state now took on a second hard nut: reform of state industry and the labour market associated with it. State-owned enterprises that were in the red – which in some estimates comprised half or more of them – were simply allowed to atrophy, and many eventually shut down. Their workers were laid off or fired outright. The state allowed a free labour market to flourish in place of the old system by which it allocated urban employment. Thus, it did not take responsibility for finding new jobs for displaced workers, though it did make some half-hearted and largely ineffective efforts to run training and re-employment schemes. Meaningful unemployment figures are impossible to come by in China; while official urban figures maintain a level of around 3 per cent, more objective estimates run from 8 per cent (if one counts only those who have been fired, but not the 'laid off' who still have some remote hope of being called back to work) to over 20 per cent. In some localities, including many in the north-east rust belt, the figure is 40 per cent or higher.

The Asian financial crisis of 1997 posed a serious challenge to the Chinese economy, but one with which it was able to cope. The country's massive size and its record of not involving itself excessively in risky overseas lending or borrowing enabled it to weather the storm far better than neighbours such as Indonesia, Japan, Korea, Malaysia or Thailand. Though China had become a massive exporter, it also possessed an even more massive domestic market that could provide an effective source of economic demand to sustain the economy. In fact, China was able to demonstrate its political and economic maturity when it joined in contributing to international emergency credit packages to help its neighbours get through the depths of the crisis. Top economic policy-makers were under a great deal of domestic and international pressure to devalue the yuan, which would have promoted Chinese export growth and limited its imports. That, however, would have cut into the recovery of its neighbours, by increasing competition for their own exports while limiting the Chinese import market for their goods. Western financial capitals kept expecting China to do so, nonetheless, to deal with its own economic slowdown. Moreover, many Chinese exporters would have benefited from devaluation. The leadership firmly resisted, however, banking instead on China's inherent economic resilience, and demonstrating the country's maturity and strength.

In the dual context of increasingly full marketization and the effects of the Asian financial crisis, the economy did slow further, though it still remained one of the most robust in the world. GDP growth slowed steadily to 7.1 per cent by 1999, rising a little to 8 per cent in 2000 but falling back to 7.3 per cent in 2001. Inflation actually came in for a rough landing. By 1998, China actually began to experience deflation, as the retail price index fell to 97.4 per cent, and it remained negative through 2000. Retail prices registered a slight rise in 2001, though they continued to fall in some key sectors such as foodgrain, clothing and transportation and communications. Deflation is a new problem for China's structural reforms, making profitability, investment and growth more difficult. Declining prices as well as several other factors – reduced investment, increasing opportunities elsewhere, rural emigration and declining arable land – have all contributed to the steady drop in foodgrain production in 1997 and 1999–2001.

The politics associated with these economic policies and results have shifted significantly from the mid-1990s onward. At first the liberalized economic policies prompted those interested in wider debate to begin by carefully calibrated steps to push the envelope open. By 1997, a lively debate on democracy 'with Chinese characteristics' was under way in political and academic journals and in discussion groups among intellectuals. No reprisals were taken against their authors. Citizens began to gain increased latitude to disagree with and complain about government policies, by outspoken grumbling, contacting officials, filing lawsuits, writing to the many newspapers that had become willing to publish certain criticisms of government policies and even joining protests and strikes. Yet this new political atmosphere did not destabilize China, an indication that perhaps the political system was maturing. The death of the supreme political patriarch Deng Xiaoping in early 1997 provoked neither popular protests nor a destructive leadership struggle. In July of that same year, the reabsorption of Hong Kong went very smoothly. There was no political crackdown in the former colony, and in fact protests against the Chinese state were permitted significant latitude there. In September 1997 came the anxiously awaited Fifteenth Party Congress, at which the shape of the post-Deng leadership was to come into focus. Predictions that Party General Secretary Jiang Zemin was a weak, inept transitional figure, and that a fierce and destructive power struggle would take place, proved wrong. The Congress went very smoothly under Jiang's adroit leadership, while Qiao Shi, his major potential rival, was shown the door and bowed out gracefully. At the end of 1997, Jiang went from strength to strength by undertaking a successful trip to the United States. His statesmanship set the stage for President Clinton's reciprocal visit to China in 1998, which brought US–China relations to new heights. In that same year, Premier Li Peng became the first top leader in Chinese history to vacate office in accordance with the Chinese constitution. In 1997 and 1998, leading dissident political prisoners Wei Jingsheng and Wang Dan were released from prison, though they were sent into exile.

At the end of 1998, however, the Party became decidedly less tolerant, cracking down on such popular political discourse and activity. Dissidents were arrested, and campaigns to promote ideological rectitude became increasingly frequent and noisy, even as they fell on the deaf ears of most officials and the public. The reasons for the hardline shift remain shrouded behind the formidable secrecy surrounding élite politics. The move was probably rooted in the leadership's concerns about the destabilizing potential of declining economic growth and grain production as well as rising urban unemployment. After all, rural and urban protest had been on the rise for several years, as we shall see in Chapter 7. Moreover, economic dislocations and political reactions to them could only be expected to increase with China's anticipated accession to the World Trade Organization. Beyond political economy, the renewed Procrusteanism may also have had to do with growing fears that opponents would seize on the upcoming fiftieth anniversary of the People's Republic of China or the eightieth anniversary of the May Fourth Movement to go on the offensive. (After all, major political anniversaries had in part triggered the 1989 protests.) Internecine politics at the top surely also contributed, as the political influence of political 'conservatives' waxed. The repressive political atmosphere continued through to the time of this writing in late 2002.

It has been broadly effective in attaining its goals. In the very last years of the twentieth century and the opening ones of the twenty-first, China has undertaken probably its most difficult structural economic reform – ending lifetime urban employment and the guarantees associated with it – during a period of relative economic slowdown. That is an impressive feat of politics and political economy. To be sure, hardline politics has not succeeded in shutting down protest entirely. Falun Dafa was an underground religious cult with millions – in many estimates, tens or even hundreds of millions – of adherents, led by a Chinese named Li Hongzhi, who had emigrated to New York under government pressure. In April 1999, ten thousand adherents unexpectedly materialized at the gates of Zhongnanhai, the top leadership's main residence and office compound, to protest the arrest of several of their members who had recently been arrested at a protest in Tianjin.[11] Premier Zhu Rongji's immediate reaction was calm and conciliatory – there were no arrests, the protesters were provided with some lunch and a few days later the Premier eventually met with several delegates, after which he ordered his staff to try to deal with their concerns. Within months, however, hardliners in the leadership had prevailed, unleashing concerted campaigns of investigation, arrests and vilification. Falungong, however, proved as tough and wily as the state. Making use of mobile phones and the internet among other organizing tools, adherents continued to stage protests in Tiananmen Square over the next few years. One dramatic case involved self-immolations. Falungong operatives even managed to get control of broadcasting equipment at regional television stations, on several occasions broadcasting their own programmes for nearly an hour.[12] In September 2002, fifteen Falungong members were sentenced to terms of up to 20 years for one such stunt.

Another spectacular series of protests occurred in the spring of 2002, this time organized by workers. In Daqing, the oilfield that was the Maoist-era model of industrial development, and in the city of Liaoyang, tens of thousands of workers simultaneously protested the meagre size of their severance packages. Demonstrations lasted several weeks. The state responded far more cautiously than it ultimately did to the Falungong. While the demonstration organizers were arrested, ordinary protesters were not targeted, and no massive crackdown was organized. Since the same hardliners were running China during both the Falungong and proletarian protests, the difference in the state's approach probably reflects the fact that it sees workers as a far more legitimate and potentially explosive group than even the tenacious Falungong zealots.

In addition to these spectacular movements, China has in recent years also seen a steady drumbeat of protest by workers and farmers. Workers are angry about layoffs, unpaid benefits and housing evictions, farmers about burdensome taxes and fees, and both about local government corruption. In far western Xinjiang, independence-minded Uighur nationalists have been a constant threat, engaging in often violent protests both locally and even in Beijing, where they bombed a central shopping district in 1997. The situation grew so serious that the state sent in several tens of thousands of troops, often keeping them on high alert.[13] That such protests large and small have continued through a period of hardline leadership and policies is a testament to the level of anger and the boldness of so many Chinese. That the state has managed to muddle through despite them is a testament to its skill in combining carrot-and-stick tactics against the protesters, in isolating the protesters from each other and from society at large and in maintaining a rate of growth high enough to satisfy sufficient numbers of Chinese so as to deny the protesters a broad base.

In fact, the leadership has acted with a great deal of self-confidence and broad effectiveness during this latest period of hardline rule from late 1998 to the time of writing in late 2002. This has, we should remind ourselves, been a period of declining though still robust economic growth, politically dangerous structural economic reform (of the labour market, and toward the WTO) and significant popular protest. Yet the state has adroitly navigated several very difficult passages. In May 1999, the bombing of China's Belgrade embassy by the USA seriously taxed the leadership's political skills. It had to take a firm stand against the USA and, indeed, all the NATO countries while still maintaining solid relations with them, as it looked forward to its treasured goal of accession to the WTO. It also had to align itself with infuriated Chinese citizens – including many students whose political potential it knew all too well – who undertook spontaneous and often unruly, destructive and potentially violent protests, while still keeping their movement from bursting out of control. It faced a similar problem in 2001 when a US spy plane was involved in a mid-air collision that brought down a Chinese fighter jet.

Popular demonstrations were more muted this time, but protracted negotiations ensued over the return of the US plane and its crew, which had made an emergency landing in China. They were successfully concluded. So were the far more important and extremely complex, multi-year negotiations to bring China into the WTO. All these problems were difficult enough in themselves, but they also required delicate and contentious interactions within the leadership as well as between the state and society. That these issues could all be brought to smooth conclusions, particularly at a time of considerable economic and political problems in China, is no small feat.

CONCLUSION

During its breathless passage through an unprecedented process of profound structural change lasting a quarter of a century, China had once again shown its penchant for swimming against the tide, breaking with its own past and seeking an innovative course. Starting in 1978 it created something new and quite unexpected: a combination of market forces, state and collective ownership and entrepreneurialism, and political repression. That can be dubbed market Stalinism. This form of political rule and economic organization was forged in a rocky process of repeated policy reversals, and in the crucible of major crises. As the Chinese Revolution and Maoist state socialism had done, market Stalinism once again broke with several previous models. It now dispensed with Maoist radicalism, Stalinist state economic control and mobilization and capitalism's insistence on extensive private ownership and marketization. In doing so, it also retained important aspects of each model, recombining them in a way that was both novel and that challenged the view that Maoism, Stalinism and capitalism were incompatible. Whatever one's view of market Stalinism may be, it was surely unprecedented and heretical.

This strange hybrid has also chalked up some impressive achievements. Market Stalinism fundamentally transformed Maoist politics, economics and society. It has lasted a good deal longer than might have been expected. It has defied Western liberals and modernization theorists, who argue that capitalism, markets and the individualism and the middle class they bring in tow ineluctably lead to democracy. Chinese market Stalinism has also outlasted its cousins in the Soviet Union and Eastern Europe, even though in 1989 it encountered a far greater seismic shock than they. It produced repeated spurts of economic growth that often surprised even its own promoters. Indeed, its major problem was its tendency to produce too much growth too quickly. Finally, market Stalinism made China a more influential force on the world stage than ever before in its history.

Yet, Chinese market Stalinism has also been shot through with contradictions that will continue for a long time. In the countryside, declining arable land, unfavourable prices and already very high yields put in doubt China's ability to grow much more food for its increasing population. In the urban areas, state-run industry faces myriad problems, unemployment is rising and the gap between rich and poor widens. Nationally, there remains a wide gulf between the advancing coastal centres and the vast hinterland. A potentially disastrous financial meltdown looms, as China's banks try to cope with a massive load of non-performing loans, some left over from years of overheated growth now past, and some still being made today to keep afloat inefficient, unprofitable enterprises whose closure would put millions more workers on the streets. Population pressures remain intense, and environmental problems profound. Corruption is deeply rooted. Politically, the survival and even success of the People's Republic does not signify political stability or social peace. Political tensions within the leadership, within society and between state and society are bound to continue in unpredictable ways that could well threaten the longevity of the present state. Economically, China's palpable industriousness and economic dynamism does not necessarily reflect the happy equilibrium of an upward spiral of development.

Will China consolidate market Stalinism or break with it? If it makes a break, will the process be smooth and gradual, or rough and sudden? And what would emerge from such a break? The world is too complex, and China's situation too unprecedented, to permit easy or sure answers. To make educated guesses, we need to analyse the many contradictory economic, social and political forces at play. They are the subjects of the rest of this book.

CHAPTER 4

The Chinese State

As we have already begun to see, in China formal institutions matter far less in shaping political outcomes than they do in many other countries. China's constitution was rewritten four times from 1954 to 1982 to reflect changing political winds. Law, institutional boundaries and administrative regulations have repeatedly taken a back seat to the will of individual leaders from the highest levels to the grass roots. They have also been sidelined by the vagaries of popular movements. Ideological principles, and even practical precedents, have been freely, often capriciously, ignored or reversed.[1]

Yet, formal institutions are far from unimportant either. At the most general level, they shape the overall nature of the state and politics.[2] The fact that China is led by a Leninist-style Communist Party committed to monopolizing power profoundly affects every single aspect of Chinese politics. Political ontology aside, institutions shape politics by providing the context within which leaders and citizens alike act politically. Even China's most powerful leaders have usually had to build a consensus among their peers in leading bodies like the Politburo or the Central Military Commission. Likewise, cadres in towns, villages and factories must reach decisions collectively. They must also eventually face their publics in annual meetings of representative assemblies. While such meetings rarely involve searching discussions of leaders' performance, the fact that they must happen can help constrain the leaders' actions in advance. Finally, while in the past meaningful popular participation was generally non (and actually anti) institutional, starting in the mid-1980s political institutions began – in the most measured and tentative way, to be sure – to be used by ordinary people to gain access to decision-making.[3]

CHINA'S INSTITUTIONAL STRUCTURE

The Chinese state is multi-layered but unitary. Unlike a federation (such as the United States), in which the central government is an historical and/or juridical creation of smaller territorial states, in China the various regional and local governments are the creatures of the centre. Below it are six levels of government. The first consists of 22 provinces, five 'autonomous regions' (administratively identical to provinces, but located on China's borders and populated heavily by minority nationalities – hence the different name) and the municipalities of Beijing, Chongqing, Shanghai and Tianjin, which are so huge that they are administered like provinces directly under the national government.

The second level comprises 331 prefectures and 236 cities so large that they are treated like prefectures. In recent years, prefectures have come into increasing disuse, for several reasons. First, they have much less historical continuity than other subunits of the Chinese state. Second, as budgets came to be more carefully tended in the Dengist period, prefectures were often seen as a unit of government with high expense and little function. Third, they were political and administrative impediments to the ability of leaders of the provinces to project their power downward. Fourth, officials in the counties below preferred a structure in which they could operate more freely if they were supervised by more distant provincial officials, while also enjoying the opportunity for direct access to their powerful provincial superiors when they needed resources or approvals.

The third level of government consists of counties and county-level cities, of which there were 2,109 plus 427 cities administered as counties in 1999. Historically, counties have been the lowest level of state organization. In imperial times, as we have seen, the bureaucracy did not reach below the county. In the Maoist and Dengist periods alike, the county has been the lowest administrative unit with a relatively full complement of state bureaucratic bureaux and commissions. It has also been the lowest level of unalloyed state organization.

Rural governments below the county have been, both formally as well as in the minds of many Chinese people and local leaders, partly of the state but also partly 'collective'. That is, on the one hand, the state reaches down to them through Party committees and certain government branch offices. Yet, on the other, most of their leaders are not state officials, but rather are selected and paid locally, and thus are responsible in significant measure to their localities as well as to the wider state. Local governments have also had some control of their own finances, and some latitude to organize themselves as they wish.

The actual situation has been in flux. Early in the Maoist period, the highest level of rural local government was the township. It was distinct from the rural co-ops, and thus did not concern itself with close regulation of day-to-day politics or production at the grass roots. During the Great Leap Forward, rural organization was transformed in accordance with the slogan 'politics in command'. Townships gave way to people's communes, which were combined units of production, government and social organization. The communes' top leaders were state officials, i.e., they were selected and paid by the county government, and therefore responsible primarily to it rather than to the locality. Most of the communes' officials, however, were local people chosen by commune leaders and paid out of commune funds. Thus, in the Maoist period, the communes were caught in a structural dilemma between serving the state and serving the locality. A complex game of cat-and-mouse often developed between locally and state-oriented officials and policies. The communes' orientation to political control of the economy became inappropriate to the Dengist reform project's emphases on economic decentralization, semi-privatization and market forces. Thus, by 1984 the communes had been completely replaced by township governments redux. In many ways this was just a change of name. Township governments are still tied to the wider state in important ways: the Party strongly influences the selection of their top leaders, and townships must fulfil all manner of government policies, such as production quotas, tax responsibilities, population control and land-use regulation. In the context of the economic reforms, however, most of township governments' work is focused on local economic development – in particular, the elaboration of the dynamic rural industries that have been the engines of so much of China's industrialization in the Dengist period. In this, the busiest and most important part of their work, the townships have had a great deal of autonomy from higher authorities. Moreover, industrially successful townships have accumulated resources and influence that make it easier to increase their autonomy from the wider state. An indicator of this is the rise of townships' own local budgetary processes and powers. Finally, townships provide some social services, such as schools and clinics. In 1999, there were 24,000 townships in China – around eleven per county.

At the grass roots, the story of institutional development has been roughly parallel. During the mid-1950s, the co-ops focused mainly on economic organization. During the Great Leap Forward, they were displaced by production brigades and teams, whose responsibilities were far wider, including political mobilization, social regulation and organization, and politicization of economic activity. With the Dengist reforms, the brigades have given way to village governments, which engage in local administration (mainly of production contracts), some social service provision (e.g., primary schools), dispute mediation and some industrial and commercial development. The teams have been replaced by rural residents' committees, which serve as subunits of the village governments.

Urban governments are, by contrast, more closely enmeshed in the wider state. As we have seen, quite a few cities and towns are administered directly by the next higher level of the state. County seats are governed directly by the county government. Urban government consists of the central city administration, district governments, street offices and neighbourhood committees. (The specific configuration varies, of course, depending on local circumstances.) The city and district governments and the street offices below them manage civil affairs (such as registering births, deaths and marriages), undertake political work, administer social services (such as schools and hospitals) for urbanites who cannot obtain them directly from their places of work and even run enterprises. The neighbourhood committees are, formally, 'self-governing mass organizations' led by the Street Office. They were established in the 1950s as de facto instruments of social control, but also took on functions such as mediation, family planning, operating small clinics, propaganda and mobilization for state campaigns and dispute mediation. With the rise of the market economy, neighbourhood committees have atrophied a good deal, though efforts to reinvigorate them are under way by the state, which is concerned about maintaining social control in a time of rapid change and its declining capacity to monitor and regulate the citizenry. For urbanites still employed in large state enterprises or organizations, social services and political functions were long organized by their places of work. These factories and bureaux have had their own apartment buildings, schools, clinics and shops. Thus they have exercised considerable control over the lives of their workers and staff members. The economic decline of many of these enterprises has meant the disappearance of these services (and the social control that went with them), turning many former employees out to the market or on to meagre public services provided by the city and district governments and the street committees.

The situation in large rural towns below the county seats is different. The downtown spaces are treated simply as parts of their townships. Since rural enterprises and organizations do not provide the same social services as urban ones, residents of rural towns are regarded as villagers who just happen to live in a town. The townships generally provide for their own housing, education and health care.

The formal institutional structure of the Chinese state is displayed in Figure 4.1.[4] Five general features can be discerned. First, the system is grid-like, with crisscrossing lines of vertical authority and horizontal (regional) coordination. Second, the key institution is the Communist Party. It penetrates the government and the legislative organs, wielding tremendous influence over them primarily through its control of their personnel. Many government officials, and certainly the leading ones within all institutions, are Party members. As such, they are subject to the tight, vertically organized political and ideological discipline that is the hallmark of Leninist Party organization. Third, the legislative branch is weak. The laws and resolutions enacted by the People's Congresses almost always reflect the will of the Party. Moreover, the legislation and pronouncements of the People's Congresses are frequently bent, undermined or ignored. Fourth, then, of course, China's judiciary is even weaker and less independent of the government. Most judges and lawyers are also Party members subject to its discipline. The courts are not a distinct, protected branch of the state, so they lack autonomy from it. Fifth, whereas in Western representative polities the people play a role in selecting and deselecting at least some political élites, and in influencing what they do while in office, in China the Communist Party monopolizes this role. It claims to act on behalf of the people, in effect arrogating sovereignty to itself as the political organization of the working classes, rather than viewing those classes or the people as a whole as sovereign.

CHINA'S CHANGING CONSTITUTIONS

The constitutions of the People's Republic of China both reflect and give formal definition to the institutional structure of the Chinese state as well as the shifting political currents that have swirled within and around it. The first, adopted only in 1954, five years after the state was founded, declared the government 'a people's democratic state led by the working class'. The role of the CCP was formally downplayed, due to the continuing united front policy of the day, under which 'democratic parties' were permitted to exist and, in fact, were given representation in the newly created National People's Congress (the successor body to the Chinese People's Political Consultative Congress, the transitional legislature). Private ownership rights were guaranteed. The document ran to 106 articles, elaborating in detail the structure of government and the mutual responsibilities of the state and the people. They were guaranteed rights including due process of law, political expression, privacy, employment, education and social welfare. This document

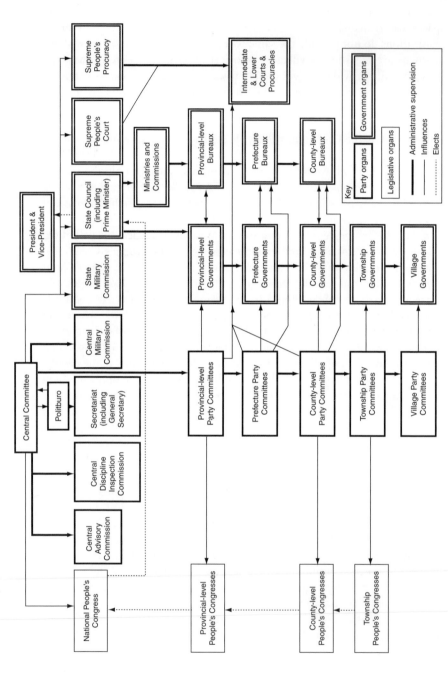

Figure 4.1 Chinese State Organization

Note: 'Provincial' and 'county-level' organs include towns and cities of various sizes. In the Maoist period, communes corresponded to what are now townships, and brigades to villages.

remained in force for two tumultuous decades, long past the time when many of its key features had become inappropriate or fallen into disuse as the country underwent fundamental changes.

By 1975, it appeared that the dust of the Cultural Revolution had cleared sufficiently to permit new constitutional efforts. It had not, however: China's second constitution, adopted by the Fourth National People's Congress in January, lasted only three years. As the child of the then still dominant left, it embodied a deep distrust of state institutions. Only 30 articles in length, it was much less detailed about state organization and procedures than its precursor. It exalted the Party above the government (in line with its view that politics ought to be 'in command'). It declared, in language that had no parallel in the 1954 constitution, that 'the Communist Party is the core leadership of the whole Chinese people' (H. Hinton, 1980: 2503). The position of Chair of the People's Republic – the functional head of state, a post last held by Liu Shaoqi – was abolished. This left the Party Chair not only unchallenged, but also vested with the power of commander-in-chief of the armed forces – a change that reflected the politicization of the military and the key role it had played in the Cultural Revolution. Locally, revolutionary committees – in which the Party held sway – were legitimated as local governments.

The defeat of the radical left in 1976 necessitated revisions to this constitution, which were made in China's third constitution. It was adopted in March 1978 (and therefore drafted earlier), well before the key Third Plenum in December at which the Dengists would triumph. Though a radical change from the second constitution, it was nevertheless a compromise document promulgated during a period of political flux. Thus, the leading role of the Party was reiterated, but a little distance was put between the Party and the government. For example, there was no mention, as there had been in 1975, of the National People's Congress being under Party leadership. More latitude was to be given to intellectuals: 'letting a hundred flowers bloom and a hundred schools of thought contend' was once again to be the official order of the day. The modernization of agriculture, industry, the military and science/technology – which, taken together, would become the Dengists' watchword 'four modernizations' – were mentioned as a 'general task for the new period'. Still, the 1978 constitution contained much with which the Dengists were dissatisfied. For example, it also included class struggle as another 'general task', specifying that '[T]he state ... punishes new-born bourgeois elements and other bad elements.' It still exalted Mao's role (Selden, 1979: 689–95).

The new leadership was soon in a position to change the constitution to its liking, and to bring it into alignment with the political, ideological and policy changes then under way. Reflecting the broad scope and rationalizing thrust of the new directions, the 1982 constitution ran to 138 articles, compared with 60 in its predecessor. That it has lasted two decades as of this writing, with no efforts in sight to supercede it, is testimony to China's relative political stability and the reduction of profound political conflict compared with Maoist days. In the spirit of political normalization, and in order to strengthen the role of the government vis-à-vis the Party, China's 1982 constitution recreated the Presidency, though in a more purely ceremonial role than had been enjoyed by Liu Shaoqi in the Maoist period. It also placed the military under firmer civilian control. It gave greater prominence to the National People's Congress and the rule of law. In the spirit of reducing political control over the economy, and in support of rural structural reform, it undercut the institution of the people's commune in favour of more limited township governments. Rights of free speech and expression, which had been used primarily by critics of the Dengist leadership, were deleted. In limiting both political control over the economy and popular participation, this was very much a market Stalinist constitution.

THE CHINESE COMMUNIST PARTY

As noted above, the Chinese Communist Party remains the linchpin of the state. The fact that the last two constitutions downplayed its formal role indicates not its decline but rather the opposite: the Party is so powerful that it does not need to be mentioned in the constitution. Rather than ruling directly, it works behind the scenes to determine the major decisions of China's legislative and governmental organs. Within them, key decision-makers and most officials are members. Significant decisions are first made within Party committees of these institutions, which then meet to affirm them formally as laws or administrative directives. Thus, our discussion of state institutions ought to begin with the Communist Party.

The Leninist model of the Party

The Chinese Communist Party was founded in the Leninist mould – and with considerable direct Soviet influence – as a highly selective, well-trained and tightly disciplined revolutionary vanguard designed to provide close leadership over the revolution. It remains as such, at least formally. One cannot simply join, but must apply. Only after a period of apprenticeship (often in the Communist Youth League), training in Party schools and evaluation is membership granted. In 2002, only 5 per cent of Chinese were Party members, a figure that has been constant for many years. Tight discipline prevails: members are expected to stick to the Party's position regardless of their own views. The principle by which the Party, like all its Leninist cousins, arrives at its positions is known, oxymoronically, as democratic centralism. In theory, this means that the Party is to arrive at decisions democratically, but that, once reached, decisions are to be carried out wholeheartedly by all Party members, including the minority who may have opposed them. Formally, the Party constitution vests power in the rank-and-file of Party members, who at each level elect delegates to local congresses; these in turn elect both the Party committees at their own level and the delegates to congresses at the next higher level. In fact, of course, power really resides at the centre and flows downward. Within each level, it rests mainly in the hands of the standing committees involved in day-to-day leadership, rather than in the larger and more infrequently convened Party committees and congresses. One reason for this is common to most political organizations, even those in formally democratic political systems: in a complex and fast-moving world, it is simply unfeasible for real power to be exercised democratically from below through infrequent elective processes or unwieldy collective deliberation. There are, however, other reasons particular to Leninist parties: the theoretical importance they place on leadership as necessary to ensure socialism's success in a dangerous world of hostile forces, the Party's political monopoly and the centralized economy, to name just a few.

The Maoist model of the Party

Leninism provides the CCP with its overall mould, but the CCP has also frequently reshaped that mould; indeed, sometimes the Party came perilously close to smashing it altogether. As we have seen, in the 1920s and 1930s, with the failures of proletarian revolution and the turn to a rural base, the Party developed a distinctive repertoire of participatory methods and institutions. The 'Yan'an Way' was grafted onto the Party's Leninist structure in ways that were not meant to threaten or displace democratic centralism, but that coexisted uneasily with them in what could be called a Maoist model of the Party. It attempted, in fascinating and original ways, to use the mass line to enhance the democratic element of democratic centralism.

The Maoist model of the Party involved four elements. First, Party members and officials were to maintain close contacts with the masses on a regular basis, by participating in productive labour and regularly soliciting their opinions and views. Second, Party members were to subject each other to criticism, and themselves to self-criticism, during Party 'rectification' movements. Third, the Party was to be made subject to criticism by non-Party members, a principle that would have shocked Lenin. After all, the major justification for a disciplined Communist Party was precisely that the masses' political consciousness was mired in the old society and therefore needed leadership from an élite group of revolutionaries. In the late 1940s, however, under a programme known as 'open door rectification', Chinese villagers were invited to criticize local Party officials (W. Hinton, 1966, parts 4 and 5). Popular criticism of the Party was encouraged again during the Cultural Revolution. Fourth, institutional methods for upward flow of views and criticisms were built into the Party. Constitutional provisions permitting Party members to appeal directly to the Chair of the Party were adopted at Party Congresses during the 1970s. Party leaders also solicited the views of their subordinates and non-Party members at the grass roots, or made themselves accessible to them, in periodic, quasi-institutionalized stints such as work teams, 'sending down to the villages' and in-depth investigations known as 'squatting on the spot' (in which leaders would take up extended residence in a locality to conduct research into the actual situation affecting policy).

The Maoist model of the Party also emphasized, probably more than its Soviet progenitor, the importance of ideological work in the development and maintenance of Party discipline and control. One basic tenet of Mao's political theory is that subjective attitudes can matter more than objective factors such as class background or institutional factors. Another is that the exercise of naked authority or coercion is not an effective way to achieve results. Accordingly, the Maoist model of the Party emphasized improving the ideological predispositions of Party members through regular propaganda and study campaigns as well as criticism and self-criticism. This is not to say that institutional approaches to Party discipline were abandoned; but they too were reshaped so that the Party would not have to rely on simple command and coercion. Thus, practices such as cadre participation in labour and periodic transfer of cadres to grass-roots work were developed in order to weaken the authoritarianism and élitism that Mao knew were inherent in the Leninist concept of a vertically structured, centralized Party. Yet no attempts were made to flatten the vertical institutional structure of the Party itself or to challenge the centralist elements of democratic centralism. Nonetheless, the Maoist approach to intra-Party affairs, and to the relationship of the Party and Chinese society, was a significant departure from Leninist and Stalinist practice. It also had enormous implications for the course of Chinese politics, by helping create the conditions for popular movements such as China's remarkable revolutions: the rural-based movement that brought the Party to state power in 1949, and the Cultural Revolution that undermined and nearly destroyed that power.

As noted above, the foundation of the Leninist conception of the Party was its putatively indispensable role in leading the class struggle. Mao developed a far more sophisticated and ultimately ambivalent view of this issue. On the one hand, he saw the Party as a breeding ground for a new bourgeoisie, which led to his call for vehement attacks on it during the Cultural Revolution. Yet at these very same moments, he insisted that the Party was a necessary bulwark against a triumph by counter-revolutionary class forces. Thus, it was to be revitalized in ideology and personnel, and was to share power with government and mass organizations through the revolutionary committees. In raising questions about the class nature of the Party, and in attempting to situate it within a less domineering relationship with non-Party political institutions, Mao strayed very far indeed from the orthodox Leninist conception of the Party.

Finally, the Maoist conception and form of the Party was affected by the Maoist strategy of economic development, which at various times emphasized popular mobilization over central planning and technological advance. This approach de-emphasized the Party's role in supervising the economic bureaucracy, in favour of work in popular education and organization. Different roles called for different personnel: in the Maoist model, the Party should prefer the revolutionary generalist (the 'red') to the administrative or technical specialist (the 'expert').

The Dengist model of the Party

One theme of this book is that the years since 1978 are not simply a radical reversal of the Maoist period. Nowhere are the continuities more in evidence than in the Party. Like its Maoist predecessors, the Dengist leadership adhered to the same Leninist principles of democratic centralism and the Party's political monopoly within the state and over society. It has also offered new twists upon some core

Maoist themes, or emphasized particular elements for its own purposes. For example, it put forward a critique of 'feudal' vestiges in the Party, but focused it on the deification of a supreme leader. Consensual, collective leadership has been emphasized instead, as a corrective to the high-handed, divisive pattern of Party leadership dating back at least as far as the co-operativization debate of 1956. As we have seen, for example, the post of Party Chair has been replaced by that of Chair of the resuscitated Party Secretariat. Yet, when push came literally to shove in 1986 and 1989, Deng was not shy about bringing his personal authority to bear.

Another Maoist theme that has been amplified so as to be put to different purposes is the emphasis on practice. Mao posited that theory could only be 'correct' – i.e., useful in promoting revolutionary progress – if based upon practice. The Dengist leadership derogated the value of theory further, adopting a hyperpragmatist position under the slogan 'practice is the sole criterion of truth'. This has meant, *inter alia*, that what people think is less important than what they do, which in turn has reduced concern with ideology in general. Behaviour can now be regulated directly – for example, through political authority or economic incentives and disincentives – without focusing, as Mao did, on underlying ideological motivation.

In Party affairs, this new hyperpragmatist orientation has had several implications. Gone is the reliance on ideological campaigns, propaganda and criticism and self-criticism as ways of enforcing discipline and political purity of the Party and its members. Party members are expected to demonstrate their political virtue through the concrete results of their work, often measured by economic indicators. Those who cannot produce satisfactory results, or who resist or transgress the new rules of the game, are now to be dealt with not so much by ideological reform as administrative methods, including retraining, strict monitoring and evaluation, demotion, retirement or expulsion. As one telling barometer of the change from the Maoist model, the frequent anti-corruption drives have emphasized punitive measures, including public humiliation and execution, far more than ideological work to reform the miscreant. For those with less glamorous 'deviations', such as political disagreements with the current Party leadership or political direction, discipline commissions have been resuscitated to identify recalcitrant members and 'help' them get in line. Lifelong tenure of Party members and office holders has been abolished. Advisory commissions have been set up as receptacles for aged Party cadres for whom demotion or expulsion would be unseemly.

The Dengists have also reduced the scope of such populistic or democratic elements as there were in the Maoist model. Internally, Party members may still appeal to leaders above their immediate superiors. This is now to be done in an orderly way, though, and criticisms are to be restricted to those that do not challenge the basic principles of the current policy line, as occurred during the Cultural Revolution. Naturally, then, Maoist forms of popular supervision and critique of the Party by non-members have also been abolished. Having been victimized by the Cultural Revolution – the most extreme form of popular attack on the Party – the Dengist leadership believes that the Party's affairs are best monitored and put in order only by the Party itself. The 1989 events demonstrate that the Party will not brook criticism from beyond its ranks. All that remains are a few indirect and harmless modes of popular expression about the Party. For example, in elections to People's Congresses, several Communist Party candidates are sometimes nominated for office, and voters may choose among them.

The view that only the Party can police itself is common to organizations everywhere. In the case of the Chinese Communist Party, though, it rests on specific arguments about the strategic position of the Party as defender of China's revolution, working people, socialism and national independence against all manner of hostile forces. This argument could be made more convincingly in the 1950s and 1960s, when external threats to China's sovereignty and internal threats to its socialist transition were palpable. Yet since the present leadership has itself criticized many aspects of state socialism, and since it believes that there are no longer any serious class-based challenges to Chinese socialism, it is far more difficult for the Party to argue persuasively that it needs to remain sacrosanct and immune from external criticism or challenge in order to protect socialism from its class enemies. Nor is it able to argue as compellingly as during the Cold War that the Party's monopoly on power is necessary to protect China's national sovereignty. To justify the Party's continuing political monopoly, it has played on many people's well-founded fears of the 'chaos' (luan) – of the kind that occurred in the Cultural Revolution, or that has occurred in Russia since the collapse of the USSR – that could result from the loss of the Party's monopoly on power. It has also argued that its commitment to maintaining political stability has been an important precondition for China's stunning economic growth since 1979. Like most good ideological arguments, both these claims have more than a little truth in them.

Another approach that the Communist Party has taken to maintaining its power is to make itself more professional and technically sophisticated. This effort grew out of the Dengist programme of economic development, which called for a new type of Party member. As economic incentive and technological advance have replaced ideological commitment and massive mobilization of labour as the linchpins of economic development, the Party has come to require members and officials who are more technically or administratively expert and competent. It has also emphasized the need to respect such expertise enough to defer to it. The Party has sought to upgrade the skills of its members in these areas, and to attract to itself younger technical experts. At the same time, it has tried to demote, retire or expel members judged to be technically incompetent. Table 4.1 shows that these efforts have met with reasonable success, at least at the top.

Party leaders hoped that such a change would not only suit the needs of economic development, but also that a more professional membership and leadership would make the Party less corrupt, less overbearing and therefore more acceptable to society. Yet it has been frustrated in this effort by countervailing trends. While its membership has become more professional and technically sophisticated, the Party has had difficulty attracting China's best and brightest, who have variously been wary of politics, disillusioned with the Party and attracted to career pathways for which Party membership is not necessary. Worse yet, corruption has been a bigger problem among the ranks of younger, more entrepreneurially minded Party members than some of the older revolutionaries who have remained more

Table 4.1 Changes in Age and Education of Party Élites

	Twelfth Party Congress (1982)	Thirteenth Party Congress (1987)	Fourteenth Party Congress (1992)	Fifteenth Party Congress (1997)
Average age of Central Committee	73	55	56	55
Percentage of college graduates on Central Committee	—	73	84	92

Sources: Blecher, 1986: 110; Saich, 1992: 1150; China Internet Information Center, '16th National Congress on the Communist Party of China' (*http://www.china.org.cn/english/features/35613.htm*).

committed to the political values and habits of the revolutionary and state socialist past.

The popular reputation of the Chinese Communist Party is at a very low ebb. Decades of rapid economic growth and restructuring have, ironically, worsened the Party's prestige rather than improved it. One reason is the rampant corruption that development and partial economic reform have brought in tow. For example, many officials have been able to make fortunes by using protected, subsidized state industries to play the market. Second is that, with the rise of market forces, the Party is increasingly seen as unnecessary, vestigial or parasitic. Third, economic reform policies, for which the Party is ultimately responsible, have been vacillating and problematical, as we have seen. Fourth are its political problems. The Party was badly tarnished by its role in 1989. It is widely seen as ideologically bankrupt and dependent for its power on little more than brute force.

It is true that the Party's coercive apparatus helped sustain it during a time that saw communist parties driven from power in most other countries. Yet the Party retained its monopoly not by brute force alone. Its formidable organizational capacity, and its ability to monitor closely the nooks and crannies of Chinese society, has helped a great deal. So has the popular anxiety that things would be even worse if the Party were driven from power. These fears are, ironically, only reinforced when ordinary Chinese look at the situation in the former Soviet Union and Yugoslavia. The Chinese Communist Party has probably lost most if not all of its base of legitimacy, and it is hard to see how it could be regained. Yet at the time of writing in late 2002, the Party still retained a workable capacity to elicit acquiescence. How thin a reed on which to stake its chances for survival this proves to be depends on the severity of the crises before it, and the sheer will of its leadership to do what will be necessary to remain in power.

THE GRIDWORK AND SIZE OF GOVERNMENT

Chinese government administration is carried out primarily by two rather different kinds of institutions: vertically organized ministries and horizontally organized regional governments. In addition, there are specialized commissions and organs in charge of functional tasks such as the military or economic planning and reform. All are overseen by the State Council. Formally elected by, and serving as the executive committee of, the National People's Congress, it is a large and somewhat unwieldy body consisting of several dozen top leaders. In 2000 it included the Premier, several Vice-Premiers, a secretary-general, the heads of 29 ministries and commissions and representatives from another 36 offices that it supervises. Its main work is carried out by an inner cabinet of the Premier, the Vice-Premiers, a secretary-general and several senior councillors.

China's ministries are vertical administrative institutions with three or four main tiers: central offices in the capital, and bureaux in provinces, prefectures and counties. As in most bureaucracies, in general authority flows downward level by level, and resources move in both directions generally on terms set by the next higher level. The number, type and relative importance of China's vertically organized ministries has varied over time in a pattern reflective of the policy emphases of the day. For example, the anti-statist themes of the Cultural Revolution found expression in demands for administrative simplification, resulting in a reduction in the number of ministries from 49 to 29. With the end of the Cultural Revolution, organizational restructuring tailored to the modernization programme has been carried out. The emphasis on streamlining administration continued after the start of the reforms, though for the very different purpose of facilitating the economic modernization programme. In 1982, 43 of the organs under the State Council were consolidated into only fourteen. Yet to foster economic development, new institutions were also created. For example, responsibilities for agriculture and forestry, formerly grouped under one ministry, were divided among two to give each greater prominence and attention. The single People's Bank was divided into four banks specializing in agriculture, industry, construction and commerce. A State Commission for Restructuring the Economic System was established. So were specialized ministries for sectors that were now to receive high priority, such as foreign trade and electronics. As we have seen, by 2000 there were 29 ministries and commissions under the State Council.

Yet the Chinese government is not organized by vertical bureaucracy alone. The people's governments of provinces, prefectures and county governments comprise large, horizontally oriented administrative infrastructures that may include various executive offices, standing committees, task forces and other bodies. Township and village governments are generally much simpler, both because of their smaller size and the fact that, following an age-old pattern, the vertical institutions do not penetrate below the county level. Innumerable government functions require horizontal coordination bringing together various organs within a region or locality. For example, when in the mid-1980s the leaders of Shulu County, in Hebei

Province, wanted to build a shopping centre, they had to bring together the local bureaux of the central Ministries of Finance and Taxation, Commercial Management, Construction and Urban Planning, as well as the banks (Blecher and Shue, 1996: Ch. 6). Such tasks have grown ever more complex as the economy and, with it, the scale of investment projects has developed. Thus, a decade later, this same county government constructed a massive production and trade centre for its famous fur and leather industry; to do so, it brought together well over a dozen local agencies, including those involved in the earlier shopping centre, but now also the police, the phone company, the education department (since the project included a school) and the foreign affairs bureau (since foreign investment and trade were involved), to mention but a few. To run the centre, it created a supervisory commission employing 160 people (Blecher and Shue, 2001). Governments from huge provinces down to minuscule villages engage in this sort of work all the time, each in different ways depending on their size and the task at hand.

Chinese government is, then, organized in a complex gridwork marked out by centralized, vertical ministries and regional, horizontal governments – a system known as 'dual rule'. At almost any point in China's vast government from the provinces on down, officials must face pressures, constraints, responsibilities and opportunities from above, below and sideways. Of course, gridworks often create gridlock. All too frequently the response of an official caught in this complex network is to do little or nothing. Yet grids also create matrices of opportunity that would not exist in a more unitary organizational structure. Most city drivers know how to find alternative routes when one is blocked, a more difficult feat when the only route available is a single strand of superhighway. To return to the example of the shopping centre, it was easier for the Shulu County government to receive permits and approval from its provincial superiors in charge of land use and construction once they had got other provincial officials to provide financial and logistical support for their project. Whether the gridwork that is Chinese government encourages or encumbers government creativity and effectiveness in any particular case depends on the problem at hand, the resources available to devote to it and the political and administrative skills and drive of the leaders involved.

The grid-like structure contributes to the expansion of government institutions and personnel. The existence of a standardized set of vertical organizations that cut through every locality means that they all tend to get a relatively full complement of central bureaux, whether they need them or not. At the same time, the need for horizontal coordination often demands the creation of task forces and committees such as those described above. Yet the expansion of government is not merely a structural effect of the way the Chinese state is organized. In the Maoist period, it sprang from the tendencies of bureaucracies everywhere, especially those with few financial constraints, to expand. In the Dengist period, contrary to the expectation in some Western and Chinese quarters that economic liberalization would shrink the state, the expanding economy actually spurred a vast expansion of the size of the state beyond anything seen in the Maoist period (Figure 4.2). Tables 4.2 and 4.3 show an example of the kinds of expansion that went along with rapid economic development in a rather ordinary rural county, some to take advantage of new

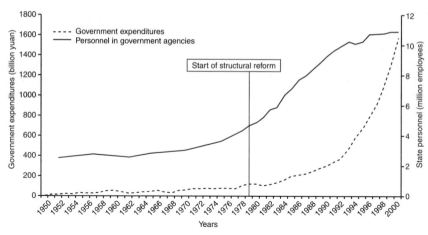

Figure 4.2 State Personnel and Expenditures, 1950–2000
Source: China Statistical Yearbook, 1987, 2001.

Table 4.2 Total State Employees, Shulu County (Hebei), 1979, 1989

	1979	1989
Administrative	1,145	2,237
Cadres	945	1,710
Support	200	527
Institutional and professional	2,357	4,285
Education	1,698	2,834
Health	306	632
Other	353	819
Enterprises	1,036	2,180
State-owned	963	1,821
Collective	73	359
Total	*4,538*	*8,702*

opportunities, and some to administer and regulate economic growth. In particular, Table 4.3 conveys the texture of the new kinds of activities in which a local government became involved as its economy took off under the structural reforms: regulation of the environment, land use, real estate and trade with distant localities; pursuit of far-off entrepreneurial opportunities; the development of new agricultural products; and the conversion of state enterprises into companies.

Table 4.3 Organization and Development of County Government Administration in Shulu County (Hebei), 1979–90

1979	1985	1990
Government Affairs Office	Government Affairs Office	Government Affairs Office
Civil Affairs Bureau	Civil Affairs Bureau	
	Labour and Personnel Bureau	Labour and Personnel Bureau
	Statistics Bureau	Statistics Bureau
	Price Bureau	Price Bureau
	Industry and Commerce Management Bureau	Industry and Commerce Management Bureau
Finance and Tax Bureau	Finance Bureau	Finance Bureau
	Tax Bureau	Tax Bureau
Commerce Bureau	Commerce Bureau	Commerce Bureau
	Grain Bureau	Grain Bureau
	Auditing Bureau	Auditing Bureau
Urban Construction Bureau	Urban Construction Bureau	Urban Construction and Environmental Protection Commission
Planning Committee	Planning Committee/ Economic Committee *	Economic Planning Committee
Industry Bureau	(see above)	(see above)
Transportation Bureau	Transportation Bureau	Transportation Bureau
Culture and Education Bureau	Cultural Affairs Bureau	Cultural Affairs Bureau
	Education Bureau	Education Bureau
Public Health Bureau	Public Health Bureau	Public Health Bureau
Agriculture and Forestry Bureau	Agriculture Bureau	Agriculture Bureau
Animal Husbandry Bureau	Forestry and Animal Husbandry Bureau	Forestry Bureau
		Animal Husbandry Bureau
Water Conservancy Bureau	Water Conservancy Bureau	Water Conservancy Bureau
Science Committee	Science Committee	Science Committee
Sports Committee	Sports Committee	Sports Committee
	Family Planning Committee	Family Planning Committee
	Township Industries Bureau	Township Industries Bureau
	Foreign Affairs Bureau	Foreign Affairs Bureau
Public Security Bureau	Public Security Bureau	Public Security Bureau
	Justice Bureau	Justice Bureau
Agricultural Machinery Bureau	Agricultural Machinery Bureau	Agricultural Machinery Bureau
	Broadcasting Affairs Bureau	Broadcast and Television Bureau

Table 4.3 continued

1979	1985	1990
	Earthquake Office	Earthquake Office
	Records Section	Records Section
Foreign Trade Bureau	Foreign Trade Company	Foreign Trade Company
Materials Bureau	Materials Company	Materials Company
Second Light Industry Bureau	Second Light Co-op Federation	Light Industries and Textiles Company
Hai River Headquarters		Huang-Huai-Hai Rivers Development Office
		Standards and Measures Bureau
		External Economic Affairs Committee
		Land Management Bureau
		Structural Reform Office
		Public Sanitation Office
		Investigations Bureau
		Nationalities and Religions Bureau
		Reception Section
		Staffing Office
		Real Estate Management Bureau
		Local Gazeteer Compilation Office
		Office of Economic Cooperation
		Shenzhen Liaison Station
		Machinery and Building Materials Company
		Chemical Company
		Tobacco Grading, Pricing and Sales Bureau
		Border Region Trade Company

* At this time, the Planning Committee and the Economic Committee – the successor to the Industry Bureau – were still formally distinct. But in practice they functioned in such close coordination that Shulu officials tended to refer to them as a single office called *jingjiwei* (literally, economic planning committee).
Source: Blecher and Shue, 1996: 30–1.

LAW AND LEGISLATION

Law and legislation are not inimical to state socialism.[5] In China, however, they have been weak. Partly this stems from the absence of a strong legal tradition in the country's long history. In the Maoist period, as we have seen, the state emphasized a contradictory combination of bureaucratic rule on the one hand and ideological, participatory politics on the other; neither placed much emphasis on law. Thus, with just a handful of notable exceptions (such as the 1950 Marriage Law, to which we will return in Chapter 5), most policies were expressed as state pronouncements and directives rather than legislation. And where disputes arose over the policies themselves or their implementation, they were hashed out not in legislatures or courts, but in Party and government meetings.

The Dengist leadership has placed a little more emphasis on what it calls 'socialist legality'. There are historical, political and economic reasons for this. First, it grows in part out of the leadership's direct experience with the highly irregular 'justice' of the Cultural Revolution, during which many people were imprisoned or punished without anything resembling a trial or even formal charges. Thus, the 1978 constitution restored the People's Procuracies, which were abolished during the Cultural Revolution. They are empowered to evaluate evidence against those arrested by the public security organs, on the basis of which they decide whether to approve the arrest and prosecute the case in a people's court. The first criminal code of the People's Republic was approved in 1979.

Second, legal development serves important political goals. Putting Party and government policies in the form of laws resonates with the Dengist leadership's commitment to procedural regularity. If laws must be clearer and more specific than the pronouncements or directives of the past, then it is easier for the state to expect and enforce accountability in implementation from its officials and ordinary people. Insofar as it has this effect, rule by law could also reduce the need for the state to exercise tight direct control over the vastness of China, a goal very much in line with the economizing and decentralizing thrusts of the reforms. The leadership also hoped that the clarity and systematic nature of law would produce a more predictable environment both for itself and as a way of reassuring the Chinese people. Finally, invigorating People's Congresses (China's legislatures) was a way of reaching out to the Chinese people. By including them, and, in particular, representatives of specific groups such as intellectuals and business people, in the institutions that approve laws, the state hopes to broaden its base of popular support, legitimacy or at least acquiescence. Moreover, having the affected people in the legislative process can help refine laws so that they are more effective in achieving the leadership's policy aims.

Third, an expanded concern with law has also been a necessary accompaniment to the structural economic reforms. A predictable environment is probably even more important to economic growth than to political stability. More specifically, the structural reforms of the economy have emphasized myriad contractual relationships – among workers and employers, buyers and sellers, investors and enterprises, and even levels of government. Initially, many reforms were hindered by the absence of legal institutions and guidelines concerning the ways in which contracts were to be drawn up or the means of resolving disputes about them that would inevitably crop up. In one rural county, for example, 70 per cent of the 80,000 contracts signed in 1984 were found to be legally invalid, according to the Chinese press (*Xinhua News Bulletin*, 10 September 1985: 14). In the countryside alone, by mid-1985, law offices had been established in over 20,000 townships, to notarize and help write contracts and to settle disputes about them. Nationally, in 1999, 8,000,000 business documents were notarized, and 1,500,000 cases of economic disputes were disposed of in courts.

China's legislature is the National People's Congress (NPC), established in 1954. It is a very large body – the fifth session of the Eighth NPC, convened in 2002, was attended by over 3,000 delegates. They comprised representatives of provincial People's Congresses as well as certain functional organizations like the army. The NPC meets late each winter in a full plenary session lasting several weeks, and is now reconstituted every five years, though during the Cultural Revolution a full decade elapsed without doing so. Between the annual plenaries, its standing committee meets several times each year to consider legislative drafts and even to adopt new laws.

In the Maoist period, the NPC served little in the way of a genuinely representative or legislative function. As in other state socialist countries, it mainly rubber-stamped policies made by the Party and imparted to them the legitimacy and formal status of 'laws'. Still, there were fleeting moments in which the NPC served as a forum for some genuine public debate. For example, critics of the 1957 anti-rightist campaign, which turned the tables on China's intellectuals, attacked Mao and the repressive policies at the NPC.

In the 1980s, the NPC was strengthened slightly. It now meets far more frequently and regularly than in the Maoist years. While in the past service as a delegate was a part-time position – which meant that delegates were mainly government officials serving primarily in other posts – now the position of delegate is a full-time post distinct from any other government office. So delegates have more time to devote to their duties, and greater independence as well. They are also now elected by provincial People's Congresses, which in turn are chosen by county congresses. Of course, as noted above, China's electoral system is still a far cry from genuine political competition. Turning to the NPC's organization, where in the past it was disabled partly by its lack of an internal committee structure, the 1982 constitution provided for six 'specialized committees' – on nationalities, law, finance and economics, foreign affairs, overseas Chinese, and education, science, culture and public health – that are to 'examine, discuss and draw up relevant bills and draft resolutions' (*Beijing Review*, 27 December 1982: 21). Delegates have also been given the right to initiate legislation themselves.

At minimum, the NPC serves as a way for the top leadership to have personal contact with a large number of the most important regional and local leaders. This is not entirely a one-way process, either. At the NPC these regional leaders have the opportunity to make their cases to each other and to the top leadership. Of course, the issues that they raise are largely circumscribed by the prevailing ideology and structure of power. No delegate to the NPC would question the state's prevailing ideological values or its current approach to them. Indeed, the delegates themselves are Party members who have been chosen because they accept the prevailing parameters of political discourse. In recognizing this, though, we would also do well to recall that the same phenomenon happens in varying degrees in most other countries. No British MP or American legislator would declare allegiance to Communism or Fascism.

Moreover, NPC delegates, in ways not entirely unlike their Western counterparts, do use the forum of the NPC to press their particular concerns – for example, the needs of their region, sector or organization for more resources, for administrative support or even for policy changes. At the second session of the Sixth NPC in 1984, no less than 2,501 'suggestions and criticisms' were put forward. It is inconceivable that all of these could have been prepared in advance by the Party or government leadership. As we saw in Chapter 3, over 200 delegates to the Seventh National People's Congress in 1988 had the temerity to reject the Party's leadership's candidate for a Vice-Premiership. Yet such displays of embryonic democracy ultimately encountered efforts to suppress them. After the 1989 crackdown, the NPC became a much tamer place. Political debate, and efforts by reformers to nibble away at the edges of state repression, have not been snuffed out altogether, however. In the run-up to the March 1996 NPC, proposals were floated to reform China's martial law statute, an extremely sensitive issue. Critics sought to tighten the conditions under which martial law could be declared, and to make it more difficult to keep martial law in effect for prolonged periods of time. Yet on the same day the *People's Daily* also reported regulations intended to control politicking at the NPC. 'State officials are forbidden to leave the capital, conduct meetings or activities unrelated to [the] congress, attend banquets thrown by delegations or deputies, [or] present unapproved written materials to the deputies or exchange gifts with delegates' (*Reuters News Service*, 29 February 1996).

The NPC is the highest level of a system of People's Congresses extending down as far as the townships. At each level, the People's Congress functions much like the NPC: as a way of rationalizing policy in the form of law, and including various groups in politics, both locally but also beyond. Each lower level selects representatives to the next higher one, though in fact the real choices are made by the local Party committees. Nonetheless, this does mean that the People's Congresses do provide a way for some local issues and interests to percolate up to the next higher level. That is why, as noted above, even the NPC itself sometimes provides a forum for localities to weigh in on policy debates.

OFFICIAL MASS ORGANIZATIONS AND CONSULTATIVE CONGRESSES

Finally, there are institutions that provide organization for specific social groups and their interests. This category includes huge operations such as the All-China Federation of Trade Unions or the Chinese Women's Association, local outfits such as the Association of Individual Entrepreneurs of the Hebei Yiji Market of Shulu County and myriad organizations in between. In fact, China's 'mass organizations' are creatures not of the masses but of the state, which selects their leadership and administers and oversees their operations. For example, union leaders in factories have generally been members of the factory management committee; and the head of the Shulu market business association in 1990 was none other than the vice-head of the county government bureau that regulated their market. Moreover, mass organizations – in particular the Communist Youth League, but also the labour unions and women's association – are not just staffed by leaders, but also serve to recruit future leaders.

The main purpose of these organizations has not been to represent their constituencies so much as to organize them to facilitate implementation of policies that the leadership has in mind for them, and to try to co-opt their political support. In the Maoist period, the state used mass organizations to mobilize particular classes and groups to take part in its various efforts at social and economic transformation. For example, during the Socialist Education Movement, Poor and Lower-Middle Peasants' Associations were formed in villages to organize opposition to 'spontaneous capitalist tendencies', criticize local cadres and reconstitute village political authority. In the earliest phase of the Cultural Revolution, as we have seen, the Red Guards were also the creations of both radical and conservative state leaders. In the Dengist period, too, mass organizations have attempted to engage popular participation and support, albeit for a rather different agenda. For example, the Hebei Yiji Entrepreneurs Association offered technical training and promulgated up-to-date market information.

China's mass organizations also play a rather more unassuming role. For example, both in the Maoist and Dengist periods, China's labour unions could be likened more to enterprise labour relations departments than to trade unions. Their major activities have been in the areas of social welfare, adult education, recreation and helping management organize and discipline the labour force. They have administered welfare subsidies for workers in economic straits, held after-work vocational and general classes, run factory libraries, recreation rooms and sports leagues and facilities, and helped promote safety and productivity drives. They have abjured from calling strikes, and in fact have been responsible for helping to settle such strikes as occur rarely and spontaneously by mediating between striking workers and factory managers. Likewise, the Women's Association is not really an association at all – there are no regular dues or meetings. Rather, it has always been a state organization concerned with what the state defines as women's issues, such as the celebration of International Women's Day, or, more controversially, population control. The emphasis of these organizations is on workers' and women's contributions to the state and the economy rather than to analysis and pursuit of their particular interests.

Yet, if these organizations do not represent the interests of their constituencies as a whole, they have sometimes represented workers' or women's individual interests. Workers who have specific complaints against their enterprises, or women who are suffering from sexist discrimination or abuse, can appeal respectively to the union or the women's association. The leaders of these organizations can make representations on their 'members'' behalf, and attempt to mediate a solution. Likewise, when private merchants of the Hebei Yiji Market feel their interests have been infringed upon, or have questions about the policies that affect them, they can address their concerns to the merchants' association, which in turn seeks to get clarification of the policy and, if necessary, to mediate any disagreements.

Hints of a wider representative role in the future may be coming dimly, tentatively and haltingly into view. In 1995, some union leaders in large enterprises were reporting that the rise of market forces and increasing economic pressure were threatening workers' interests in ways that forced the unions to take far more seriously than ever before their role of defending workers' interests. The director of the union in a bureau employing 30,000 workers reported that he found himself disagreeing with his fellow leaders in ways that had not happened in his many decades of working with them. Moreover, his position as union director, which had been equivalent to that of a bureau vice-director, was being moved to the municipal union organization, so that he could do a better job of representing the workers (author's interview, Tianjin, 1995). Since that time, however, China's labour unions have not delivered much, if anything, that advances the interests of the country's working class. In 1999, an official in the union's national office said privately and candidly that its main role was to promote 'stability' at a time of rising worker discontent and protest (author's interview, Beijing, 1999).

Another organization by which the state tries to connect itself with society is the Chinese People's Political Consultative Conference (CPPCC). It originated in the Party's historic united front policy during and after the revolution. Indeed, in 1954 China's first National People's Congress grew directly out of it. Formally the CPPCC remained in existence until the mid-1960s, presided over by Premier Zhou Enlai, and serving as a way of linking non-Communist political figures to the state. It was not heard from during the Cultural Revolution. It reappeared in 1978, this time with Deng Xiaoping as its president. By 1982, it had over 100,000 members and 1,600 organs at the provincial and county levels. According to the *Beijing Review*, the CPPCC

consists of the various democratic parties, non-Party democrats, people's organizations, public figures of national minorities as well as patriotic personages from all walks of life, including compatriots in Taiwan, Xianggang (Hong Kong) and Aomen (Macao) and Chinese nationals residing abroad.

(*Beijing Review*, 20 December 1982: 5)

In 1996, for example, it included Gong Li, China's leading movie star, a good example of the state's efforts to make highly visible links with society. Yet the CPPCC also includes a heavy dose of Party members – e.g., 40 per cent in its 1982 session, a figure which rose to around 95 per cent in 2000 (reflecting the Party's efforts over the intervening years to attract more of China's social and economic élites). It operates according to a state corporatist principle of organization (Womack, 1984: 430), under which delegates are chosen not by the members but rather by its constituent organizations. It convenes concurrently with the NPC, so that CPPCC delegates can mingle and meet with the country's lawmakers.

The CPPCC serves several political functions. It is a way for the state to co-opt such non-Communist political forces as have survived from the past or emerged out of the structural reforms. It lends a veneer of popular legitimacy to the state. As suggested by the passage quoted above, it is especially useful as a way of institutionalizing linkages between the state and overseas Chinese, especially wealthy businesspersons, who are given membership on the CPPCC in order to win their support in promoting investment and in the hopes of smoothing the reunifications with Hong Kong and Taiwan. Finally, the CPPCC serves to percolate opinions and information upward, thereby keeping the state leadership abreast of a range, however limited, of political interests and concerns.

Of course, none of China's mass organizations or consultative bodies has any significant autonomy. Thus, they are not forums for serious, vigorous criticism, nor do they provide a basis for true political competition or opposition. As we have seen, the Chinese socialist state has always opposed independent organizations of any kind. It was on this point that it drew its line in the bloody sand of 1989. This fact does not necessarily render China's official quasi-state organizations utterly useless. Whether such organizations can open up spaces for more genuine representation and regularized disagreement is an unprecedented problem. There are few reasons to be optimistic. Yet Chinese politics has developed in surprising ways many times before.

CHAPTER 5

Chinese Society

CLASS

Both China's revolution and its state socialism grappled with the question of class and class struggle more profoundly than perhaps any other country ever has. As we saw in Chapter 1, the revolution faced complex and compelling issues of how far to press class struggle and how to identify classes on the ground. It was often difficult, for example, to decide who was a landlord or rich peasant, and, once people were classified, how to treat them. A misstep could, and frequently did, set back the revolution for years. For example, the Party blamed its radical class policy for the failure of the Jiangxi Soviet, which led to the debacle of the Long March and nearly put an end to the revolution. During the Maoist period, China struggled hard to develop a new brand of socialism that would overcome old class cleavages and prevent new ones – efforts which, as we saw in Chapter 2, produced genuine theoretical and practical innovations, some notable successes and several disasters. In the Dengist years, the state set aside class as a political project precisely at the time that its policies were creating new classes and sharp inequalities among them.

Analysis of the class structure of state socialism involves thorny theoretical problems. The standard notions of class are based on the experience of Western capitalism. In the Marxian tradition, class is based on structures of property relations: those who own the means of production are the bourgeois class; those who do not, and must, therefore, work for those who do, are the working class; those who are self-employed are the petit bourgeoisie; and so forth. In Weberian theory, which informs most social science and, indeed, most popular conceptions in capitalist countries, class refers to one's resources: those with more money, education and social position have a higher class standing than those with less. While both of these approaches have some applicability to state socialist countries, they also require rethinking. For Marxian theory, there is the question of what it means to say that the means of production are owned by the state or a collective, and what it means to work for the state or a collective. For Weberian theory, money, education and status were much more difficult to translate into class differences in a state socialist country, where many of the commodities that people want were not up for sale on markets, or the opportunities for advancement in work or social position were not distributed strictly according to merit-related criteria such as education. Moreover, Marxian and Weberian theory tend to see political power as a result of class differences, while of course in state socialist countries it was, as Mao recognized, often their source.

These are not idle questions. The ink that social scientists and socialist theorists have spilled struggling for a coherent, robust theory of class in state socialism is nothing compared with the blood, sweat and tears that have been shed in actual political struggles over this question in those countries. These issues have had the profoundest impact in China, where they were taken most seriously, both by the Maoist leadership but ultimately by many ordinary Chinese as well. They are also important since they left crucial legacies that have shaped the structural reforms.

To analyse the class structure and struggles of Chinese state socialism, it is best to take as a starting point not theoretical questions but rather the actual situation. Theories of class in state socialism – especially those generated and debated in China – have been fascinating, innovative and iconoclastic; but ultimately they have been unsatisfying in that they proved unable either to reflect complex reality coherently or to provide a guide to effective socialist transformation. If Chairman Mao's theory of class was ultimately flawed, we would do better to follow his theory of social science and social action: that theory should be based on practice (Mao, 1967, 1: 295–309). Of course, no study of social realities can be theoretically innocent. What we choose to include and exclude, and how we define and analyse society, always reflects our prior theories, often implicitly and in ways of which we are not always aware. Given the complexity, uncertainty and controversy that swirl around the class structure of Chinese state socialism, we would do best to be consciously eclectic and open-ended. Thus, we will draw on both the Marxian and Weberian traditions, while also being aware of the need to develop a new approach to grapple with the question of the political roots of class structure.

The revolutionary and Maoist periods

The countryside

As we saw in Chapter 1, the central class struggle of the Chinese Revolution took place in the countryside. Naturally, the Communist Party understood this in Marxian terms, as a conflict between those who owned the means of production – primarily, land – and those who did not and who therefore worked for or paid rent to them. Seeing the world in class terms did not come naturally to many Chinese peasants. The Party often found that the poor had trouble tracing the source of their poverty to land ownership, even though it was right before their eyes. A classic account of the revolution by Jack Belden, an American journalist who travelled extensively in the Communist base areas, is revealing.

> Ever since the Ching [sic] dynasty, Ma revealed, his family had been poor tenants, renting land and never having any of their own. Every year he raised eight piculs of millet and every year he had to give four of these piculs to Landlord Wang. He could afford no medicine for his wife whom he feared was dying. Two years before, his father had died and he had not been able to buy the old man a coffin, but had to wrap him in straw. Now he was thirty-five and still poor and it looked as if he would always be poor. 'I guess I have a bad brain,' he would say in summing up the reasons for his poverty.
>
> Then the cadres would ask: 'Are you poor because you have a bad brain or because your father left you no property?'
>
> 'I guess that's the reason; my father left me no property.'

'Really is that the reason?' asked the cadres. 'Let us make an account. You pay four piculs of grain every year to the landlord. Your family has rented land for sixty years. That's 240 piculs of grain. If you had not given this to the landlord, you would be rich. The reason you are poor, then, is because you have been exploited by the landlord.'

They would talk like this for hours and Ma would finally acknowledge that he was exploited by the landlord . . .

For fifteen days the cadres talked with Ma. In this period they had twenty-three formal talks with him besides the numerous evening talks . . . From this it can be seen it is not easy to move a Chinese peasant.

(Belden, 1973: 244–5)

Of course Ma knew he was poor. He also knew he was paying a great deal of rent to the landlord. He could not, however, draw the causal link between the two the way the Party did. The concept of class did not come naturally or easily to him. It was foreign to traditional, Confucian Chinese thought, which emphasized the unity of society, the naturalness and virtuousness of the social order (including even its deep inequalities) and the mutual obligations of people in society even when they are in very unequal positions. While this social theory was clearly a creation of the élites whom it benefited, it also exerted a hegemonic influence on the ordinary people who suffered from it.[1] The novelty and unfamiliarity of the concept of class among so many ordinary Chinese had important implications. As we saw in Chapter 1, it meant that the Party had much work to do in persuading Chinese peasants to rise up against their landlords. It also left the Party with a great deal of flexibility in shaping the concept of class and the practice of class struggle. Finally, it opened considerable space for some rather murky, confused thinking and action by the people as well as the leadership on class issues, especially during the Cultural Revolution.

During the revolution, the Party vacillated between very radical class policies that almost sunk it, and extraordinary flexibility on class issues that was an important key to its ultimate success. After its call for radical attacks on landlords and rich peasants in the Jiangxi Soviet fell on deaf, baffled or frightened ears, its united front policy of allying with 'patriotic' landlords and rich peasants during the Anti-Japanese War won it broad support and much needed breathing space. This cycle was repeated after the defeat of Japan, during the final phases of the revolution.

With the establishment of the People's Republic, every Chinese was given a formal class status based on the person's position in the structure of ownership in the last three years before the victory of the revolution in the locality. In the countryside, this happened during the land reform, which also broke the back of the landlord class' power, as we have seen in Chapter 1. We also saw how the rich peasant class was undermined during co-operativization. In the aftermath of the Great Leap Forward, in some villages former landlords and rich peasants did make something of a comeback. Their opposition to socialism found ready confirmation in the realities of economic collapse, and their residual fount of skills and social contacts could be put to use to help fuel the recovery (Thurston, 1977). This in turn induced Mao and his followers to call for a new mobilization of poor peasants against their former class enemies. In the Socialist Education Movement, former landlords and rich peasants came in for public criticism and ostracism. For example, during

139

festivals they were required to work in the fields while everyone else celebrated. They were also frequently blamed for all manner of problems.

During the last decade and a half of the Maoist period, when the people's communes were consolidated, rural China achieved very high levels of economic and social equality in many important respects. Because all productive resources were collectively owned, no one was getting rich simply by virtue of owning land, draught animals or machinery. Everyone was paid according to work. Moreover, individuals' pay was generally set in a public process in which members of production teams – the lowest level of collective organization – rated how much their neighbours ought to receive per day. There was strong social pressure to minimize differences. Thus, within the teams, income differences among families were mainly a function of how many family members were working, and how many non-working dependants they had to support. That is, they were a function of each family's size and where it was in the life cycle (i.e., how many retired elderly parents there were, and whether the children were small or old enough to work). Moreover, the teams tried to compensate for the effects of different positions in the life cycle by making long-term loans of foodgrain to families with many dependants, to be paid back when more members were old enough to work. Finally, a safety net guaranteeing minimal but adequate supplies of crucial items like food, shelter, clothing and even burial services was provided by the teams. Thus, within villages, economic equality was extremely high.

Yet because income was accounted and divided within the production teams, the commune system left room for economic inequality among villages. Those with better land or access to water and other needed inputs produced more, so they had more to divide up. Within a brigade or commune, rich teams' average incomes could frequently run to two or three times those of their neighbours'. The collectives undertook some measures to counteract this fact of nature. Health care and education, and sometimes childcare and even housing, were provided as collective goods by brigades and communes. Thus, access to these services was equalized among the teams of a brigade or commune regardless of the teams' own production and income levels. Some very limited efforts were made to amalgamate teams, so that income would be accounted and divided up on a brigade or even commune-wide basis, but they were resisted both by richer villages and by those who recalled China's experiences with overly large collectives in the Great Leap Forward. Yet the state never tried to use simpler redistributive measures such as a progressive taxation system to resolve inequalities among rich and poor villages.

Meanwhile, social inequality was significantly reduced. There was nothing corresponding to the old landlord, rich peasant or poor peasant classes anymore. Education and health care were distributed very equally at least within brigades and communes. Even local officials lived in conditions quite similar to those of ordinary peasants. Because the social distance between them was low, there were few obstacles to peasants expressing their complaints and disagreements to their local leaders, and many did so quite freely, as we shall see in Chapter 7.

Overall, then, by eliminating inequalities originating in ownership, and by adopting collective institutions and policies to help counteract some of the remaining inequalities that occur due to geography and life cycle, Maoist China achieved levels of economic and social equality that have rarely been seen in the rural areas of a developing country. Of course, in a country as large, diverse and poor as China, serious inequalities nonetheless remained among regions. These are difficult to ameliorate for any country – even the wealthy UK and USA still have their Yorkshires and Mississippis – much less for one as poor as China. Maoist China can be credited for making some efforts nonetheless. It developed the 'third front' industrialization programme to locate major investments in the hinterlands. Though many of these enterprises proved unable to stand up to the test of the market in the 1990s, for decades they did provide employment and livelihood for millions of people, and they did lay down infrastructure and the basis for industrialization in areas that would not otherwise have had them. It operated a programme to supply impoverished areas with foodgrain. Most prominently, starting in the mid-1960s its core strategy for rural development was the campaign to 'learn from Dazhai', a poor, mountainous village that had pulled itself up by its bootstraps. Since, however, the Dazhai model stressed local hard work, ideological commitment, strong leadership and the virtues of making do with local resources rather than relying on the state, the campaign around it is not an example of state-led redistribution so much as an effort to promulgate a development strategy appropriate to poor areas. That the Maoist state took this route distinguishes it from the rural development strategies of most other poor countries of the day. The dominant model used elsewhere – most prominently, India – was the 'green revolution', a package of advanced technological inputs that was appropriate mainly to wealthier areas.

The urban areas

After its defeat in the Shanghai 'White Terror' in 1927, the Communist Party was unable to lead a class struggle in China's cities. Unions under the thumb of the Nationalist Party came to the fore, as the Republican government crushed radical labour opposition. With the Communist victory in 1949, many capitalists fled to Taiwan, leaving their factories to become the property of the new state. Quite a few stayed, though. In some of their factories, workers at last rose up to seize the plant or attack the owners and managers. The Party actually discouraged such moves, concerned about their effect on an economy already in crisis. It took a more moderate position, forming joint ventures with the capitalists and keeping them on as managers. Indeed, as business partners with the new state, many members of the Chinese bourgeoisie actually received shares of the profits of their former factories until the Cultural Revolution. Of course, all was not cushy for China's capitalists. They were targeted during state-sponsored political campaigns such as the *wu fan* ('five-anti') campaign of 1952 against 'tax evasion, bribery, cheating in government contracts, thefts of economic intelligence and stealing of state assets'. They and their children were discriminated against in the distribution of housing, health care and educational opportunities. Yet on the whole they were spared the systematic, face-to-face attacks and public humiliations visited on the landlords. Meanwhile, China's small businesspeople and self-employed artisans, who were not generally regarded as class enemies, were organized into co-ops in 1956.

With the consolidation of the urban state socialist economy, the working class became basically homogeneous. Workers were employed by state enterprises on more or less similar terms, including a nationally standardized wage scale. Unemployment was minimal. Their 'units' were not just places of employment, but little welfare states providing lifetime guarantees of cash income and free or nominally priced housing, food, education and health care, all distributed in a highly equal fashion. There were, naturally, some differences in the quality of goods and services provided by various enterprises, but they were relatively small. Thus, economic and social inequality among urban workers reached very low levels through the end of the Maoist period. Inequalities between them and rural migrants who took up jobs in many urban factories were more pronounced, and became a serious source of conflict during the Cultural Revolution. There are few good studies of the social distance between workers and managers in the Maoist period; but judging from managers' subsequent complaints that they often had trouble getting their workers to follow directives, it may well be that Chinese workplaces were less authoritarian than many capitalist firms. By all indications, then, during the Maoist period, social and economic inequality in China's cities was even lower than it was in the countryside.[2]

The reconceptualization of class and the denouement of class struggle during the Cultural Revolution

Given the high levels of class equality that had been achieved even by the mid-1960s, the explosion of class conflict during the Cultural Revolution is deeply puzzling. When Mao and fellow leftists called for uprisings against 'those in authority who are taking the capitalist road', they were offering an iconoclastic innovation in the theory of class and the practice of class struggle. Moving against the tide of Marxist tradition, which generally sees political power fundamentally as a reflection of class power rooted in economic relations, they argued that in a socialist country new class formations could actually originate in politics. They did not think that everyone in power was a new class enemy, of course – the Maoists were not anarchists. They were proposing, though, that key determinants of class included a person's political attitude and behaviour, not just one's (or one's parents') class status, rooted in property ownership, at a time now almost two decades in the past. If one sided with the workers and peasants, then it did not matter into what class one had been born. Likewise, being born into an exploited class and even becoming a leader of the socialist state was no guarantee that one was on the right side of the class struggle, even if one were a leading official.[3]

This approach made some sense in theory. In a state socialist country, where the economy is run politically, and where the state is so powerful, the unequal distribution of political power, and in particular the ways it is exercised, can of course be a source of social cleavage. Yet if class is defined in terms of subjective criteria such as attitude and behaviour, it becomes difficult in practice to distinguish one 'class' from another – to determine who is for the working classes and socialism and who is against them. This uncertainty opened the door to indiscriminate attacks on all leaders by anyone who resented them for any reason. And of course even the best leaders must sometimes make unpopular decisions that anger some people. During the Cultural Revolution, foremost among the attackers were many former 'class enemies' and their children, who, after all, had suffered many indignities over the previous decades. Moreover, many of these people possessed leadership skills – such as education, self-confidence and organizational ability – that were valuable in the mass movements of the Cultural Revolution. Thus, former capitalists, landlords and rich peasants and their children were disproportionately found among the most radical groups, and often their leading ranks, in the Cultural Revolution. This in turn made it easier for state officials under attack to defend themselves by shifting the focus of the Cultural Revolution to struggles against former 'class enemies'. When that happened, Mao and his fellow leftists actually tried to protect radicalized children of former capitalists, landlords and rich peasants, and to legitimate their role in the Cultural Revolution. The Maoists condemned 'blood theory', which held that class was indelibly determined by birth. In doing so, the Maoists were drawing on the Party's tradition of flexibility on class struggle issues. They were also following one of Mao's tactical rules of politics and war: one should try where possible to unite with all those who oppose the main enemy, which in this case was the 'capitalist roaders' among the state bureaucratic élite.

Several conclusions emerge from this complex story. First, the meaning of class and class struggle, and efforts to reinterpret them in a fundamental way, lay at the epicentre of the Cultural Revolution. Second, the actual political activities of the millions of ordinary people who took part in the Cultural Revolution were deeply affected by class issues. Statistically, class background was the most significant factor accounting for people's decisions to join one faction or another during the Cultural Revolution (Blecher and White, 1979). Third, the politics that swirled around class in the Cultural Revolution was confusing, and led to some strange coalitions. The left leadership allied itself with the former enemies of the revolution. Often unintentionally, their position fostered indiscriminate, unbridled and unprincipled attacks against the leadership of the socialist state, including many honest officials. This in turn led to equally vituperative and reprehensible attacks on many people with 'bad class backgrounds' who had long ceased to exploit anyone or, in the case of their children, who had never done so but were simply being held responsible for their forebears' behaviour. Fourth, then, it is no wonder that the most far-reaching effort ever seen to grapple with the conundrum of old and new class formations in state socialism ended tragically, without making China a less class-ridden society. Fifth, and going still further, it is also no surprise that the Cultural Revolution discredited the whole concept of class and class struggle in China, which, ironically, is also one of the last, and surely the largest, country in the world led by a Communist Party. This is no mere theoretical point. The fact that 'class' and 'class conflict' were so profoundly discredited during the Cultural Revolution has gone far to pre-empt protest against the stark new class inequalities that have emerged under the structural reforms.

The Dengist period

The Dengist state shelved class politics precisely at the time that its policies were actively and purposefully promoting the rise of new classes, the differentiation of old ones and the increase of inequality among them. This was no mere irony. The leadership's plan for economic development was expressly predicated on the principle of 'allowing some to get rich first'. In order to encourage them, the Dengists had to offer convincing assurances that the state would not encourage class struggle. They took some truly iconoclastic steps. Starting immediately after the landmark Third Plenum in 1978, propaganda campaigns glorified the newly rich '¥10,000 [annual income] households', condemned the class politics of the Cultural Revolution as a 'leftist deviation' and extolled the material prosperity of compatriots in capitalist Taiwan. In the realm of policy, the state began a process in which it would, over two decades, encourage the development of lucrative specialties and sidelines, material incentives and disincentives, a more entrepreneurial approach to managing state and collective firms, and even the rise of private enterprise.

The countryside

Increased economic inequality was nothing less than an explicit objective of the rural reforms. Criticizing collective agriculture for damaging incentives by being excessively egalitarian – a questionable claim, as we shall see in Chapter 6 – reform leaders began very early in the process to speak of 'allowing some farmers to get rich first'. New social cleavages began to grow up both within the responsibility system and outside it. When the communes' productive assets began to be contracted out, some were of course much more valuable and potentially lucrative than others. The best land and the most profitable sidelines often tended to go to the local officials, who were in control of the contracting process. Sometimes they were put up for bid, and it was often former landlords, rich peasants and 'speculators' (i.e., traders) who possessed the entrepreneurial skills and self-confidence to contract for business resources that others saw as too risky. Sometimes, too, former landlords and rich peasants benefited as land contracts were drawn up to replicate pre-collectivization holdings, despite a quarter of a century having elapsed. In still other instances, where land was contracted out according to households' ability to work it, those peasants who were lucky enough to have an abundance of labour power in their families at the time benefited. Thus, a new stratum of prosperous farmers began to develop, some out of the pre-1949 élites, some from the Maoist-period leadership and some from ordinary farmers.

Other people opted out of the agricultural responsibility system altogether. Some started small businesses in the countryside engaged in artisan production or services like barbering or bicycle repair. Others went into trade – rural China was suddenly awash with pedlars, roadside stands and shops. Many set out with a cart and, if they were lucky, a donkey, to do transport work for their neighbours or local enterprises large and small. Some took up waged employment in the proliferating rural industries and even on fields for which others had contracted. Quite a few took advantage of the lifting of Maoist-period migration controls, setting off for the cities, to seek their fortune in factories, markets and construction sites. The re-emergence of many former village social and economic élites is eloquent testimony to the tenacity of entrepreneurial inclinations and skills passed down through families. Traders, moneylenders and rich peasants also benefited from the revival of pre-existing socio-commercial networks, in which they were well situated.

All this quickly produced a rural society that was far more complex and differentiated than it had been in the Maoist period. In the Marxian sense of class as rooted in the structure of production, there were now several classes, where before there had been only one. By 2000, 29,000,000 rural Chinese had become self-employed – a new petit bourgeoisie. Others became employers profiting from the work of people they hired as wage labourers – a new bourgeoisie, at least in part.[4] Still others were those wage workers – a new working class. Some were employed to work the land, but most – 128,000,000 in 2000 – worked in rural collective enterprises. As the 1990s wore on, another growing phalanx – 11,400,000 in 2000 – were employed in burgeoning rural private enterprises. Working conditions in these plants are often difficult, due to primitive technology, little attention to safety and environmental protection and the absence of a labour union branch, which in the cities does sometimes enforce the minimal guarantees stipulated in the Labour Law. Rural plants offer no benefits or job guarantees. The fact that the workers generally hail from the same town or village as the managers can cut both ways: in many instances it can provide the basis for patriarchal despotism on the shop floor, while in others it can help ensure a minimal level of protection. Where these plants employ workers from other places, the tougher approach is likely to prevail, and the outsiders tend to be given the worst jobs for the lowest pay.

In the Weberian sense of class defined as rooted in one's possessions and resources, the picture is equally complex. In some senses, the rural structural reforms opened up opportunities for people in poor localities. Some of them could now avoid state cropping controls emphasizing grain production, turning instead to more lucrative local specialities. Others could unseat unpopular or ineffective local leaders who had been mismanaging the collective economy. Still others could simply leave, enriching themselves (and, for the many who remitted some of their earnings back home, their localities) while reducing the pressures on the local economy to provide for so many people. Such mobility actually worked to ameliorate some economic inequalities that had been embedded in the Maoist-period collectivist structure. While the inequality of the distribution of household income has many sources besides the gap among rich and poor places, some data suggest that this effect was so strong as actually to reduce overall inequality in household income below the already low level that had been achieved by 1978 (Khan *et al.*, 1992: 1056–8).

By the early 1980s, however, statistical measures of rural household income inequality began to rise again (Rozelle, 1996), for several reasons. Within villages, those who had contracted for the most lucrative property began to develop their operations, producing much higher and more rapidly growing incomes than their neighbours, who were simply contracting ordinary cropland. Businesspeople started to profit from employing labour and from corruption. In a startling development, the new rich included a disproportionate number of former rich peasants (Putterman, 1989: 308). In 1995, the poorest 10 per cent of people in the Chinese countryside received only 2 per cent of income, while the richest 10 per cent got 34 per cent (Khan and Riskin, 2001: 31) – a huge increase in inequality compared with Maoist days, and high even in comparison with other late industrializing countries.

The urban areas

In the cities and towns too, the class structure has become more diversified and unequal. Starting in the late 1970s, urbanites without jobs were urged to become self-employed in petty retail and service trades, selling vegetables, repairing bicycles, taking photographs of tourists and the like. All over China, 'getihu' – individual entrepreneurs – began opening little businesses. By 1986, there were already nearly 5,000,000 in both urban and rural areas, and by 2000 there were 21,000,000 in urban areas alone. At first, the private sector was restricted to self-employment, including family enterprises. Gradually, though, it was given greater latitude to hire labour – a huge change, in view of the fact that Marxist theory begins its critique of capitalism by treating wage labour as 'exploitation'. Numerical limits for the permissible numbers of employees started small and were increased by stages. By the mid-1990s there were no more limits, and individual private firms were employing thousands of workers. In 2000, nearly 13,000,000 workers were employed in urban private firms.

All this private enterprise led, on the one side, to the rise of a new bourgeoisie. Their numbers are difficult to measure, but the order of magnitude may be inferred from the fact that in 2000 there were 2,500,000 private enterprises in urban China, many with multiple owners and employing large staffs of managers. Some of China's new bourgeoisie had been managers and officials in the Maoist period, some hailed from the old capitalist class and some arose from the working class itself. Their incomes and wealth are also hard to ascertain. Dazzling anecdotal accounts of fabulous wealth – such as the case of Li Qinfu, a textile and printing tycoon whose office is modelled on the US Capitol building and who drives a Lamborghini, a Bentley, two Mercedes-Benzes and several BMWs and Japanese luxury cars – are not utterly atypical; China now has thousands of multimillionaires (Smith, 2002). Even in a more modest rural area such as Hebei Province's Shulu County, there are a number of newly rich entrepreneurs who were farmers or petty businesspeople just a decade ago. They are able to sport flashy Western clothes, furnish their offices lavishly, travel abroad several times each year and attempt to enrol their children in expensive Western private schools (author's interview, 1999). However, most of China's new bourgeoisie are more modest members of a growing middle class.

As regards the working class, in 1986 workers in state enterprises were put on fixed-term contracts, replacing their lifetime guarantees of employment. This change threatened the basic livelihood of the China's working class, who had grown accustomed to the guarantees of the Maoist period, and had been planning their lives accordingly. Managers feared the consequences – both for production and for themselves – of actually threatening their workers' livelihood. Thus the new contract system was treated as a mere formality: fixed-term contracts were signed, but both managers and workers still expected them to be automatically renewed for life.

Profound change for China's proletariat did, however, begin quietly and sporadically in the late 1980s. Until this time, state enterprise workers were on a standardized eight-grade wage system. The differentials were relatively small, and were determined mainly by seniority; a coalition of left-oriented party leaders above and workers below had managed to blunt most efforts to differentiate by skill or assiduity. As state enterprises were gradually cut loose from planning and given greater autonomy and financial responsibility, wages began to be affected by the financial health of the firms. Those that were doing well of course had more financial resources with which to pay their workers, and they often tended to raise wages and benefits, in order to maintain smooth production by stoking workers' morale, and to prevent their more skilled workers from leaving for more lucrative jobs. Firms that were struggling in the new competitive environment, by contrast, often now had no choice but to cut wages, since the state no longer took responsibility for them. The result was a transformation as massive as it was quiet: China's state enterprise workers' entire livelihood, which had been dependent on the state, now became dependent instead on their individual firms. Those fortunate enough to work in enterprises that were prospering or at least surviving in the newly marketizing environment could keep their jobs and the housing, health and retirement benefits that went with them. Those with equal skills and assiduity who simply happened to work for firms that could not compete found their lives thrown into deep crisis. Unemployment is impossible to measure in China, but it has grown significantly, as we saw in Chapter 3. The state has provided meagre allowances to laid-off and unemployed workers – in the range of ¥250–300 (≈$30–35) per month. By the late 1990s, it was actively encouraging bankrupt firms to close, and offering workers severance packages in lieu of further payments. Anger about the size of those packages has triggered several sustained, organized demonstrations by infuriated, dispirited workers, as we saw in Chapter 3.

China's cities are also increasingly packed with migrants from the countryside. Two hundred million had moved in the first two decades of the structural reforms. Many work in factories, shops and construction sites, many are self-employed as pedlars and maids, and some even own businesses and employ other migrants. Migrants' legal status is often murky. The state still formally categorizes the entire Chinese population as either rural or urban. Rural designees have to get permits to work or reside in cities. In practice, about half do not, which consigns them to living in a legal and administrative netherworld, subject to paying high prices for necessities such as health care or education for their children so long as they remain in town. Many rural migrants have taken up semi-permanent residence, often in shanty towns on the edge of the city. Some of these can be quite large, replete with their own factories, shopping zones, schools, hospitals, restaurants and so forth. We shall return to them below, when we consider China's rural–urban cleavage.

Finally, there is China's lumpenproletariat. Beggars have begun appearing on the streets of urban China since the start of the structural reforms. Just as disturbing is the rise in the number of criminals, including pickpockets and petty thieves, con artists, illegal money changers, sellers of contraband (such as pirated CDs), prostitutes, drug traffickers and members of gangs (some of which are revivals of pre-1949 criminal organizations and secret societies).

Like rural China, then, urban China is also a vastly more differentiated, stratified society than it was in 1978. On the positive side, this stunning development is often seen as a necessary condition of the rapid economic growth of the urban economy. Urban residents now face a greater range of possible occupations and forms of employment than they did in the Maoist period, though many of these are not available due to individuals' low qualifications or to tight labour markets. From a Weberian point of view, these changes involve vastly increased inequality. In 1995, the top 10 per cent of urban Chinese earned 27 per cent of income, while the lowest 10 per cent earned only 3 per cent (Khan and Riskin, 2001: 36). Moreover, looked at through Marxist lenses, many of these inequalities are rooted in exploitation redux, both as private-sector employment has returned to the urban economy, and as a portion of the profits of collective and state-run firms falls increasingly into the hands of corrupt officials. From 1988 to 1995, and perhaps beyond, inequality increased faster in the urban areas than in the countryside. By 1995, overall inequality in China, including both urban and rural areas, was greater than in India, Pakistan or Indonesia (Khan and Riskin, 2001: 49). That is a stunning development, and one fraught with political consequences to which we shall return in Chapters 7 and 8.

GENDER

The Chinese revolution and Maoist state socialism took class, not gender, as the fundamental focus of their efforts to transform Chinese society. The Dengist structural reforms downplayed state-led social transformation altogether, including both class and gender relations. Thus, relations between women and men have never been particularly high on the state's political agenda, and significant political and economic resources have never been devoted specifically to attacking the deep patriarchy of traditional China. All this has limited the country's progress toward gender equality. Nevertheless, extremely significant gains have been made. Gender equality in urban China may well be as great as anywhere in the world, as we shall see. A recent comprehensive study found greater equality in China than in Taiwan in the 1990s in a range of areas including employment, childcare, household chores and attitudes. This finding confounds modernization theory, which would posit the reverse outcome due to Taiwan's much higher level of economic development. The authors attribute their finding to the positive effects of changes in the Maoist period (Tang and Parish, 2000). In the countryside, there is, not surprisingly, much more patriarchy and gender inequality. Yet even there China may compare favourably with most late industrializing countries. For example, female illiteracy, a key indicator of women's welfare and opportunity, was 24 per cent in 2001 – triple the male rate, but still significantly below the 32 per cent average for developing countries (World Bank, 2002). This progress is only partly the result of specific efforts to transform gender relations. It also owes much to some unintended effects of China's socialist transformation.

The revolutionary and Maoist periods

Mao Zedong is famous for coining the slogan 'women hold up half of heaven'. He was right when he wrote as early as 1927 that:

> A man in China is usually subjected to the domination of . . . political authority, . . . clan authority . . . and . . . religious authority . . . As for women, they are also dominated by the men. These . . . are the embodiment of the whole feudal–patriarchal system and ideology.
>
> (Mao, 1967, 1: 44)

Traditional Chinese society was indeed profoundly patriarchal and downright abusive. Under the system of patrilocal exogamy, women married into their husbands' households, which were customarily located outside their home villages. Thus, from birth girls were regarded as a financial burden, since the resources involved in raising them would never be recouped. Emotionally, too, parents resisted getting too attached to their daughters, since after marriage they would rarely if ever see them. Boys were much preferred because they would remain in their home villages – indeed, usually in their natal household – where they could be relied on eventually to take care of their elderly parents. To conform to patriarchal standards of beauty that were also requisites for marriageability, mothers bound their daughters' feet by breaking the toe knuckles and bending them under. This not only caused excruciating pain, but also limited women's physical mobility for life. Once married, women remained inferior. They were outsiders to their new villages and households, in a society deeply suspicious of strangers. Women suffered abuse at every turn. Their husbands ordered them about, frequently beat them and demanded sexual subservience. Even their mothers-in-law, who might be expected to be empathetic, were often harsh, either out of jealousy or because this was their one opportunity to be domineering. Young wives were often literally imprisoned in their homes, forbidden to venture out into the street without permission even just to do a little shopping or deal with an itinerant pedlar or repairman.

During the revolution, the Party, like middle-class reformers, of course campaigned against footbinding. In its liberated zones, it also conducted propaganda work against wife-beating and in favour of women's participation in the movement. Not surprisingly, though, such participation often reflected traditional gender roles, with women sewing uniforms or providing food. Even these efforts on the gender front never became more than sidelines to the Party's main work of fighting the landlords, the Guomindang and the Japanese, for several reasons. Ideologically, Marx had of course emphasized class struggle, and had much less to say about gender. Engels paid far more explicit attention to the issue, but argued that patriarchy was a function of private property; thus, the best way to struggle against it was to struggle for socialism (Engels, 1972). Insofar as the transition to socialism itself had important positive consequences for women – an argument we shall be exploring – Engels had a point. Yet the main reasons the Party did not take gender as seriously as class had less to do with theory than with practice. The Party cadres themselves were predominantly male, and as such could objectively be threatened by a transformation of gender relations. And even where leaders' subjective commitment was strong enough to overcome their objective interest, efforts to lead their localities toward progress on gender issues could alienate male peasants who, as heads of their households, were the revolution's main political base. Poor farmers, who already faced many obstacles in joining the class struggle, were not likely to be receptive to the programmes of an outside leadership that was mobilizing wives and daughters against husbands and fathers.

With the establishment of the People's Republic, the leadership turned its attention to building a new society. In the 1950s, class struggle became less central a concern than it had been during the revolution and land reform. Thus, more attention could be paid to overcoming China's historical patriarchy. The first major piece of legislation promulgated after the establishment of the People's Republic was the 1950 Marriage Law. It outlawed 'bigamy, concubinage, child betrothal, interference with the remarriage of widows and the exaction of money or gifts in connection with marriages' ('Marriage Law, 1950'). It made divorce legal and available on demand by mutual consent, or by court decree if reconciliation failed and grounds – that were not specified – were judged warranted. Men were not permitted, however, to divorce their wives when they were pregnant or within one year of the birth of a child. Women were granted 'equal rights in the possession and management of family property', including inheritance. They were to possess 'the right to free choice of occupation and free participation in work or social activities'. Infanticide, which had predominantly affected baby girls, was outlawed. Of course, this legislation did not translate perfectly into practice. Bride prices have never disappeared, for example, and men generally continued to control family property. Nevertheless, the Marriage Law marked a sharp break from the past, by making it clear that the state would or at least could throw its weight against some of the worst depredations perpetrated by men and traditional patriarchy against women.

As the socialist state broadened education, it encouraged parents to send their daughters as well as their sons to school. In a modernizing society, educational attainment for girls can open opportunities for occupational advancement and political participation that hold the greatest promise of any single factor for breaking the grip of patriarchy (Drèze and Sen, 1995: Ch. 7). Naturally, educational inequality was greatest in the countryside. There, parents lacked incentive to educate their daughters, who would be leaving home anyway when they married. It was far more advantageous to have girls go out to work as early as possible. Yet huge gains in girls' educational attainment were produced by the combination of political encouragement and the fact that now it was the collective that was controlling labour assignments and remuneration for girls. In one sample of rural girls who started school between 1929 and 1949, only 38 per cent completed their primary education; but 100 per cent of those who started after 1959 did so. By 1978, 45 per cent of all primary school students, including town and countryside alike, were female. Yet educational attainment grew more unequal as one moved up the ladder. Only 20 per cent of rural girls who started middle school after 1959 completed it, compared with 54 per cent of males. In 1978, 41 per cent of all middle school students and 24 per cent of college and university students were women (Parish and Whyte, 1978: 83; *China Statistical Yearbook*, State Statistical Bureau, 1995: 597).

Population control policies, too, helped women. By reducing the number of pregnancies women would have during their childbearing years, the risks of injury or death for the mothers declined. Moreover, having fewer children to care for reduced their burden of work. Once again, though, the picture was mixed. Women also tended to be made more heavily responsible than men for birth control: IUDs and pills, both of which carry risks for women, were more commonly used than condoms. Moreover, with fewer children being born to each family, women were placed under intense psychological pressure to give birth to boys, and often suffered serious abuse when they gave birth to girls.

The Maoist state's ideological policies probably also helped increase gender equality, though how and how much is hard to evaluate in a society without object-ive survey research. The official position of the Chinese state that women are the legal equals of men is well ahead of many other countries (including the USA, which, after protracted debate, rejected adding the Equal Rights Amendment to its constitution). Yet even as a concept, legal equality is not the same as social equality. The content of ideological campaigns on gender shifted with the changing eco-nomic policies. During the Great Leap Forward, women were encouraged to par-ticipate in labour outside the home, and so they were portrayed as co-equal contri-butors with men to socialist economic development. (Yet in the wake of that movement's collapse, when dire realities and recovery policies favoured returning farm work to men, women were pictured in more traditional roles.) Maoist period ideological postures on issues other than gender also had some positive, if unintended, effects on gender equality. Cynical Westerners enjoyed condemning or poking fun at Maoist China's Spartan clothing design and the taboo against public discussion or imagery that contained even a hint about sex. Likewise, anti-consumerism meant a complete absence of advertising. These policies, though, prevented the kind of offensive sexist iconography that is so common in the West, such as barely clad young ladies lounging on the hoods of automobiles. (Such images began to be seen in China starting in the 1980s.)

Women did make some political gains in the Maoist period. At the grass roots, by the 1970s each rural production team had a position known as women's team head. The person filling it was elected by the women of the team, sat on the team management committee and was charged with overseeing women's issues, which included population control, labour allocations, physical abuse and celebration of International Women's Day. She also served as an advocate for women's interests in team affairs. At the village level, women were increasingly elected to other positions of responsibility in production teams during and after the Cultural Revolution. In one sample of several hundred team cadres, women comprised between 8 and 12 per cent from 1958 to 1966, but between 16 and 21 per cent from 1970 to 1974 (Blecher, 1978: 61).

At the higher levels of the state, there were two patterns of women holding leadership posts, each reflecting an aspect of latent patriarchy. Most women officials occupied posts specifically concerned with women's work (i.e., in the Women's Association or the population control apparatus). Some held other positions by virtue of being married to key leaders. For example, Deng Yingchao and Wang Guangmei, married to Zhou Enlai and Liu Shaoqi respectively, also achieved political influence in the top leadership ranks. So did Song Qingling, Sun Yatsen's wife, who became a major figure in the Chinese People's Political Consultative Congress (see Chapter 4). The most prominent example was Jiang Qing, the prominent radical and member of the Gang of Four, who was also Mao's wife. Jiang was more widely hated than her three colleagues not only because she was the only woman among them, but the attacks on her had a salacious quality that is one indicator of lingering sexism.[5]

Some of the greatest gains made by women in the Maoist period were unintended effects of the socialist reorganization of the economy. Collective agriculture and socialist industry, in which tasks were assigned by village leaders or factory managers, helped limit the patriarchal power of male household heads to control women's labour. Of course, most grass-roots leaders were men; but, because they were Party members or had been trained by and were responsible to the Party, they were likely to be a little more progressive on gender questions than ordinary rural men. Moreover, decisions about women's labour assignments were made in public, which made it harder to discriminate. In the countryside, women were often organized into specialized teams to do tasks for which it was thought they were best suited, such as picking mulberry leaves or cotton, which requires great manual dexterity. Whether it was right or wrong to do so, such organization had a positive effect in promoting female solidarity by putting women together during extended periods of work. This was a far cry from the situation just a generation earlier, in which many women were literally trapped in their homes. Factories and farm collectives also provided a range of social services, such as prenatal check-ups and day care, that were a boon to women. Finally, women's participation in labour outside the home meant they were making a palpable, often important, contribution to the household's income.

Of course, the socialist economy did not completely liberate Chinese women. Having employment outside the home now left women with the 'double burden' – so familiar in most countries – of also being primarily responsible for housework. The macroeconomic emphasis on accumulation and investment over consumption goods reduced the availability of appliances, such as washing machines, to ease that burden. Likewise, restrictions on marketing made shopping more difficult, and required women to spend more time producing household necessities themselves. There were also inequalities of pay. In the countryside, women generally earned around 80 per cent of the number of work points given to men.[6]

Moreover, at the structural level, aspects of the socialist economy actually benefited from and in turn helped reinforce the patriarchal family system. The male-dominated extended family proved well suited to the mobilization of women into labour outside the home. In teams without collective day care, it provided a way for children to be tended at no cost to the collective – i.e., by grandmother – during the day. At women's expense, the family system also gave the collective flexibility in labour management, which is so important in highly seasonal and variable work such as agriculture. Women were drawn into collective work as needed (e.g., during busy planting and harvest seasons), and then shunted back to their homes when work slackened. The latitude given to the small, village-sized collective unit to run many of its own internal affairs vested considerable local power in the hands of male village leaders. Though, as argued above, they were likely to be a little more enlightened on gender relations than most husbands, these men could still effectively obstruct feminist offensives. One prominent example was the collapse of the Women's Association's effort to use the campaign to criticize Lin Biao and Confucius in the early 1970s to press for matrilocal marriage.

In terms of politics, this failed proposal points up the ways in which further progress on gender issues was limited by one structural feature of the state and one 'non-decision'.[7] The structural feature is that women were never able to form their own autonomous organizations to pursue their interests.[8] Thus, as we have seen, gains in gender equality occurred only as a result of the initiatives of the leadership or as unintended effects of institutional changes and policies on other issues. Chinese women had a difficult time formulating their own liberatory agendas. If they had had some autonomous organizational space, perhaps the 'non-decision' to leave patrilocal exogamy in place would have been challenged. As we have seen, the practice of women marrying out of their natal families into households in other villages is the firm foundation on which rest myriad forms of oppression of girls and women. Moreover, the elimination of patrilocal exogamy would have had the welcome side effect of reduced upward pressure on population (since people would not need only sons to support them in their old age). China's revolution and its socialism were bold in overturning numerous deeply entrenched structures of political, economic, social and cultural domination. Yet no serious movement against patrilocal exogamy ever occurred in this, one of the most radically transformative polities ever seen. Reasons can be adduced for why this did not happen: it would have disrupted society at its foundations, interfering with class struggle or economic development; the male leadership was not sensitive enough to the problem; China's society was too patriarchal to offer any realistic hope of change. Yet in an historical context when many impossibilities and unimaginable transformations occurred, it is hard not to question the state's failure to challenge this linchpin of the status quo.

The Dengist period

If China were ever going to witness a frontal attack on patrilocal exogamy, the Maoist period was the moment. The Dengist state is, as we have seen, neither interested in nor capable of using political power to press for fundamental social transformation. Its approach is to transform society mainly through economic changes such as marketization. Like its Maoist predecessor, the effects on women have been decidedly mixed. Marketization and the development of commerce and industry, especially in the rural areas and the special economic zones, have vastly expanded employment opportunities for women. This has given them incomes and, for those in industry, physical and psychological space that they share with other women away from patriarchal fathers and husbands. Yet the men often retain some control over their wives and especially their daughters' incomes, though, as we shall see, such power may be weakening a little. Many of the factories are sweatshops, and work there is in dead-end jobs; young women often quit or are fired when they get married. More broadly, the burgeoning market combined with declining state attention and commitment to socialist values has meant the return of prostitution, trafficking in women and pornography and other forms of sexist iconography.

The collapse of rural collectives has had several effects. It has restored the position of the male household head. Yet given the changes of the Maoist period, and the development of the market-based economy that keeps many men on the road and puts women into employment outside the home, it is unlikely that most Chinese households are quite as patriarchal as they were before 1949. In 1995, women earned 80 per cent of what men earned in agriculture, but only 51 per cent as much in rural industry (Liu and Chai, 1996). According to one Chinese researcher, 'the status of women farmers is rising along with their income . . . women now don't have to ask permission from their husbands when they want to buy something. For big purchases, husbands and wives discuss it and decide together' (*AP News Service*, 17 February 1996). The willingness of local and national governments to relax their control of day-to-day social activity has permitted the return of all manner of traditional patriarchal practices, such as wedding ceremonies demeaning to women. Women have been hit particularly hard by the decline of collectively funded education. Without the pressure of the collective to send girls to school, and with both the rise of school fees and increased opportunities to put girls into remunerative work, there has been a sharp decline in female school enrolment. The number of girls attending primary school dropped from 65,000,000 to 57,000,000 from 1980 to 1990, and had only recovered to 62,000,000 by 2000, even though the female population grew by 27 per cent over the twenty-year period. As noted above, in 2001, the illiteracy rate was 24 per cent for women, but only 8 per cent for men. With the decline of local governments' capacity, and their reorientation to a more exclusive concern with the economy as opposed to social and political transformation, it is probably more difficult for women to get protection against or redress for sexist discrimination and crimes.

A recent comprehensive study by Western social scientists concluded that 'urban women continue to gain on men in education, jobs and . . . bargaining power at home.' From 1980 to 1997, women's share of high school enrolment rose from 40 to 46 per cent, and college enrolment from one-quarter to one-third. Thus, in 1997, they earned 80 per cent as much as men, the highest ratio in Asia, with Japan coming in at 51 per cent and Hong Kong 63 per cent. This income enables them to reduce their 'double burden' by inducing their husbands to take up a greater share of household chores and childcare than in, for example, the culturally similar but economically more advanced Taiwan (Tang and Parish, 2000: 62, 227, 315–16).

Yet in the urban areas, sexism in employment persists. Women are becoming concentrated in 'pink-collar ghettos' of low-level and relatively poorly paid clerical work, though many such niches of the labour market still constitute an improvement on the recent past (Tang and Parish, 2000: 226). In early 1996, *China Women's News* reported that 27 of 42 government organizations it surveyed admitted to violating government policy by limiting or refusing to hire female university graduates. The reasons offered by male supervisors included women's allegedly lower physical strength, the difficulty in sending them on business trips due to their household responsibilities and their need for maternity leave (*AP News Service*, 8 January 1996). Only a few women have begun to take up positions in their own right in urban, regional and national government. Of the 44 members of the State Council in 2000, only three were women.[9] Likewise, at the National People's Congress, only three of the top 49 leaders and committee chairs and vice-chairs of the National People's Congress were women.[10]

Violence against women is an even more troubling problem. In 2002, the official All-China Women's Federation reported that family violence occurs in 30 per cent of households (*Xinhua*, 27 April 2002). According to government figures, over a quarter of divorces in China in 1994 involved family violence. Two-thirds of the women who threw themselves into Shanghai's Huangpu River in 1995 were victims of domestic violence. China is now starting to develop shelters and hotlines for battered women (*Reuters News Service*, 11 March 1996). In the countryside, 250,000 women per year commit suicide, and another 2,000,000 attempt to do so. China is the only country in the world where more women than men end their own lives. Many are victims of the growing market in young women, some of whom are lured away by empty promises of employment or marriage to well-off men, and some of whom are actually forcibly abducted. The demand for young women is intense and growing, due to rising gender imbalances that run as high as over 125:100 in some provinces. Those imbalances are in turn the result of female infanticide or abortion of female foetuses (identified through ultrasound) caused by the dual pressures of unreformed patrilocal exogamy and the one-child policy. There is also an international market in Chinese women. By one estimate, 10,000 young women are sold into virtual slave labour or prostitution in South-East Asia, Japan and the USA each year (Fackler, 2002). The state – focused primarily on economic development, feeling ever more serious budgetary constraints and evincing a declining interest in socialist or even basic social values – lacks the capacity and perhaps also the will to deal with these problems in anything approaching their fullness.

URBAN AND RURAL

A third cleavage cutting through Chinese society is that between urban and rural people. In the early 1950s, the government classified people as either 'rural' or 'non-rural householders'. One important motivation was simply to distinguish who would be entitled to purchase grain through state distribution networks, and who would have to produce their own grain.[11] Gradually, this distinction took on larger, unintended proportions. In the 1950s, socialist institutions developed completely differently in the cities and the countryside. Peasants became members of co-ops and then communes, and as such their incomes were shares of collective income. If their co-op or team did poorly, so did they. Moreover, they had to provide for their own housing. Yet in the cities, the new state industries and urban governments offered workers in state firms lifetime guarantees not only of their wages but also housing, health care and education for their children. These structural inequalities created tremendous pressures for migration from the countryside. The countryside began to be emptied of its most skilled, assiduous and entrepreneurial workers. Cities that were already having trouble employing and feeding their residents were becoming even more crowded. Thus, in 1958, 'rural householders' were forbidden to move to cities.

When urban factories needed to expand their labour forces, they were permitted to contract with communes to send some of their members. The communes received a cash payment from the factory, and in turn paid their peasant-workers in the same work points as other commune members, often augmented by a little cash stipend. This often created significant inequalities within the plants, since the work points were worth much less than urban workers' wages. The peasant-workers of course received none of the benefits that the urban workers did. This perceived injustice was the source of much radical protest during the Cultural Revolution.

During the Maoist period, there were other economic and social inequalities between urban and rural areas. In most years, roughly 90 per cent of state investment went into the urban areas; even in 1962, in the wake of the disastrous effects of the Great Leap Forward, only 21 per cent of investment went to the countryside. Communes were expected to finance their own investment. Urban personal incomes were two to three times higher than rural ones. In terms of social status, urbanites continued to look down on the farmers as country bumpkins. In the run-up to the Cultural Revolution, Chairman Mao criticized the urban bias in the provision of government services, acerbically accusing the Ministry of Public Health of being in fact a 'Ministry of Urban Gentlemen's Health' (Schram, 1974: 232). The Maoist state waged campaigns to overcome urban bias by sending officials, students and intellectuals to the countryside for resettlement. Many were shocked by the gap in living standards that they encountered, and some actually gained a new respect for the peasants or at least stopped condescending to them quite so unkindly.

In the Dengist period, the basic structural gap between workers in urban state enterprises and rural residents remained in place through the 1980s, though at the end of the decade it began partly to erode. The workers retained their guarantees of employment, wages and benefits until the late 1980s, and often into the 1990s. As we have seen, however, by the mid-1990s most state industry workers' wages and benefits were, like those of workers in rural industries, tied to the economic well-being of their individual enterprises, rather than being guaranteed by the state. Many still continued to receive subsidized housing, health insurance and even education for their children; if their firms were not doing well, however, the quality of housing or schooling often declined, or health benefits shrivelled or went into arrears. Aside from state industry workers, an increasing number of 'non-rural householders' are, like rural people, living without any such benefits.[12] Meanwhile, the rural people too have to fend for themselves, now without even the meagre security once provided by the communes. With the decline of both the communes and the capacity of the state to regulate daily life, roughly 120 million rural people have been able to make their way to towns and cities. There they engage in trade or take up employment in the informal sector, in non-state enterprises, or as a substratum within state enterprises. In addition, an increasing number of 'rural householders' who stayed in the countryside – 34 per cent in 2000 – are no longer engaged in agriculture. Thus, the urban–rural divide no longer corresponds so perfectly as it did in the Mao period with a clear difference in terms and privileges of employment and social benefits.

With increasing migration of rural people to towns and cities, daily intercourse between them and urbanites has increased sharply. This has often provoked resentment. In some cases, the ill will has a material basis. Rural people often have jobs that threaten urbanites' employment. For example, migrants who were driving minibuses in the city have been beaten up and had their vehicles wrecked by Beijing bus drivers. Yet it is also true that rural migrants do many jobs that urbanites would not do themselves but are glad to have others do for them, such as maid service or nightsoil collection. Many urban people also believe, sometimes correctly, that rural migrants are partly responsible for rising crime and social decay. For example, the growing ranks of prostitutes are fuelled by migrants (*AP News Service*, 4 November 1995). In a bizarre example that would be humorous were it not so dangerous, manhole covers in many Chinese cities are being stolen by rural migrants, who sell them to rural factories for scrap metal. Two hundred Beijing residents were injured in 1994 when they fell down open manholes (*Jingji ribao*, 13 September 1995). Victimization, however, does not run just in one direction. Many rural migrants find themselves swindled or exploited by urban merchants, employers and landlords. Another dimension of the animosity between urbanites and rural migrants is simply social and cultural. Rural and urban people often appear strange and obnoxious to each other. For example, quite a few Beijingers stopped riding the subway, preferring not to be in close proximity to the many unkempt peasants who were taking refuge there; eventually the police started to expel these homeless migrants. Of course, not all contacts are negative. Many urbanites also quite appreciate the range of goods available in burgeoning farmers' markets.

Migration to cities has also posed a problem for China's urban governments. An area on the fringes of Beijing, known as 'Zhejiang Village' because it is peopled by migrant garment traders and workers from Zhejiang Province, became a headache for the Beijing government because of the serious traffic problems it caused, over-crowding due to rapid population growth fuelled by illegal births, and terrible public health and sanitation conditions. The markets and businesses there were also very difficult for local commercial and tax authorities to regulate (Reuters News Service, 6 November 1995). In 1995, the Beijing city government passed extensive new regulations to stop migrants from 'straining resources and threatening social stability'. It required all rural migrants to carry temporary residence cards issued by the Public Security Bureau, and landlords to take out licences to rent space to migrants. Employers are also expected to assure migrants' compliance with popula-tion control policies (*China News Digest*, 13 April 1995). The situation is so ser-ious that some very radical and disturbing steps have been contemplated and even implemented. The threat of rampant, unregulated population growth among migrants caused the government to consider developing birth control vaccines to use on them. In the Zhuhai Special Economic Zone near Hong Kong, the local government erected a 24-mile, 9-foot-high fence to keep out poverty-stricken migrants.

The economic gap between rural and urban areas, which shrunk a bit in the early 1980s as agriculture took off, has worsened dramatically starting in the mid-1980s (see Figure 5.1). The urban areas are attracting the lion's share of new investment, as we shall see in Chapter 6. With such inequality rising precisely at a time when the capacity of the state to regulate migration is on the decline, it is no wonder that rural people are flocking to cities in ever greater numbers. The problems cities have coping with them, and the potential for conflict between city and country folk, are growing commensurately.

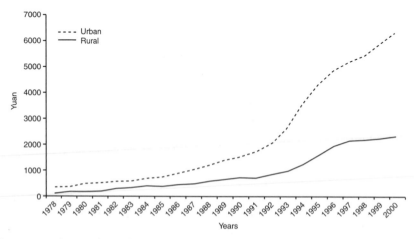

Figure 5.1 Urban and Rural Per Capita Annual Income, 1978–2000

Source: China Statistical Yearbook, 2001, Table 10-3.

NATIONALITY

China is, by and large, a nationally homogeneous country. In 2000, Han people made up 91.6 per cent of the population. Government statistics list 56 minority nationalities, the largest of which are Zhuang, Man and Moslems. Tibetans may be China's most famous minority, but they rank ninth in population. The vast majority of China's national minorities live in border provinces: Mongols to the north and north-east, adjacent to Mongolia, Tibetans to the south-west and a host of others along China's borders with South-East Asia. Because of the minority peoples' concentration along the country's borders, their importance in national politics is greater than their small size would otherwise suggest. Yet for this same reason, only a very small proportion of Han Chinese have significant contact with them. In short, the minority question looms much larger in Chinese politics than in Chinese society as a whole.

Historically, minority nationalities have lived in relative peace in China for millennia. Examples of violent confrontation and deep conflict between them and the Han are rare. Most Chinese governments have not practised systematic discrimination against national minorities. In general, the greatest threat to minorities has been assimilation. Even the massive invasion of Manchus, which brought down the Ming Dynasty and established the Qing Dynasty in 1644, is an exception that proves the rule. The new Manchu emperors did not try to impose an alien culture on China. They were forced to rely on many Han to run the state, and they left Han economic élites in place as well. Gradually, it was the Manchu rulers who were assimilated by the Han subjects. When the Qing collapsed in the 1911 Revolution, there was, to be sure, a great deal of nationalistic, anti-Manchu politics. Yet there was little in the way of pogroms or 'ethnic cleansing' by Han against ordinary Manchus. Chinese revolutionaries wished to destroy the Manchu (Qing) state, but by and large they did not wish to eradicate or take revenge against the Manchu people.

From its inception, the People's Republic, with Mao's urging, continued this long tradition of toleration. Land reform and class struggle were moderated or shelved, and pre-existing native élites were co-opted into the new local governments. Chinese language was not actively promoted until the Great Leap Forward. As the state became more serious about promoting co-ops and began to label as 'rightists' those seeking to preserve autonomy for nationality areas, social and political tension rose, and there were armed clashes in Tibet and Xinjiang. After some initial relaxation in the first part of the 1960s, the Cultural Revolution saw the return to ideologically driven efforts to wipe out 'feudal' remnants and to assimilate national minorities more fully. Those offensives petered out with the end of the radical mass movements, and the top leadership soon returned to a more accommodating policy, in part out of its concern that border areas not be destabilized. More minority élites started appearing at the top levels of the state. Today education includes instruction in native languages as well as Chinese, though many minority students actually prefer studying Chinese since it advances their economic prospects. National minorities are also exempted from the strict population control policies, out of concern that they need to grow. Perhaps the greatest threat to minority cultures and societies comes from modernization itself, as the rise of commerce, travel and communications threatens to swamp traditional ways of life. That, of course, is not specific to China.

Tibet is a different kind of case. It was an independent kingdom thirteen centuries ago. After the Mongol conquest, China exercised suzerainty, which meant a great deal of local autonomy alongside dependence in external affairs. Tibet declared independence when the Qing Dynasty fell in 1911. Chinese troops reoccupied it in 1950. Until 1959, the People's Republic treated Tibet with lenience similar to its approach to other minorities' areas and people. The hardline policies of the Great Leap, however, provoked uprisings that elicited a Chinese military crackdown. The Dalai Lama, Tibet's traditional spiritual and political leader, fled to India, establishing a government in exile. The situation has remained tense ever since. On the one side, the Dalai Lama has put a great deal of energy into cultivating an international following that includes many Western movie stars, writers and celebrities, while his relations with Beijing have sometimes waxed but mostly waned. On the other, the Chinese state has remained adamant in resisting any moves toward independence or significant autonomy. It has, therefore, made sure that Tibet is ruled by Han Chinese. Beijing permits religious practice, but it is tough on priests and monks who maintain political and religious loyalty – which in the traditional Tibetan view are inseparable – to the Dalai Lama. It has put down all political protests, going so far as to declare martial law in March 1989. At the time, the Governor of Tibet was Hu Jintao, who become China's top leader in 2002. Tibet, then, afforded Hu the opportunity to establish his bona fides as a tough leader. In 1995, as we have seen, Beijing even arrested the boy selected by the Dalai Lama's loyalists as the next Panchen Lama (the second most powerful Tibetan leader), and anointed its own successor. Beijing has also promoted economic modernization, including the influx of Han businesspeople and workers and the development of transport links to the rest of the country. Tibetan exiles believe, no doubt correctly, that such modernization is a greater threat to Tibetan culture, and to the power of Tibetans in the regional government and economy, even than the Red Guard attacks of the Cultural Revolution. The state has not, of course, promoted modernization only to gain political or cultural domination. Tibet is rich in minerals and ores, which the eastern parts of the country and the central government would like to exploit.

Tensions also run high in Xinjiang, in China's far north-west. In 1990, at the height of the post-1989 crackdown, the state restricted mosque construction and announced that national minorities would henceforth have to carry ID cards. The Islamic Party of East Turkestan, based across the border but operating on the Chinese side, called for a jihad – an armed uprising. China's armed forces were mobilized, and over twenty Uighur protesters were killed. Subsequent years have seen sporadic violence from both sides, including hundreds of executions and thousands of arrests. Independence advocates in return have set off bombs in Beijing. In the wake of the September 11 2001 attacks by al Qaeda, China declared that the Uighur independence activists were 'terrorists', a position they even persuaded the USA to endorse in late 2002.

The overt tensions in Tibet and Xinjiang have to do with the fact that there are active movements seeking political independence in both regions. Beijing sees both as matters of national sovereignty, an issue on which there can be no compromise. By contrast, relations between the Han majority and minority nationalities in other parts of China are far less troubled, and state policy far more accommodating.

CONCLUSION

Chinese society has undergone profound structural change twice since 1949. In the Maoist period, relations between classes and genders were radically equalized, while urbanites and farmers, and national minorities on the one hand and Han people and the state on the other, were brought into much more intimate contact, resulting in both harmony and serious conflict. The Dengist period ushered in the rise of new classes and yawning inequalities between them. Maoist policies that had helped women were abolished, resulting in massive and literally murderous disparities in population dynamics, as well as serious inequalities in education, the arena that development economists identify as crucial for women's overall welfare. Yet the rise of markets has also created new opportunities for women to earn income for themselves and, at least in the cities, leverage that into more equal relations with their husbands. The urban–rural gap has widened significantly, and relations between Han and national minorities have generated deadly flashpoints. China is now straining under these multiple new cleavages. How they have affected China's politics is the subject of Chapter 7. First, however, we must look at political economy, which shapes both the society we have analysed and the politics we will study.

CHAPTER 6

Political Economy

China's political economy, in the Maoist period and even more so in the Dengist era, forms a complex structure involving political leaders, planners, enterprises, markets and resources. To analyse it, we must have some conceptual tools to organize thinking and discussion. One is economic ownership and organization. Are enterprises owned by the state (and if so, by which level thereof)? Or are they owned collectively by the people who live and work in them? What role is there for private ownership? For foreign ownership? Do workers receive a wage or a share of the profits (or both)? What are the responsibilities of collectively owned firms to the wider state in terms of taxes, planning and regulation? How do firms with different forms of ownership relate to each other?

Second is planning. There are two main issues here. First, is it done on a centralized scale, taking the whole country as a unit, or in a more decentralized way, focusing on regional subunits? Centralized planning can promote greater evenness of development nationally, but may involve more inefficiencies and irrationalities. Yet insofar as decentralization requires or encourages each regional subunit to produce more of its own needs whether or not its conditions are suited to doing so, other inefficiencies and irrationalities can come into play. There are also major implications for politics in the question of centralization and decentralization. Centralized planning keeps power in Beijing, whereas decentralization potentially creates rivals to the central leadership as well as rivalries among localities. The second issue related to planning has to do with its goals and motivations. To what extent is planning done with political goals in mind, such as equality, social welfare, national defence or socialist ideology? And to what extent is it informed by more purely economic goals, and in recognition of economic constraints?

The third conceptual tool for analysing political economy is the relationship of planning and markets. Here again there are two distinct though related issues: the extent of planning vs. markets, and the ways in which planning does or does not take market forces and market rationality into account. Does planning try to encompass all economic activity? If so, how does it deal with the sheer volume and complexity of the task? How does it cope with hidden but inescapable market-like forces? For example, what happens when planned production does not serve the needs of those for whom the production is intended? If goods are supplied through the plan at little cost, how can the tendency to waste those goods be combated? Yet if some markets are permitted to exist, how can planning coexist with and take account of them? How are the political consequences of markets, including the potential rise of inequalities and a bourgeoisie, to be dealt with?

Fourth is the question of economic priorities. What decisions are made about the balance of industry and agriculture? Of heavy and light industry? These sectors are interdependent, after all, supplying inputs, capital and markets for each other.

Some level of balance must be maintained. Yet they also compete for scarce resources. Another balance is that between production and consumption. How much of what the country produces should be set aside to invest in development? If too little is set aside, the economy will stagnate in the medium or long run. Yet if too much is set aside, public discontent may grow; moreover, returning to the issue of market-like forces, capital may be wasted if the economy is too flush with it.

Fifth is the issue of enterprise management. Should a socialist enterprise concentrate on production and efficiency, or on making the workplace more humane and democratic? How authoritarian should it be? If enterprises are run more democratically, which is surely one goal of socialism, what would be the effect on fulfilment of state plans or on the enterprise's own prosperity, which is another socialist objective?

A sixth question is domestic and international self-reliance. Socialist economies have often pursued economic nationalism. Sometimes they have done so as a matter of politics, to make up for the effects of imperialism. They also have done so to reduce the leverage of capitalist countries to shape their development or extract resources through trade and investment. Economic nationalism envisions a country with a relatively comprehensive economy able to provide for its needs. Finally, economic nationalism may be conceived as a transitional step that helps to shelter domestic enterprises until they can stand on their own feet. Yet this objective has costs. Tariff barriers or trade controls can put inexpensive imports beyond reach. They can also protect domestic industries from the competition that induces improvement, and restrict their access to advanced technology that could make them more productive.

Seventh, there is the question of performance. How much, and in what ways, did Maoist state socialism and Dengist structural reform develop the Chinese economy?

To organize our analysis of the complexities of China's state socialist economy we take up these questions one at a time, first for the Maoist and then the Dengist periods. For each era we will gradually weave them together into an increasingly comprehensive picture.

THE MAOIST PERIOD

Ownership and organization

As we saw in Chapter 2, the state tolerated private ownership so long as it was concerned about restoring the economy and maintaining political control during the first few years of transition to state socialism. By 1956, however, private ownership of the means of production was abolished in both the cities and the countryside. (People still owned their personal effects, savings accounts and, in the rural areas, their homes.) Farms, factories and shops came under two forms of socialist ownership and organization. In the countryside, 'collective' ownership by the local farmers themselves predominated, whereas, in the cities, 'state' ownership prevailed. The coexistence of these two very different forms of socialist organization did create some problems, as we have seen. Widely disparate growth rates of industry and agriculture during the First Five Year Plan – the former growing about seven times faster – raised concerns about the sustainability of rapid industrial growth and the burgeoning inequality between town and country. In the Great Leap Forward and then again in the Dazhai campaign (discussed below), the state made concerted but ultimately failed efforts to bring agriculture under more direct political control.

Agriculture and rural industry

Mutual aid teams and agricultural producers' co-ops were owned by the farmers who comprised them, not by the state or local governments. While the co-ops had their responsibilities to the state (such as tax remissions and quotas for grain sales), their assets, including land, belonged to them, and could not be seized or reallocated by state fiat. The lower-stage co-ops managed their own internal affairs. Management decisions were made through various combinations of local leadership and popular participation. The lower-stage co-ops distributed their income based on both share ownership and labour contribution, using proportions and formulae they determined themselves. The higher-stage co-ops abolished share ownership, but otherwise used the same distributive principles and processes as their predecessors.

During the Great Leap Forward, co-ops became subsumed under the huge new people's communes, which combined the political functions previously discharged by township governments and the economic ones handled by co-ops. The entire concept of ownership was effectively abolished. Land, tools, machinery and other assets were merged, and decisions about their use were made, often haphazardly, by commune leaders. Even some private property was contributed to or appropriated by the communes; for example, iron pots and pans were melted down to make steel. The very concept of personal income also atrophied, as farmers received food without charge in collective dining halls in lieu of individual compensation, at least until the food ran out.

Once the institutional and policy readjustments after the Great Leap were complete, collective agriculture in China settled down to a fairly standard pattern for the next fifteen years. Within the three-tiered commune, the lowest level, called the production team, was a small, face-to-face group averaging between 20 and 40 households – roughly 100 to 200 people, around the size of a former lower-stage co-op. It resumed ownership of the land and most basic productive resources; if the brigade, commune or higher levels of government wanted the team's property (e.g., to build a canal, road or railway), they had to purchase it for a negotiated price. The team was the unit of income sharing among team members; i.e., each farmer's income was a share of the net distributed income of the team.[1] The size of shares was determined, often in quite a participatory way, according to work points earned for labour done in a day or on a job. In addition, teams, brigades and communes also provided public goods, such as guaranteed minima of food and housing, education and health care. Major economic decisions – about cropping and investment – were heavily circumscribed by state plans administered by brigade and commune authorities.

The brigades and communes did not engage in farming. In addition to their political and social functions (such as running schools and clinics), they ran shops, built and maintained infrastructure such as roads and waterworks, and ran small factories. The profits of these enterprises were used to help fund the brigade's or commune's operations. The farmers who worked in these 'collective' firms were paid work points from their teams, which in turn received money from the brigade or commune to fund those work points.

Teams chose their own leadership, who were paid in work points like their fellow villagers. That had the effect of linking team leaders' livelihoods to the team economy, which imparted something of a localist orientation to the team leadership. By contrast, at the brigade and commune level the key officials were paid by the state (and therefore were more oriented to its interests than to those of the village). The key institution at the brigade and commune was the Communist Party. Its local committees made sure that local governments adhered to assigned responsibilities, while also carrying out mobilization campaigns that included everything from eradicating schistosomiasis and counter-revolutionaries to extolling the virtues of Mao's thought.

Urban industry and commerce

Unlike co-ops, teams, brigades and communes, which maintained *de jure* and even some de facto separation from the state, industrial enterprises were owned and controlled by various levels of government. Those run by the central ministries or their provincial government bureaux, and many run by county-level bureaux, were considered 'state-owned'. They were subject to strict, vertically organized state plans, their investment capital came from the central, provincial or county agencies, and their profits belonged to those bureaux, which absorbed their losses as well. Managers were also appointed by their parent bureau. Alongside them were industrial and commercial enterprises owned and operated by local governments rather than centrally oriented ministries. They were often known as 'collective' firms, though in fact those who worked in them had no ownership rights or significant involvement in running them (as farmers did in their collectives). Their workers, like those in 'state-owned' firms, simply received a wage. Urban 'collective' firms were often less subject to central planning and regulation, though. Their products often helped fill gaps left by state planning. Their after-tax profits went to the local governments that owned them, and those governments were also responsible for covering their losses.

Planning

In the Maoist period, planning in the state sector of the Chinese economy varied over two analytical dimensions. Structurally, it was sometimes highly centralized, emphasizing national level coordination and locating economic authority in Beijing. At other times, it was more decentralized, passing authority downward to regional levels of government or to enterprises. The underlying rationale of planning also changed. At some moments, political considerations such as regional balance or preferred sectoral priorities held sway, while at other times economic considerations such as profitability, efficiency or comparative advantage did. Figure 6.1 sums up the shifts.

Central planning of the Chinese economy proceeded only on a year-by-year basis through mid-1955, when the First Five Year Plan was enunciated retroactively to 1953 – an odd way to begin 'planning', certainly, but one that suggested the leadership's recognition of the need to start off incrementally and pragmatically. The First Five Year Plan emphasized centralized planning using a political rationale. Following the Soviet model, the State Planning and Economic Commissions formulated mandatory targets and norms concerning industrial output, employment, wages, other production costs, labour productivity, profit, production techniques, innovation of product lines and other indicators. They were passed down level by level until they reached the enterprise, which had to abide by them.

At the heart of this kind of industrial planning were several political visions and logics. The visions included the desire to emulate the USSR, and the belief among planners and political leaders in the theory that economic development proceeds most rapidly and securely from a foundation of basic, modern industries. Thus, 90 per cent of capital investment was to be devoted to heavy industry. Leaders and planners also envisioned a China with a high level of economic balance among regions, for several reasons. As socialists, they were committed to some level of economic equity, in this case among people living in different parts of the country. As statespersons, they wished to create industrial bases beyond the reach of hostile foreign powers. After all, Japan had occupied China's Manchurian and Shanghai industrial bases in the 1930s and 1940s, and the Korean War threatened Manchuria once again. Thus, the First Five Year Plan called for locating much new industry inland, away from the more prosperous, industrially developed and militarily vulnerable coast and north-east.

Behind these visions lay several political logics favouring centralization. China had been torn apart territorially starting a century earlier with the loss of the Opium War, and continuing with concessions to multiple imperialists, battles

	Centralized	Regionally decentralized	Decentralized to enterprises
Political logic	First Five Year Plan	Second Five Year Plan Great Leap Forward Cultural Revolution decade	
Economic logic	Post-Leap recovery		Dengist structural reforms

Figure 6.1 Levels and logics of economic planning

among warlords, the Japanese occupation and several phases of civil war. The new government was still consolidating its control over some provinces as late as 1951. It faced a hostile and interventionist West, and, as we saw in Chapter 2, concerns about the Soviet Union's ambitions in China. Moreover, the new state had inherent centralizing tendencies, which can be understood as complementary functions of its growing bureaucracy and its historic Leninist organization.

In the countryside, by contrast, co-ops were given quotas for tax remissions and sales to the state, and were also required to sell some of their above-quota output to the state, albeit at bonus prices. Yet they were also allowed considerable latitude to plan their own production once they had fulfilled those responsibilities. Still, at this time of limited market development and no rural industrialization to speak of, most co-ops did not have many options about what to produce or how to produce it.

The First Five Year Plan's régime of centralized industrial planning and adminis-tration resulted in many of the problems characteristic of centralized planning throughout the socialist world. If anything, the problems in China were somewhat more daunting than, for example, Eastern Europe, because of China's huge size and wide range of variation in natural and developmental conditions. Economic coordination on a national level was hampered by China's poorly developed trans-port system. Technical norms set in Beijing planning offices proved inappropriate to many factories. Planners sometimes allocated excessive or insufficient resources. Production targets were sometimes set irrationally, producing surpluses of some items that were not needed, in weak demand or unsuitable to their planned purposes, while leaving shortages of needed ones.

China's Second Five Year Plan, enunciated in November 1957, was intended to deal with some of these problems on both the industrial and agricultural sides. It occasioned a shift in China's economic strategy toward decentralization, though still based mainly around a political rationale. The number of mandatory targets was reduced from twelve to four: output, employment, wages and profit. Middle-level planners, in particular at the provincial levels, were given greater leeway over technical aspects of production, diversification of production lines, cost reduction and other ways of improving productivity. Coordination was to emphasize the hori-zontal principle of integration with the needs of the province more than the vertical principle of functional integration with the needs of the central ministry. Many firms producing light industrial products, textiles and agricultural machinery were put under the complete control of provincial and local authorities, leaving the centre with only 'basic' sectors such as mining, iron and steel, transportation and defence industries. The primacy of political over economic planning principles remained, as in the First Five Year Plan. Their actual content, however, was to shift somewhat, for example to a slightly greater emphasis on agriculture and light industry.

The Great Leap Forward quickly expanded on the directions charted by the 1958 decentralization. More emphasis was placed on provinces as regional units of industrial planning and economic integration. In the countryside, communes were placed under more direct political control, in the form of centrally sponsored cam-paigns for close planting and the use of political and administrative power to extract great quantities of foodgrain despite rapidly plummeting output (resulting in widespread starvation). The initial wild enthusiasm of the Leap, and the deep crisis that followed it, crippled the planning mechanism for both agriculture and industry, though. The Second Five Year Plan was replaced by annual and even quarterly plans that reflected efforts to cope and survive rather than to project order and political will on the economy.

Planning began to function again in 1961. Planners and politicians abandoned their discredited efforts to control China's farms. Industrial planning became more centralized but, now, began to function with more of an economic rationale. During the next several years, advocates of central planning began to press for a greater role for vertical (functional) rather than horizontal (territorial) coordination. They coined the slogan, 'the whole country is a chessboard', to express the view that the Chinese economy was one integrated entity in which changes in any one part affected all the other parts. In the wake of the dislocations of the Great Leap, whose emphasis on local and regional autarky had heightened regional inequalities and made manifest the need for central control and resource allocation, their arguments found adherents. In 1963, 'trusts' – in effect, large public corporations organized centrally (and functionally) in various industrial sectors – began to appear. As an example of the new use of economic criteria for planning, the trusts were given authority to allocate investment capital wherever it was most productive. The trusts also resonated to growing concerns about improving technical specialization and comparative advantage. Naturally, the trusts favoured the more technologically advanced firms, which generally were located in the wealthier areas. Thus, unlike the politically driven centralization of the First Five Year Plan, this form of central planning based more fully than before on an economic rationale was prone to exacerbating regional inequalities. In this sense it resembled the more decentralized, politically motivated mode of planning that had preceded it during the Great Leap Forward.

Because of both the inequalities they involved and the bureaucratic centralization they embodied, the trusts came to be criticized bitterly during the Cultural Revolution. Planning of any sort was hampered from above by Red Guard attacks on planning officials, and from below by the breakdown of production in the factories. During the early, most radical years of 1967–69, planning was rendered nearly impossible when many factories stopped regular production while their workers preoccupied themselves with the political struggles of the movement in their factories and cities. In the countryside there were renewed efforts to shape production politically. Villages were urged to 'learn from Dazhai', a poor village that had prospered thanks to extraordinary hard work and vigorous local leadership in production but mainly on farmland and infrastructure development. Dazhai also embodied values of local self-reliance, which attenuated somewhat the extent of planned exchanges between town and countryside.

The Dazhai campaign continued inconclusively through the early 1970s. In the cities, industrial planning remained obstructed by poor labour discipline and ongoing political campaigns. To the extent that planning took place, decentralization and politicization predominated. The emergence of revolutionary committees gave strong impetus to horizontal coordination, while the disruptions of the

Cultural Revolution and its attacks on the state weakened capacities for vertical control. Thus, decentralization was pushed further than ever before, with even very large firms in key sectors – such as the huge Anshan Steel Complex, then China's largest – turned over to provincial administration. Profits and efficiency were eschewed vociferously as appropriate goals of planning. One slogan alleged to have been put forward by the left leadership of the time was: 'Better a socialist train running late than a capitalist train running on time.' Planners emphasized raising output without particular regard for costs, markets or quality control, and factory managers struggled to meet even this simple objective.

Markets

Starting in its early years, the People's Republic moved incrementally but systematically to restrict markets and control prices. By issuing new currency and applying strict price controls, it rapidly brought one of the worst inflations in history under control. This was necessary to make government possible at all, but it also earned the new state a good deal of public adulation. As the state gradually socialized China's factories and wholesale commercial enterprises, and began to build new ones, it began to substitute planned allocation for market exchange. Retail markets too gradually came under price regulation, a process that was completed with the 1956 co-operativization of small urban enterprises. As we have seen, actual planning was driven by explicit political goals, which left little room for planners to take underlying market realities into account.

As we saw in Chapter 2, markets made a brief return to the Chinese countryside in the wake of the Great Leap Forward, as a response to the economic disasters that had taken place. Yet they did not put in even a brief appearance in the urban economy until the dawn of the Dengist period. Moreover, planning did not attempt to take underlying market forces into account, or to mimic market mechanisms. For example, one goal of the trusts was to improve technical efficiency and allocative rationality. The way they were to achieve these goals, however, was not through market-like mechanisms such as better cost accounting or tighter budgets. Instead, the trusts embodied an organizational approach, in which it was thought that gains would occur if decisions were made by managers and ministry executives rather than planning bureaucrats.

Economic priorities

Industry and agriculture

The Maoist state placed its priority on industry over agriculture. As we have seen, this was partly a matter of its political vision, in which industry was the key to socialist economic development and the guarantor of national security. The priority on industry was also a function of the way the state structured China's state socialist political economy. Agriculture was organized collectively, with productive resources owned and operated by co-ops and communes, as we shall discuss next.

The state expected these grass-roots units to provide the means for their own development. Industry, by contrast, was owned by the central, provincial, prefecture and county governments, and so it had nowhere else to turn for its developmental needs.

Accordingly, state investment in agriculture was very low in the Maoist period, averaging just 12 per cent of total investment from 1953–78 (compared with 54 per cent for industry). During the First Five Year Plan, it was under 8 per cent. The imbalances between agriculture and industry during the First Five Year Plan (see Chapter 2) and the disasters of the Great Leap Forward led to a significant readjustment. In post-Leap recovery (1963–65), agriculture took nearly 19 per cent of total investment, more than double the level during the mid-1950s. Yet it remained slighted in national priorities. Ironically, as Mao himself predicted (Mao, 1977: 284–307), this may have damaged industry and the overall national economy as much as it hurt agriculture. One scholar has argued that since the industry–agriculture imbalance of investment was greater than the imbalance in their growth rates, Chinese state investment policy has been irrational: i.e., 'the rate of growth of national income would have been higher if a larger share of investment resources had been allocated to agriculture' (Lardy, 1983: 129). Students of economic development more generally will recognize this as an instance of the common phenomenon of 'urban bias' (Lipton, 1976).

The capacity of the rural areas to provide their own investment was also undercut by state pricing policies. In particular, agricultural outputs were priced low, and industrial outputs high – the 'scissors' pattern familiar to students of Soviet economic history.[2] So long as agriculture used few industrial outputs and peasants bought little in the way of industrially produced consumer goods – which was the case through the 1950s and early 1960s – scissors pricing was of limited significance. Of course, peasants were probably receiving less than what the free market price would have been for their marketable surplus. Yet they were also taxed at low and declining rates and offered credit on favourable terms. From about the mid-1960s on, though, as agriculture began to use larger doses of industrial inputs such as chemical fertilizer, cement and farm machinery, it began to suffer more from scissors pricing (though to some extent this was offset by agriculture's self-provision of some of these inputs through its own rural collective industries). The problem of rising prices for industrial inputs into agriculture reached explosive proportions in the Dengist period, as we shall see in Chapter 7.

Heavy and light industry

Within state industry, investment in the Maoist period overwhelmingly favoured heavy industry, by a factor of nearly ten to one. As we have seen, this reflected a policy decision made in the early and mid-1950s. It is reflected in the sharply declining ratio of light to heavy industrial output through the 1950s (Figure 6.2). Before the First Five Year Plan was even complete, Mao attempted to scale back the state's emphasis on heavy industry. In his famous speech 'On the Ten Major Relationships', in which he began to express his worries about China's burgeoning bureaucracy and urban bias, he called, among other things, for more emphasis on

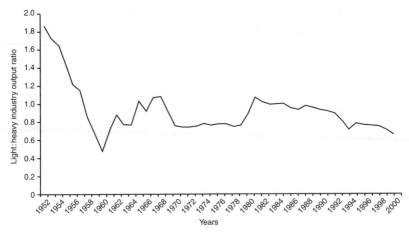

Figure 6.2 Ratio of Light to Heavy Industry Gross Output Value, 1952–2000

Source: China Statistical Yearbook, various years.

light industry (Mao, 1977: 284–307). His speech proved so controversial that it could not be published for many years. One reason for the controversy, and for Mao's ultimate failure to reverse the priority on heavy industry (see Figure 6.2), is that, once the decision to prioritize heavy industry had been made, it became self-perpetuating politically. Representatives of the heavy industrial ministries had become the most powerful voices in the Party leadership and the planning organs that were making the key decisions about investment. Finally, as with agriculture, the priority on heavy over light industry was partly an effect of institutional arrangements. The state was the only source of heavy industrial investment and production, so naturally it emphasized this sector in its policies. By contrast, much light industry tended to be owned by local governments and, after the Great Leap, rural collectives, and the state was content to leave responsibility for it to them.

Figure 6.2 demonstrates two other significant phenomena of the Maoist period. First, heavy industry suffered more than light industry during the Cultural Revolution. It was, after all, dependent on the smooth operation of the central planning bureaucracy. By contrast, light industrial production tended to be subject to local administration by county, city and even commune governments. It may also have been the case that workers in heavy industrial enterprises participated more in Cultural Revolution politics. Second, heavy industry recovered strongly relative to light industry during the 1970s, helped by the resuscitation of China's planning institutions and greater political stability nationwide.

Accumulation and consumption

Finally, there is the question of accumulation vs. consumption: how much should be set aside for investment in the future, and how much for spending here and now? The People's Republic inherited an economy whose growth had been seriously hampered by very low rates of capital investment, due to low rates of growth and production, wartime destruction and capital flight.[3] Ironically, therefore, it was left to the People's Republic – as to other socialist states in poor, late industrializing countries – to depress consumption in order to extract a large surplus from the Chinese people with which to finance investment.

By 1957 it had done so: accumulation was up to a quarter of gross domestic product (see Figure 6.3). Some of this was relatively painless to most people. For example, the land reform eliminated a class that had been consuming around one-quarter of national income, and the expropriation of the small Chinese bourgeoisie helped too. These were one-time gains, however, and soon the Chinese people would begin to feel the effects of the need to invest in industrialization. During the Great Leap, investment surged to the astronomical figure of 43.8 per cent of national income in 1959 and 39.6 per cent in 1960, which contributed to the massive declines in consumption – in human terms, to the spread of hunger and even starvation in many places. To make up for this, accumulation declined to only 10.4 per cent in 1962. During 1967–69, the most radical years of the Cultural Revolution, it averaged 21.9 per cent, as the planning bureaucracy, which was a major mechanism for extracting a surplus for accumulation, fell into chaos. Through the 1970s it rose again to about one-third of GDP.

The reasons for Maoist China's very high rate of accumulation are not hard to find. To some extent they were common to state socialist economies elsewhere. These economies tightly regulated consumption through strict control of income, production and prices, but they were less good at regulating investment. Capital goods allocated through central plans were not charged as costs to enterprises, so factory managers had no incentive to limit their requests for capital. On the contrary, managers had every reason make requests greatly in excess of their needs. They could never be sure how much they would be allocated. They could easily store any excess or, still better, cannibalize it for spare parts or use it to trade sub rosa for other scarce goods that they did not receive in sufficient quantities through

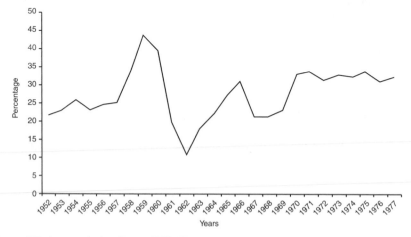

Figure 6.3 Accumulation Rate, 1952–77

Source: China Statistical Yearbook, various years.

the plan. Visitors to China in the late 1970s saw factories awash in lathes, many going unused.

These accumulative tendencies inherent in state socialism were exacerbated by specific features of the Maoist strategy of economic development. In general, Maoism eschewed high levels of consumption (though it was not as ascetic as its opponents frequently charged, emphasizing rather the fulfilment of basic needs). The emphasis on collective rather than individual consumption, intended partly to foster community solidarity, also had the effect of reducing the costs of popular consumption. Finally, the generally low levels and poor quality of consumer goods production further discouraged consumption.

Enterprise management

Agriculture and rural industry

China's farm collectives operated with a combination of leadership by village cadres and state officials on the one hand and popular participation on the other. Many team leaders were not Party members, and both they and even many brigade officials, including Communists, frequently acted to protect their villages from state interventions that they deemed harmful. Team leaders were often elected democratically, and it was not uncommon for villagers to ignore the wishes of state officials in making their choices. Decisions about the management of the production team and the public life of the village were often taken very democratically. Farmers generally showed little temerity in talking with, making suggestions to and even criticizing team and brigade officials, as we shall explore further in Chapter 7. These participatory habits, along with grass-roots leaders' capacity to protect their localities, were in many ways products of the way the Communist Party had led the revolution and organized post-revolutionary rural institutions. Over time, however, that same Party gradually restricted the scope of local politics and the latitude available to local leaders, even while continuing to encourage and often even demand popular participation. Farmers were left to debate questions such as minuscule differences in the size of their village reserve fund, whether their neighbour should receive 9 or 9.5 work points per day or how (but not whether) they should 'learn from Dazhai'. The contradiction between farmers' participatory inclinations (fuelled by their revolutionary experience) and the state's promotion thereof on the one hand, and the straitjacket in which it placed that participation by the 1970s on the other, fuelled increasing political disillusionment in the villages, and helped pave the way for the collapse of collective farming (Blecher, 1991).

In urban industry, Maoist China experimented with participatory management, but was never able to institutionalize it into an ongoing system of workplace democracy. In the early 1950s, the East China or Shanghai system involved a wide range of practices under which factory managers were made responsible to management committees of workers, technicians and even factory owners. This system served a variety of purposes in specific instances, sometimes simultaneously. It could be used to win over or harness the cooperation of factory owners and technicians. It could encourage and institutionalize worker participation and

173

mobilization. It drew in the trade unions and assigned an important role to the Party committee of the enterprise.

In 1953, the East China system began to be overshadowed by 'one-man management', a form of industrial management inspired, as so much else in early 1950s China, by the Soviet Union. Premised on the primacy of scientific management principles and the need to integrate the internal operations of each enterprise with the larger directions of the economy – including the new central planning mechanisms such as central targets and uniform technical and labour norms – one-man management vested authority almost completely in the hands of factory directors. Vertical lines of authority were drawn within enterprises, with each sub-manager having complete authority over those below while also being fully responsible for all facets of work to those above. In this sense it replicated the patterns of bureaucratic and hierarchical authority used in the central planning apparatus of the day.

One-man management ran into several difficulties. It grated against the participatory and mobilizational sensibilities of many revolutionaries in the Party, including especially the proponents of the East China system. It required large reservoirs of scientific, managerial and technical expertise and data that China lacked. It passed significant authority into the hands of Soviet advisers. These problems led many to oppose the system and to propose around 1956 that one-man management be supplemented by closer Party authority. The effect of this change was not to increase workplace democracy or to challenge the principles of technocratic, scientific management; rather, it put the Party in overall charge of the factories. The Party used its authority to ensure compliance with national plans and to shore up its own political position vis-à-vis its rivals in the industrial professions and the state bureaucracy.

During the Great Leap, a plethora of criticism surfaced about bureaucratism, excessive rules and regulations, irrationalities resulting from one-man management (both with and without Party supervision), mind-numbing division of labour and élitism of factory officials. The Party called for 'two participations, one reform and triple combination', which meant: (1) participation of all cadres in productive labour and worker participation in management; (2) reform of old workplace rules and structures; and (3) management by teams of workers, experts and cadres.

Managers' participation in production was an interesting counterpoint to worker participation in management. By taking part in labour on the shop floor, managers were to gain a different perspective on factory affairs, come to understand the workers' point of view and interests and therefore be better able to take them into account in running the factory. This was a form of political solicitation, in which the managers would take the initiative to discover and experience the workers' situation. As such it contrasts with worker participation in management, also urged at this time, under which the workers were called on express their views to managers through meetings of committees that included worker representatives.[4]

Reform of work rules meant reorganization of factories into small, collaborative workshop-sized teams comprising managers, technicians and workers. They were given operational latitude to tackle and structure tasks collectively. The combination of managerial, technical, practical and political perspectives from each respective group in the teams would, it was hoped, unleash the initiative and creativity of all and arrive at the most efficient, dynamic and democratic outcomes.

With the decline in industrial production in 1961 and 1962, these management policies were called into question. The reassertion of central planning exerted definite pressure to change the 'two participations, one reform and triple combination'. Yet no clear alternative could be found or agreed upon by the Party. A return to one-man management was even more difficult, since the detailed data, strong managerial authority, technical resources and Soviet advice that it required were now more lacking than ever. Extensive debates were carried on in these years about the proper role of worker participation in management, the relationship of political to technical values, calculus and authority – known as the problem of 'red vs. expert' – and the organization and division of labour in the workplace.

The Cultural Revolution saw these debates turn into, and in turn become inundated by, a radical mass movement whose scope included but transcended the issue of enterprise management. For a time in many factories there was little or no management in which to participate, as production slowed to a trickle or ceased altogether. There were spontaneous attempts to institutionalize new forms of management based on some of the principles enunciated and tried during the Great Leap. These were integrated into broader and more radical efforts to politicize workplaces more generally – for example, over issues such as political study, ideological campaigns and recruitment and training of workers to be managers and technicians.

These experiments in broad democracy in workplace political communities conflicted with counter-trends toward rationalization of authority and management in the hands of managers and technicians under the supervision of the revolutionary committees, which in many places came to be dominated by former party and government leaders or their sympathizers. The situation resembled that of the post-Leap period, in which there was a contradiction between the participatory and democratic elements embodied in the Great Leap innovations ('two participations, one reform and triple combination') and the needs of an increasingly complex modern industry for efficiency, predictability and standardization (embodied in 'one-man management'). Efforts to reconcile the two were generally unsuccessful, and the Maoist period ended in a conflictual stalemate on the question of enterprise management. With the general triumph of the conservative side in the early and mid-1970s, many managers tried to assert their authority. Yet with the fresh memory of activated, angry workers defying authority during the Cultural Revolution, most managers tended to do so only with the greatest care. Meanwhile, many workers felt free to defy work rules. This situation, which frustrated managers, economists and development-minded political leaders, faced the Dengists as they ascended to power in 1978.

Economic integration and self-reliance

Maoist-period economic development emphasized self-reliance. Domestically, this meant creating local or regional units – provinces in the 1958 decentralization, communes during the Great Leap Forward – that would provide broadly for their own needs. Internationally, self-reliance meant minimizing external trade. Maoist China's efforts to create self-reliant economies at both levels attracted widespread attention from students of economic development in the Third World. For those concerned with the depredations wrought on peasants by agricultural specialization – for example, the common phenomenon of peasants who produce large surpluses of bananas or coffee but still hunger for basic foodgrains – China appeared as a model of a country that had got its priorities straight by producing 'food first' (Lappé and Collins, 1977). And for those who believed that integration into the world economy can only make Third World countries dependent and underdeveloped, China presented a model of autocentric, independent development.

It is not so clear that Maoist-period Chinese leaders and planners thought of their self-reliance policies in quite these ways. Both domestic and international self-reliance were founded partly upon concerns with national security. Indeed, it can even be argued that the emphasis on self-reliance was not only a political choice made by Chinese leaders, but also a way of making a virtue of necessities imposed by a hostile world.[5] Starting in the late 1950s, as the Sino-Soviet split was growing and tensions with the United States were running high in the Taiwan Straits, Chinese leaders began to seek ways to disperse industry away from a few established centres. That way, no invader could choke off China's industrial capacity by occupying one or two parts of the country, as Japan had done in the 1930s. Commune-level industrialization was one concrete response. Another was the 'third front' industrialization programme of the early 1960s, in which billions of yuan were poured into investments in huge factories located well out into the hinterlands of central China. (Much of this investment was wasted, as the projects proved too remote or irrationally planned to be efficient. Today many are hot spots of labour protest against efforts to close them down.)

National security aside, regional and local self-reliance was also based on a solid appreciation of the low level of development of China's transportation infrastructure. It was very difficult to move large quantities of commodities from place to place over the vastness and complexity of Chinese geography (which was one reason for the failure of the 'third front'). While local production of various goods might be less efficient and more costly than concentrated production in a few larger, more modern plants, the differential could often be more than made up for by the high cost and unreliability of shipping the goods from their production centres to a multiplicity of widely dispersed users and consumers. Local self-reliance also helped supply collectives and peasants with simple producer and consumer goods that the cumbersome central planning system was unable to provide. The cement, fertilizer, herbicide and insecticide that the late Maoist-period rural factories made, and the agricultural machinery repairs they carried out and parts they produced, were invaluable in advancing water conservancy work, mechanization and, ultimately, agricultural production. As we shall see, these plants also provided the basis for much of China's industrial growth in the Dengist period.

Performance

When all is said and done, how did China's economy perform during its first three decades?

Agriculture and rural industry

China's great experiment with collective agriculture could point to several solid achievements. Grain production managed to stay slightly ahead of population growth, rising from 288 kg per capita per year in 1952 to 319 kg in 1978. Faster than that were per capita production of meat (rising 54 per cent for hogs) and fish (64 per cent). Chinese scientists and farmers created their own 'green revolution' – a package of high-yielding crops and the modern pumps, chemicals and machinery needed to grow them – quite independent of that developed in the West, raising land yields of grain 55 per cent between 1965 and 1978. Enormous improvements in rural infrastructure were made, including land reclamation and water conservancy. The countryside also began to industrialize: in 1978, 23 per cent of the output of China's communes, brigades and teams came from industry. Economic inequality within production teams and among teams within communes reached very low levels by the end of the Maoist period (Blecher, 1976; Putterman, 1989). Life expectancy at birth, the best all-round indicator of health, which in 1950 was 41 years for the country as a whole, reached into the mid-60s in the countryside by 1978.

Yet all was not rosy. The Maoist policy of local self-reliance in grain production cut into comparative advantage, hurting productivity and income in many areas. Restrictions on rural markets and on trade among production units made it difficult for farmers and their collectives to obtain what they needed for consumption and production. These constraints also blocked the entrepreneurial potential of individuals and collectives, as did direct controls on development of rural collective enterprises. In the absence of careful attention by the state to technical support and cost accounting, the emphasis on rapid, labour-intensive construction by rural collectives of infrastructure projects such as dams, canals and reservoirs led to a definite degree of wasted effort, as many of these projects piled up high expenses or ultimately failed to produce the intended benefits.

This reflects a much wider motif that is also seen in Maoist-period industry, which economists term low labour productivity, and which farmers experienced as backbreaking work year after year for incommensurately low returns. The frequently heard argument that Chinese agricultural collectives did not provide labour incentives is dubious both in theory and in practice. An economic model of rational behaviour under conditions of uncertainty can suggest, on the contrary, that the payment structure of Chinese collectives gave farmers incentives to work too hard. Since they did not know until the end of the year how much their work points would be worth, farmers worked harder and longer than made sense from the point

177

of view of labour efficiency (Putterman, 1983). This theory conforms to practice. During the 1970s, farmers and rural cadres did not complain primarily about indolence among their fellow villagers; on the contrary, their biggest complaint was that they worked very hard but did not seem to be reaping much in the way of rewards (author's interviews, Hong Kong, 1974–75 and 1978). With growth rates slow or stagnant, China's farmers, like the country's workers, were running at top speed just to stay in place. Little wonder, then, that they were ready to try something else.

Urban industry

During the Maoist period, China did accomplish a major feat by creating a great deal of modern industrial plant and infrastructure. Industrial output grew at an average annual rate of 10.7 per cent per year from the start of the First Five Year Plan in 1953 until 1978. Figure 6.4 charts this growth. As it makes plain, growth would have been even faster but for the obvious downturns of the Great Leap Forward and the Cultural Revolution.[6] It also demonstrates the rapid growth of collective industry – most of it rural – in the 1970s. Indeed, a good part of China's industrial growth in the last decade of the Maoist period came from rural industry.

A tremendous price was paid for all this growth. The average rate of accumulation – how much of total production (measured by gross domestic product) was reinvested or wasted, but not consumed – was 28 per cent. This is extremely high by comparison with other countries. These funds reflect a gargantuan sacrifice by the Chinese people. Much of China's enormous accumulation was genuine investment; after all, industrial growth was indeed impressive. Sadly, though, much of the sweat and blood represented by China's accumulation rate was wasted through ill-conceived projects, poor allocation of resources and political disruptions.

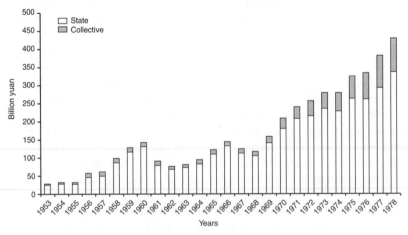

Figure 6.4 Gross Value of Industrial Output, 1953–78 (in 1980 yuan)

Source: China Statistical Yearbook, various years.

The reasons for this high rate of accumulation were adduced earlier in this chapter. Where did all this money go? What was not wasted was devoted to expanding Chinese industry in an extensive but not an intensive way. That is, more and more factories and production lines were built, turning out more and more products, but the efficiency and quality of production did not rise as fast as output. Value-added per worker – a measure of how much a worker produces in a given period of time – doubled from 1949 to 1964, as China began to create a large-scale industrial economy. Yet from 1965 to 1975 it declined by 5 per cent. The value-added per unit of capital – a measure of how much return there is to each yuan invested – declined by almost 40 per cent from 1957 to 1977. These are shocking figures, since they show that a great many of the sacrifices that the Chinese people were making (as measured by both the accumulation rate and by their toil) were not going into infrastructure, machinery or technology that would enable them to be more productive. This was another form of waste – of human effort and sacrifice, and of scarce resources. From the workers' point of view, the faster they ran, the less productive they became. From the economy's and the leadership's point of view, China's extensive economic growth was not sustainable over the long run, and would eventually slow down. This realization, brought home to the leadership at the end of the Maoist period by economists to whom they listened, but also by their own experience, was a factor inclining them to seek a new pathway for the Chinese economy.

Living standards offer another perspective on the human costs of Maoist-period growth. China's workers did not get a pay rise from 1957 until after the end of the Maoist period. As another indicator, by 1978 an average urban Chinese family of four lived in only 4.2 square metres – roughly the size of a college dormitory room – at least partly because the emphasis had been placed on building factories rather than apartments. The promise of a better material life was, therefore, one relatively feasible way for the new leadership to gain the support of the Chinese people.

THE DENGIST PERIOD

The rubrics under which the Maoist-period political economy has been discussed can also guide analysis of the Dengist period. However, the complexities of reform require that our discussion sometimes be organized a little differently. Planning and markets became too intertwined to be discussed separately. Moreover, the rise of markets means we must look at price reform and inflation.

Ownership and organization

Industry
Soon after the Third Plenum, the state encouraged communes, urban neighbourhood governments and even private individuals to expand existing enterprises and start new ones. By 2000, of the 134,000 domestically owned industrial enterprises

in urban China, only 42,000 were state-owned, and 22,000 were privately owned. The remaining 70,000 constitute what can be called an intermediate sector that includes the 'collective' firms owned by local governments as well as several new categories: 'co-operative' firms (partnerships), limited liability companies and firms owned jointly by state ministries, local governments and individuals. State-owned firms only produced one-third of the output value of domestically owned urban industrial firms, purely private firms 8 per cent and the rest a full 60 per cent. A major motivation for permitting and encouraging the development of the urban intermediate and private sectors was to absorb the huge part of China's labour force that was allocated unproductively. In the countryside alone, the figure of 100 million surplus workers was frequently heard in the 1980s. (It still is, though the cited figure is now often higher.) Moreover, many people who had been sent to the countryside in the 1960s and 1970s were now returning to their home cities, where they were having trouble finding jobs. Open unemployment appeared in urban China for the first time in decades. If people without work could start their own little businesses, they could contribute to production, and solve the state's problem of finding work for them. Finally, reformers knew that many urban factories had more workers than they could use efficiently. This was partly because, under Maoist-period planning, wages (like capital, discussed above) were not charged as a real cost to firms, who therefore had no reason to restrict their payrolls. In addition, labour bureaux charged with finding jobs for urbanites often simply allocated them to enterprises without regard to need. Reformers hoped that some of these workers would be enticed by the opportunities of self-employment or employment in workshops owned by their local governments and even their neighbours.

The development of small collective and private businesses had other advantages. They could fill the many gaps in the state-run economy, particularly in the consumer goods and services sectors that the Maoist economy, with its orientation to production and accumulation over consumption, had slighted. They could subcontract work that state-run firms could not do, could not afford to do or did not wish to do. One prominent example is that much of the construction labour that has built China's shining new skyscrapers and roadways since 1978 was done by migrant rural workers supplied by labour service companies that are owned privately or by rural governments. Some reformers, especially those with a more aggressive attitude toward state industry, wanted private and collective firms to provide lively competition for state firms.

Collective and private firms have brought problems too. Not everyone views the competition they provide for state industry so positively, which is one reason that so many were shut down during the 1989 crackdown, when more 'conservative' leaders – that is, those more inclined to preserve some of the Maoist-period political economy – were riding high. Many of these firms exploit labour: sub-standard wages, child labour and sweatshop conditions have returned to Chinese industry. These small firms also pose serious environmental threats, since they have low levels of technology and poor knowledge of waste disposal, and are very difficult to regulate because of their huge numbers and small size. Finally, for some of these same reasons, they pose a major problem for commercial regulators and tax agencies.

In addition to the rise of a much more heterogeneous set of domestic ownership forms, China has expanded the opportunities for foreign ownership of enterprises in the country. In 2000, a full 10 per cent of industrial enterprises were owned by businesspeople from Hong Kong, Macao and Taiwan, and another 7 per cent by entrepreneurs from elsewhere. Some were joint ventures with Chinese government agencies, some with Chinese businesspeople, but the largest category by far – 54 per cent in 2000 – are those that were owned outright by foreigners. These firms operate strictly as capitalist enterprises, paying taxes to the state (often on conciliatory terms negotiated at the time of the investment) and employing workers on terms determined by the labour market with little if any state regulation. In fact, foreign firms have been instrumental in ending the labour protections of state socialism (Gallagher, 2002).

Agriculture

The process of decollectivization has been discussed in Chapter 3. By the mid-1980s, the vast majority of villages had adopted the most extreme form of responsibility system known as 'household production contracting' (*bao chan dao hu*), from which no major change is in sight. Under this system, individual households enter into long-term contracts for the use of a plot of land, a piece of machinery or even a workshop or enterprise. The contracting villagers keep all net profits, but must also bear all losses. Land contracts specify a quota of particular crops to be grown, which must be turned over to the state partly as taxes and partly as a fee for use of the land; contracts to run workshops or machinery specify a cash fee. Formally, the land remains owned by the state, not by the farmers, who only have long-term leases to it. Informally, however, farmers think of the land as their property, and in practical terms it is. When local authorities want to acquire a piece of land for some developmental purpose, they speak not of cancelling the contract but of 'buying' the land, and farmers say they are 'selling' it. And what they do looks a lot like that: they negotiate a price under which the land formally reverts from being contracted to the farmer back to the government. Moreover, farmers who want to work off the land can and do sub-let their contracted land to other farmers.

Economic and political administration have been separated institutionally. Communes were first stripped of their political control over agricultural production, and by 1984 they were abolished altogether, replaced by township governments. Brigades have become 'village committees'. They both were to have far more modest roles in economic life than the communes, but in fact they have remained important in enforcing state cropping policy and developing and managing rural industrial enterprises. The state has also maintained its control over local affairs through the Communist Party, whose rural work departments maintain considerable power in areas such as finance, land allocation and reallocation, leadership recruitment and evaluation, technical and industrial development and political reform, among others.

Planning and markets

Industry

The Dengist political leadership, and the economists advising it, shared a consensus that Maoist-period economic planning was a major impediment to industrial development. They believed that the only way forward toward more rational production and greater efficiency was to grant more power to enterprises to make economic decisions. Where the Maoist period had gone no further than regional decentralizations that still operated with a political logic, now enterprise decentralization with an economic logic was placed on the drawing boards (Figure 6.1). Behind this shared vision lay many difficult questions provoking profound disagreement. How much latitude should enterprises be given? What role should planning continue to play, and how should it be organized? How should market forces be introduced, and how would they be reconciled with planning?

One proposal was to divide the economy into planned and unplanned segments. Economic policy leaders such as Chen Yun, who had presided over China's five-year plans, sought to maintain planning more or less in the form in which they had developed it, but now agreed that such planning could not possibly cover all of China's immense economy. They were willing to jettison control over vast sectors that they deemed to be of relatively less strategic importance to overall development and national security, such as petty production, services and retail trade. Key sectors – such as basic heavy industries, national transportation networks and energy – would remain under central plans more or less as before. This proposal came to be known as the 'birdcage' approach because, in the words of its proponents, the economy would be freed up to follow market forces within limits, just as a bird can fly freely within its cage. It involved two problems. First, how would the planned sectors become more efficient and rational? Second, how would they intersect with the unplanned sectors, which they would eventually have to meet? For example, if steel or energy were produced as inefficiently as before, the unplanned sectors that relied on their output would surely be affected.

Another approach attempted to solve these problems by putting individual enterprises simultaneously both within and outside the planned sector. Firms would be given production quotas well below their capacity, and they would be permitted to orient the balance of their production to the developing markets. They would also be permitted to retain a significant portion of their profits, as an incentive to produce efficiently for the market. This way, the state would be guaranteed that its basic goals for production of strategic products would be met through the planned part of the enterprises' production, while production for market would make the enterprises more efficient.

This planning reform resulted in a what came to be known as 'two-tier pricing'. The output of the planned portion of an enterprise's production was sold to the state at prices inherited from the Maoist period, perhaps with some small adjustments. These prices were generally much lower than those on the burgeoning markets, where scarcities were driving them up. Enterprises and the state alike realized that in order to sell to the state at the old, planned prices, the enterprises also had to receive inputs on those same terms. Chinese industry thus began to develop something like two parallel economies. In the planned one, the state provided inexpensive inputs, and in turn purchased the products that factories made with them at low prices. In the unplanned one, firms had to buy their inputs at higher market prices, and they could sell their output accordingly. The problem was that, unlike parallel lines, which never touch, these two economies bumped into each other every day. The temptation for enterprises to use low-priced state inputs to turn out products for the high-priced market was simply too great. Two-tier pricing created irresistible opportunities for corruption and abuse of state resources. Even where managers were honourable, they often faced difficult problems. If a surplus of inputs was received through the plan, could it be used for non-plan production? If choices had to be made about which sector to prioritize, how should they be made, especially at a time when the state was urging enterprises both to meet their production quotas but also to increase their profitability? Yet, two-tier pricing also had unintended benefits. It eased enterprises' transition to the market, giving them time to adjust. It also permitted a political compromise between leaders more committed to planning and those urging market reform (Naughton, 1995: 8,190).

Still another issue was how planning should be done. As we saw in Chapter 3, some reform economists proposed that planning and markets be combined right inside the planning process, by making plans in a way that reflected market realities and constraints. For example, if a problem with planning was that the state-set prices were irrational, why not raise them to something that more closely reflected actual costs of production and scarcities? Specifically, if, as was the case, Chinese coal mines could almost never make a profit because the state price for coal was set too low (to allow big coal users like steel mills to show large profits on their books), why not raise it? This kind of proposal ran into heavy opposition. Ministries in sectors that had benefited from the irrationalities of the Maoist-period price structure of course balked; moreover, the political legacy of the Maoist-period political economy was that many of their leaders, e.g., those in highly prioritized heavy industry, were extremely powerful. Ironically, leaders in sectors that stood to gain from readjustment in the state price structure often objected as well, fearing that with price reform they would lose the subsidies to which they had become accustomed for decades, and instead would be forced to sink or swim in the uncertainties of the emerging market. Finally, many leaders and economists worried about the inflation that would certainly result from state price adjustment.

The planning reform that caused the least debate was the change from production quotas to profitability quotas. Ironically, though, it involved some of the thorniest problems. It was widely agreed that Soviet-style production planning created serious irrationalities and inefficiencies by locating decision-making in bureaucratic offices too far removed from the realities of the enterprise. Tremendous gains could be realized simply by telling firms to turn over to the state not a certain number of nails or shoes, for which there might be no carpenters in need or feet that fitted, but rather a certain amount of profits made by factories that knew far better from their retailers what carpenters and consumers needed. Yet how would those profits be collected by the state in ways that left firms' incentives but did not bankrupt the government by undermining its most crucial revenue stream? So long as the state continued to claim a share of firms' profits, the firms' incentive to maximize their profits was undermined. Gradually, then, the state moved in the direction of replacing profit claims with taxes, which were to be more predictable for both the state and the firms, and which provided the enterprises more incentives to seek their profits, since they could now retain them all. This problem with profit quotas was not nearly as knotty, though, as the issue of price reform, to which we shall turn soon.

By the late 1990s, planning of the old state socialist type, in which the state issued commands for the allocation of goods and services, was practically dead. Except for a very small number of strategic products, most goods and services in China today exchange on the market, and most economic decisions are made by enterprise managers who look solely to the market. The market has also replaced planned allocation of labour. Enterprises are now free to hire and fire workers, and to set wages according to the labour market rather than state-set pay scales. The result has been massive increases in unemployment and declining income for many workers, both of which have fuelled significant protest (discussed in Chapters 3 and 7).

Agriculture

1985 dawned with Document #1, published on the first of the year to highlight its importance, announcing the abolition of the state grain procurement system. It was to be replaced by a contractual relationship between the state and the farmers covering part of the harvest, with free markets taking up the rest. The state's interest was not just with market reform, though. An unexpectedly large harvest in 1984 had overwhelmed the state's procurement system, which found itself short of drying and storage facilities and of cash to pay for required purchases. Thus, many leaders and officials were happy at the prospect of getting out of the procurement business. Yet, as we saw in Chapter 3, many were not, fearing that China's food security would become threatened. And with the prices on grain markets plummeting, farmers did not necessarily experience Document #1 as a liberation. The farmers responded by cutting back on grain significantly in subsequent years. In 1985, grain production was down 7 per cent. Thus, the deregulatory fanfare of 1985 was reversed in 1986, when the state reimposed mandatory grain quotas, which remain in place.

The farmers, however, did not just grin and bear the state's renewed efforts to control the crops they grew. On the contrary, they have resisted in several ways. Often they have simply ignored the quotas. They have also commonly purchased grain on the free market, reselling it to the state in order to meet their quotas. The costs of such transactions are usually more than made up by profits from the cash crops they plant or the money they make working outside agriculture. When urban grain prices were still subsidized, they could sometimes even make money by buying it there (illegally) and reselling it to the state at the higher rural purchase price. Sometimes farmers have lied to procurement officials, saying that their best efforts to meet their quotas were frustrated by drought, flood or blight. The state became so frustrated with these tactics that by 1990 procurement policy began to switch from output to area quotas, backed up with inspections of fields to make sure the farmers had actually put into the ground the crops the state demanded. Still the farmers were not beaten. Some responded by refusing to tend those crops assiduously, diverting their energy and investment to other, more profitable pursuits. In this game, intermediate and grass-roots officials often work for the benefit of their localities, even when this means undercutting the plans assigned them by central and provincial governments (Blecher and Wang, 1994). In general, the state has won this battle with its farmers, since China was flush with grain by the late 1990s. This permitted the state to reduce its control over grain prices and to permit the market to set them. The low level of these prices has depressed rural incomes, however, fuelling discontent.

Price reform and inflation

As we have seen, the reforms tried to increase the productivity of the Chinese economy by inducing firms to make more rational, cost-based decisions, and by using profitability both to measure how well they did so and as a basis for state revenue extraction. None of this could happen in the absence of price reform. First, markets cannot serve as rational allocators unless market prices reflect demand, supply and real costs of production. For example, factory managers cannot make wise choices about alternative inputs if the prices of those inputs do not reflect the costs of producing them. If, as was the case, the price of coal is set way below the cost of producing it, factory managers will continue to use more coal than another fuel that might have lower real production costs but higher state-set prices. This only encourages and reproduces inefficiency in the energy sector. It also produces waste, since managers will have less incentive to use coal wisely if it comes to them so cheaply. Second, profits cannot serve their function of reflecting efficiency if they can be generated by manipulating price differentials. For example, heavy industries, which were favoured with low input prices and high output prices set during the First Five Year Plan, could hardly fail to make a profit, whether they were efficient or not. Conversely, since the price of coal was so low, Chinese coal mines could almost never make a profit no matter how efficient they were. In short, price reform was necessary for the Dengist economic reforms to reach their goal of overcoming the inefficiencies and irrationalities of central planning.

Yet, as we have seen in Chapter 3, price reform has been a very hot issue in the politics both among China's leadership and between the state and society. At the élite level, price reform would hurt precisely those sectors that were most powerful in the pre-reform period and beyond. At the level of society, it brought about repeated bouts of consumer inflation in almost perfect rhythm with the openings and retrenchments of economic reform discussed in Chapter 3 (Figure 6.5). These two levels of élite and élite–mass politics interacted repeatedly, as leaders opposed to reform frequently pointed to popular discontent and the spectre and, indeed, the reality of resulting political instability in their efforts to scuttle price reform. As we saw in Chapter 3, failed price reform contributed directly to the massive popular protests of 1989.

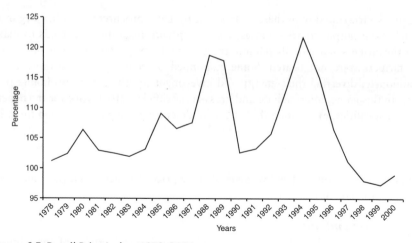

Figure 6.5 Retail Price Index, 1978–2000

Source: China Statistical Yearbook, various years.

Yet a countermovement took place as well. The 1989 crackdown and the resulting political deep-freeze created the political conditions for the state to pursue the very price reform that had helped occasion the protests in the first place. Once the state had demonstrated its willingness to use force against its own people, consumers were much less likely to protest against price reforms. That is one reason why prices rose rapidly in the years immediately following 1989 (Figure 6.5). In other words, in contrast to the Western liberal view that markets and democracy go hand in hand, in China's transition from radical state socialism to capitalism, political repression proved to be an indispensable precondition for the price reform, which was in turn necessary for the rise of the market.

By the turn of the century, China began, surprisingly, to experience the opposite problem: price deflation (Figure 6.5). Consumer spending began to drop, as rising unemployment cut into workers' buying power and sent shivers up the spines of many others about possible lay-offs, inducing them to save rather than spend. Moreover, many state and collective enterprises tried to avoid cutbacks or shutdowns by continuing to produce more than could be sold and running up inventories. Finally, China lowered many tariffs as part of its gradual approach to its expected accession to the WTO. That made imports of some key inputs cheaper, which lowered costs of production and, therefore, prices. Together, dropping demand, rising supply and reduced costs drove prices downward. Deflation can be as serious a problem as inflation, since it undermines the profitability of all producers, which, in China's new market-oriented environment, can lead to serious difficulties, including declining investment, further closures and still more lay-offs.

Economic priorities

Industry and agriculture

Economic reform has not shifted the orientation of government investment away from industry. Capital construction in agriculture, which was only 3.7 per cent of the total in 1978, averaged only 1.4 per cent from 1985 to 1998. It recovered to 2.7 per cent in 2000, as the state began to recognize agriculture's impending economic and political crisis. In part, the government's continued orientation to investment in industry is a result of the same institutional factors that prevailed in the Maoist period: the state still owns a great many industrial enterprises. Yet, whereas at that time investment priorities were also a matter of ideological commitment to socialist industrialization, now they have much more to do with politics and profits: politics in that the big state-run firms still loom large in the Chinese political firmament, both because of the powerful people who run them and also out of fear of the potentially disruptive power of the workers whom they employ; and profits in that parts of the industrial sector remain much better investments than agriculture.

In Maoist China, agriculture was expected basically to take care of itself. In Dengist China, it has lost most of its capacity to do so. Many village governments, which are responsible for collecting funds and organizing construction and maintenance work at the grass roots, are in financial crisis. Quite a few are literally bankrupt. One survey in five Hubei counties found a full one-third of village governments 'have suffered severe economic losses, reducing their collective economies to mere skeletons'. One-eighth of those in a Heilongjiang rural survey were classified as 'empty shells', with debts outpacing assets by over ¥100,000 per village (*Inside China Mainland*, February 1991: 20–1). The reasons were losses by collective enterprises, financial mismanagement, lack of managerial talent as specialists leave local government service for more lucrative pursuits and, of course, declining agricultural prices.

Declining agricultural investment threatens calamity. Shortages of funding and administrative support for water conservancy have contributed to massive flooding. While some in the leadership have blamed the farmers for neglecting water conservancy, no less a luminary than Chen Yun pinned the responsibility clearly on the reforms (*China News Digest*, 6 and 21 September 1991). The tragedy is that, as we shall discuss below, while there is plenty of investment going on in China, very little is going to the sector that supports the livelihoods of most Chinese.

Heavy and light industry

Within industry, the Dengist claim to improve standards of living should by definition have gone hand in hand with an increased role for light industry. Light industry's share of total industrial output did in fact burst during the first few years of the Dengist period (see Figure 6.2). And even though it then began a slow decline through the 1980s, it remained significantly higher than in the 1970s. Partly this is a result of a change in the priorities of state-owned industry, whose investment policy shifted from favouring heavy industry by an average annual ratio of 8.9:1 from 1953–75 to only 5.7:1 from 1981–88. The rise of light industry is also rooted

187

in the enormous expansion in rural and urban collective and private industry that Dengist policy encouraged (but in which the state did not invest, leaving that to local governments and private entrepreneurs).

The relative resurgence of heavy industry starting after the 1989 crackdown (Figure 6.2) is also startling. It reflects the increased power of the Party 'conservatives' rooted in the heavy industrial ministries during that time. In the middle and later 1980s, policy on heavy, state-owned industry emphasized its profound problems and the need for structural reform. However, with the rise of hardline 'conservative' leaders in the early 1990s, there was a noticeable shift to underscoring the significance of this sector to the national economy and, therefore, the importance of investing in it. This was also a time when many rural enterprises, which had been competing with state-owned firms for very scarce investment funds as well as in product markets, were ordered to close down.

Nonetheless, this is a relative trend. In absolute terms, light industrial production continued to grow 11.8 per cent per year from 1988 to 2000. The rapid development of light industry during the Dengist period remains apparent to the naked eye in marketplaces and homes all over China, where consumer goods now proliferate in a range and quantity unheard of in the 1970s.

Accumulation and consumption

The very high rate of accumulation and investment in the Maoist period was an effect of planners' emphasis on rapid industrialization, the structure of the state socialist economy and Maoist values. The Dengist leadership came to power committed to raising the level of consumption, to pursuing industrialization more efficiently (thereby reducing the need for and waste of investment capital) and to a very different set of social values. The huge costs that the Chinese people paid for rapid development during the Maoist period, as measured by the high rate of accumulation, could now be expected to be reduced. Standards of living would rise at long last; the Chinese people would begin to enjoy the fruits of their previous sacrifices. At stake were not only people's livelihoods, but, potentially, the fate of the state, which based so much of its claim to power on making material life better. How well have the Dengist economic policies done in righting the balance of consumption and accumulation during their first decade and a half?

Figure 6.6 shows that they have not done well at all.[7] The accumulation rate dipped noticeably from 1978 to 1982. Factory managers began raising wages and paying bonuses. Individual entrepreneurs started small businesses that required little investment but earned significant incomes. Unemployment and underemployment began to decline, raising the overall level of income. Yet accumulation began to roar back in 1983. It peaked in 1985, as the economy went into a time of overheated growth. After some levelling, it spiked again in 1993, another moment of overheating in response to Deng Xiaoping's shift away from the post-1989 economic retrenchment symbolized by his 'southern tour'. Though it then declined gradually, in the 1990s it has maintained an overall level significantly higher than in the 1980s.

As before, the reasons can be traced in large part to the structure of the economy, even though that structure was now very different. With market opportunities

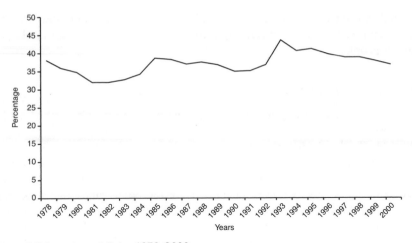

Figure 6.6 Investment Rate, 1978–2000

Source: China Statistical Yearbook, various years.

being opened for the first time in decades, China's investment rate would have been high in any event. The economic growth that has occurred since 1978 required a good deal of investment, after all. Yet the accumulation rate in the first fifteen years of the Dengist period was far higher than even China's rapid growth required. Like their Maoist-period predecessors, economic bureaucrats in the half-reformed Dengist system continued to exhibit a powerful tendency to overinvest. The reasons were now quite different, though. The burgeoning market offered rich opportunities for expansion and entrepreneurship. The people best placed to take advantage of them were provincial and local governments. After all, they had the most expertise, information and experience. Most important of all, their budgets and their influence with their colleagues in the state-owned banks afforded them access to the necessary capital. By contrast, in the absence of capital markets, the collective and private sectors were desperately squeezed for investment funds. Yet China's factories, provincial and local governments and ministries and bureaus did not need to be responsible investors. Their leaders lacked fiduciary or personal responsibility for the monies they invested. If a project went belly up, the red ink appeared on the books of the enterprise or state organ for which they worked, and by which they could rarely be fired or demoted. Moreover, in an economy where material inputs were in very short supply, a good strategy to procure needed inputs was to start the project and then hope to appeal to the supply agency about how urgently their help was needed to complete it. The result of this structure of investment and development was similar to that of the Maoist period: many poorly planned projects were begun, and quite a few proved unprofitable or difficult to complete. (By contrast, in a capitalist economy investors and banks would want to see everything assembled in advance.) Central and regional planners, deprived of many levers of economic control, and told not to interfere excessively in the spontaneous economic pursuits unleashed by the reforms, have been poorly positioned to regulate accumulation

189

even if they wanted to do so. As in the Maoist period, the source of this high level of accumulation and investment is the appropriation and waste of the hard toil of the Chinese people.

Enterprise management

During the Dengist period, there have been some experiments with limited worker participation, this time in the form of workers' congresses and election of factory managers. Workers' congresses are not new; they existed at various times during the socialist period, and were revived in 1975 after their abandonment during the Cultural Revolution. Their formal powers include the right to review budgets and production plans, specify uses of safety, welfare and bonus funds, make decisions about management structure, wage systems and training programmes and oversee the election and conduct of cadres. Yet it is also specified that the higher levels of the Party and economic administration are under no obligation to abide by these decisions. Elections of factory managers are not recognizably democratic: they are rarely contested or conducted with secret ballots, nominations are generally controlled by existing factory leaders or Party officials and the selection of the representatives who vote is influenced by the factory leadership. The best that can probably be said for them is that the prospect of having to face the workers' congress once a year may place a modicum of pressure on some managers to conduct their affairs in a responsible and careful way.

In general, then, it appears at present that workers have no power to run factories, to participate in a meaningful way in their operation or to structure their organization. Yet this does not mean that all Chinese factories are oppressive places to work. In some older, established state-owned plants, the terms and conditions of work continue to be relatively favourable to workers, who also still enjoy some de facto employment guarantees and social welfare benefits such as housing and health care. These firms are also subject to the Labour Law, whose occasional enforcement by state labour unions can help prevent at least some egregious depredations. By contrast, some urban private, collective and foreign joint-venture plants as well as rural factories are more likely to be dictatorial sweatshops. They have none of the workerist traditions of the Maoist period. Their union organizations are even more likely to be ineffective or non-existent. These enterprises are beyond the reach of regulatory agencies such as the industrial or labour ministries. Their workers have no employment guarantees, which makes it easier to intimidate them; they usually also lack social welfare benefits from their enterprises. These firms are more likely to employ young women and children, who, unfortunately, remain an extremely vulnerable labour force.

Economic integration and self-reliance at home and in the world

The Dengist leadership came to power committed to ending Maoist policies of self-reliance, both domestically and internationally. It is perhaps most noted outside China for its opening to the international economy. Foreign direct investment comprised 15 per cent of total investment in the mid-1990s. For the 1990s as a whole, China attracted almost twice as much foreign investment as Brazil and Mexico combined, countries known for being attractive to foreign investors (Gallagher, 2002: 346). In 2002, it is expected to attract $450 billion in foreign direct investment, making it the largest such magnet in the world. (To put that figure in perspective, all of South-East Asia will draw only $12 billion.) International trade volume comprised 45 per cent of gross national product in 2000, an enormous figure.[8] This policy appears to be in the objective interest of virtually every major constituency in China. For workers, it means expanded employment. For farmers, it has meant some relief from the heavy emphasis on grain production – foodgrain imports have risen sharply since 1978 – and more latitude to produce cash crops or to engage in non-agricultural work. Consumers, especially in the urban areas, have gained vastly increased access to prized imports, from cigarettes and clothing to adventure films and music cassettes. For officials and intellectuals, the open policies offer expanded contacts with foreigners and the possibility of international travel, both of which are important sources of information, social status and resources for career mobility.

China's economic opening has been distributed very unevenly. It has occurred most heavily in some coastal cities and regions, especially Guangdong and Fujian Provinces and the Yangzi Delta. There it fuelled the development of regional economies whose economic growth rivals that of the export-led developmental success stories such as Hong Kong, South Korea and Taiwan. The effects on China's vast hinterland have been far slower in coming. The resulting inequality between coast and inland has in turn undercut the Dengist programme for reducing regional self-reliance and its putative inefficiencies through marketization. As industry and commerce grew apace along the coast, inland provinces found their role more as suppliers of raw materials, which is far less remunerative. Investment funds too flowed from inland to coast, lured by the prospect of higher returns. Local and especially provincial leaders, many engaged in the investment boom discussed above, sought to prevent the outflow of capital and raw materials, preferring to mobilize them for their own enterprises. In a startling development, in the 1990s China saw the rise of trade barriers between provinces, including not only policies and financial incentives, but also checkpoints on major roadways. In 2002, for example, it was illegal for all SUVs except Beijing Jeeps to ply three main Beijing thoroughfares. As with the question of accumulation vs. consumption, the Dengist reforms have unexpectedly produced an outcome with an odd resonance to the Maoist period – in this case, market-based 'self-reliance' – albeit for very different reasons.

Expanded international trade has also brought in tow the proliferation of Western goods and the culture of consumption that goes with them. Many Chinese and most Westerners view this as positive, since it helps overcome some of the drudgery of daily life and work, creates competition for Chinese industry that forces it to become more efficient and in general puts China closer to par with other countries. Some 'conservatives' have worried about the effects of Western-led consumerism in eroding China's collectivist social values, threatening China's historic civilization, increasing alienation and crime and endangering the natural environment. The ensuing debate provoked more than one campaign against 'spiritual pollution', as we saw in Chapter 3. Though these campaigns did not gain much popular support, it is possible to foresee the development, at a moment of crisis, of an anti-foreign, hyperpatriotic backlash building on China's deep sense of national pride, a phenomenon that has occurred more than once in the past century and a half. Indeed, trade disagreements with the USA in mid-1996 did appear to gain some genuine purchase on Chinese public opinion, which began voicing strident hostility toward America. Such a response could also be based on concerns about China becoming economically dependent on foreign powers, fears that, as we saw in Chapter 3, erupted in 1985 in an open split among the top leadership, and public criticism of Deng Xiaoping, over the extremely sensitive question of whether China ought to rely on foreigners for its food.

Such a crisis and backlash is a real danger in the wake of China's accession to membership in the World Trade Organization in December 2001. Over the five-year phase-in period, tariffs are to drop further.[9] Restrictions on foreign ownership and investment in many sectors are to be dropped. So are import restrictions of all kinds, including domestic content regulations and requirements that some imports of high-tech goods be accompanied by transfer of information, training and use rights to the technology. Industrial policies constituting subsidies that put domestic producers at an advantage vis-à-vis foreign producers, such as low-interest loans, are to stop. Foreign firms are to be given access to set up sales and distribution networks in China.

China's aggressively pro-reform leaders sought these massive changes for several reasons. The mercantilist (state-regulated) foreign trade régime that prevailed in the 1980s and 1990s created myriad opportunities for corruption. Officials responsible for issuing needed permits could charge various 'fees' and other emoluments, some legitimate but many simply corrupt. That could discourage foreign investment and operations, weaken profitability and, most seriously, undercut the state's legitimacy in the eyes of the public. Moreover, many leaders felt that they had to subject the economy to foreign competition in order to promote the deep restructuration they felt it needed to make the transition from the extensive, technologically primitive, low-productivity development of state socialist days to a more intensive, technologically advanced and productive pattern demanded by the world economy of the twenty-first century.

Overall, WTO membership is expected to increase economic growth, though how much is a matter of debate – estimates run from as little as one-tenth of 1 per cent to as much as 3 per cent per year for the proximate future. The biggest winners will probably be apparel and textile producers, who will now be able to export to the USA and Europe without the restrictions and quotas that were in effect in the 1990s. Other labour-intensive export producers, such as those in electronics, leather and footwear, will probably also gain, though not as much, since they have not faced as many export restrictions in the past. (Indeed, some economists argue that, with the possible exception of textiles and apparel, China did not need to join the WTO in order to boost exports, which were already very strong [Nolan 2001:

213]. The biggest losers are expected to be agriculture and heavy industry. Grain farmers, who are already suffering from low purchase prices, will now face stiff competition from even lower-priced imports. Twenty-five million of them stand to lose ¥100–130 in annual income, a huge amount for those who are already subsisting on ¥1,000 or less (*South China Morning Post*, 14 February 2002).[10] Hardest hit will be poor farmers in China's interior, while those in coastal areas, who produce cash crops, will fare better. This is just one aspect of the way that WTO accession will increase regional inequality in China. Another is that the beleaguered old, technologically backward heavy industrial plants in China's hinterland – which were built as part of the 'third front' strategy of the 1960s (see Chapter 2) – and in its north-east will go into even deeper crisis due to their high costs of production, low profitability, poor quality and, therefore, general inability to compete with domestic, much less foreign, producers. Steel mills, automobile plants and many others that have managed to cling to life through the turn of the century will now die. They, together with other uncompetitive enterprises of various kinds, will take with them the jobs of up to 40 million of China's workers. While WTO membership will foster new enterprises and employment, that cannot solve the problem, for two reasons. First, projections for employment creation due to WTO accession range from a mere 1.5 million jobs to, at most, 15 million jobs. Second, even those jobs will generally not go to the tens of millions of unemployed industrial workers, who are on the whole not qualified for them; instead, they will go to the next generation of younger, better educated proletarians (Solinger, 2002, 2003). Meanwhile, China's banks, still rooted in the ways of the state socialist past, are burdened with a frequently unbusinesslike approach, massive bad loans on their books and dismal technology and marketing skills. They stand to lose a huge share of the financial services market to aggressive foreign banks. That threatens a financial implosion of mythic and terrifying proportions.

These difficulties and potential crises have engendered considerable opposition within China. Impoverished workers and farmers have already been protesting their lot. While those protests have generally not explicitly targeted the decision to join the WTO, accession will worsen their lives and probably induce further protest. Middle-level officials in the bureaucracy and the enterprises threatened by accession are in a better position to throw a spanner in the works, and they began to do so even as the ink was drying on the WTO agreement. In July 2002, the USA complained that China's State Development Planning Commission had reneged on its promise to raise import quotas on corn and wheat, and that farmers were still receiving export subsidies. The Ministry of Information Industry was accused of dragging its feet on promises to treat foreign and domestic technology companies equally. Foreign automobile companies had trouble setting up finance companies to encourage Chinese drivers to purchase their cars. The government was demanding local content quotas on electronic goods produced by foreign companies in China. The Ministry of Agriculture's opposition to imports on genetically modified grains, ostensibly on the grounds of health concerns, is probably also motivated by protectionist impulses.

WTO accession also faced opposition from political leaders in China's hinterland, who argued, with good reason, that they could actually lose out not just relatively – as coastal areas drew the lion's share of new investment and services – but also absolutely, as local business and investment capital would be sucked into the booming Eastern vortex. The top leadership, which had aggressively promoted WTO accession – responded with a 'Western Development Strategy'. That included tax breaks, liberalized credit and land-use policies and restrictions on capital outflow, all designed to promote development in the hinterlands. The plan faces huge obstacles, however. Poor transport and communications networks and Western officials' less capitalistically minded economic predispositions combine to discourage eastern and foreign investment there.

China will need to exercise considerable central state power to enforce its WTO commitments and to survive them. The whole purpose of joining the WTO is to weaken the power of local political authorities who promote development in ways that protect their regions and pet projects or that line their pockets. The central leaders who aggressively promoted accession did so because they did not have the political capacity to break down such obstacles to fuller marketization. It is hard, therefore, to see how they will muster the power to enforce the myriad demands of WTO compliance. Likewise, their ability to ameliorate its effects on China's poor farmers and workers is limited. To prevent or cope with potentially massive protest, they will have to rely on persuasion, repression and the hope that the discontented will be so dispirited that they will just give up – questions to which we shall return in Chapter 7.

Performance

Industry

Growth rates in Chinese industry in the Dengist period (Figure 6.7) mirror the undulations of reform policies (discussed in Chapter 3). They have often been astonishing, and for significant periods have also been nearly flat. During the early 1980s, they were generally modest, reflecting the irresolution of reform policy and the continuing strength of opponents of rapid marketization. Small bursts are detectable during the moments of opening at the beginning and middle of the decade, and the levellings in 1981 and 1983 correspond to the policy of retrenchment at those times. In the later 1980s, reform policy gathered momentum, led by and reflected in the rising fortunes of Zhao Ziyang. The overheating of the economy – excessively rapid, unsustainable growth accompanied by inflation – is clearly visible in 1988. So are the effects of the austerity policies of 1989–91, whose economic logic was the effort to slow overheating and whose political logic was a victory for or pay-off to 'conservative' leaders who participated in and supported the 1989 crackdown. Finally, the effects of the end of austerity policies in 1992 and the opening signalled by Deng's 'southern tour' are stunningly visible.

Figure 6.7 also shows that much of this growth, both in the later 1980s and especially the 1990s, has been fuelled by the extraordinary development of non-

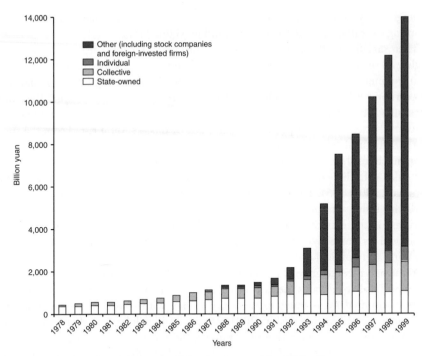

Figure 6.7 Gross Industrial Output Value by Ownership, 1978–99

Source: China Statistical Yearbook, various years.

state-owned enterprises. By the mid-1990s they were looming a good deal larger than state-owned firms in overall industrial output value. The dynamic collective sector includes enterprises owned by rural and urban local governments, bureaux and even state-owned firms who formed subsidiaries. Especially noticeable is the rise of firms owned variously by individuals, private and institutional stockholders and foreign investors. The non-state sectors have been able to take advantage of China's rapidly proliferating market opportunities. They are highly entrepreneurial by nature, since they are owned and run by gumptious businesspeople rather than government officials. They are also far less constrained by state regulations, and their labour costs are far lower. As we have seen, for example, the flip side of their dynamism is a higher incidence of environmental degradation and generally more draconian labour régimes.

The fast pace of growth in Chinese industry cannot only be chalked up to mar-ketization and privatization, as is so popularly thought. It is also the result of enormously high levels of accumulation, discussed above.[11] With only around two-thirds of everything that is produced being consumed, a good part of the rest is being invested in new plant, equipment and infrastructure projects, all of which fuel growth. In a very real sense, then, China's success in raising industrial output is an achievement not just of something as abstract as the market, but also something as real as the extremely arduous efforts of tens of millions of Chinese who are, on average, only consuming two-thirds of the value of what they produce while working overall much harder than they did in Maoist days.

Their sacrifice is all the greater in light of the fact that a good deal of China's very high level of accumulation is not invested at all, but, rather, wasted through corruption and inefficiency. There are, of course, no reliable estimates of the financial cost of corruption; but there is wide agreement that the problem is endemic. If all this accumulation is being used to positive economic effect, labour productivity – the amount that each worker produces in an hour or day – should rise. From the start of the structural reforms through the early 1990s, it rose only a few per cent per year, much less than it should have given all the changes that were taking place.[12] It did take off, thereafter, reaching 13.6 per cent per year from 1991 to 1996 (Bramall, 2000: 185). The timing suggests that the leap had a great deal more to do with the influx of foreign investment and technology than with the structural reforms of the economy per se. In short, the economic reforms – which were promoted as correctives to the gross inefficiencies of Maoist-period centralized planning and political dislocations – have had only modest success at best.

Yet urban income growth has been robust. Figure 6.8, based on official Chinese data, probably overstates the rate at which urban incomes have risen; yet even if it were discounted by as much as one-third in line with some Western economists' estimates (e.g., Khan and Riskin, 2001: 25), it would still be remarkable. The trend line shows the effects of the rhythms of market Stalinist policy: some fluctuations in the early and mid-1980s, a definite slowdown in both the run-up to and the aftermath of 1989, and a definite and sustained take-off after 1993. This stunning achievement, even amid bouts of inflation and deflation, no doubt helps account for the urban public's broad willingness to put up with continued political repression and corruption. Yet these aggregate figures conceal tremendous inequality. In 1995, the top 10 per cent of urban income earners took 60 per cent of total urban income, while the lowest 10 per cent earned only 1.7 per cent. This level of inequality

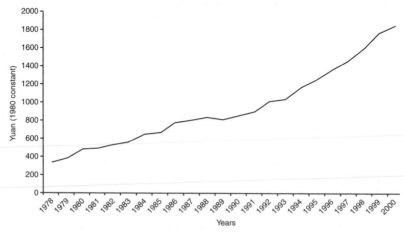

Figure 6.8 Urban Per Capita Income, 1978–2000

Source: China Statistical Yearbook, 2001: Table 10-3.

is significantly greater than it was in 1988. The reasons are increasingly unequal wages, declining and increasingly unequal state subsidies (particularly for housing), growing inequalities in the housing market and the growing returns to investments of China's rising bourgeoisie (Khan and Riskin, 2001: 36–40). Urban poverty has also been on the rise. In 1995, almost 15 per cent of urbanites were living in poverty, up from just under 7 per cent in 1988. A major cause of the increase was unemployment (Khan and Riskin, 2001: 147–8), which has roared ahead even further since then. The serious political implications of these problems, and difficult and uncertain prospects for dealing with them, are discussed in Chapters 7 and 8.

Agriculture

Under the structural reforms, grain production has been highly erratic, reflecting shifting policies, incentives and the cat-and-mouse game between the state, which demanded grain production, and the farmers, who often found it less profitable than other pursuits (Figure 6.9). After a false start, it rose to an all-time peak in 1984. The glut, plus the state's flirtation with deregulation of cropping and procurement (discussed above), brought production back to earth. The 1990 peak is probably due to a combination of the draconian political environment of the day and the decline of alternative activities under the prevailing hardline economic policies. Growth picked up again in the late 1990s, due in part to technological advances, but those gains were not sustained in subsequent years. Overall, in eight years grain production did not keep pace with population growth.

After years of the Maoist period's heavy emphasis on grain production at the expense of other products, farm output has diversified dramatically (Figure 6.10). Obviously, non-grain production rose and fell much more erratically than grain production, which of course remains the anchor of agriculture. Significantly, and not surprisingly, output of cotton, which is unpopular with farmers due to its low sale price and the inherent difficulties of growing it, had the greatest variability and

Figure 6.9 Grain Production, 1978–2000

Source: China Statistical Yearbook, various years.

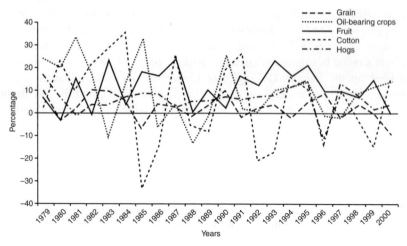

Figure 6.10 Growth Rates of Key Agricultural Products, 1979–2000

Source: China Statistical Yearbook, various years.

the biggest annual drops. Fruit and hog production, which are far more popular and profitable, generally did better that cotton and grain. Figure 6.10, then, tells a story of farmers having gained considerable latitude over what they produce in the Dengist period.

With each passing year it grows harder to raise farm output. According to official statistics, the sown area declined 1.6 per cent from 1978 to 1993.[13] Some of the problem came from the construction of factories, shops, roads and new housing. An increasing amount of cultivated land has also been ruined by emissions from rural industry. China's Huai River Basin is home to 110 million people, who produce around one-fifth of China's grain each year. Four-fifths of the water in the river and its 200 tributaries have been rendered undrinkable by pollution from paper mills, tanneries and distilleries. Cancer and intestinal disease are rising rapidly, and crop damage is serious. Lake Tai, one of China's best-known and most beloved scenic spots, is so polluted that the water has actually developed a foul odour. The problem has attracted the attention of China's State Council, which in early 1996 announced regulations that require rural enterprises to comply with environmental regulations within two years or face closure (*UPI News Service*, 17 April 1996). Yet rural industry remains popular with both leaders and farmers because of the production, income and employment it generates. The government became alarmed at this trend, and strengthened land-use regulation, investment in rural infrastructure and environmental regulation. For example, irrigated area, which had increased at an average annual rate of 0.5 per cent per year from 1978 to 1993, rose 1.3 per cent per year from 1993 to 2000. As a result, sown area actually increased 5.8 per cent from 1993 to 2000, at least according to official statistics. That would help account for the renewed increases in grain production in the late 1990s (Figure 6.9).

The other hope for continued growth in agricultural output is to increase yields per unit of land. In many of China's most fertile areas, yields are already reaching and sometimes exceeding the capacity of the land even with modern inputs in use. In Jilin Province, for example, the ratio of inputs to profits declined 41 per cent from 1983 to 1988. Soils in some places are becoming 'burned' by excessive application of chemical fertilizer (whose use increased 4.7 times from 1978 to 2000), or poisoned by excessive use of insecticides and herbicides. Elsewhere, yields could be increased, but only at costs that are beyond the reach of the farmers who now make decisions about investment and production. In many places, farming is neglected as rural industry attracts the lion's share of investment and labour. Irrationalities in land contracting and state cropping policy have sometimes even resulted in farmland being left idle by those who have contracted for it, a stunning development in a country where arable land is so terribly scarce and precious.

China's agriculture has undeniably performed well under the structural reforms. While simplistic analyses often fall victim to the ideological urge to attribute increases in crop production to decollectivization, it is in fact difficult to do so. For, at the same time that the collectives were being broken up, procurement prices were being raised, markets were being opened and the amount of chemical fertilizer applied doubled. Some economists, even politically conservative ones, have argued that decollectivization was not necessarily a major cause of post-1978 growth. It may, in fact, have actually restricted growth in some ways, since the small size of the farm plots it created was not well suited to some modern inputs. Post-1978 growth can be explained perfectly well by rising prices, which gave individual farmers much greater incentives – incentives that could have worked just as well on small collectives, which were, in effect, like little business partnerships since the farmers in them shared the income.

Whatever the causes of the spurt of agricultural and industrial production may have been, it combined with continued growth in rural industry to cause rural incomes to rise significantly (Figure 6.11). Like urban income, however, these gains have been distributed extremely and increasingly unequally. In 1995, rural income inequality was higher in China than in any Asian country. The bottom 10 per cent of rural income earners that year only brought in 2.3 per cent of income, whereas the top 10 per cent brought in 34 per cent (Khan and Riskin, 2001: 29–31). These numbers are significantly worse than in the urban areas.

The structural reforms have both revealed the enormousness of China's rural underemployment and unemployment problem, and begun to address it. According to the socialist ideology that prevailed during the Maoist period, labour was not considered a commodity to be sold. Therefore, it could not be figured as a cost of production. Thus, there was little incentive to economize on labour or to use it efficiently. While this had the advantage of providing work and income very broadly, it also meant that a great deal of underemployment and unemployment remained hidden. With the onset of the structural reforms, the state's economists began to calculate the value and cost of labour. Estimates of agricultural under-employment and unemployment have consistently run in the neighbourhood of

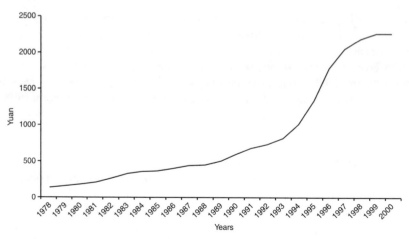

Figure 6.11 Per Capita Rural Household Income, 1978–2000

Source: China Statistical Yearbook, various years.
NB Data throughout 1985 are current yuan, and thereafter constant yuan.

100 to 120 million, despite the ongoing outflow of labour to rural industry and the cities.

If the reforms can be credited with revealing the problem, they have also gone some way toward ameliorating it. Rural industry, a Maoist-period innovation that started in the Great Leap Forward and has undergone tremendous growth in the Dengist period, employed 128 million villagers in 2000. Without it, rural unemployment would be astronomical.[14] The reforms have also permitted and, indeed, promoted the migration of approximately another 120 million farmers to towns and cities, where they generally live better than they did at home, but still as second-class urban citizens, disadvantaged in labour and housing markets and in access to education and health care.

CONCLUSION

China's economic reforms have been truly structural. Today China's economy is in many respects capitalist. Private ownership is growing apace, and many economic decisions even by government-owned enterprises are made with reference to markets. Workers and farmers no longer participate in collective economic institutions or decision-making. The Chinese economy is becoming tightly integrated into the world market. It has performed in many of the ways that capitalist economies tend to perform, by increasing growth, efficiency and inequality. In a society that had been organized in a radical, politically mobilized form of state socialism, these sea changes have created profound political tensions, both within the state and between state and society. We now turn to those issues.

CHAPTER 7

Politics

Despite the hierarchical, Party-centred nature of the Chinese state, the absence of elections and the extraordinary power of China's leadership, there has, paradoxically, been no shortage of lively political conflict. Indeed, the People's Republic of China has experienced broader and more intense political conflict than most countries, both within its leadership and between the state and society. Even the contrast only with other state socialist countries is striking. Where the Soviet Union, Cuba and many of the Eastern European countries underwent prolonged periods of political quiescence lasting decades, until the 1990s and beyond, the longest time that China did so was less than a decade – the years from 1949 until the Great Leap Forward in 1958, and the first years of the Dengist structural reforms, from their beginning in late 1978 until late 1986, when widespread student demonstrations broke out. No country, state socialist or capitalist, has ever experienced anything like the Cultural Revolution.

The bases and forms of political conflict in China have changed over time. These various political conflicts within the leadership, and between the state and society, have profoundly shaped the decisions of the state and, more broadly, the political outcomes of those decisions for the state and society. Yet, paradoxically, despite all this, state socialism in China has outlived that in the Soviet Union and Eastern Europe. Its longevity, and its prospects for the future, are puzzles to which we shall return in Chapter 8.

ÉLITE POLITICS

Before 1949, the Chinese Communist Party had a long tradition of strife, sometimes over ideology, sometimes over particular policies and sometimes over power itself. These battles were variously resolved by internal manoeuvring, votes in meetings of key Party organs (such as the Politburo) and then dismissal of the losers and criticism campaigns against them. For a time, Mao himself was held in a Party lockup in the Jiangxi Soviet for criticizing Party leaders whom he thought were too influenced by Soviet advisers. In the early days of the People's Republic, the state leadership was relatively unified, and society (including even many former social and economic élites) was relatively calm and optimistic. As we have seen, though, the advent of industrialization and rural co-operativization soon began to create serious divisions within the leadership (e.g., between the 'two lines' and among government institutions), within society (between town and countryside, between former 'good' and 'bad' classes) and between state and society (over the disasters of the Great Leap Forward, the corruption and backpedalling in the post-Leap recovery, the Cultural Revolution and the structural reforms). The state found itself, then, making decisions in an increasingly conflictual environment. Thus, over time it was less and less able to make decisions that would mould China's society and economy according to its own vision, and more and more preoccupied with making decisions in response to crises.

Conflict among China's political élites has occurred along three main lines of cleavage. One was over what was called 'political line', which is an ideologically informed approach to the political process. A second occurred between government officials in different bureaucratic posts, and usually involved disputes over specific policies. Finally, there have been the political differences among generations of Chinese leaders and citizens.

'Political line': conflict over ideology and political process

The Chinese leadership has experienced sharp ideological cleavages since 1949. The most prominent was known as 'the struggle between two lines'. It emerged at the centre of politics in the wake of the Great Leap Forward, though proponents of this theory in China then tried to read it back into the entire history of the Party and the Communist movement that began in 1921. On the one side were those leaders, led by Liu Shaoqi, who believed in centralized economic planning of the economy, and a role for bureaucratic, technocratic organizational rationality. On the other were those, led by Mao, who were more concerned with developing the economy through mass mobilization and local self-reliant communities, and who emphasized popular participation and class struggle in social, political and organizational life. There were also differences in political style, with the 'Liuists'[1] believing in stable adminis-tration and incremental change, and the 'Maoists' preferring to take 'two steps forward and one step back', i.e., rapid, even ill-prepared political offensives to overcome inertia, followed by clean-up operations to correct excesses and mistakes.

This difference in 'line' found repeated expression during the Maoist period. Mao argued successfully for rapid rural co-operativization in 1955, believing that it was a good thing in itself, a step toward socialism and a way to conclude the class struggle by absorbing rich peasants; Liu and others urged a more cautious pace, arguing that co-ops could only work if they had farm machinery, which was just starting to become available. Mao criticized growing bureaucratization associated with the First Five Year Plan and the Soviet model, while his opponents had built that model in the first place and then, after the disastrous Great Leap Forward, tried to restore political and administrative order through reassertion of centralized organization and control. In the Socialist Education Movement, 'work teams' – ad hoc urban-based task forces of Party and government officials – were sent to the countryside to combat the decline of collective farming in the wake of the Great Leap Forward. 'Liuist' work teams operated with a top-down style, carrying out their own investigations and then replacing grass-roots officials they deemed cor-rupt, incompetent or misguided. By contrast, 'Maoist' work teams, who saw the problem through the lens of class struggle, tried to work from below by mobilizing a mass movement to attack those they saw as reactionaries who had allegedly taken over in the communes. The rival work teams often clashed, setting the stage for the Cultural Revolution to come.

During the Cultural Revolution, ideological cleavages and debates became extremely confused, since all sides used Mao's ideas to express and legitimate their positions. Making matters even worse, from the 1920s onward Mao's ideas were themselves organized around problems (which he called 'contradictions') more than clear prescriptions. He was concerned, for example, with the need to balance local initiative with central control, popular initiative with Party leadership, individual with collective interest, expertise with common sense and chaos with stability. In different contexts, he could say 'oppose book worship' but then 'read more books'. Little wonder, then, that, by the 1960s, Red Guard organizations could attack each other vehemently while they all carried Maoist banners.

Nevertheless, there were identifiable ideological differences during the Cultural Revolution. The conservative factions conceived of class in terms of official categories based on pre-revolutionary economic position, while the rebels felt that class was more malleable, based on one's attitude toward the peasants, workers and socialism. To deflect criticisms that they had lost touch with the masses despite their good formal class backgrounds, the conservatives focused their Cultural Revolution attacks on China's ancient tradition, while the rebels focused on the élitism of the state leadership. The rebels were also more interested in participatory forms of politics and work (such as criticism campaigns, ideological reform of leaders and leaders' participation in production), while the conservatives tended to want to return to the forms of organization that had been established since 1949.

If the theory of the 'two-line struggle' helps describe a major ideological cleavage of the Maoist period, it cannot explain the advent of the Dengist structural reforms. The pro-market orientation of the post-1979 leadership is not captured by either 'line'. The reformists have critiqued both the 'Maoist' model of political and economic mobilization and the 'Liuist' model of intense, centralized state control. While they are not interested in democracy or even liberal rights, the reformers have been very concerned with depoliticization – i.e., the withdrawal of the state and politics from many spheres of private life into which they had penetrated (such as ideological rectitude and direct economic management). In the economy, what could be called the 'Dengist' reformers have assailed both ('Liuist') central planning and state ownership on the one hand, and ('Maoist') local self-reliance and collective ownership on the other, in favour of mixed forms of ownership (including private enterprise) and markets. If we take the history of state socialist China as a whole, then, it may make more sense to talk about a 'three-line struggle'.

And a struggle it has remained, for the 'Maoist' and 'Liuist' approaches did not roll over and die once the 'Dengist' reforms began. The 'Liuist' tendency has been more prominent. During the 1980s there was still a huge planning bureaucracy, and into the twenty-first century there remains a panoply of state-owned enterprises employing millions of workers, managers and technicians. They have often been a potent political force. Particularly during periods of economic austerity since 1979 (and especially during the post-1989 crackdown), these bureaucracies and enterprises have come to the fore with their claim to be the core of Chinese state socialism, and have demanded priority in planning and in the allocation of investment capital and other resources. Moreover, as we have seen, some prominent Party leaders have worried about the effects of market forces on China's ability to feed itself, its rising regional inequalities, the economic squeeze on many peasants and workers and the social protests resulting from these problems. Hu Jintao, China's top leader, reiterated these themes forcefully soon after his accession in late 2002.

After the Dengists' victory in 1978, it was widely assumed in the West that Maoism was dead, and that the major conflict in post-1979 China was the one we have just discussed: between those committed to the planned economy (whom many journalists and scholars began calling 'conservatives') and 'Dengist' marketeers (whom they dubbed 'reformers'). This analysis was proven wrong in 1989, when many people, particularly workers, again marched under Maoist banners and expressed a collective disgust with the political corruption and the cultural venality and hedonism that had been more or less eliminated from 1949 to 1976. There have been several Mao crazes since 1978, and while many aspects are parodic and trivializing, there is a serious undertone as well. Certainly there was a connection in popular consciousness between the massive popular protests of 1989 and those that filled Tiananmen Square during the Cultural Revolution, when Mao mobilized mass protest against an élitist, bureaucratic and corrupt leadership. In early 1996, Party General Secretary Jiang Zemin repeatedly invoked another side of Mao, the one that emphasized ideological rectitude and opposition to corruption and 'spiritual pollution'. In the 1990s, farmers in more than one Chinese village built temples honouring Mao.

In short, then, all three general ideological tendencies – loosely dubbed Maoism, Liuism and Dengism – are alive in China. Each has material bases of social support. Workers and clerks in state enterprises and the remaining economic bureaucracy have a stake in 'Liuist' state economic regulation and rationalization, if no longer in command central planning. 'Dengism' obviously has broad support from the vast majority who benefit from marketization and the very rapid economic growth of the post-1978 years. 'Maoism' is recalled fondly by those critical of corruption and the many degrading outcomes of social and cultural liberalization. Each of these ideological tendencies will continue to find expression as the country gropes toward its uncertain future.

Bureaucratic pluralism

'Line' theory may be useful to explain some of the conflict over ideology and political style in China at a general level. However, it is more limited in its capacity to capture the full richness of concrete political conflict, much of which does not depend directly or mainly on ideology. As in any complex organization, there has been and still is a great deal of contestation within the Chinese state over bureaucratic turf and policy goals, none of which can be explored if one assumes that all state officials are part of a 'Liuist' line. Such conflicts are sometimes described by political scientists with the term 'bureaucratic pluralism', to suggest that under state socialism government organizations conflict in ways that resemble interest-group conflicts in other systems. These disputes have been going on since quite early in the history of Chinese state socialism. They are also extremely varied, taking place between officials in organs responsible for industry vs. agriculture, heavy vs. light industry, production vs. consumption, services and commerce (e.g., housing, health, trade), military vs. civilian work and technical vs. bureaucratic and political tasks, to name just a few.

Sometimes these conflicts have occurred over competition for scarce resources. For one small example, in Shulu County (Hebei Province) the Water Conservancy Bureau, which was responsible for supplying water to farmers, was alarmed by the rapidly dropping water-table. Wells are a major source of water there, and the bureau was having to dig them deeper with each passing year. This was both increasingly expensive and also very worrisome to bureau engineers who feared that underground supplies might soon dry up. Thus the bureau placed very tight regulations on irrigation. That put a crimp in the plans of the Forestry and Orchard Bureau, which was responsible for increasing fruit production. Fruit growing is very profitable – some Shulu peaches are even renowned enough to be exported – but it also demands a huge amount of water. Thus officials of this bureau developed their own estimates of water availability that were much more optimistic than those of the Water Conservancy Bureau, and they were using them to argue openly within the county government against the tight regulations. They were also touting the bright economic returns of fruit to argue for high priority in water rationing (Blecher and Shue, 1996: 178–9). Another example occurred around the policy of restricting families to one child to curb China's burgeoning population. In the early 1980s, as soon as the very first generation of single children was starting school, teachers and Education Ministry officials began to write articles in newspapers complaining bitterly about the one-child policy. It seems that these single children were being spoiled rotten at home by parents and grandparents, who poured all their affection and doting onto what would be their only offspring. Teachers coined the phrase 'little emperors and empresses' to describe these brats, whom they regarded as a significant educational problem.

The rise of the market has also increased bureaucratic rivalry. Returning to the Shulu example, the County Industry Bureau was responsible for the development of collective enterprises. It saw an opportunity to start a barium salts plant in the county seat's Eighth Street neighbourhood by using attractive wages to lure workers, technicians, managers and marketing officials who had retired from the state-run Xinji Chemical Factory. The new plant was so successful that Xinji Chemical began to fear for its future. It sent up howls of protest to the Hebei Province Chemical Industry Bureau, questioning the quality of Eighth Street's barium salts. Yet Eighth Street was defended by the County Industry Bureau. Ultimately the Chemical Industry Bureau's inspection team could find no problem at Eighth Street, and it closed the matter with a public statement calling for collaboration between the competitors. Yet bureaucratic and political obstacles, including the hurt pride of Xinji Chemical's director, prevented so happy an outcome (Blecher and Shue, 1996: 184–5).

If markets can be the cause of bureaucratic rivalries, the rivalries can also threaten the operation of markets, which poses a profound challenge to the entire reform project. The rise of local and regional trade protection has been a headache for reformers. Inland or primarily agrarian provinces specializing in the production of industrial raw materials (such as wool or cotton) have been unhappy to see the huge profits that coastal firms can make processing these relatively inexpensive inputs into semi-finished or finished goods (such as textiles). They have sometimes tried to impose 'duties' in the form of surcharges or taxes on their 'exports' to more industrialized places. In extreme cases, they have even forbidden the movement of goods at all, hoping that this will force up the price, or waiting until they can construct their own processing industries. This sort of regional rivalry pit against each other producers and users of energy, fuels, ores, foodstuffs, industrial crops, chemicals, machinery, finished goods and much else. These conflicts have damaged economic growth and market development, and created often serious political conflict.

Generational conflict

The Chinese Communist Party was founded in 1921, and the People's Republic of China in 1949. The movement's three-quarters of a century have seen four generations of political leaders and politically active people.[2] First of course are the eldest of the Party elders, who forged close bonds in the early days of the revolution, particularly during the cataclysmic experiences of the Long March. As we saw in Chapter 3, even in 'retirement' in the 1980s and 1990s, these leaders still exerted huge influence over the overall direction of the state and the leadership succession. Their backgrounds were long and varied, including experience with the rural and underground urban mobilizations of revolutionary days as well as the systematization of state institutions in the 1950s. Many were badly hurt – emotionally, politically and often even physically – in the Cultural Revolution. The resulting disillusion with both the politics of mobilization and of bureaucratization helped incline many of them toward the reformist alternative after 1978, though they never forgot the crucial role of the Party in organizing society and disciplining and defeating enemies.

To carry out structural reform, they needed to ally with those in the next generation, who were in their fifties and sixties when the process began. These people came of age during the last days of the revolution and the first decade of the socialist state. Many of them received technical training in the Soviet Union or in Chinese universities. Premier Li Peng, for example, was head of the Chinese Students' Association in Moscow in the 1940s, where he took an engineering degree. This generation of officials subsequently garnered long experience working its way up through the Party and government bureaucracies. Many of these people too were attacked in the Cultural Revolution, and, like their elders, were also inclined toward a new alternative that would involve neither the broad Maoist political mobilization that had lambasted them nor the worst aspects of the bureaucratic politics for which they had been lambasted. Given their age, they would have to be the ones to take the lead in running reformist China on a day-to-day basis.

However, they lacked the prestige and authority to set key directions on their own. For this they needed the imprimatur of their elders, who retained the capacity all through the 1980s and early 1990s to make or break their political careers. Party General Secretary Hu Yaobang learned this the hard way when he fell from Deng's grace in 1987. Premier Li Peng and Party General Secretary Zhao Ziyang also learned it in 1989, when Li's star rose for supporting the crackdown, while Zhao fell from power when Deng blamed him for the 'turmoil'.

Next comes the generation that was in high school or university during the 1960s. It provided the core of Cultural Revolution activists and participants. These people are, in general, much more dubious than their elders about the state, both because of the their Cultural Revolution experience of protest, as well as the punishment meted out to many of them (often involving years in the countryside to 'learn from the peasants') by the state leadership for those same activities. Yet the Cultural Revolution was also a grave disappointment to many of them for rather different reasons: its failure to achieve its goal of undermining élitism and bureaucracy. Unlike their elders, who have direct experience in the state institutions, many of these people tend to be more anti-bureaucratic. This may help explain why so many of them eventually joined the ranks of the 1989 protesters. They were dubious about the protests at first because of their sourness about the Cultural Revolution. Yet once they saw that this time social protest would probably not turn toward the personalistic and factional excesses that had derailed the Cultural Revolution, many became supportive of a new movement that held out the prospect of reaching some of the anti-élitist, participatory goals that had motivated them in their youth, goals that many of them had not yet abandoned. This generation is more inclined than its predecessors toward independent thinking and action. That could affect China over the next quarter of a century, insofar as they accede to the leading positions in the Chinese state and economy. One serious problem, however, is that many of these people – especially the freer-thinking ones – had their education interrupted, and their careers ruined, by the Cultural Revolution. Foreign scholars of this age cohort who visit China often do not find very many colleagues their own age, for example. Those Chinese in this group who did survive to become political élites tend to be those with a less independent cast of mind in their youth, who were willing in the 1960s and 1970s to keep their heads down and play along with the establishment. These are the men (and a few women) who are acceding to the top positions in the Chinese state as the twenty-first century dawns. Little surprise, then, that this group looks as bland and cautious as the second-generation leaders it is gradually succeeding. On the other hand, the bolder, more creative inclinations of some members of this generation have found expression in economic entrepreneurship.

Finally, there is the generation that has come of age under the structural reforms. It was reared in an increasingly consumeristic society, under a state that remained pervasive but that has also pulled back from close supervision of daily life and massive efforts to transform society. Thus its inclinations run toward growing personal ambition and self-absorption, to which it views the state as a significant but gradually weakening obstacle. In some ways, its protests in 1989 were even more audacious than those of the Cultural Revolution, because it did not have the specific encouragement of the supreme leader of the country, as the Red Guards did. With only the backing of the international media and his fellow students in Tiananmen Square, student leader Wu'er Kaixi, only in his early twenties, had the temerity to excoriate Premier Li Peng to his face on national and international television, even though the Premier had his finger poised on the trigger of a military crackdown. The inexperienced student leaders and participants of 1989 would soon learn that they had overestimated their strength, and after the crackdown they were humiliated and disillusioned. During the years following, many have turned back toward the privatism and self-absorption that characterized the 1980s, their formative decade. For example, Chai Ling, a firebrand of the 1989 movement who advocated provoking the state into a bloody crackdown, ended up graduating from Harvard Business School; she now believes that 'China's democracy and free-market economy will require people with a solid understanding of capital markets, advanced management skills, and experience in global competition' (*Harvard Business School Bulletin*, 1998). However, pundits and cynics to the contrary notwithstanding, these young people are not all members of a Chinese 'Generation X'. Many still remain patriotic and idealistic at least in their wish for a state that will allow them more latitude to pursue their private pursuits. Some probably maintain fond attachments to the public-spiritedness and collective action they experienced in 1989, as many of their immediate elders do to the Cultural Revolution. However the sentiments and inclinations of this young generation play out, they are certainly not in general a positive force for the strength of the state.

STATE AND SOCIETY

Political culture: the rise and fall of class-based hegemony

Conceptual issues

The unusual features of Chinese politics are often attributed to Chinese culture, which is, of course, also regarded by most Westerners as distinct from their own. Such an approach is understandable enough; after all, we have an intuitive sense that different countries have different cultures, and that these cultures affect their politics. Yet the concept of political culture also contains several pitfalls of which we should be very careful. They require us to undertake a methodological and conceptual excursus before proceeding to actual analysis of its relationship to Chinese politics.

First, cultural explanations can distance us from the subject of our study. They may prevent us from treating China the way we would treat other political systems in parts of the world culturally closer to our own. In other, sharper words, we may inadvertently partake in old stereotypes by coming to regard China not just as different but as strange, because of its alien and – dare we say it? – inscrutable culture. In discussing political culture, then, we must guard closely against the dangers of implicit ethnocentrism.

Second and more complex, cultures are rarely unambiguous or seamless. They often contain contradictory values and assumptions, which can make their political implications quite indeterminate. For example, Confucianism, with its collectivistic, conservative and anti-developmental commitments, was used until very recently to explain why industrialization was so slow in developing in East Asia compared with Western Europe. Now, it is used to explain precisely the opposite – why East Asia, with its subservient, disciplined and highly educated labour force, and its strong family systems that encourage savings, has had such remarkable economic development of late.

Third, most countries contain more than one culture. In our 'multicultural' age, we are reminded daily that women and men, various racial and ethnic groups and people with many other kinds of differences often have disparate values, assumptions and ways of perceiving and thinking. In the face of the proliferation of international migration and the rise of long-oppressed groups, it is getting harder and harder to say words like 'British' or 'American' culture. These changes are not just modern (or, better, postmodern) ones; they also force us to look at history very differently than we used to do. If we say that 'Chinese culture' was (and in many ways still is) heavily Confucian, we ignore the country's vast panoply of grass-roots values, assumptions and rituals, many of which are rather at odds with Confucianism. For example, a Confucianist perspective on something as mundane but important as tax collection would begin with the assumption that the Chinese people are subservient to authority, thus making them obedient and inclining China toward a relatively unproblematic system of state finance. Yet, if we were more attuned to grass-roots traditions that justify opposition to the state when necessary to protect one's village and family, we would expect a good deal more problems for the state in raising the money that is its lifeblood. (The problem is complicated by the fact that Confucianism itself also legitimated popular protest when leaders were not acting properly. As we shall see below, even dominant cultures have their built-in contradictions.) The reality is that China had both one of the most well-developed and well-functioning taxation systems of any pre-industrial country, and also one characterized by regular and elaborate traditions of tax evasion and popular resistance.

Fourth, this example also shows us the danger of treating the élite cultures as if they were nothing but abstract values and norms. Cultures are also forms of power used by élites to ground, legitimate and justify their rule. As we saw in Chapter 1, Confucian values played a significant role in keeping the Chinese people politically subservient to the authority of the imperial state and to local landlords for millennia. We need to recognize that culture does not just shape politics, but is often shaped and used by politics – a point to which we shall return.

Fifth, following from this point, a problem arises with the effort to relate culture to institutions. As mentioned in Chapter 1, it is certainly valid and valuable to see culture as shaping the actions people take within the institutional boundaries in which they find themselves. Yet there is another relationship of culture and institutions that those who live in liberal, representative states tend to miss. Such systems are built around the idea that the values citizens hold and the choices they make are logically and analytically prior to the state and politics. In methodological terms, people in liberal states tend to take culture and values as 'given', and to assume that democratic government reflects and conforms itself to them. As we have already glimpsed above, however, leaders and state institutions also shape political culture to fit their own wishes, needs and beliefs. We often think of this as occurring more in 'totalitarian' countries, where the state engages in regular programmes of propaganda and what used to be called 'thought control'. Yet we ought to remember that this also occurs – often more subtly – in liberal political systems, through mechanisms that run the gamut from patriotic rituals to campaign advertising to the use of political 'spin'.

Sixth, in the face of all this complex texture, there is the very real danger that what we call the political culture of a country might inadvertently be a way of giving social scientific window dressing to old-fashioned national stereotyping. This of course can have extremely negative consequences for actual politics. In the Vietnam War, General William Westmoreland, the commander of American forces, argued publicly that the Vietnamese people value human life less than Americans do – an outrageous fabrication about Vietnamese culture that he nevertheless used to justify barbaric bombing and napalm attacks. And even when cultural stereotyping is more implicit and is used to analyse rather than attack other countries, it can, as we have seen, lead us to some rather one-sided and downright wrong understandings of other countries and, therefore, of ourselves.

Yet none of this is an argument for dispensing with culture in our efforts to understand politics. On the contrary, these points tell us precisely that there are important links between culture and politics. They demand that we look at political culture in a way that takes full account of its multiplicity and ambiguity, and that strives for an appreciation of its complex relationship to politics.

One way to do so is to look at culture less as a set of positive statements about the values of a whole people – which, as we have seen, is simplistic and dangerous – and more as a way of looking at the world and asking questions about it. To quote Thomas Metzger, culture can be defined as 'an historically transmitted pattern of meanings . . . a system of inherited conceptions . . . [by which people] communicate, perpetuate and develop their knowledge about and attitudes toward life' (Metzger, 1977: 14). It does not provide answers so much as ways of formulating questions and political agendas, and providing the terms and language for debates over them. In other words, we can avoid many of the problems involved in analysing political culture by thinking of it in terms of the premises on which politics takes place.

According to the great Italian Marxist, Antonio Gramsci, a social group or class can be said to have hegemony over others when it has succeeded in persuading them to accept its political and cultural premises. Hegemony does not, then, involve deterministic, totalistic control of thought or action. To adopt a sports metaphor, hegemony lies not in the plays people make or the feats they accomplish, but in the rules of the game. Thus, the Chinese Revolution can be seen not as trying to change what people thought so much as the way people thought. In Gramscian terms, the Chinese Communist Party undertook a counter-hegemonic project during this cen-

tury to transform Chinese political culture. In fact, it undertook two rather different such projects: one during the Maoist years, and another during the Dengist
period. Each had a good deal of success, but each effort also ran into deep contradictions, some of which are still being played out, as we shall see.

A common hegemonic or counter-hegemonic strategy for a leadership is

> to view the society from the lens of a single sociocultural divide. All political conflict
> can then be interpreted in terms of that divide. Cultural hegemony has been estab-
> lished when members of all social strata interpret politics and choose strategies of
> participation in terms of the divide favored by the élite group.
>
> (Laitin, 1986: 107)

Since China's Communist Party leaders were Marxists, the divide they used was, of
course, class.

Political culture and China's socialist state

Until the revolution, Chinese political culture, including both Confucianism and
popular, grass-roots ways of thinking, did not have a prominent concept of class.
Historically, the Chinese word for class – *jieji* – does not appear to have been a
regular part either of day-to-day language or official discourse. Class has no place
in Confucianism. Many ordinary people partook of Confucian thinking, which is
what made it hegemonic. Yet many others subscribed at various times to a wide
range of local, popular cultures that emphasized the primacy and virtue of ordinary
people. Though these were very different world-views from Confucianism, like it
they too did not have a prominent concept of class and class conflict. Grass-roots
political cultures also seemed to hold that the greater power and wealth of government officials and landlords was part of the natural order of things rather than a
result of exploitation or political usurpation.[3] When times were rough people could
speak of oppression by landlords, usurers and corrupt officials; and they could go
so far as to conceive and justify resistance and sometimes even rebellion. Yet they
did so not in terms of overthrowing exploiters or despots so much as attacking
people who, through evil or excessive behaviour, had lost the moral or natural right
to collect rent or to rule. By saying that the gentry élite was rich and powerful
precisely because it kept the people poor and weak, the CCP's counter-hegemonic
concept of class and class conflict was a genuine departure from Confucianism, of
course; but it was also fundamentally different from previous popular cultures of
resistance and revolt.

The Party put its new cultural premise to many political uses. It based its claim to
leadership on its representation of the interests of poor, exploited peasants and
workers against landlords and capitalists. It tried to make the language of class and
class conflict a part of everyday discourse. The Party sought to make class into a
moral system, coming to speak eventually not just of 'objective' class categories
(peasant, landlord, worker, capitalist) but also of 'good' and 'bad' classes. Class
and class conflict also became a political agenda: in order to carry out the land
reform, people had to be sorted into classes by where they stood in the structure
of economic power. Then class conflict repeatedly became a goal of political

movements and specific policies pursued by the state. It even became a principle for running the economy, since socialism itself is understood as the form of economic organization favourable to the working classes. Finally, of course, class and class conflict defined and shaped political organization. The very concept of a single Communist Party that monopolizes power and organizational life originates in Marx's and especially Lenin's idea, shared by the CCP, that parties represent classes. Therefore, a multi-party system would only ensure the continued organization of capitalists, thus institutionalizing and prolonging class conflict.[4] The CCP also does not permit any other kinds of autonomous political associations or interest groups to exist, again justifying its monopoly by the need to preserve socialism, which, of course, is the working classes' mode of production.[5]

However, as we have seen, by the early 1960s, Maoists reversed this theory by seeing state socialist organization itself as the source of a new kind of class conflict. They began to speak of the bureaucracy as a class, coining the phrase 'Party persons in authority taking the capitalist road'. Maoists' calls for attacks on these new class enemies instigated the Cultural Revolution. The concept of bureaucratic class formations under socialism struck a responsive chord with many people frustrated with bureaucracy, technocracy and élitism. However, it was too murky to be put into practice. For while the class categories of the revolution – such as landlord or poor peasant, capitalist or worker – had an identifiable material basis, the new Maoist concept relied heavily on one's attitude and actions. Not all 'Party persons in authority' were class enemies, only those who had 'taken the capitalist road'. The examinations of leaders' dispositions and styles of work undertaken by Red Guard organizations to find out what road officials had taken soon deteriorated into unprincipled personal attacks and demagogic inquisitions. Mao's effort to view socialism through the lens of class struggle, which had driven the Party's hegemonic project to redefine social conflict around class struggle, and to reorganize society accordingly, collapsed.

As we have been arguing throughout this book, what replaced it is far more than mere 'reform', as it is commonly known. The Dengists have proposed nothing less than a new hegemonic project, China's second effort since 1949 to restructure its political culture and organization. This one dispenses with the basic social cleavage of class around which the Party had conceived and reorganized society and the state. As we have seen, one of the first acts of the Dengist leadership after consolidating its power at the Third Plenum of the Eleventh Central Committee in December 1978 was to abolish the formal class categories with which every Chinese citizen had been tagged for three decades, and to drop any further talk of class or any policy based on it. In 2000, Jiang Zemin went further, enunciating the theory of 'three represents', which holds that the Party stands for 'advanced productive forces', 'advanced culture' and 'the fundamental interests of the broadest masses' – all of which do not merely include but actually feature capitalism and the bourgeoisie. He subsequently promoted the admission of leading capitalists to the Communist Party, an initiative that elicited furious opposition in the Party and was soon shelved. The central problem, though, has now been clearly redefined as China's poverty and backwardness.

Politically, however, the state uses this profoundly transformed ideological tenet in the very same way that it used class conflict in the past: to justify monopolistic Party rule and to reorganize the polity and the economy. Socialism has been retained as a formal goal, for which, following a simplistic Marxian theory of stages, economic modernization is seen as a necessary precondition.[6] This modernization is not to be capitalist, even though it will make use of markets and strong material incentives in order to develop the economy rapidly. Continuing CCP control is justified as necessary to make sure that these capitalistic elements do not themselves become hegemonic, and to keep the goal of socialism clearly in view as modernization proceeds.

Because of the erosion in the leadership's commitment to a set of goals, a vision or even a shared pattern of meanings and a set of lenses through which to view the world, it is having difficulty organizing a hegemonic project that can rally people to its side. Indeed, it has little way of distinguishing its allies from its enemies. Insofar as the state has little sense of what to struggle for or even what to struggle over, it does not know whom to lead to do what. In this situation, society has descended into mere self-interest. With the exception of nationalism, the sense of belonging to some larger whole – a community, a work unit, a class struggling against its exploiters, a socialist project – that had begun to develop in the Maoist period, albeit often in very problematic ways, is practically gone. So are the values of social commitment and political and moral integrity. Once the Communist Party prided itself on being incorruptible; now an honest official is viewed, sadly by many, as an increasingly rare and quaint anachronism. In one small but poignant example, in the early 1990s an older woman who had been a loyal Communist all her life refused to pay the small bribe necessary to procure a bag of cement she needed to expand her home after many years of scrimping and planning. After waiting in vain for a long time for the building supplies dealer to fulfil her order, she broke down and, with tears in her eyes and outrage in her heart, finally lifted one from a huge pile at a nearby construction site. She reflected angrily that the system for which she had struggled for a lifetime, and to whose values of honesty and 'serving the people' she had committed herself and her hopes for China, was ultimately a failure because it forced even people like her to steal. She did not feel disillusioned, because her beliefs were not illusions – for a significant period of time she and many others had lived them. Rather, she felt betrayed at having the meaning and values taken out of her life. Not everyone in China shares this woman's noble values and historical commitments. Yet so many share her feelings of being lost and alienated from the state and society, of the profound uprooting of cultural moorings provided by shared values, commitments and identity, that we can speak of a cultural crisis in China.

Politics between state and society

The Maoist period: participation, mobilization and mass-line leadership

During the revolution, as we have seen, the Party developed the 'mass line', according to which its leadership was expected to pay close attention to the people's situation and demands, encourage them to express themselves and participate in politics, formulate its policies accordingly and, provided it had done all this, implement those policies with what it expected would be the people's active consent and participation. Mao summed this up in 1943 with the phrase 'from the masses, to the masses' (Mao, 1967, 3: 119). Though, as we shall see, the mass line was ultimately a method of leadership, it did encourage both some significant popular participation in politics as well as serious efforts by leaders to solicit the views of the people whether or not they took the initiative to participate.

During the land reform and much of the Maoist period, a broad range of daily decisions was left to localities which, at least in the countryside, deliberated and decided on them quite autonomously and even democratically. State authority set the parameters for local democracy, but did not eliminate it. For example, while certain methods of organizing production (such as subcontracting to households) were forbidden, production teams were also given definite latitude to conduct their affairs as they wished among a meaningful range of choices. They could choose time or piece-rate distribution, set their own norms for allocating work points and adjust their accumulation rates and welfare spending within certain ranges. They could also choose their own officials, even to the point of ignoring Party nominees. They arranged their own work on a day-to-day basis. Villages also often found ways to protect their own interests against those of the state. Grass-roots leaders frequently had an interest in doing so, since in many cases their loyalties were first to the villages in which they had grown up. Moreover, team and brigade leaders received their incomes from their collective units, not the state, which gave them a direct material stake in the economic fortunes of the locality. For example, during the 1970s one production brigade was forbidden to build a cement factory because the leftist regional leadership regarded the project as 'capitalist'. Because the brigade leader knew that rural enterprises that directly served agriculture were favoured under official policy, he then applied to build a chemical fertilizer plant instead – even though he knew that the raw materials for such a venture were very scarce and would soon run out. He got the approval, the plant was built and indeed soon faced shutdown. As had been his plan all along, he then switched the equipment over to cement making, arguing successfully that leaving the plant idle was wasteful of scarce collective resources (C. Hinton, 1986).

Within the production teams, decisions were often made by direct democracy. Team meetings were held frequently, and many were scenes of lively debate over how to organize and run local affairs. Team cadres were ordinary peasants from the village who earned their livelihoods by working in the team, so there were few obstacles (save personality and leadership style) to peasants' approaching them with questions, complaints and suggestions. They did so in myriad settings: when the villagers congregated informally in the evenings, during rest breaks or even while working, on the way to work in the fields, at local shops and so forth. Peasants also made conscious use of indirect methods, such as village grapevines and anonymous big-character posters, to make known views that they expected to be unwelcome to their leaders. A wide range of peasants utilized these various channels of political expression. They could and frequently did bring up issues of concern to them (rather than restricting themselves to agendas set by their leaders), frequently disagreed with their leaders (not to mention each other) and were often successful in influencing local decisions. In general, strong norms of consensus operated within Chinese production teams, and the most effective leaders were those who could forge such broad agreement (Blecher, 1978, 1979, 1983). There were also numerous channels by which peasants' views could reach the ears of brigade and commune leaders and even state officials at the county level. They were not shy about marching right up to brigade and commune officials when they saw them in their own village or in the local market town. They could have their views represented by delegates to the meetings frequently held at the brigade, commune or county levels. They could write letters to local officials or newspapers.

The mass line included not only political participation but also what could be called political solicitation (see Chapter 6). That is, in the Maoist period the Chinese state did not always wait for its citizens to take the initiative. Leaders frequently sought out the people's views through numerous mechanisms that provided the main conduit for expression of popular opinions and sentiments to leaders beyond the village. For example, 'work teams' periodically visited villages, often with the expressed purpose of ascertaining the contours and nature of popular political discontent. Higher-level cadres were regularly sent down to villages to 'squat on the spot' (*dun dian*), which meant that they moved into villages for extended stays of several weeks or even months, living in peasants' homes and working in the fields alongside them. Leaders were also sent to villages for shorter visits to conduct interviews or to attend team meetings. 'On-the-spot conferences' (*xian chang huiyi*) were held to investigate specific problems. In these ways, the views and concerns of peasants who lacked the inclination or ability to make themselves heard could be ascertained, and their situations experienced, by local and middle-level leaders. As a result, the state did not merely receive information from its own sympathizers or from those with greater political resources and energies. It could tap into a wider range of mass expression.[7]

The situation in the urban areas differed from the countryside, in that there is a greater separation of work and home, the unity of which in the countryside helped promote participatory politics there. In workplaces, there were experiments with the mass line, such as the famous constitution of the Anshan Steel Mill, much lauded by Mao. It institutionalized the participation of workers in management and managers in work, and combined managers, workers and technicians in workshop organization. During the Cultural Revolution, the Beijing General Knitwear Factory, where a management committee comprised equal numbers of political and production cadres, and where factory officials regularly rotated jobs in and out of the office, became an exemplar of new forms of management based on participatory politics and management solicitation and investigation. Such experiments were short-lived, and little is known about their effects on China's factories more broadly. Worker participation along Yugoslav lines was never broadly pursued in China. Outside factories, urban neighbourhood committees were generally preoccupied with carrying out propaganda and public health and information campaigns, exercising social control and mediating disputes. The extent to which they have provided the means for political expression or leadership solicitation of popular views also remains little studied.

However, the mass line was at bottom a method of leadership developed by a Leninist party, not a form of democracy guaranteed by rights, laws and institutions. The popular participation and leadership solicitation it encouraged were limited by the wishes, inclinations and capacities of the state. Over time, through the post-Leap recovery and the highly conflictual and ideologically strident Cultural Revolution decade, the state gradually placed narrower and narrower limits on the latitude within which villages could run themselves. By the mid-1970s, they were left only with the power to decide, for example, whether to place 3 or 4 per cent of their earnings into a welfare fund. Gradually, then, farmers became disillusioned with local participation. In some ways, their reaction resembles the disinterest that college students the world over show in student government or 'dormitory democracy', because there is so little at stake. In Chinese villages, however, the problem was worse, because nothing less than farmers' livelihoods depended on the decisions that they were increasingly unable to make. Their disgust with empty collective-level political participation was an important factor in their willingness to abandon collective farming altogether (Blecher, 1991). Likewise, Chinese leaders, not unlike politicians in many other countries, all too often had a tendency to solicit or pay attention to the views that they wanted to hear, or to filter what they heard through their own preferences, values and ways of thinking.

The mass line was also used by leaders consciously as a mobilizational tool. When they were determined to accomplish something, they would find or encourage the development of a locality that seemed to exemplify their proposed course of action, and then hold it up as a model for national emulation. This too could be legitimated under the mass-line principle of 'from the masses, to the masses'. The Great Leap Forward started this way, when Mao visited a rural area where peasants and local leaders were experimenting with what they called Weixing ('Sputnik') Commune. Mao was overheard by a reporter saying 'people's communes are good', the remark was reported in the newspapers and then villages all over China were exhorted to follow suit. The Cultural Revolution too got a strong push from Mao's order that the *People's Daily* publish a big-character poster put up by Nie Yuanzi, the young Beijing University philosophy instructor who stridently criticized her Party committee. From the mid-1960s through to the end of the Maoist period, farms and factories all over China were exhorted and pressured to pattern themselves after models such as the Dazhai Brigade and the Daqing Oilfields respectively. In other words, the mass-line principle of 'from the masses to the masses' gradually lost much of the participatory, locally democratic character it had originally had in the 1940s and the early 1950s. Instead, it became a way for the state to promote selected policies by finding localities that were exemplars of its wishes ('from the masses') and then mobilizing everyone else to follow them ('to the masses').

Here we see the operation of a very problematic political dynamic, known in Chinese as 'one cut of the knife' (*yi dao qie*), under which every locality is expected to follow the same guidelines in the same way. It seems to result from a combination of a general tendency toward bureaucratic uniformity with the specific activist ideological drive of Chinese state socialism. Sometimes, there has been a strong bottom-up dynamic. For example, when, after observing Weixing Commune, Mao uttered 'people's communes are good', officials and even many farmers did not even wait to be ordered; instead, they rushed to outdo each other in following the direction pointed out by the Chairman. At other times, the state imposed the uniformity, as during the 'Learn from Dazhai' campaign in rural development. Officials from all over China were mobilized to pay visits to this remote model village to see what they could bring home. The emulation campaign became rather mechanistic. One local leader from Guangdong said his village could not emulate Dazhai because his home was on flat land while Dazhai was mountainous. 'One cut of the knife' was a surprising development for a Party that during its revolution had learned the advantages and even necessity of decentralized operations and close attention to local differences.

The Dengist period

The Dengist leadership continued to make its own uniform knife cuts. While decollectivization began spontaneously from below, by the early 1980s the state forced every village in China to decollectivize, even though decollectivization was resisted by local leaders and farmers in many places where collectives had been prosperous. By allowing and then demanding the abolition of the collective units that had lain at the centre of the participatory, solicitative and mobilizational mass-line politics, the Dengists destroyed those politics. Farmers now spend their days working on household plots and in other individuated work processes, or else in the authoritarian setting of rural enterprises. They are no longer interdependent during work and in the processes that determine their income. In addition, the scope of political life has been reduced by the general depoliticization pursued by the Dengist leadership. Moreover, political functions have been hived off from economic ones and transferred to the more distant township governments. In the cities, there is no longer even any talk of mass-line innovations such as worker participation in management or shop-floor combinations of workers, technicians and leaders. Workers' representative assemblies may sometimes serve as a check against egregious managerial practices, but by and large they do not represent a form of workplace democracy. In short, since 1978, day-to-day life and production have become less directly and intimately regulated by collective, potentially participatory political processes.

Yet neither the structural reforms' institutional changes nor the rapid economic growth they produced have stilled popular political expression. As we have seen in earlier chapters, there are ample, palpable sources of political discontent in China. Corruption and unemployment are reaching serious levels, as did inflation for a time. Farmers are squeezed between rising input prices and state demands that they grow crops with low selling prices. They are also angry at the proliferation of unpredictable taxes and fees. Many workers have been furloughed or fired, and many more face the same prospect. The general decline of public services threatens the health and welfare of an increasing number of people. Since 1978, many Chinese have struggled to find new ways to give political expression to their concerns about these issues.

Many people in China and the West have been hopeful about the rise of 'civil society' – the realm that lies between the state and private life consisting of autonomous organizations formed to advance the interests of members of society. Throughout the reform period there have been wisps of such a development, particularly among intellectuals. For example, artists have organized their own associations and even held unauthorized art exhibits – a significant break from the Maoist past, when art and literature were considered supremely political, and their production and promulgation were closely controlled by the state. In the 1980s, one such exhibit raised eyebrows and caused long queues in Beijing because it depicted nudes.[8] On the whole, though, the actual development of a civil society in China has disappointed those who hoped for it. In 1989, political leaders associated both with Zhao Ziyang as well as his hardline enemies opposed students' and workers' efforts to form autonomous organizations. Insofar as society is organized at all to express itself to the state, the more common pattern resembles only remotely even the least democratic form of interest organization in non-Leninist systems, known as 'state corporatism', in which single-interest groups for each social group are established and directed by the state. For example, as we saw in Chapter 4, in Shulu County (Hebei) the head of a merchants' association was also the vice-director of the bureau that regulates private commerce. Of course, this pattern limits expression of social interests, but it does not choke them off altogether. In the early 1990s, for example, China's official labour union federation and its locals began openly to complain to factory managers, state officials and even the public (through the press) about the effects of lay-offs and deteriorating wages and working conditions. Some even threatened to organize strikes.

If civil society as a realm of popular self-organization and representation has been slow in coming, disorganized and spontaneous social protest has been much more common. Groups of disaffected citizens regularly hold sit-down protests on the steps of Party and government offices. For just one example, in February 1993, at the time of the symbolically important Chinese New Year,

> In a sign of unrest over labour reforms, as many as 200 retired women workers from China's leading steel company staged a daring protest at the offices of Chinese leaders to demand pensions ... The protest occurred ... at the main gate of the walled Zhongnanhai compound in central Beijing, where senior Chinese government and party leaders have their offices and some reside ... The women were among up to 400 retired workers from the giant Capital Iron and Steel Corporation, who have protested repeatedly since last autumn at the main gate of its mammoth complex in western Beijing to demand pensions they claim are owed to them.
>
> (*China News Digest*, 17 February 1993)

Likewise, in the summer of 1993, homeless people in the city of Wuhan gathered in front of city hall to express their outrage that their apartments had been torn down before new ones were built. Such forms of protest are difficult for the state to cope with, because they are peaceful, they raise concrete material issues that are much harder to discredit ideologically than specifically political demands and they are staged by groups that are politically impeccable (unlike intellectuals) and that are core parts of the state's social base.

Labour protest has been on the rise as well. As we saw in Chapter 3, many workers participated in the 1989 protests, and in late May began to organize autonomous unions. Indeed, the timing of the crackdown just days later seems to have been related to the leadership's panic that the protests would spread to the working class. Much of the violence on the night of 3–4 June involved workers and lumpenproletarians, and the harshest punishments of the crackdown, including the only executions, were reserved for them. Yet even in the face of the state's most draconian crackdown, China's workers were not cowed. In the second half of 1989, strikes occurred in all but four provinces, involving up to 80,000 workers. Since then, labour protest has become ubiquitous. The Chinese press reported over 400 strikes in 1992 alone. The Ministry of Labour admitted that in 1994:

> the number of large-scale labour-management disputes exceeded 12,000. In some 2,500 cases, workers besieged plants, set fire to facilities, staged strikes or detained bosses or leaders. Such events directly threatened the personal safety of Party leaders in various factories and mines. In the Jixi Mining Bureau, enterprise leaders did not dare go to the pits for fear that they might be attacked by the workers.
>
> (*Dangdai*, 15 May 1994)

In 1996, the number of protests rose 50 per cent over the previous year. In March 1997, 20,000 workers in Nanchong City joined a protest against a factory manager, who had not paid workers their wages for months, just as he was about to depart on a so-called business trip abroad. For a day and a half they took him hostage, paraded him through town tied up and bent over (in a manner reminiscent of the Cultural Revolution), and besieged city hall, where a bomb was also exploded (*Far Eastern Economic Review*, 26 June 1997). As we saw in Chapter 3, in 2002 a massive series of loosely coordinated labour protests in China's northeast, involving tens of thousands of workers, mesmerized the world.

In the countryside, too, many farmers have become politically active, often in novel and creative ways. In some cases, they respond to ad hoc exactions by informing themselves about state tax policies, and, armed with documents that support their case, remonstrate in a number of ways. They may first protest to village officials and, if they are not successful, then on up the ladder to the township and the county authorities. Many stage peaceful sit-ins in front of government offices. Thousands upon thousands have written letters (or hired scribes to do so) to magazines telling their stories. In some cases these letters attract the attention of editors and investigative journalists interested in publishing exposés. Some farmers even go to court seeking redress against local officials whom they accuse of acting improperly. These peaceful, legal and legalistic forms of protest may portend a new form of political participation in China (O'Brien, 1994; O'Brien and Li, 1995). Thus far they have not transcended their parochial concern with individualistic complaints by contributing to civic organizations that engage in advocacy on policy formation rather than just implementation. In view of the state's firm opposition to

219

any kind of autonomous political organization, the prospects for their doing so seem remote.

To these peaceful forms of rural protest can be added the violent uprisings by peasants caught in a tightening economic vice between higher input costs and rising government exactions on the one hand and declining crop revenues on the other. These became increasingly common in the late 1980s and, like the urban protests, continued past the 1989 crackdown. In one example that became prominent in the Chinese press, spontaneous protests by farmers in June 1993 in Renshou County (Sichuan Province) against road construction levies led to 'beating, smashing and looting . . . [in which] some people . . . stormed the district and township governments and schools, beat up cadres and teachers, smashed public and private property, and illegally detained grass-roots cadres and public security personnel'. When police responded with tear gas, some were taken hostage by the angry crowd, and police cars were set on fire (*BBC Daily Report*, 14 June 1993). Farmers are not the only perpetrators of rural violence. In Anhui Province, a villager who had the temerity to complain about 'unreasonable retention of funds' was beaten to death by several village cadres in April 1991 (*BBC Daily Report*, 30 May 1991). In a Hunan village, a farmer too poor to pay more than ¥220 of a ¥319 levy was hounded daily by local cadres until he committed suicide. A riot ensued when his body was pulled from the pond in which he had drowned himself (*BBC Daily Report*, 3 May 1993).

Rural violence has broken out around a range of issues besides local government levies. An effort in July 1993 by a county government in Hunan to requisition land along a railway line prompted farmers to seize weapons, including semi-automatic rifles, from the local armoury; several hundred troops and armed police were drawn into a battle in which 35 people were wounded (*BBC Daily Report*, 6 July 1993). Farmers have been slaughtering and maiming tax collectors: in 1989 in Shandong Province alone, five were killed and over 3,000 wounded, 353 permanently (*China News Digest*, 6 October 1990). During flooding in 1991 farmers were enraged by what they perceived to be insufficient state attention to water conservancy work and its mismanagement of relief efforts. They engaged in over 100 incidents of mass rallies, looting of state warehouses, armed clashes and even efforts to set prisoners free in four provinces. In Guizhou Province alone 30 people were killed (*China News Digest*, 8 August 1991). In September 2002, 30,000 Guizhou farmers, 'enraged' about low purchase prices and delayed payments for previous harvests, 'stormed the government building and smashed plaques hung on the walls. One read "Serve the People" and the other concerned Jiang Zemin's "Three Represents Theory". The farmers also blocked the main Guizhou–Guangxi railway for six hours' (*China Labour Bulletin*, 31 October 2002).

Violence is spreading in other forms, for other reasons and with other targets. Even routine work by local officials, in land reallocation, population control, dispute mediation and public welfare work, is sometimes met with reprisals from farmers, including vandalism and beatings. Battles have broken out between villages over property rights and access to water. Secret societies are making a strong comeback, which ought to frighten the leadership most of all because they portend a possibility of organized protest (*Inside China Mainland*, October 1990: 8–9; *BBC Daily Report*, 30 April 1991; *China News Digest*, 26 January 1993).

CONCLUSION: AUTONOMY IN STATE–SOCIETY RELATIONS

In all state socialist countries and other forms of authoritarianism, society has little autonomy from the state. Self-organization of civil society, and political competition and rights, are eliminated or severely restricted. The state uses a mixture of intensive surveillance and coercive power to control politics and public life. All this has been true of Chinese state socialism, though, as in all countries, the way in which society was deprived of autonomy from the state took a form specific to the country's society and history. However, society's autonomy from the state is a different question from the state's autonomy from society. While most authoritarian states seek to insulate themselves from society by repressing it into quiescence, the Maoist state chose instead to rule by activating society. It demanded not mere obedience, but active, mobilized assent. It wanted believers, not subjects. It sought to control not just what the Chinese people did, but how they thought. It wanted them to combine theory and practice, to put their commitments to socialism into action. From the early days of the revolution, when 'open-door rectification' broke with Leninism by encouraging popular criticism of local officials and Party leaders, through the Cultural Revolution, Maoism was opposed to keeping the state too autonomous from society.

As we have seen, the Maoist commitment to popular participation and mobilization came into frequent and increasingly sharp contradiction with its commitment to a specific, radical form of socialist transformation. Naturally, the flaw in the Maoist project was the assumption that overall the people were naturally inclined to the leadership's socialist vision. They often were not. As Maoist theory itself often professed but did not really grasp, real material and social life was far more complex than theories, including Maoist theory with its emphasis on practice. Even where people tried honestly to make Maoist concerns their own and put them into practice, as in their genuine concern about élitism, corruption and urban bias during the Cultural Revolution, their efforts to prosecute a 'class struggle' around these issues became inevitably and fatally intertwined with issues of personal revenge, factional power struggles, leadership opportunism and genuine confusion about who the enemy really was and how it should be dealt with. Thus, on the one hand, by opening itself to attacks from society, the Maoist state was almost directly brought down by social protest. On the other, it only survived by frequently stepping in to repress the very popular outpourings it had encouraged – most notably, in the anti-rightist campaign in 1957 and the deradicalization and military suppression of the Cultural Revolution. In short, the Maoist state's renunciation of autonomy from society provoked crises that ultimately undermined it. The Maoist state

221

opened itself to society but it also gave society the opportunity to ravage the state.

The Dengist leadership came to power determined to reverse this structural contradiction. It sought to extricate the state from being so tightly enmeshed with society, and to open a greater distance between them. One approach was the depoliticization of social and economic life, i.e., narrowing the definition of what counts as political, and expanding what Tang Tsou has called its 'zone of indifference' to many aspects of daily life (Tsou, 1986: xxiv). Thus, the state no longer cares much about ideological rectitude or transformation, it abolished class labels and renounced class struggle, it does not try to run the economy so directly or exclusively and it permits a much wider range of social and cultural forms. A second way of creating distance between state and society has been economic development. As we know from the experience of capitalist development, consumer goods have tremendous power to distract people from social concerns, and to atomize and privatize social life. Marketization and privatization induce and often force people to be intensely preoccupied with procuring and advancing their material lives. Third, institutions such as representative assemblies in workplaces and local governments have been established to canalize, co-opt and control political participation. Fourth, of course, occasional doses of ruthless repression – of dissidents on an ongoing basis, and of protest movements as they arise – have been added into the mix.

These efforts have transformed the structure of state–society relations. In general, ordinary Chinese see state officials much less often and from a much further distance than they did in the Maoist period. They spend far less time engaged in political activity. The increased distance compared with Maoist days is apparent in the comparison between the Cultural Revolution and the 1989 protests. In the Cultural Revolution, people hauled out 'capitalist roaders' right in their neighbourhoods, workplaces and schools; in 1989, they held signs denouncing Premier Li Peng, who was safe inside well-fortified government compounds, and they inflicted pain on themselves rather than upon their enemy. By politicizing the most concrete issues of daily life in a very direct and broad way, the Cultural Revolution more easily deprived the state of its capacity to bring matters back under control; it was far easier to order in the troops in 1989.

However, implicit in this comparison, of course, is that the widened gap between state and society has not always translated into political stabilization or quiescence. That depends on far more than the strategies of state autonomy. It hinges on the severity of China's social and economic crises, the social coalitions they do or do not bring together in common cause and the institutional setting for coping with dissatisfaction. To those issues we turn in our final chapter.

CHAPTER 8

Toward the Future

Don't think it won't happen just because it hasn't happened yet.
– Jackson Browne

As we began, so let us end with some puzzles. China has surprised many people – including even its own leaders and people as well as foreign observers – more often than most care to remember. Its fall from the apex of world civilization for millennia to the lowly status of the 'sick man of Asia' by the late nineteenth century still baffles. Subsequently, China could not consolidate a capitalist economy or a polity at a time when some of its neighbours did so. Instead, the most sturdy and continuous political system in world history, and a deeply conservative one at that, produced a massive socialist revolution and transformation. China's socialism has experienced several dramatic shifts. Departing early from the Soviet model, for years it evinced a driving impulse for 'continuing revolution' that put it at the extreme left among state socialist countries. Then, in 1979, it switched course, pioneering broad-gauged structural reform way ahead of them. In 1989, it switched back, moving sternly, decisively and successfully against popular demands for reform precisely at a time when most other state socialist countries were being destroyed by such popular movements for change. Predicting China's future is a hazardous occupation. The safer course is also the more intellectually defensible one of analysing some of the important forces that will be in play as China moves through the first decades of the twenty-first century.

Can the People's Republic of China maintain the political quiescence it so desperately seeks? A good place to begin is with the factors that occasioned the 1989 protests and enabled the state to survive them. The protests began with demonstrations around symbolic issues (honouring Hu Yaobang and recalling the May Fourth Movement) by students favouring political reform. The students' boldness was rooted in the apparent divisions among the leadership and in the indecisiveness and lack of will that the state had shown the previous year over economic policy – specifically, the key issue of price reform. The students' agenda soon spread to include corruption, which was to a significant degree a structural effect of China's half-reformed economy. So were many other problems: stagnating productivity, cyclical overheating and austerity, growing inequality, mounting state deficits and a generalized credit squeeze. Social problems such as rising crime, increasingly expensive education and health care, an ongoing housing shortage and cultural ambivalence about Westernization, were also rife. All these issues had created discontent. In the contexts of the presence of Western journalists, as well as the continuing divisions and the palpable indecisiveness of the leadership, the movement gradually broadened to include many other urbanites.

China continues to experience most of the problems that underlay the 1989 protests. Inequality is worsening. Corruption is harder to measure, but clearly is still a major problem. From 1997 to 2002, Chinese courts handled almost 120,000 corruption cases; many more were dealt with extralegally within the Party. Nineteen provincial or ministerial level officials were sentenced for their crimes. Education remains expensive yet in high demand. Other problems loom as well. Inflation has abated, but it has been replaced by massive and growing unemployment. A cataclysmic banking crisis looms on the horizon, capable of plunging the economy into recession or even depression. If the independence-minded political authorities in Taiwan, who have so far acted with restraint, decide for whatever reason, including domestic political advantage, to declare formal independence, war could break out in the Taiwan Straits. That would bring China into direct confrontation with the USA and the rest of the world, and plunge the economy and the political system into the profoundest crisis.

Meanwhile, protest by farmers, workers and ordinary urbanites is now endemic. Students have shown that they can start their own demonstrations unexpectedly and at the drop of a hat. They have proved throughout recent Chinese history to be capable of drawing wide support from urban society, a task that would be easier now that many workers and ordinary urbanites are already mobilized themselves. Reports of political apathy among the Chinese people due to the triumph of consumerist hedonism and alienated self-absorption were heard in the run-up to 1989, and may be as premature now as they were inaccurate then.

Ultimately, the People's Republic of China survived the challenge of 1989, and the reasons that it could do so may also point to the countervailing forces that still mitigate against a political movement to bring down the state. First, in the USSR and Eastern Europe, state socialism was associated with national subjugation: by Russians over multiple nationalities in the Soviet Empire, and by the USSR over Eastern Europe. By contrast, in China – as in Vietnam, Korea and Cuba, all survivors too – state socialism was part and parcel of a movement for national liberation and economic development. The People's Republic continues to enhance its legitimacy at home by effectively advancing China's position of independence and self-respect in the world. This tactic was in evidence most recently in its efforts to host the 2008 Olympics, the prospect of which now provides a political asset on which it can draw for several more years. Second, there are few, if any, immediately apparent sources of social identification around which broad opposition can rally. In particular, nationality, though often deeply felt in China, is not an issue dividing society internally, as it was in the USSR, Czechoslovakia and Yugoslavia. Third, the history of Chinese state socialism, from the Great Leap Forward to the Cultural Revolution to 1989, has impressed on many Chinese, often in the most personal ways, the profound dangers of political disorder. The 1989 protesters were clearly on much better behaviour than the Red Guards. Fourth, and following from that point, the living example of the myriad problems of the former Soviet states and Yugoslavia reinforce this view. Many Chinese, including quite a few of the most radical participants in the 1989 protests, are deeply fearful that the collapse of the People's Republic could result in the collapse of the country and a renewal of the internecine warfare that wracked China as recently as the years of warlordism earlier in the twentieth century.

Fifth is the question of political institutions and the culture associated with them. In Russia and especially Eastern Europe, there were distinct, if suppressed, historical traditions of civil society. By contrast, imperial China basically did not possess even the conceptual distinction between public and private, much less an organizational tradition of civil society. After 1911, social organizations devoted to political representation developed only weakly among intellectuals and workers, and barely at all among farmers. Civil society has been suppressed since 1949. The absence of institutions and even a cultural concept of civil society was evident in the inability of the 1989 demonstrators to give coherent answers when Western journalists asked them what they meant by democracy. It also helps explain why, in a fashion resembling the traditional Chinese practice of petitioning officials but not challenging their legitimacy, demonstrators' demands focused on changing the leadership and reforming the Party and bureaucracy rather than on creating a multi-party system. Nothing that has happened since 1989 suggests that China's political opposition has become differently inclined. By contrast, the Chinese Communist Party, for all its corruption, crisis of morale and declining capacity to control the economy and society, proved itself in 1989 to be a powerful organizational weapon in the Leninist mould. Its leaders showed their determination and even their ruthlessness. The crackdown, and the years since then, have not only vindicated them politically – they won, after all, and the economy has boomed since – but also demoralized and undermined the opposition and strengthened the state's self-confidence and resolve.

Thus, there are formidable forces operating in opposite directions on the question of the survivability of the People's Republic of China. How they will balance out in practice cannot be predicted, but the field of play that will concretely determine the outcome can be specified. It will involve the complex interaction among various social classes and groups. Students and intellectuals may be able to start a broad political movement, but they cannot end it. In 1989, the state survived because the working class remained quiescent until very late, while the farmers were passive at best and downright hostile at worst. Thus, the students, intellectuals and their urban sympathizers could be isolated and cut down during the crackdown.

In the years since 1989, as we have seen, the material bases and expressions of discontent among farmers and workers have been growing. Yet they have mostly remained localized. The wave of proletarian protests in the spring of 2002 appeared for a time to herald a new and portentous potentiality for a broad workers' movement; yet the state managed to cope with them and put the genie back in the bottle at least for the time being. But if a renewed round of coordinated or contagious urban demonstrations were to occur, a strong signal would be sent, and a powerful opportunity would be presented, to discontented students, other urbanites and even farmers that their moment had arrived. What would be required in this scenario is not an organized alliance of urban and rural popular protest. The cultural gap, historical antagonism, existential gulf and economic contradictions between town and country, or even between students and workers, remain far too great for that. But as Barrington Moore has shown, even unorganized rural revolt, triggered by an urban uprising but separate from it in form and content, directed against very different targets, and oriented to very different goals, can nonetheless be an indispensable element in undermining the structure of a state (Moore, 1966). The danger in China would be still greater if rural protest were to grow so serious as to undercut the capacity of the military to command its troops, who hail mainly from the countryside.

If even the survivability of the People's Republic cannot be predicted with much accuracy, harder still is it to foresee how China's politics would develop under the present state or some successor. Four main scenarios can be charted, two if the state collapses and two if it survives. In the former case, a new and weaker state based on some form of elections could begin to develop, perhaps broadly along the lines seen in Russia and Eastern Europe. It would face several obstacles. As we have seen, China is poorly equipped with the cultural traditions and institutions of civil society. The country's workers and farmers have weak links at best, and suspicious and hostile relations at worst, with the urban intellectuals and politicians who would organize and operate such a state. Unless the Communist Party had been totally devastated by the transition, which is unlikely, it would probably be in the best position to win elections, if not immediately then at least within a short time – a development already taking place in Eastern Europe.

An alternative outcome is collapse into competing provinces. China has always been a country with strong regional differentiation. People from different regions look different, eat different foods and some even speak different languages.[1] A great deal of decentralization has already occurred both in the Maoist and Dengist periods. Regional inequality is worsening. Trade barriers have cropped up. The prospect of China becoming as bloody a battleground as Yugoslavia may be overstated, since in China the Han nationality is so predominant. But in these politically centrifugal times, the decomposition of China into a loose, weak federation cannot be ruled out.

If the People's Republic of China survives, two other scenarios suggest themselves. One would be a gradual, élite-led liberalization, along the lines of the changes that took place in South Korea or Taiwan in the 1980s and 1990s. In this model, the Party would gradually open the political system to limited competition and some sharing of power with other élites that it already knew and whom it hoped to control in the process. But the geographic proximity of the South Korean and Taiwan cases may obscure a huge structural gulf between them and China. Their authoritarian élites who moved toward limited liberalization were not leaders of a Communist Party, with all its ideological strictures and its intensely disciplined, hierarchical institutional culture and structure of authority.[2] It is difficult to see how any CCP leader who hoped to maintain significant political power for the foreseeable future could take the first step across the sharp line that the Party has always drawn against any degree of autonomy for any political group outside itself. As with the Chinese view of the USSR and Eastern Europe, the earliest living results of liberalization in South Korea and Taiwan – the disgrace and imprisonment of former presidents in Korea, and a lively separatist movement threatening national sovereignty in Taiwan – further mitigate against any such impulse.

The final scenario is the most obvious: that the current state will muddle through its difficulties and crises. This could happen for positive or negative reasons. Market Stalinism has achieved proven results in China over almost two decades, and its combination of economic inducements and hardline politics enabled it successfully to survive the formidable challenges and apparent impasses of the 1980s and 1990s. More negatively, the consensus that seems to have emerged in China in the last decade – that the People's Republic, however problematic, is preferable to the alternative – could continue to hold sway. Certainly the history of many former state socialist countries in the 1990s makes this a reasonable view.

Muddling through does not mean that China would necessarily remain a tightly repressive one-party state. As we have seen, in the mid-1990s individuals began to experience much greater personal control over their social and economic lives, and some limited space to discuss politics critically. Until late 1998, the state demonstrated its growing maturity and confidence in allowing the expansion, very slowly but steadily, of the range of public discourse and debate open to both leaders and citizens. Even after the rise of a harder line toward opponents starting in 1999, the state, while still not brooking rivals for power, nonetheless seeks to be somewhat responsive to the needs and wishes of society. For example, it has made a major public issue of corruption, encouraged village elections of local officials and begun to erect new social insurance systems. It sees its role as something of a benevolent despot. It believes that it needs to monopolize political power, because it thinks that competitive politics will weaken the country's ability to grow rapidly and to manage the urgent problems that arise daily along the way. Put more positively, it believes that if it can succeed at strengthening the country by promoting prosperity and efficiently managing problems, the Chinese people will permit it its monopoly. That is a formula on which China's emperors predicated their own rule for millennia. It is not a common political configuration in the modern world, but it is one that comes almost naturally to the Chinese state and to many ordinary Chinese. In trying to bring it forward into the tempestuous twenty-first century, the Chinese state may again be setting out on a new and unique political pathway.

The wise observer will, therefore, be prudent in making predictions or commitments. When it comes to China's future, social science can help direct us where to look, but is, like many natural sciences such as meteorology, limited in its ability to tell us what we will see. Perhaps, after China's repeated penchant to swim against shifting tides in the past 150 years, and all the spectacular innovation that has generated, the best one can do is to expect the unexpected.

Notes

INTRODUCTION

1. 'Socialism' is a broad term that covers a range of actual and potential economic systems involving public ownership of the means of production and economic decision-making through planning rather than markets. It can include everything from highly democratic, autonomous Utopian communities and syndicalist, anarchistic experiments in worker ownership and management of factories to the highly organized, authoritarian systems based on the Soviet model. (The word is also often used in connection with capitalist welfare states such as Sweden, though such systems are more properly classified as social democracies.) Many critics, including some on the political left, argue that what developed in the Soviet Union, Eastern Europe, China and several other countries was not 'socialist' at all, since ownership and economic decisions were not handled democratically, as the founders of socialism clearly intended. In order to avoid this debate while still taking account of it, we will use the term 'state socialist' to characterize China's political economy during both the Maoist period and much, if not all, of the subsequent period of structural reform starting in 1978, since during both life was organized mainly (though not exclusively, as we shall see) by a strong, centralized state in control of the economy. By the 1990s, as China's economy became ever more fully marketized, and as privatization grew to significant proportions, the term began to fit less and less well. The country is coming to resemble capitalist authoritarianism, though the fact of continued rule by the Communist Party sets limits to the power of the new bourgeoisie and still lends a socialistic cast to some areas of policy.
2. Yugoslavia, with its system of workers' councils and political decentralization, was a major exception.
3. Poland also experienced a massive popular movement – Solidarity – that attacked the state and ultimately brought about martial law. But where Solidarity was formed by society in opposition to the state, the Cultural Revolution attacks were inspired and led by radical state leaders.
4. Again, Yugoslavia was an exception. But since it never adopted the standard model of political and economic centralization seen in the Soviet Union, the rest of Eastern Europe and the Asian state socialist countries, it did not require the same sort of broad reform.
5. In 1979, China's average life expectancy at birth was 64 years, compared with 52 for India and 57 for all low-income countries. Its rate of adult literacy in the mid-1970s was 66 per cent, compared with 36 for India and 51 for all low-income countries (World Bank, 1981: 134).
6. Of course, the voices of many Chinese intellectuals contributed to this

analytical miscue. Western observers who hoped for a democratic break-through in China tended to give these Chinese democrats undue weight, and abstracted them from the wider context of Chinese politics. Those observers who were more attuned to the thinking of China's farmers, workers and bureaucrats, and who kept in view the power of the Chinese state and the perspective of most of its Party leaders, were rather less surprised by the crackdown and survival of the People's Republic.

7. The term 'Maoist period' is unfortunate for two reasons. First, it focuses too heavily on the character of the dominant leader of the time; as we shall see, developments in state socialist China were shaped not just by the state acting on society, but rather by complex politics within the state and by the reciprocal, active relationship of the state and society. Second, 'Maoist period' focuses too heavily on one leader – Mao Zedong – who in fact faced significant opposition with which he had to compromise, and to which he even lost out, through much of the period. Nonetheless, when all is said in done, the overriding character of the three decades between 1949 and 1978 bears the indelible stamp of Mao's leadership. Thus, lacking an equally parsimonious term, this shorthand is appropriate enough to bear using, so long as these provisos are kept in mind.

8. Though Deng Xiaoping did not face the same level of opposition from other leaders as Mao did, most of the other provisos in the previous note also apply to the term 'Dengist period'.

1. IMPERIAL LEGACY, CAPITALIST FAILURE AND SOCIALIST TRIUMPH

1. No country has ever achieved stable representative democracy without capitalism. As Barrington Moore has written about the historic rise of the liberal state: 'no bourgeois, no democracy' (Moore, 1966: 418). But capitalism has, of course, actually produced a representative state in only a small number of cases. In East Asia, home to some of the world's most vibrant capitalist development, representative democracy is only beginning to develop in just a few countries. Even in Japan, the modern constitution was imposed by the USA after the Second World War. Thus, any analysis of the question of democracy in China should not look at China alone.

2. The terms 'imperial' and 'empire' have two different meanings in our discussion. On the one hand, they refer to the social and political structures that existed within China for thousands of years until the early part of the twentieth century. The Chinese word for its monarch is commonly translated into English as 'emperor'. Moreover, the state was indeed an empire in the strict sense of the word, in that it was controlled mainly by Han Chinese, and it dominated many other small nationalities. But probably the major reason that Westerners termed historical China an empire is simply because of the

country's vast size and centralized rule. In any event, this sense of the 'imperial' character of the traditional Chinese state and society contrasts sharply with that of Western and Japanese imperialism, which played a major role in undermining the Chinese 'empire', as we shall see. Which meaning is operative at any particular point in our discussion should be clear enough from the context.

3. 'His' is not sexist usage here. In patriarchal China, bureaucracy and politics were exclusively male domains.

4. Confucianism is a philosophical and ethical system that has had wide currency in China for many centuries, especially among the gentry and the imperial court, but also to a large extent among the broad population. It emphasizes the natural harmony among the various parts of society, based on family metaphors for the relationship between rulers and ruled, and between landlords and tenants. Confucianism painted the emperor and imperial officials as well as landowners as wiser, more virtuous and, therefore, deserving of more power than ordinary people; but, like a good father (never a mother, since Confucianism was also deeply patriarchal), these élites also had responsibilities to nurture their 'children'. For their part, the people were expected to obey the élites, to understand their own inferiority and to appreciate that doing so would promote social harmony.

5. Of course, peasants often resisted, usually in small ways such as cheating landlords at harvest time. They also expressed their opposition in grass-roots cultural forms known as the 'little tradition' (see Thaxton, 1983). Sometimes they also staged uprisings, though, interestingly, these often had an essentially conservative character: they generally demanded not the abolition of landlordism or the state, but instead called on landlords and officials to respect the proper traditional limits and obligations of their roles.

6. Of course, this process occurred in very different ways in different countries.

7. The case of Sheng Xuanhuai is instructive. See Feuerwerker, 1958.

8. Actually, this alliance continues to the present on Taiwan, where the Republic of China moved after losing control of the mainland. Indeed, it is one of the important reasons for the economic successes registered there.

9. Moore, 1966: 183. Skocpol makes the controversial case that, in France, the state rather than the bourgeoisie played the major role in the transformation to industrial capitalism. See Skocpol, 1979, Ch. 5.

10. The Nazis, it will be remembered, had their 'Brown Shirts' and the Italian Fascists their 'Black Shirts'.

11. This is not to deny the considerable differences among these régimes, or between them and the Guomindang. Barrington Moore summarizes the major reasons why the Guomindang ought not be considered Fascist, though it had affinities with Fascism. See Moore, 1966: 196–201.

12. Interestingly, history would later show that the Party did not also conclude from this debacle that it ought never again contract a marriage of convenience with the Guomindang. In fact, it did so just ten years later. But by then the CCP had its defences up, in the form of the Red Army.

13. His major statement on the matter is his famous essay, written to criticize Moscow-trained cadres who had no experience in the field of actual revolutionary action, entitled 'On Practice' (Mao, 1967, 1: 295–310).

14. In Marxian lingo, the lumpenproletariat refers to the lowest subclass of urban society, including the likes of criminals, gang members, prostitutes and drug addicts and dealers. Marx saw them as not particularly revolutionary, and, in fact, potentially reactionary. After all, they could not form revolutionary consciousness based on the degradations of wage labour. Moreover, they often preyed on the working class, by providing them with 'pleasures' that distracted workers from their misery and their efforts to attack the capitalists, by stealing from them and even by serving as hired thugs to attack working-class moments.

15. The term 'cadre' – the common translation of the Chinese term *ganbu* – includes the broad range of leaders and officials, from the highest levels of the state down to local activists and grass-roots leaders. It can even include people who are not Communist Party members.

16. The Communists finally did permit such sales in 1937 as part of the more moderate policies they adopted after the nearly fatal Long March.

17. 'Kulak' is the Russian term for better-off farmers.

18. As we shall see in Chapter 7, the shared experience of the Long March would also have a significant impact on élite politics. The survivors were widely revered, and many maintained powerful positions in the leadership for the rest of their lives, which continued through the 1990s. Quite a few formed an informal group that acted as a bulwark against significant political reform in the Dengist period.

19. In Marxist categories, petit bourgeoisie refers to self-employed people operating small businesses. The CCP also spoke of the national capitalists (sometimes also translated as 'national bourgeoisie'): Chinese businessmen who were patriotic (i.e., anti-Japanese) and not closely tied to the Guomindang (which would place them in the category of bureaucratic capitalists).

20. Though the translation uses the male pronoun, the original Chinese is gender-neutral.

21. Theda Skocpol has pushed this line of argumentation – especially on the latter two points – to its limits (Skocpol, 1979: 246, 252 and *passim*).

22. Skocpol comes close to such a position in the following statement:

> Precisely because this military strategy [of popular, peasant-based guerrilla warfare] was the only one possible in the circumstances, the Chinese Communist Party after 1927 was forced to come to terms with the peasantry in a way far different from what happened in France and Russia.
>
> (Skocpol, 1979: 252)

But how do we know that this was the only strategy possible? Or if it was, that the CCP adopted it because it knew this?

23. Skocpol, 1979: 4. I have left out the word 'rapid' used by Skocpol, because it does not fit the protracted nature of the Chinese Revolution – something which she takes into account in her analysis but not in her definition.

24. This is not a lesson which could be learned directly from the Russian Revolution. The Bolsheviks organized the Tsarist armies from within, and ultimately took them over. The need for revolutionaries to have their own military forces is, then, a contribution to revolutionary practice made first by the Chinese Revolution.

2. THE TRIUMPH AND CRISES OF MAOIST SOCIALISM, 1949–78

1. The best study of the Chinese land reform, depicting both the range and complexity of problems as well as the triumphs, remains William Hinton's eyewitness account *Fanshen* (W. Hinton, 1966).
2. In Chapter 1, we spoke of the gentry as China's traditional ruling class, and the landlords as an integral part of the gentry. By 1949, the other components of the gentry – the officials and the scholars – had been dispatched from the scene for decades. It is possible, then, to speak of the landlords as a class in and of themselves by this time.
3. The Chinese term for this system was *yi zhang zhi*, which literally means direction or rule by one head person. Thus it is not sexist in Chinese. Yet the universal translation into English is, unfortunately, the sexist term 'one-man management'. For that reason, and because most of the managers were in fact male, that translation is followed here, regrettably and with this proviso.
4. For a perceptive and moving first-hand account of the effects of piece-rates in a Hungarian factory, see Haraszti, 1978.
5. This speech was not published in China until after Mao's death, another signal of the ambivalence and possible controversy swirling around the First Five Year Plan.
6. Of course, former landlords were also excluded, but more for political reasons than out of concern with economic exploitation. After land reform, landlords had little property to contribute.
7. 'On the Correct Handling of Contradictions Among the People' (Mao, 1977: 384–421). This version, published months later, contains important changes made subsequently during the 'anti-rightist movement' in order to deal with unanticipatedly harsh criticisms of the state that the original speech helped unleash during the Hundred Flowers campaign. It even admits this, stating in a footnote (on page 384) that Mao 'went over the verbatim record and made certain additions before its publication in the *People's Daily* on 19 June 1957'.
8. The term 'brigade' (*shengchan dui*) has the same martial overtones in Chinese as in English, reflecting the military imagery of the day. Likewise, the production groups (*zu*) were soon redubbed 'teams' (*xiao dui*). These terms stuck even after commune organization and operations settled down to greater normalcy in the mid-1960s.
9. As we shall see in Chapter 6, this did not entail a shift in state investment

priorities. Rather, agriculture received more prominence in political campaigns, and light industry was helped simply by granting communes some flexibility and latitude to start their own workshops.

10. 'Private plot' is an inaccurate though common translation of *ziliudi*, which literally means 'self-retained plot'. It was not privately owned in the sense of being property which peasants could purchase, sell or rent. Rather, it was a piece of the collective's land which was allocated temporarily to individual households on a per capita basis. (Under the stabilized communes of the 1960s and 1970s, the plots were reallocated every three years to make adjustments for changes in household size.) Peasants could grow whatever they wished on these plots. The product was not subject to taxation or collective distribution. It was, then, a sphere of private production and consumption, but not private ownership.

11. In some places, former landlords also experienced rising fortunes in this period. Yet because they were more thoroughly and overtly attacked in the land reform than the former middle and rich peasants were in the co-operativization, and because as a former leisure class they generally had less to contribute to economic growth, the landlords staged much less of a comeback.

12. The translation has been altered slightly to improve grammar.

13. Lin was the main proponent of the ubiquitous *Quotations from Chairman Mao*, the *Little Red Book* that political activists in their tens of millions carried everywhere.

14. In a graphic example of the political fluidity and incoherence of the day, Wang's actual position remained murky for some time. He made public appearances welcoming foreign heads of state, but, when asked, high Chinese officials were unable to explain what position he held or why he was qualified to do so. See MacFarquhar, 1993: 281 n.

15. Liu Shaoqi, his superior, had died in prison in 1969.

3. THE TRIUMPH AND CRISES OF STRUCTURAL REFORM, 1979 TO THE PRESENT

1. This is not to say that material and political factors were not extremely important, and indeed often primary, in shaping Chinese socialism. Indeed, such factors were stressed very heavily in the arguments in the previous chapters. But, as we have already begun to glimpse, for example, the Maoist concept of class and class struggle was more heavily infused with ideological components than it is in more standard Marxist materialist theories. As we shall discuss more fully in Chapter 5, for Mao and his followers, proletarian and socialist values could be determinants of class status, not merely results of it. In another example, the Cultural Revolution focused as much or more on ideological issues as on material ones.

2. Note the use of inverted commas, which clearly signify the view that the Cultural Revolution was neither about culture nor was it a true revolution.

3. The reasons for the popularity of decollectivization among so many farmers and leaders, the positive economic results that were achieved, the effects on the state's ability to govern the countryside and the problems decollectivization created are analysed in Chapters 6 and 7.
4. The exception was Tibet, where they continued a while longer.
5. See Chapter 1 for an explanation of this uniquely Chinese form of popular political expression.
6. Certainly, the term 'Stalinism' fits Dengist China only imperfectly. As we have already seen, for example, in 1980s China fallen leaders enjoyed far more favourable treatment than did those of the 1930s Soviet Union. And, of course, Stalinism involved command central planning, which was being abolished in China. Yet insofar (and only insofar) as Stalinism evokes some of the major structural outlines of politics and the state in Dengist China – monopolistic rule by a Leninist-style Communist Party, strictures against civil liberties and civil society (i.e., autonomous political organization) and the use of political repression in the service of the overriding goal of rapid economic development – the 'Stalinist' part of the term 'market Stalinism' can be advanced. It has been used, for example, by White, 1993: 256 and *passim*.
7. Note that this occurred in August 1988, almost a year before martial law would actually be declared to close down the Tiananmen protests.
8. The concept that democratization could only be born in China with the help of an authoritarian midwife goes back to the reformers of the early twentieth century, including Sun Yatsen, who spoke of the need for a period of 'tutelage' before democracy could emerge.
9. This alliance had been a key to the success of Solidarity in Poland, a phenomenon about which the leadership was and still is well and very anxiously aware.
10. As we have seen, a similar trip in 1984 had also ushered in a period of renewed economic expansion and marketization.
11. According to one informant, they were arrested because they started a punch-up with staff of a magazine that had published a criticism by a professor critical of cults.
12. One such programme even accused the government of staging the self-immolations.
13. In 2002, it was even claiming that the separatists were in cahoots with al-Qaeda, and that the government had established a special anti-terrorist unit to deal with the threat.

4. THE CHINESE STATE

1. To mention just two examples, in 1956 Mao urged that 'a hundred flowers bloom', but by 1957 he called for an 'anti-rightist campaign' to uproot what he (along with other leaders) then decided were actually 'poisonous weeds'

(see Chapter 2). Deng did something very similar, making statements that encouraged democratic expression in 1978 and then shutting down criticism and arresting dissidents in 1979 (see Chapter 3).

2. A terminological inconsistency extant in Western political science should be noted here. The term 'state' generally refers to the structural totality of political institutions, including the Party or parties. But in the sub-field of socialist and communist studies, the term 'state' has often been used to refer more specifically to *government* institutions such as ministries, bureaux, commissions as distinct from the Party. In the interests of consistency with the broader literature of political science, and because the term 'government' is more precise a way of referring to executive institutions, it is used in the rest of this book with that denotation, while the term 'state' is reserved to refer to the totality of political institutions in China, including the Party, government, military and mass organizations.

3. See, for example, the discussions in Chapter 7 on new forms of political participation by peasants.

4. This simplified sketch omits a number of organs, perhaps the most important of which are the standing committees that exist within many of China's political institutions. Not only do these subgroups of key leaders oversee or carry out day-to-day business, they also make many of the most important decisions, either on their own or as 'proposals' which are then ratified by their parent body. This phenomenon is not unique to China; it is, of course, fairly common in Western organizations as well.

5. Indeed, the Soviet Union was rather legalistic. Not only government pronouncements and directives but also laws were used to organize and regulate the economy and society. Courts were generally not filled with kangaroos, nor did most engage in show trials. On the contrary, they were often places in which all manner of day-to-day social and economic disagreements were adjudicated.

5. CHINESE SOCIETY

1. Antonio Gramsci, the great Italian Marxist, developed the concept of hegemony to describe a situation in which the oppressed come to accept the oppressors' view of the world. We shall explore this issue much more fully in Chapter 7.

2. In this respect, China once again bucks the pattern of development in most other late industrializing countries, where urban inequality is usually greater than rural (Khan *et al.*, 1992: 1058–9).

3. A Chinese joke that revolved around precisely this point. During a meeting, Nikita Khrushchev needles Zhou Enlai by comparing his own proletarian roots to Zhou's upbringing in a wealthy rural home. Zhou shoots back that nonetheless they have something in common: they have both betrayed their class backgrounds!

4. Individuals can, strictly speaking, be members of more than one class. In fact, most of us are. If a shop owner both worked hard in her or his own shop while also hiring shop assistants for a wage, s/he would be both bourgeois and petit bourgeois. Erik Olin Wright has developed the theoretical concept of 'contradictory class location' to deal with this. See Wright, 1985.

5. One rumour circulated during the Cultural Revolution had it that Jiang closed Beihai Park, a beautiful and popular spot in downtown Beijing, so that she could ride her white horse while naked.

6. This figure nonetheless stacks up favourably with the gender wage gap in, for example, the United States, which is under 70 per cent. Of course, these two indicators are not strictly comparable, but they do provide a rough sense of the relative gender pay gaps.

7. A 'non-decision' refers to those aspects of policy which are so ingrained that no consideration is ever given to them, much less to changing them. See Bachrach and Baratz (1963).

8. Although, women were not alone in this inability to organize themselves outside the purview of the state. No groups were permitted to do so.

9. They were: Chen Zhili (Minister of Education), Wu Yi (State Councillor) and Zhu Lilan (Minister of Science and Technology).

10. They were He Luli and Peng Peiyun (Standing Committee Vice-Chairs) and Wu Yi.

11. Those in the latter category could still be entitled to food aid in the event of crop failures.

12. Some are employed in 'collective' firms (i.e., those owned by local governments), some in private firms and some in the informal sector, while many others are furloughed from their jobs or are formally unemployed.

6. POLITICAL ECONOMY

1. Income was not ordinarily shared among the larger brigades or communes of which the teams were a part. Thus, as we saw in Chapter 5, farmers' incomes could differ simply because they were members of teams with different levels of economic development. The Great Leap had taught Chinese leaders and villagers much about the dangers of sharing income within too large a collective unit (see Chapter 3).

2. The term 'scissors' comes from the shape of a graph charting rising industrial prices and falling agricultural prices over time.

3. Even without a serious problem of war or political instability, investment rates under the Republic were far too low to catalyse modern economic development. In current prices, investment was only around 5 per cent of gross domestic product (GDP) in 1933. Economic development requires an accumulation rate in the range of 12 to 20 per cent or more. See Kuznets (1966), cited

in Cheng, 1982: 420. Of course, it is likely that investment rates would have been higher in a more stable political environment.

4. The difference between political solicitation and political participation is an interesting analytical problem. Western political scientists generally think that polling – a form of political solicitation – provides élites with greater control over the information that moves from the citizens to the leaders, since the questions can be closely shaped and used to induce certain responses. In revolutionary and Maoist China, however, political solicitation was used by leaders to expand the range of popular political thinking. The line of questioning used by grass-roots cadres with farmer Ma (Chapter 5) is a good example. How the messages conveyed by participation and solicitation differed in various contexts – which channel was broader or franker – is a fascinating question. As we shall see in Chapter 7, the Maoist state also developed a repertoire of methods of political solicitation in the countryside. One example of research focusing on it in the countryside is Blecher (1978, 1983 and 1991). Unfortunately, similar work was not done on factories. The research that comes closest to examining shop-floor politics in Maoist China is Andors (1977), Frazier (2002) and Richman (1969).

5. After all, when the international situation presented possibilities for expanded economic relations with foreign countries, China took advantage of them. Through much of the Maoist period, China tried to maintain trade relations with Western Europe. In the early 1970s, China did not hesitate to improve its relations, including trade, with the United States.

6. The output data for 1958–60 are probably misleadingly high. A great deal of overreporting took place during the Great Leap, and much of what was produced was of unusually poor quality.

7. The data in Figure 6.6 are not precisely consonant with those in Figure 6.3, due to changes in the way the statistics were calculated.

8. Of course, these figures overstate somewhat the total amount of economic activity (such as labour days or proportions of commodity production and sales) represented by international economic relations, since foreign assets and commodities are relatively highly priced compared with their Chinese counterparts.

9. As noted above, China had already reduced tariffs significantly in the 1990s as part of its plan to ease its transition to the WTO and in order to enable its producers to take advantage of inexpensive, high-quality imported inputs. Nominally, they are to drop from an average rate of 11 per cent to 7 per cent. In fact, though, since only around 30 per cent are actually collected, the effective rate will drop from around 3.6 per cent to 2.3 per cent.

10. Average per capita farm incomes were ¥2,400 in 2001, but the grain farmers who will suffer most tend to be the poorer ones.

11. The discussion of accumulation in this paragraph and the next refers to both industry and agriculture. Available data on accumulation do not distinguish sufficiently between these two sectors. As we have seen, however, industry does take the lion's share of investment.

12. According to Chris Bramall, labour productivity for the whole economy (not just industry) rose at a maximum rate of 4.6 per cent per year, and probably less (since the GDP figures on which it is based are probably inflated) from 1978 to 1991. Jefferson and Rawski estimate that total factor productivity – the returns to all inputs, including capital and labour – rose only an average of 2.4 per cent per year from 1980 to 1992. See Bramall, 2000: 185; Jefferson and Rawski, 1994: 57.
13. Data on land use in China are highly suspect, however. Some analysts believe that farmers and local officials significantly understate the amount of land they cultivate, to avoid taxes and required sales to the state.
14. According to one estimate, in 1993 it would have reached about 48 per cent (*China News Digest*, 8 September 1993).

7. POLITICS

1. This term, and its opposite ('Maoists'), are unfortunate ones, insofar as they imply that 'the struggle between two lines' was mainly a power struggle between two leaders and their groups of supporters. A broader conception is that it was a struggle over the ideology and style of political organization and leadership that played itself out during the Cultural Revolution partly as a power struggle. We will use the terms 'Maoists' and 'Liuists' anyway, because the diffuseness of the concept of 'line' makes it difficult to find another terminology. The one used by the Maoist protagonists – 'mass line' versus 'black line' – is obviously too polemical.
2. This discussion refers mainly to the urban areas. Little is known about generational changes in relation to politics in the countryside.
3. The account of farmer Ma (Chapter 5) is a good example. He had great difficulty grasping the concept of exploitation as party cadres explained it to him. The expression *bo xue*, which is the Chinese term used for the Marxian concept of exploitation, is translated in the *Mathews' Chinese–English Dictionary*, which was compiled in 1931, as 'to fleece; to cut down, as wages' (Mathews, 1931, 733). Its pre-revolutionary usage, then, seems to carry a specific implication of cheating, which is alien both to the strict Marxian concept of exploitation and also to Ma's understanding of normal land rent. Indeed, to the extent that he thought about it, Ma seems to have been conscious of his rent either as a legitimate prerogative of land ownership, or more simply as a customary fact of life or part of the natural order that, like the weather, is simply not subject to change through human agency or appropriate to moral or political judgement.
4. As we saw in Chapter 4, the CCP has in fact permitted minor non-Communist political parties to exist, a policy reflecting its pragmatic approach to winning over as well as attacking its rivals. They are, however, politically insignificant.
5. Thus, during the 1989 demonstrations, the Party leadership's *bête noire* was

the effort of students and workers to organize their own autonomous associations.

6. Marx did argue that in the industrialized countries socialism would be a product of capitalism. That is very different from saying that capitalist industrialization is a necessary condition for socialism, or that all countries must take the same path as the industrialized capitalist ones of the North Atlantic. Such a theory is sometimes dubbed 'vulgar Marxism' by its opponents (including other Marxists). In fact, Marx himself was ambiguous on the question of whether more than one route to socialism and Communism exists.

7. For a detailed discussion of this kind of politics during the rural co-operativization of the 1950s, see Shue, 1980. For a discussion set in the countryside during the late 1960s and early 1970s, that is specifically attentive to the issue of political solicitation, see Blecher, 1978 and 1991.

8. While this was interpreted in the Western press as a blow for artistic freedom, it was clear from the works and the artists' demeanour that the more important motivation was financial: the paintings sold like hotcakes!

8. TOWARD THE FUTURE

1. Spoken Cantonese, and even a thick Shanghai dialect, are unintelligible to a Mandarin speaker, for example.

2. The Guomindang on Taiwan was in fact formed along Leninist lines (due to its cooperation with the Soviet Union and the CCP in the 1920s), and it retained some of its Leninist institutional character even through the 1990s. But, in part because it existed within a capitalist economy, the Guomindang's ideological and internal discipline, and its domination of society, ultimately became less draconian and comprehensive than the CCP's.

Bibliography

Andors, S. (1977) *China's Industrial Revolution: Politics, Planning, and Management, 1949 to the Present*. New York: Pantheon.

AP (Associated Press) News Service.

Ash, R. (1991) 'The peasant and the state', *China Quarterly* 127: 493–526.

—— (1992) 'The agricultural sector in China: performance and policy dilemmas during the 1990s', *China Quarterly* 131: 545–76.

Bachman, D. (1991) *Bureaucracy, Economy, and Leadership in China: The Institutional Origins of the Great Leap Forward*. Cambridge: Cambridge University Press.

Bachrach, P. and Baratz, M. (1963) 'Decisions and nondecisions: an analytical framework', *American Political Science Review* 57: 632–42.

BBC Daily Report (Summary of World Broadcasts).

Beijing Review.

Belden, J. (1973) *China Shakes the World*. Harmondsworth: Penguin.

Blecher, M. (1976) 'Income distribution in small rural Chinese communities', *China Quarterly* 68: 797–816.

—— (1978) 'Leader–mass relations in rural Chinese communities: local politics in a revolutionary society'. PhD dissertation, University of Chicago.

—— (1979) 'Consensual politics in rural Chinese communities', *Modern China* 5: 105–26.

—— (1983) 'The mass line and leader–mass relations and communication in basic-level rural communities', in G. Chu and F. Hsu, *China's New Social Fabric*. London: Kegan Paul International.

—— (1986) *China: Politics, Economics and Society*. London: Pinter.

—— (1991) 'The contradictions of grassroots participation and undemocratic statism in Maoist China and their fate', in B. Womack, *Contemporary Chinese Politics in Historical Perspective*. New York: Cambridge University Press.

—— and Shue, V. (1996) *Tethered Deer: Government and Economy in a Chinese County*. Stanford: Stanford University Press.

—— and Shue, V. (2001) 'Into leather: state-led development and the private sector in Xinji', *China Quarterly* 166: 368–93.

—— and Wang S. (1994) 'The political economy of cropping in Shulu County, China, 1949–1990', *China Quarterly* 137: 63–98.

—— and White, G. (1979) *Micropolitics in Contemporary China: A Technical Unit During and After the Cultural Revolution*. Armonk, NY: M. E. Sharpe.

Bo Y. (1952) 'Three years of achievements of the People's Republic of China', in *New China's Economic Achievements, 1949–52*. Beijing: China Committee for the Promotion of International Trade; cited in Lippit (1974).

Bramall, C. (2000) *Sources of Chinese Economic Growth 1978–1996*. Oxford: Oxford University Press.

Chang C. (1962) *The Income of the Chinese Gentry*. Seattle: University of Washington Press.

Cheng, C. (1982) *China's Economic Development*. Boulder, CO: Westview.

China Daily (Beijing).

China News Digest.

China Quarterly.

China Women's News (Beijing).

Coble, P. (1980) *The Shanghai Capitalists and the Nationalist Government, 1927–1937*. Cambridge: Harvard Council of East Asian Studies.

Dangdai (Hong Kong).

Drèze, J. and Sen, A. (1995) *India: Economic Development and Social Opportunity*. Delhi and New York: Oxford University Press.

Eckstein, A. (ed.) (1980) *Quantitative Measures of China's Economic Output*. Ann Arbor: University of Michigan Press.

Elvin, M. (1973) *The Pattern of the Chinese Past*. Stanford: Stanford University Press.

Engels, F. (1972) *The Origin of the Family, Private Property, and the State*. New York: Pathfinder.

Esherick, J. (1981) 'Number games: a note on land distribution in prerevolutionary China', *Modern China* 7: 387–412.

Fackler, M. (2002) 'Flesh industry turns to China for slave labour', *South China Morning Post*, 12 January 2002.

Far Eastern Economic Review (Hong Kong).

Fei H. (1953) *China's Gentry*. Chicago: University of Chicago Press.

Feuerwerker, A. (1958) *China's Early Industrialization*. Cambridge: Harvard University Press.

Frazier, M. (2002) *The Making of the Chinese Industrial Workplace*. Cambridge and New York: Cambridge University Press.

Gallagher, M. (2002) ' "Reform and openness": why China's economic reforms have delayed democracy', *World Politics* 54 (April): 338–72.

Haraszti, M. (1978) *A Worker in a Worker's State*. New York: Universe Books.

Harvard Business School Bulletin (1998) 'Chai Ling: the meaning of freedom'. *http://www.alumni.hbs.edu/bulletin/1998/june/salute/ling.html*

Hinton, C. (1986) *All Under Heaven* [film]. Pittsburgh: New Day Films.

Hinton, H. (1980) *The People's Republic of China, 1949–79: A Documentary Survey*. Wilmington: Scholarly Resources.

Hinton, W. (1966) *Fanshen*. New York: Vintage.

—— (1984) *Shenfan*. New York: Vintage.

Inside China Mainland (Taibei).

Jefferson, G. and Rawski, T. (1994) 'Enterprise reform in Chinese industry', *Journal of Economic Perspectives* 8: 47–70.

Jingji ribao (*Economic Daily News*) (Beijing).

Johnson, C. (1962) *Peasant Nationalism and Communist Power*. Stanford: Stanford University Press.

Judd, E. (1992) 'Land divided, land united', *China Quarterly* 130: 338–56.

Kelliher, D. (1992) *Peasant Power in China: The Era of Rural Reform, 1979–89*. New Haven, CT: Yale University Press.

Khan, A., Griffin, K., Riskin, C. and Zhao R. (1992) 'Household income and its distribution in China', *China Quarterly* 132: 1029–61.

Khan, A. and Riskin, C. (2001) *Inequality and Poverty in China in the Age of Globalization*. Oxford and New York: Oxford University Press.

Kuznets, S. (1966) *Modern Economic Growth*. New York: Norton.

Laitin, D. (1986) *Hegemony and Culture: Politics and Religious Change Among the Yoruba*. Chicago: University of Chicago Press.

Lappé, F. and Collins, J. (1977) *Food First*. New York: Ballantine.

Lardy, N. (1983) *Agriculture in China's Modern Economic Development*. Cambridge: Cambridge University Press.

Li F. (1955) 'Report on the Five-Year Plan for development of the national economy of the People's Republic of China in 1953–57', in R. Bowie and J. Fairbank (eds) (1962), *Communist China, 1955–1959: Policy Documents with Analysis*. Cambridge: Harvard University Center for International Affairs and East Asian Research Center.

Lian bao (*United Daily News*) (Taibei).

Lippit, V. (1974) *Land Reform and Economic Development in China*. White Plains, NY: International Arts and Sciences Press.

—— (1978) 'The development of underdevelopment in China', *Modern China* 4: 251–328.

Lipton, M. (1976) *Why Poor People Stay Poor*. Cambridge: Harvard University Press.

Liu D. and Chai H. (1996) 'Equality and women workers' rights', paper for International Labour Standards Seminar, Beijing, 21–24 May; cited in United Nations Development Programme (1999) *The China Human Development Report*. New York and Oxford: Oxford University Press.

MacFarquhar, R. (ed.) (1993) *The Politics of China, 1949–1989*. Cambridge: Cambridge University Press.

Mao Z. (1966) *Oppose Book Worship*. Beijing: Foreign Languages Press.

—— (1967) *Selected Works*. Beijing: Foreign Languages Press.

—— (1969) *Mao Zedong Sixiang Wansui* (*Long Live the Thought of Mao Zedong*). Np.

—— (1977) *Selected Works*, Volume V. Beijing: Foreign Languages Press.

'Marriage Law of the People's Republic of China (1950)', in A. Blaustein (ed.) (1962), *Fundamental Legal Documents of Communist China*. South Hackensack, NJ: Fred. B. Rothman and Co.

Marx, K. (1959) 'Theses on Feuerbach', in L. Feuer (ed.), *Marx and Engels: Basic Writings on Politics and Philosophy*. Garden City, NY: Anchor/Doubleday.

Mathews, R. (1931) *Mathews' Chinese–English Dictionary*. Shanghai: China Inland Mission and Presbyterian Mission Press; revised American edn. (1963). Cambridge: Harvard University Press.

Metzger, T. (1977) *Escape from Predicament*. New York: Columbia University Press.

Moore, B. (1966) *Social Origins of Dictatorship and Democracy*. Boston: Beacon Press.

Munro, R. (1990) 'Who died in Beijing, and why?', *The Nation*, 11 June.

Naughton, B. (1995) *Growing Out of the Plan: Chinese Economic Reform, 1978–1993*. Cambridge: Cambridge University Press.

Nolan, P. (2001) *China and the Global Economy*. Houndsmills: Palgrave.

Nongmin ribao (Farmers' Daily).

O'Brien, K. (1994) 'Implementing political reform in China's villages', *Australian Journal of Chinese Studies* 32: 33–59.

—— and Li Lianjiang (1995) 'The politics of lodging complaints in Chinese villages', *China Quarterly* 143: 756–83.

Parish, W. and Whyte, M. (1978) *Village and Family in Contemporary China*. Chicago: University of Chicago Press.

Perkins, D. (1975) 'The growth and changing structure of China's twentieth-century economy', in D. Perkins (ed.), *China's Modern Economy in Historical Perspective*. Stanford: Stanford University Press.

Putterman, L. (1983) 'A modified collective agriculture in rural growth-with-equity', *World Development* 11: 77–100.

—— (1989) 'Entering the post-collective era in North China: Dahe township', *Modern China* 15: 275–320.

Renmin ribao (People's Daily) (Beijing).

Reuters News Service.

Richman, B. (1969) *Industrial Society in Communist China: A Firsthand Study of Chinese Economic Development and Management*. New York: Random House.

Riskin, C. (1975) 'Surplus and stagnation in modern China', in D. Perkins (ed.), *China's Modern Economy in Historical Perspective*. Stanford: Stanford University Press.

Rozelle, S. (1996) 'Stagnation without equity: patterns of growth and inequality in China's rural economy', *The China Journal* 35: 63–92.

Saich, T. (1992) 'The Fourteenth Party Congress: a programme for authoritarian rule', *China Quarterly* 132: 1136–60.

Schram, S. (ed.) (1974) *Mao Tse-tung Unrehearsed*. Harmondsworth: Penguin.

Selden, M. (1979) *The People's Republic of China: A Documentary History of Revolutionary Change*. New York: Monthly Review Press.

—— (1982) 'Cooperation and conflict: cooperative and collective formation in China's countryside', in M. Selden and V. Lippit (eds), *The Transition to Socialism in China*. Armonk, NY: M. E. Sharpe.

Shue, V. (1980) *Peasant China in Transition: The Dynamics of Development Toward Socialism, 1949–56*. Berkeley: University of California Press.

Skocpol, T. (1979) *States and Social Revolutions*. Cambridge: Cambridge University Press.

Smith, C. (2002) 'For China's Wealthy, All but Fruited Plain', *New York Times*, 15 May 2002.

Solinger, D. (2002) 'The cost of China's entry into WTO', *Asian Wall Street Journal*, 4 January 2002.

—— (2003) 'Chinese urban jobs and the WTO', *China Journal* 49: 61–87.

State Statistical Bureau (various years) *China Statistical Yearbook*. Beijing: China Statistical Publishing House.

Tang, W. and Parish, W. (2000) *Chinese Urban Life Under Reform: The Changing Social Contract*. Cambridge: Cambridge University Press.

Thaxton, R. (1983) *China Turned Rightside Up*. New Haven: Yale University Press.

Thurston, A. (1977) 'The revival of classes in rural Kwangtung: production team politics in a period of crisis'. Unpublished paper.

Tsou, T. (1986) *The Cultural Revolution and the Post-Mao Reforms*. Chicago: University of Chicago Press.

UPI (United Press International) News Service.

Wang, R. (1983) 'Wei rendaozhuyi bianhu' (In defence of humanism), *Wenhui bao* (Shanghai), 17 January; quoted in MacFarquhar (ed.) (1993): 351–2.

White, G. (1993) *Riding the Tiger: The Politics of Economic Reform in Post-Mao China*. London: Macmillan.

White III, L. (1989) *Policies of Chaos: The Organizational Causes of Violence in China's Cultural Revolution*. Princeton: Princeton University Press.

Womack, B. (1984) 'Modernization and democratic reform in China', *Journal of Asian Studies* 43: 417–39.

World Bank (1978) *World Development Report*. New York and Oxford: Oxford University Press.

World Bank (1981) *World Development Report*. New York and Oxford: Oxford University Press.

World Bank (2002) *http://devdata.worldbank.org/external/dgsector.asp? W=0&RMDK=110&SMDK=473885*

Wright, E. (1985) *Classes*. London and New York: Verso.

Xinhua News Bulletin.

Yao W. (1975) *On the Social Basis of the Lin Piao Anti-Party Clique*. Beijing: Foreign Languages Press.

Zhang C. (1975) *On Exercising All-Round Dictatorship over the Bourgeoisie*. Beijing: Foreign Languages Press.

Index

Index